A·N·N·U·A·L EDITIONS

Women's Studies

99/00

First Edition

EDITORS

Patricia Ojea
Rutgers University-Camden

Patricia Ojea currently teaches at Rutgers University, Camden, in the Department of Political Science. She brings to *Annual Editions* valuable perspectives on Women's Studies gained from her experience as a scholar and community activist.

Barbara Quigley
Lehigh Carbon Community College

Barbara Quigley received her Ph.D in psychology from the State University of New York at Albany. She has taught at the University of Montana and Morehead College. Dr. Quigley currently teaches and writes about social behavior and statistical application.

Dushkin/McGraw-Hill
Sluice Dock, Guilford, Connecticut 06437

Visit us on the Internet
http://www.dushkin.com/annualeditions/

Credits

1. Women's Movement, History, and Feminist Theory
Facing overview—Reproduced from the collections of the Library of Congress.
2. Education and Psychology
Facing overview—AP/Wide World Photo by Carlos Osorlo.
3. Medicine, Health, and Sports
Facing overview—PhotoDisc, Inc.
4. Religion and Philosophy
Facing overview—United Nations photo by Ian Steele.
5. Political Science, Law, and Criminal Justice; Public Policy and Administration
Facing overview—PhotoDisc, Inc.
6. Business, Economics, Labor, and Employment
Facing overview—PhotoDisc, Inc. 159, 161, 162, 164—photos courtesy of Jocelyn W. Knowles.
7. Sociology and Anthropology
Facing overview—© 1998 by Cleo Photography.

Cataloging in Publication Data
Main entry under title: Annual Editions: Women's Studies. 1999/2000.
1. Women's Studies. 2. Women—United States—20th century. I. Ojea, Patricia, *comp.* II. Quigley, Barbara, *comp.* III.
Title: Women's Studies.
ISBN 0–07–303197–6   305.42'0973

Members of the Advisory Board are instrumental in the final selection of articles for each edition of ANNUAL EDITIONS. Their review of articles for content, level, currentness, and appropriateness provides critical direction to the editor and staff. We think that you will find their careful consideration well reflected in this volume.

Editors/Advisory Board

Staff

To the Reader

In publishing ANNUAL EDITIONS we recognize the enormous role played by the magazines, newspapers, and journals of the public press in providing current, first-rate educational information in a broad spectrum of interest areas. Many of these articles are appropriate for students, researchers, and professionals seeking accurate, current material to help bridge the gap between principles and theories and the real world. These articles, however, become more useful for study when those of lasting value are carefully collected, organized, indexed, and reproduced in a low-cost format, which provides easy and permanent access when the material is needed. That is the role played by ANNUAL EDITIONS.

New to ANNUAL EDITIONS is the inclusion of related World Wide Web sites. These sites have been selected by our editorial staff to represent some of the best resources found on the World Wide Web today. Through our carefully developed topic guide, we have linked these Web resources to the articles covered in this ANNUAL EDITIONS reader. We think that you will find this volume useful, and we hope that you will take a moment to visit us on the Web at *http://www.dushkin.com/* to tell us what you think.

From the late 1960s and throughout the 1970s, eager feminist inquiries began evolving into a mature field of women's studies with all the accoutrements of any other academic discipline, including conferences, professional organizations, journals, and reference tools. During this same period, colleges and universities began developing separate courses and departments for Women's Studies. As the separation proliferated, issues and perspectives were compartmentalized or incorporated into separate academic fields.

The first edition of *Annual Editions: Women's Studies* attempts to keep pace with these growing interests by covering a variety of topics, issues, and societal domains, most but not all presented from an American cultural perspective. For instance, women throughout the world today in general live longer, healthier lives, are better educated, enjoy more job opportunities, and earn higher salaries than ever before. More women than men are enrolled in college and more women than ever are assuming top-level leadership roles, both in business and in public life. Also, the past several decades have witnessed tremendous improvements in women's literacy, longevity, education, employment opportunities, and general standard of living. A positive correlation of this improvement is that families and communities have become better educated, better nourished, healthier, and more productive.

Yet progress has not always been even, and some parts of the world have suffered reversals. There are, for instance, many places in the world where a women's average life expectancy is less than 50 years and where the great majority of women can neither read nor write. In most developing countries, women constitute the majority of the poor, accounting for more than 70 percent of the world's 1.3 billion people living in poverty.

Moreover, despite having made many great strides in attaining women's rights and improving their lives, all too often girls and women find their access to education, employment, health care, political influence, and sometimes even food or life itself limited solely because of their gender. In China and some other parts of the world, it is not uncommon for a fetus to be aborted or a baby killed for no other reason than her gender. Likewise, millions of women live in societies where centuries-old social and religious laws, customs, and traditions have created insurmountable barriers to education, jobs, and health care, as well as having deprived them of their political and civil rights.

In areas where women have limited access to schooling, health care, and economic opportunities, their families tend to be larger, poorer, less educated, and more debilitated by malnutrition and disease. Literary views and fundamental information necessary for a general understanding of these situations are discussed in this volume. The articles do not contain references to all of the past or current women's studies research topics nor does it include articles for every significant woman, place, event, organization, or concept within the field. *Annual Editions: Women's Studies* does attempt to provide coverage of issues, events, organizations, individuals, and concepts that constitute a core of pertinent information regarding basic facts, theoretical views, materials, and resources.

In order to facilitate easy reference, we have divided *Annual Editions: Women's Studies* into seven units. Unit 1 introduces several historic roles of women in American society, and variations of American feminism. At the heart of these roles is the notion that women's perspectives, interpretations, and roles are defined by women. Unit 2 examines females' attitudes, roles, and outcomes in education, as well as the speculation about differences in the cognitive abilities of adults, and employment issues for women.

Health care issues and hospital policies, plastic surgery for beautification, abortion, and behavior during pregnancy are examined in unit 3. You will find these topics intense and controversial. As for female participation in sports, questions concerned with sports sponsorship by schools and Title IX are examined. Unit 4 covers feminine religious roles. The evolution of women in the early Church depicts women playing a spiritual role but not given credit. Also, various church and religious roles, real and mythical, are contemplated. Unit 5 covers politics, law, and issues related to women in the military, sexual harassment, and pregnancy in the workplace.

Unit 6 examines women and employment historically. Also, gender networking and female to female mentors issues are reviewed. Unit 7 examines issues of the 1990s, including gay families, domestic violence, abortion, and the Million Woman March.

In the first edition of *Annual Editions: Women's Studies 99/00* we have included a topic guide and a list of selected World Wide Web sites that relate to areas of traditional concern in the field of women's studies. They should be very useful for locating interrelated articles and Web sites through our *Dushkin Online* support site at *http://www.dushkin.com/online/*.

Whether you are someone who is currently pursuing women's studies, or are just a casual reader eager to learn more about the major issues and concerns, you will find the first edition of *Annual Editions: Women's Studies 99/00* to be one of the most informative, useful, and up-to-date anthologies available. Your input can be valuable for the next edition. Please offer your opinions by filling out and returning to us the prepaid *article rating form* on the last page of this book.

Patricia Ojea

Patricia Ojea

Barbara Quigley

Barbara Quigley
Editors

Contents

UNIT 1

Women's Movement, History, and Feminist Theory

Seven articles discuss unusual roles and accomplishments of women and various feminist theories.

The concepts in bold italics are developed in the article. For further expansion please refer to the Topic Guide and the Index.

UNIT 2

Education and Psychology

Five selections examine the importance of changing practices within education to open opportunities for women, behavioral and emotional differences between men and women, and the status of working environments.

The concepts in bold italics are developed in the article. For further expansion please refer to the Topic Guide and the Index.

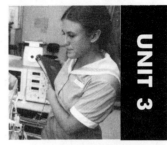

UNIT 3

Medicine, Health, and Sports

Six articles examine
inequities in medical care,
health, and women's sports.

UNIT 4

Religion and Philosophy

Six articles look at some of the
historical roles and portrayals
of women in religious activities.

UNIT 5

Political Science, Law, and Criminal Justice; Public Policy and Administration

Seven selections examine women in public office and the military, as well as women involved in political and social activism.

The concepts in bold italics are developed in the article. For further expansion please refer to the Topic Guide and the Index.

UNIT 6

Business, Economics, Labor, and Employment

Four articles consider the changes and problems that women are experiencing in all phases of the workplace.

The concepts in bold italics are developed in the article. For further expansion please refer to the Topic Guide and the Index.

ix

UNIT 7

Sociology and Anthropology

Nine articles discuss the cultural roles, stations, and social conditions of women in such areas as domestic violence, gay parenting, and social bonding.

The concepts in bold italics are developed in the article. For further expansion please refer to the Topic Guide and the Index.

through enhancing the economic position of women have put the male labor force at an economic disadvantage.

The concepts in bold italics are developed in the article. For further expansion please refer to the Topic Guide and the Index.

This topic guide suggests how the selections and World Wide Web sites found in the next section of this book relate to topics of traditional concern to psychology students and professionals involved in the field of women studies. It is useful for locating interrelated articles and Web sites for reading and research. The guide is arranged alphabetically according to topic.

The relevant Web sites, which are numbered and annotated on pages 4 and 5, are easily identified by the Web icon (◎) under the topic articles. By linking the articles and the Web sites by topic, this ANNUAL EDITIONS reader becomes a powerful learning and research tool.

TOPIC AREA	TREATED IN	TOPIC AREA	TREATED IN
Abused/ Battered Women	29. Women and War 31. Legal Evolution of Sexual Harassment 39. Behind [Closed] Doors ◎ **2, 3, 12, 18, 29**	**Business**	2. African-American Women on the Western Frontier 12. Myth of the Miserable Working Woman 33. Separate and Unequal 35. Female Entrepreneurs ◎ **24, 25, 26, 27**
Activism	1. Why Suffrage for American Women Was Not Enough 3. "Rights as Well as Duties" 5. Beyond Gender 6. Women of the Future 7. Farewell to Feminism 13. Warning: Feminism Is Hazardous to Your Health 15. Women's Health Movements 18. Fair Game 21. Goddess Myth 28. Women's Work 30. Women in Power 31. Legal Evolution of Sexual Harassment 43. Desperately Seeking Sisterhood ◎ **4, 5, 6, 7, 8, 23**	**Christianity**	14. Blocking Women's Health Care 19. Women and the Early Church 20. No Humanitarian: A Portrait of Mother Teresa 23. Whatever Happened to Sister Jane? 24. Labor of Compassion ◎ **17, 18**
African American Women	1. Why Suffrage for American Women Was Not Enough 2. African-American Women on the Western Frontier 31. Legal Evolution of Sexual Harassment 36. (R)Evolution of the American Woman ◎ **4, 5, 7, 20, 27**	**Criminal/ Criminal Justice/ Legal**	1. Why Suffrage for American Women Was Not Enough 16. Abortion in American History 25. Future of *Roe v. Wade* 31. Legal Evolution of Sexual Harassment 39. Behind [Closed] Doors ◎ **12, 22, 23, 29**
Asian and African Women	20. No Humanitarian: A Portrait of Mother Teresa 22. Islam's Shame 24. Labor of Compassion 43. Desperately Seeking Sisterhood	**Culture/Customs**	3. "Rights as Well as Duties" 4. Women, War, and the Limits of Change 5. Beyond Gender 9. Man's World, Woman's World 19. Women and the Early Church 21. Goddess Myth 22. Islam's Shame 23. Whatever Happened to Sister Jane? 24. Labor of Compassion 36. (R)Evolution of the American Woman 42. Housewives' Choice 43. Desperately Seeking Sisterhood 44. Beyond 'It's a Baby' ◎ **1, 2, 3, 4, 17, 18**
Athletes	17. Females in Sports 18. Fair Game ◎ **14, 15, 16, 19**		
Birth Control/ Contraceptives	14. Blocking Women's Health Care 15. Women's Health Movements 16. Abortion in American History 22. Islam's Shame 25. Future of *Roe v. Wade* 34. Managing Pregnancy in the Workplace 36. (R)Evolution of the American Women 44. Beyond 'It's a Baby' ◎ **2, 3, 8, 13, 14, 29**	**Discrimination**	1. Why Suffrage for American Women Was Not Enough 2. African-American Women on the Western Frontier 3. "Rights as Well as Duties" 4. Women, War, and the Limits of Change 5. Beyond Gender 18. Fair Game 19. Women and the Early Church 22. Islam's Shame 24. Labor of Compassion

◎ Annual Editions: Women's Studies

The following World Wide Web sites have been carefully researched and selected to support the articles found in this reader. If you are interested in learning more about specific topics found in this book, these Web sites are a good place to start. The sites are cross-referenced by number and appear in the topic guide on the previous two pages. Also, you can link to these Web sites through our DUSHKIN ONLINE support site at *http://www.dushkin.com/online/*.

The following sites were available at the time of publication. Visit our Web site—we update DUSHKIN ONLINE regularly to reflect any changes.

General Sources

1. Social Science Information Gateway
http://sosig.esrc.bris.ac.uk/
This is an online catalogue of Internet resources relevant to social education and research. Every resource is selected and described by a librarian or subject specialist.

2. University of Amsterdam/Sociology Department
http://www.pscw.uva.nl/sociosite/TOPICS/Women.html
Open this enormous sociology site—with a strongly feminist orientation—to gain insights into a number of issues that affect both men and women. It provides links in affirmative action; gender, family, and children's issues; and much more.

3. University of Maryland/Women's Studies
http://www.inform.umd.edu/EdRes/Topic/WomensStudies/
This site provides a wealth of resources related to women and their concerns. You can find links to such topics as body image, comfort (or discomfort) with sexuality, personal relationships, pornography, and more.

Women's Movement, History, and Feminist Theory

4. American Studies Web
http://www.georgetown.edu/crossroads/asw/
This eclectic site provides links to a wealth of resources on the Internet related to prominent social issues, from gender studies, to education, to race and ethnicity. It is of great help when doing research in demography and population.

5. Black Women's Manifesto; Documents from the Women's Liberation Movement
http://scriptorium.lib.duke.edu/wlm/blkmanif/index.html#double/
For information from a black feminist perspective, explore this online archival collection from Duke University.

6. League of Women Voters
http://www.lwv.org/
This home page of the League of Women Voters, a national organization, describes the League's purposes and principles, explains its current activities and programs, and suggests how individuals can make a difference.

7. National Women's History Project
http://www.nwhp.org/
This Web site, entitled "Living the Legacy: The Women's Rights Movement, 1848–1998," has useful history links and provides recent news about women and history.

8. Q Web Sweden: A Women's Empowerment Base
http://www.qweb.kvinnoforum.se/activity/thagemar.htm
This site from a Swedish organization will lead you to pages about women's health and societal issues. It provides interesting cross-cultural perspectives.

Education and Psychology

9. American Psychoanalytic Association
http://www.apsa.org/pubinfo/female.htm
This site provides information on the American Psychoanalytic Association's supplement, "The Psychology of Women: Psychoanalytic Perspectives," regarding current Freudian perspectives on women.

10. Educational Resources Information Center
http://www.aspensys.com/eric/index.html
This invaluable site provides links to all ERIC sites: clearinghouses, support components, and publishers of ERIC materials. You can search the ERIC database, find out what is new, and ask questions about ERIC.

11. Sex and Gender
http://bioanth.cam.ac.uk/pip4amod3.html
Use the syllabus, lecture titles, and readings noted in this site as a jumping-off point to explore sexual differentiation in human culture as well as the genetics of sexual differentiation.

12. Sexual Assault Information Page
http://www.cs.utk.edu/~bartley/saInfoPage.html
This invaluable site provides dozens of links to information and resources on a variety of sexual assault–related topics, from child sexual abuse, to date rape, to incest, to secondary victims, to offenders. It also provides some material of interest in the pornography debate.

Medicine, Health, and Sports

13. Carnegie Mellon University/Center for the Advancement of Applied Ethics/Philosophy Department
http://caae.phil.cmu.edu/caae/Home/Multimedia/Abortion/IssueofAbortion.html
Open this site to learn about a CD-ROM that is being developed regarding "The Issue of Abortion in America." Reading the pages of this site will give you an introduction to important historical and social perspectives, legal issues, medical facts, and philosophical arguments related to the abortion debate.

14. Starting Point: Health
http://www.stpt.com/health/health.html
Search engine to excellent resources on health and fitness. Click on Women's Health for complete menu of links to relevant sites.

15. World Health Organization
http://www.who.ch/Welcome.html
This home page of the World Health Organization will provide you with links to a wealth of statistical and analytical information about health in the developing world.

16. U.S. National Institutes of Health
http://www.nih.gov/
Consult this site for links to extensive health information and scientific resources. The NIH is one of eight health agencies of the Public Health Service.

Religion and Philosophy

17. Association of College and Research Libraries/Women's Studies Section
http://www.nd.edu/~colldev/subjects/wss.html
Explore the many materials available through this "Women and Philosophy Web Site." It provides Internet collections of resources, ethics updates, bibliographies, information on organizations, and access to newsletters and journals.

18. Columbia University
http://www.columbia.edu/cu/libraries/subjects/womenstudies/
Open this site, which is updated frequently, to click on extensive links to information about women in religion and philosophy as well as a wealth of other topics, including domestic violence and bisexual, gay, and lesbian studies.

Political Science, Law and Criminal Justice, Public Policy and Administration

19. The Feminist Majority Foundation Online
http://www.feminist.org/
This site provides a wealth of information and a variety of links on such topics as women's sports, "gender apartheid," and international feminism.

20. The North-South Institute
http://www.nsi-ins.ca/info.html
Searching this site of the North-South Institute—which works to strengthen international development cooperation and enhance gender and social equity—will help you find information and debates on a variety of topics of interest in women's studies.

21. University of Maryland
http://www.umd.edu/cgi-bin/post-query/
Open this site from the University of Maryland's "inforM Pages" to read articles related to women in the military and other topics of interest in women's studies.

22. Women's Law Journal of Legal Theory and Practice
http://gort.ucsd.edu/newjour/w/msg02265.html
Sponsored by the University of Pennsylvania, this journal keeps abreast of current women's legal issues. The journal aims to provide a meaningful forum for women's and men's voices on a variety of issues surrounding women's relationship to jurisprudence. This is also a valuable site for exploring business topics of concern to women.

Business, Economics, Labor, and Employment

23. American Civil Liberties Union
http://www.aclu.org/issues/worker/campaign.html
The ACLU provides this interesting page on workplace rights in its "Campaign for Fairness in the Workplace." Briefing papers on workplace issues cover such privacy issues as lifestyle discrimination, workplace drug testing, and electronic monitoring.

24. Cybergrrl Webstation/Women on the Web
http://www.cybergrrl.com/
Investigate this site and its many links to find "female-friendly" resources on the Internet. It covers a wealth of topics, such as career development and networking.

25. Michigan State University/School of Labor and Industrial Relations
http://www.ssc.msu.edu/~lir/hotlink.htm
This MSU/SLIR "Hot Links" home page takes you to sites regarding industrial relations throughout the world. It has links from U.S. government and statistics, to newspapers and libraries, and to international intergovernmental organizations. With this level of access, you should be able to research virtually every labor-related topic.

26. Society for Economic Anthropology Homepage
http://www.lawrence.edu/~peregrip/seahome.html
This is the home page of the Society for Economic Anthropology, an association that strives to understand diversity and change in the economic systems of the world—and, hence, in the organization of society and culture.

27. U.S. Equal Employment Opportunity Commission
http://www.eeoc.gov/
The EEOC's mission "is to ensure equality of opportunity by vigorously enforcing federal legislation prohibiting discrimination in employment." Consult this site for small business information, facts about employment discrimination, and enforcement and litigation.

Sociology and Anthropology

28. American Psychological Association
http://www.apa.org/books/homepage.html
Search this site to find references and discussion of important workplace issues for the 1990s and beyond, including restructuring and revitalization of businesses and how these affect women.

29. National Network for Family Resiliency
http://www.nnfr.org/nnfr/
This organization's home page will lead you to a number of resource areas of interest in learning about resiliency, including "General Family Resiliency," "Violence Prevention," and "Family Economics."

30. The University of Minnesota's Children, Youth and Family Consortium
http://www.cyfc.umn.edu/Parenting/parentlink.html
By clicking on the various links, this site will lead you to many organizations and other resources related to divorce, single parenting, and stepfamilies, as well as information about other topics of interest in women's studies.

31. University of Plymouth/Department of Psychology
http://www.psy.plym.ac.uk/year2/maternal.htm
This site presents an interesting summary of a study on maternal behavior as studied in rats. It includes brief discussions and instructive graphs of such topics as the impact of hormones on maternal behavior, maternal self-image, and mothers' ability to recognize their babies' smell.

We highly recommend that you review our Web site for expanded information and our other product lines. We are continually updating and adding links to our Web site in order to offer you the most usable and useful information that will support and expand the value of your Annual Editions. You can reach us at: *http://www.dushkin.com/annualeditions/*.

www.dushkin.com/online/

5

Unit 1

Unit Selections

1. **Why Suffrage for American Women Was Not Enough,** Elisabeth Perry
2. **African-American Women on the Western Frontier,** Roger D. Hardaway
3. **"Rights as Well as Duties": The Rhetoric of Leonora O'Reilly,** Anne F. Mattina
4. **Women, War, and the Limits of Change,** Susan M. Hartmann
5. **Beyond Gender,** Betty Friedan
6. **Women of the Future: Alternative Scenarios,** Christopher B. Jones
7. **A Farewell to Feminism,** Elizabeth Powers

Key Points to Consider

❖ Why were women unable to break through in politics between the two world wars? In what ways are the roles of women more focused today?

❖ How does the diversity of women's roles in America affect feminism as a collective goal?

❖ Why should women be concerned about how far to go with gender equality?

 **Links** **www.dushkin.com/online/**

4. **American Studies Web**
   http://www.georgetown.edu/crossroads/asw/
5. **Black Women's Manifesto: Documents from the Women's Liberation Movement**
   http://scriptorium.lib.duke.edu/wlm/blkmanif/index.html#double/
6. **League of Women Voters**
   http://www.lwv.org/
7. **National Women's History Project**
   http://www.nwhp.org/
8. **Q Web Sweden: A Women's Empowerment Base**
   http://www.qweb.kvinnoforum.se/activity/thagemar.htm

These sites are annotated on pages 4 and 5.

Our purpose in the first unit of this anthology is to describe the great diversity that makes up feminism, one of the basic movements for human dignity. To view it in any less serious manner would be a shocking ignorance of the history of one-half of the human race. But the vast majority of women and men are unaware of the great feminist accomplishments of the past and are only minimally acquainted with the struggles and achievements of contemporary American feminism. For instance, most of us were taught less about the public role of women in America than about the queens of Europe. Yet access to scholarly writings, describing the significant tribal roles portrayed by the first American women (the Iroquois and others), or the "Republican Mothers," who died alongside the soldiers they fed and bandaged, was limited.[1]

The suffrage movement is a historical event that transformed the annals of American history. Suffragettes deserve a great deal of credit for their political astuteness, courageousness, and willingness to go against the grain of the most powerful patriarchial system in the world. However, we hear less about the indignities they suffered—imprisonment, physical assault, and scorn—than about the contractual arrangements between Queen Isabella of Spain and Christopher Columbus.

Ironically, soon after women received the right to vote, feminism was put on hold for more than 35 years. Its decline is attributable, in part, to its concentration on the single narrow issue of suffrage. Other factors cited are the inability of the suffragettes to recoup their membership, postwar economic depression, the growing influence of antifeminism by Freudians, and the development of authoritarian governments that tended to foster male supremacist values. Beginning in the late 1960s, an exploratory outgrowth of these situations developed into a contemporary women's studies field—just as the black power movement of the 1960s spawned an intellectual wing called black studies. The women's movement itself was as much influenced by the earlier civil rights and black power activism as all, in turn, were influenced by the nineteenth century women's rights movement in the United States and the abolitionist movement within which the women's rights movement took root. From this interlocking set of influences and conflicts, the twentieth-century women's movement took inspirational style, slogans, and even tactics.

The first unit opens, appropriately, with a historical overview of the American feminist movement from its early stages to the present. Author Elisabeth Perry concludes her essay with a

[1] Linda Kerber, *Women of the Republic*, Chapter 7, passim.

listing of contemporary feminist activities that are more focused and sophisticated. Then Roger D. Hardaway, in "African-American Women on the Western Frontier," describes the lives of seven women who were born slaves and became successful businesswomen. Next, Anna Mattina, in " 'Rights as Well as Duties': The Rhetoric of Leonora O'Reilly," examines working class feminism, describing an oratory style quite different from that of upper middle-class reformers. The shortage of men in the labor force during World War II forced a shift in gender roles. Susan M. Hartmann views this as a positive change that brought forth new opportunity and outlooks, which in turn helped create a renewed spirit in women as workers and professionals.

The unit ends with Betty Friedan, who, in "Beyond Gender," issues a 1990s' warning against overly ambitious feminism, which calls for equal loss as well as equal gains. Friedan asks whether advancing the interests of women as equals is worth the loss of husbands and children.

Unit 1 ends with two articles, "Women of the Future: Alternative Scenarios," by Christopher Jones, and "A Farewell to Feminism," by Elizabeth Powers, which discuss how far radical concepts of feminism will continue to go, and whether women will regret winning some of their demands.

Why Suffrage for American Women Was Not Enough

With Hillary Clinton in the White House as the most political First Lady since Eleanor Roosevelt, the role of women in American politics is in sharp focus. Elisabeth Perry *explains here, via four case-histories, why American women did not break through in politics between the wars, despite having won the vote.*

Elisabeth Perry

Elisabeth Perry directs the graduate programme in Women's History at Sarah Lawrence College, in Bronxville, N.Y. Her most recent publication, The Challenge of Feminist Biography: Writing the Lives of Modern American Women *(Champaign: University of Illinois, 1992) was co-edited with Sara Alpern, Joyce Antler, and Ingrid Winther Scobie.*

As a result of the autumn elections in 1992, a year the American media billed as 'The Year of the Woman', the numbers of women holding elective office in the United States rose to unprecedented heights. The percentage of women office holders at state level climbed to 22.2 per cent for state-wide elected executives and 20.4 per cent for legislators. At the national level, the number of female US Senators tripled (from two to six), while the number in the House of Representatives rose from twenty-eight to forty-seven (there is a forty-eighth, who represents the District of Columbia, but she has no vote). Even with this impressive progress, however, women's share of elective office in the United States remains relatively small.

It is not hard to explain why. Deeply ingrained global traditions have long kept women out of public, authoritative roles. But why have these traditions remained so entrenched in the United States, ostensibly one of the most advanced, modernised countries of the world? A close look at American women's political history in the imme-

diate post-suffrage era might provide a few clues.

American women won the vote in 1920 with the ratification of the Nineteenth Amendment to the federal Constitution. Women had worked for this goal since 1848, when Elizabeth Cady Stanton, a reformer active in the campaigns to abolish slavery and also a temperance advocate, organised a public meeting in Seneca Falls, New York, to discuss women's rights. Many observers ridiculed her demand for the vote. By the turn of the century, this demand had become the focal point of the entire women's movement. Suffrage for women was eventually won in a number of the states, and then nationwide in August, 1920.

By the time this event occurred, women were no longer political novices. For decades they had been organising conventions, giving public speeches, writing editorials, campaigning door-to-door, petitioning and marching. These activities gave them vast political expertise, as well as access to wide networks of other women activists and of male political leaders. This combination of expertise and contacts ought to have placed them at the centre of American political life. It did not.

The winning of female suffrage did not mark the end of prejudice and discrimination against women in public life. Women still lacked equal access with men to those professions, especially the law, which provide the chief routes to political power. Further, when

women ran for office—and many did in the immediate post-suffrage era—they often lacked major party backing, hard to come by for any newcomer but for women almost impossible unless she belonged to a prominent political family. Even if successful in winning backing, when women ran for office they usually had to oppose incumbents. When, as was often the case, they lost their first attempts, their reputation as 'losers' made re-endorsement impossible.

American political parties did try to integrate women into their power structures after suffrage. They courted women's votes, especially in the early 1920s, when a 'woman's voting bloc' seemed real. In addition, the parties formed 'women's divisions' or created a committee system of equal numbers of committee women and committee men (with the latter usually choosing the former). But when party leaders sought a candidate for preferment, they tended to look for 'a good man', seldom imagining that a woman might qualify. In short, in the years immediately after suffrage most party leaders confined women to auxiliary, service roles. They expected women to help elect men but not seek office themselves. That party men in the early 1920s held to such an expectation is hardly surprising. That many of the most politically 'savvy' American women went along with them is more difficult to understand.

In the post-suffrage United States, although there were many strong, executive-type women with considerable political

Courtesy of Elisabeth Perry

Belle Moskowitz with Eleanor Roosevelt at a 1924 political meeting, and (right) a 1931 portrait of Belle Moskowitz by the celebrated photographer, Lewis Hine.

expertise, none of them became the vanguard of a new, office-seeking female political leadership. Because of women's long exclusion from the vote and political parties, these women had worked for change only in a nonpartisan fashion from within their own gender sphere. After suffrage, in part because men kept them there, they accepted the notion that separate roles for women in politics ought to continue.

The reasons for this acceptance are complex, and probably differ from woman to woman. Some women felt most comfortable operating from within their own sphere. In single-sex groups, they made lifelong friendships with women who shared their interests and problems. In addition, in women's groups they did not have to compete with men for positions of authority. A deep suspicion of electoral politics was yet another important factor. Political women distrusted the world of electoral politics. It was a man's world, a world filled with 'dirty games' that men had been trained to play, and indeed were forced to play, if they wanted to 'get ahead'. For these women, it held few allures. Educated and middle-class, they had not been brought up to be career-orientated or personally ambitious. Rather, they had been taught that their proper role was to serve others and to work for idealistic causes. The winning of the vote did little to change this socialisation.

These were some of the views of women's role in politics held by both

men and women in the 1920s. The careers of four suffragists, all politically active in the post-suffrage era and all of whom could have held elective office had circumstances differed, serve to illustrate how these views affected individual lives. The four do not comprise a balanced 'sample', for they were all based in New York City and were all active in the Democratic Party. They are exemplars, however, because they thrived in a hot-bed of women's activism in the post-suffrage era. If any woman could have risen into electoral political prominence during that era, she would have been a New York City Democrat.

My first example is Belle Lindner Moskowitz (1877–1933). A shopkeeper's daughter born in Harlem, New York, she spent her early career as a social worker on the city's Lower East Side. After her marriage in 1903, while her children were growing up, she did volunteer work until, by the 1910s, she had developed a city-wide reputation as an effective social and industrial reformer. Although considering herself an independent Republican, in 1918, the first year New York State women voted, because of Democrat Alfred E. Smith's reputation as an advocate for labour, she supported him for governor.

After organising the women's vote for him, Moskowitz proposed that Gov-

ernor-elect Smith establish a 'Reconstruction Commission' to identify and propose solutions for the state's administrative, social, and economic problems. Smith not only formed the Commission but appointed her its executive director. During the one year of its existence (1919–20), it outlined Smith's legislative programme and launched Moskowitz's career as his closest political advisor. From 1923 on, she ran his state re-election campaigns and guided the legislative enactment of his policies, all the while preparing the ground for his nomination by the Democratic Party as presidential candidate in 1928. In that year, she directed national publicity for the campaign and served as the only woman on the national Democratic Party executive committee.

Al Smith lost that election to Herbert Hoover. But because Belle Moskowitz had played such a central role in his career throughout the 1920s, by the time of his presidential race she was a nationally known political figure. Still, her fame depended on his. Smith had offered her a number of government posts

Courtesy of Elisabeth Perry

but she had refused them. She believed, and rightly so, that her work from behind the scenes would in the end give her more power than the holding of any bureaucratic, appointive office. Thanks to her, Smith, a man whose formal education had ended at the age of thirteen, was able to pursue his legislative programme with enough success to become a viable presidential candidate. But because of her self-effacement, when Smith failed to win the presidency and then lost his party leadership role to Franklin Delano Roosevelt, her career was eclipsed along with his. Future generations of political women would not see her example as an inspiration or model for their own careers.

More famous than Moskowitz, Anna Eleanor Roosevelt (1884–1962) became known worldwide for the role she played as the wife of Franklin Roosevelt, four-term president during the Great Depression and Second World War. Most portraits of Eleanor focus on her activities after 1933, when Franklin became president, until his death in 1945, when she became a United Nations delegate and moral force in world politics. What is less well known is that, before FDR became president, even before he became governor of New York, she had accumulated a vast amount of political experience and influence in her own right.

Unlike Moskowitz, Eleanor Roosevelt was born into wealth and privilege, but endured an unhappy childhood. A measure of fulfillment came to her through her education and volunteer social work. She married Franklin in 1905, bore him several children, and fostered her husband's promising political career. In 1920, this career reached its first culmination when he ran, unsuccessfully, for vice-president. By then their marriage was on shaky ground. Although in 1918 Eleanor had discovered Franklin's affair with Lucy Mercer, the couple had resolved to keep the marriage together. In 1921, Franklin was stricken with polio and withdrew from politics. Franklin's political manager and publicist, Louis Howe, convinced Eleanor to keep her husband's name alive by becoming active herself in women's organisations. Once involved in this work, Eleanor confirmed what she had discovered during her husband's earlier campaigns. She liked politics.

But primarily from within her own sphere. She took up volunteer work for four New York City women's groups: the League of Women Voters and Women's City Club, the Women's Trade Union League, and the Women's Division of the State Democratic Party. For this latter group, from 1925 to 1928 she developed and edited a newspaper that, in bridging the gap between upstate and downstate Democrats, formed a critical base for Al Smith and her husband's future support. Through her other groups she worked for legislation on a variety of important issues: public housing for low-income workers; the dissemination of birth control information, the reorganisation of the state government, and shorter hours and minimum wages for women workers.

To accomplish her goals, she gave talks on the radio and published articles. Journalists interviewed her. She travelled all around the state during and in between campaigns to keep local party leaders connected with one another. She ran the women's campaigns for the Democrats at the state level in 1924 and national level in 1928. As a result, she became a well known figure, almost as well known as her husband, at both state and national level. But when her husband won the governorship in 1928, she gave up all activity. She knew where her duty lay—to become Albany's First Lady, not to hold office herself.

By 1928, in the crucible of New York women's politics, Eleanor Roosevelt had forged for herself acute political skills. These would serve her well as she continued until her husband's death to support his political agendas and afterwards to pursue more directly her own. By 1928, however, she herself had become so prominent that had she wanted she could have run for office and probably won. It did not even occur to her to do so. That was not what women did, especially not women married to ambitious men.

The first woman in the United States to hold cabinet rank was Frances Perkins (1880–1965). Even though she held public office my argument holds true for her as well: her post was appointive, not elective, and she asserted to the end of her life that she had never been interested in a political career. Better educated than either Moskowitz or Roosevelt (she graduated from Mt. Holyoke College), Perkins had a background similar to theirs. After working as a teacher and in a social settlement, she became secretary of the New York Consumers' League, a group seeking labour legislation to improve factory safety and health conditions for all workers. Although always known as 'Miss' Perkins, she was married and bore one child, but her husband suffered from mental illness and was later unable to earn a living. This circumstance gave her a keen interest in finding well paid jobs. Like Moskowitz, she came to admire Al Smith and in 1918 worked for his election as governor. Unlike Moskowitz, when Smith offered her a job as a State Industrial Commissioner, she ac-cepted. This post became the launching pad from which she entered Roosevelt's cabinet in 1933.

Still, when she reflected on her career years later, she denied being a 'career woman' with political ambitions. Doors had opened for her and she had gone through them. She had never dreamed of being Secretary of Labor or Industrial Commissioner, she said. A 'series of circumstances' and her 'own energies' had thrown her into 'situations' where she had assumed responsibility and then was asked to assume more. Before she knew it she 'had a career'.

Here again is an accomplished, talented woman who had matured through social reform and suffrage politics in the 1910s and then moved into appointive office. As she plied her way, although she wanted and needed to work, ideas of personal advancement or career ambition were seldom at the forefront of her thinking. Convinced even at the moment of Roosevelt's elevation of her that she was probably unworthy, she accepted the offer as a 'call to service'. Once she attained office, fearful that men would resist answering to her, she took on the look, dress, and behaviour of a schoolmarm so as to appear less threatening to them. Despite all of her accomplishments, the gender stereotypes and constraints of her time prevailed.

My last example from the period is Mary W. (Molly) Dewson (1874–1962). Like Perkins, Dewson was well educated. After graduating from Wellesley College and holding some research jobs, she became Superintendent of Probation at the nation's first reform school for girls and then executive secretary of the Massachusetts Commission on the Minimum Wage. Never married, she maintained a lifelong partnership with a friend, Polly Porter, with whom she farmed in Massachusetts and did suffrage and war work. Eventually, under the mentorship of Eleanor Roosevelt, Dewson moved into Democratic state and then national politics. Her personal ambitions remained severely limited, however.

When Dewson assessed women's political progress since suffrage, she confessed that their opportunities had barely expanded. usually on the basis of their 'looks, money', or a 'late husband's service to the party', they had received only ceremonial party positions. In these circumstances, Dewson decided that the

Courtesy of Elisabeth Perry

A 1917 photograph of Molly Dewson who co-ordinated a separate women's effort in the Democratic Party between the wars, but from a traditionalist standpoint.

only way to build women's political strength was through separate women's divisions. As head of the Women's Division of the Democratic National Committee, she organised women workers for FDR's campaigns and co-ordinated support for his programmes between elections. In so doing, she played roles essential to the success of the Democratic Party during the New Deal initiative. Like Perkins, Dewson followed a cautious philosophy in working with men: she took on a maternal or 'aunty' pose and disclaimed any relationship to feminism. She also turned down posts when they threatened her partnership with Polly Porter. Only in her old age did she finally enter a political race in her own right. But the race she chose was in a solidly-Republican district where she had no chance of winning.

Among the most politically adept of their generation, all four of these women pursued political goals in the 1920s but none as a man would have done. Moskowitz achieved an important advisory role but lost all her power at the fall of her mentor. Roosevelt sacrificed her own needs to those of her husband. Perkins reached high office but masked her strength and denied personal ambition. Dewson often put domestic happiness before career fulfilment and, like

Perkins, downplayed her feminism. Others of their generation who had been leaders in the suffrage struggle acted similarly.

When younger women growing up in the 1920s and 30s looked at their political forbears, Belle Moskowitz, Eleanor Roosevelt, Frances Perkins, and Molly Dewson were among the few successful ones they saw. But younger women wanted real careers, not roles as an amanuensis to a man or as a behind-the-scenes campaigner. But 'real careers' were denied them. Either men discriminated against them and kept them out of the central circles of power, or when they married they discovered that domestic life and a political career just did not mix.

The door was open to women in politics in the 1920s. But, as Molly Dewson once said, the battle was uphill and most women got quickly discouraged. By accommodating themselves to a reality they could not control, they participated in the perpetuation of a 'separate spheres ideology' long after it had outlived its relevance. Looking back at them from the standpoint of 1993 we might judge these women as 'old fashioned'. But we ought not reject them as important role models. As smart, wily, and skilled political strategists, they have much to teach us. We must reject not them but the constraints that held them back.

Some of those constraints are still with us. Throughout the 1992 campaign, questions about women's appropriate roles in politics continued to surface. They dominated the controversies that swirled around Hillary Clinton, wife of Democratic presidential candidate, Bill Clinton. What role had she played in his years as governor of Arkansas? Why did she keep her maiden name when they were married? What was the quality of their married life together? Had she been a good mother or was she one of those career-orientated, ambitious feminists?

At its national convention in August, the Republican Party exploited popular doubts about Hillary Clinton's ability to operate in the traditional mode of the political wife. In an unprecedented move, convention organisers asked the wives of its candidates, Barbara Bush and Marilyn Quayle, to speak. The shared theme of the women's speeches, 'traditional' family values, sent out a clear message: political wives must adhere strictly to giving priority to their husbands' careers.

The Democratic Party response disturbed many feminists, but it was probably essential to victory. Hillary Clinton got a makeover. She baked cookies and, in response to rumours that she was childless, trotted out her daughter Chelsea at every possible occasion. Still, when Bill Clinton and his running mate, Albert Gore, Jr., made their victory speeches on election night, women heard some new words on national television. In describing their future government, for the first time in history both president and vice-president-elect included the category of 'gender' as an important test of the diversity they envisioned.

Despite their personal openness to women in government, Hillary Clinton remained vulnerable to further attacks. As a lawyer with a distinguished record of accomplishment concerning the rights of children, she took active part in her husband's transition team discussions. Later, she received an appointment as unpaid head of a task force addressing one of the nation's most pressing problems, the lack of a national health insurance system. In response to a query by the press as to how reporters should refer to her, she asked them to use all three of her names, Hillary Rodham Clinton. The charges flew. Ambitious feminist. Power mad. Who is in charge here? In March 1993, on a flight over Washington DC, an airline pilot joked over the loud-speaker, 'Down below you can see the White House, where the president and her husband live'.

If, on the brink of the twenty-first century, the wife of the President of the United States still cannot perform in an authoritative role without questions being raised about the appropriateness of her behaviour how could the women of the 1920s have stood a chance? Today's 'Hillary factor' shows just how far we have come and how far we have to go before women can at last take up citizenship roles equal to those of men.

FOR FURTHER READING:

Blanche W. Cook, *Eleanor Roosevelt,* volume I (Viking, 1992); J. Stanley Lemons, *The Woman Citizen. Social Feminism in the 1920's* (University of Illinois, 1973); George W. Martin, *Madam Secretary Frances Perkins* (Houghton Mifflin, 1976); Elisabeth Israels Perry, *Belle Moskowitz: Feminine Politics and the Exercise of Power in the Age of Alfred E. Smith* (Routlege, 1992); Susan Ware, *Partner and I: Molly Dewson, Feminism, and New Deal Politics* (Yale University Press, 1987).

AFRICAN AMERICAN WOMEN ON THE WESTERN FRONTIER

by Roger D. Hardaway
Associate Professor of History
Northwestern Oklahoma State University

African Americans have been in the American West for as long as European Americans have been. Africans came to the New World with Columbus and other Spanish explorers in the late fifteenth and sixteenth centuries. In the early nineteenth century, an African American named York was a member of the Lewis and Clark Expedition that went to Oregon. A few black "mountain men," including Jim Beckworth and Edward Rose, worked in the Rocky Mountain fur trade that flourished in the years following the Lewis and Clark exploration.

In the 1840s and succeeding decades, the number of blacks in the American West increased substantially. African Americans were miners in California, Colorado, Nevada, and Arizona; cowboys on the trails from Texas to Montana and the Dakotas; military scouts in the Indian Wars; soldiers in the frontier army; homesteaders on the Great Plains; community builders from Nebraska to Oregon and from Texas to California; and elected public officials in several western territories and states including Kansas, Wyoming, and Washington. They were prostitutes, barbers, beauticians, hoteliers, cooks, nannies, stagecoach drivers, Pony Express riders, preachers, outlaws, lawmen, porters, newspaper publishers, real estate developers, lumberjacks, domestic servants, and laborers. In short, they were a small—but significant—part of those who settled and developed the American West.[1]

Compared to European Americans, the number of African Americans on the western frontier of the late nineteenth and early twentieth centuries was not great. In most western territories and states, African Americans comprised less than one percent of the population during the frontier era. Moreover, the number of black women in the West compared to black men was also small.

These two facts have led most historians of the American West and of the African American experience in the United States to make two interrelated omissions. First, they have basically ignored the black presence in the West. And secondly, when they have mentioned western blacks, they have concentrated upon the male experience—mountain men, cowboys, buffalo soldiers—and neglected to discuss those intrepid black females who were western pioneers. Discussing a few black women who lived on the western frontier can alleviate partially this unfortunate situation and make a contribution to a body of work being developed by only a few historians.[2]

One of the first black women who went west was Jane Elizabeth Manning James. Jane Manning was born in Connecticut in 1818 and converted to Mormonism in about 1842. She went to the Mormon community at Nauvoo, Illinois, where she worked as a domestic servant in Joseph Smith's home and married another black Mormon, Isaac James. She, her husband, and their baby son followed the Latter-day Saints to Utah in 1847. Although Jane and Isaac James later divorced, they struggled together for years to develop a farm, accumulate some property, and raise a family of seven children.

When she was fifty-three years old, Jane sold her farm and built a house in a residential area of Salt Lake City. She worked as a domestic servant and laundress to support several of her children and grandchildren. She

From the *Negro History Bulletin,* January-March 1997, pp. 8-13. © 1997 by the Association for the Study of Negro Life and History. Reprinted by permission.

also made and sold soap and raised garden vegetables in order to eke out a sparse livelihood. In the meantime, she was active in her church, joining the ladies' auxiliary, doing charity work, and pleading in vain for church leaders to end the religion's discriminatory treatment of its few black members. She died as she lived—poor but devout—in 1908, just a few days shy of her ninetieth birthday.[3]

Another African American woman to travel with Mormons to Utah led a life almost totally different from that of Jane James. This woman, known originally only as "Bridget," was born the same year as James—1818. But Bridget was born a slave in Mississippi, and she went to Utah in 1848 with her master, Robert Smith, who had converted to Mormonism. Smith took Bridget and several other slaves to California in 1851 where another Mormon community was being established at San Bernardino.

Although California had entered the Union in 1850 as a free state, several slave owners took their human chattels to the state apparently assuming that the law would not be enforced. Unfortunately, this was often the case, and Bridget and several other blacks—including some of her children—labored in involuntary servitude for Smith in California for five years. In 1856 Smith decided to move to Texas where his status as a slaveholder would be more secure. At this point, however, Bridget and the law intervened and thwarted his plans.

With the help of some African American and Caucasian friends, Bridget sued for her freedom and that of Robert Smith's other slaves. In a landmark case, the judge agreed with the black plaintiffs, and Bridget became a free woman. She adopted the last name of "Mason," and was known throughout the remainder of her life as "Biddy Mason"—"Biddy" apparently being a diminutive version of "Bridget."

Biddy Mason moved to Los Angeles where she became a well-known pioneer and community leader. She worked as a nurse and midwife for a local doctor and helped him deliver hundreds of babies. She managed to save a few dollars a year from her meager salary and began investing in real estate. First, she purchased two vacant lots for a total of two hundred and fifty dollars. Then she bought some rental houses and a commercial building. Her wealth began to grow along with her fame as one of the first African American female landowners in Los Angeles.

Like Jane James, Biddy Mason was a religious woman. Unlike James, however, Mason had no love for Mormonism. In 1872 a few Los Angeles blacks met in Biddy Mason's home and organized the city's first African Methodist Episcopal church. Mason also donated much money during her lifetime to poor people who needed it. This intelligent and determined woman, who was a slave for the first thirty-seven and a half years of her life, remained unpretentious as she grew wealthy. She lived a rather simple and basic existence until her death in 1891 at the age of seventy-two. Her descendants, however, parlayed her small fortune into a much larger one and became members of Los Angeles's black elite community in the late nineteenth and early twentieth centuries.[4]

One other black female California pioneer has become as well-known to historians as Biddy Mason. This woman was Mary Ellen Pleasant, often called "Mammy" by both her friends and her numerous enemies. Pleasant, like Mason, became a wealthy business woman and the plaintiff in an important California civil rights case.

The facts of Mary Pleasant's life are shrouded in mystery. She was a controversial figure about whom many rumors circulated. She contributed to the confusion herself by being deliberately vague about the facts of her background prior to her arrival in California in about 1849. Perhaps the best guess about her early life is that she was born in Pennsylvania in 1814. From her first husband, a wealthy (supposedly Cuban) planter, she inherited several thousand dollars. She then married John Pleasant, and they were active in the abolition movement in New England before moving to San Francisco during the California gold rush.

Mary Pleasant worked at several jobs in California that were typical for African American women on the frontier. She was first a cook and housekeeper for several white men; later, she operated boardinghouses, restaurants, and laundries. What was rather untypical about her was that she, like Biddy Mason, invested her money wisely and became wealthy. Rumors alleged that she was the mistress of one of her rich white business partners, that she practiced voodoo, and that her boardinghouses were really brothels. But, like the details of her early years, the truth is elusive and will probably never be known.

Like many other black women in the West, Mary Pleasant was active in church and charity work—helping whites as well as her fellow African Americans. Perhaps her most significant contribution to life for blacks in California, however, was that she helped secure a measure of legal equality for them in several instances. She reportedly helped free some members of her race who were being enslaved illegally in California, and she aided in the fight to permit blacks to testify in the state's courts. In the late 1860s, she sued a streetcar company that refused to allow her and other blacks to ride, and she won in a case that went all the way to the California supreme court.

Mary Pleasant's later years were sad ones. She suffered several business setbacks and may have been cheated out of some of her money by unscrupulous associates. She died impoverished in San Francisco in January 1904 at the age of eighty-nine.[5]

Like those of James, Mason, and Pleasant, the lives of two Colorado women serve also to highlight the generosity and kindheartedness many African American women exhibited toward their fellow humans in the late nineteenth-century American West. Both endured the brutality of slavery and unbelievable human suffering in their lives, yet each was blessed with the strength of character to find the goodness in others and to work to make the world a better place. Because of this, both earned the respect of almost all who knew them regardless of race or social and economic standing.

Clara Brown was born a slave in Tennessee around 1800 and moved to Kentucky as a child. At the age of eighteen, she married a fellow slave, and they eventually had several children. In 1835 her master died, and his heirs decided to sell all of his property including his human chattels. Clara, her husband, and their children were sold to several different slaveholders and she never saw most of them again (although, when she was in her eighties, she was able to reunite with one of her daughters and learn that she had grandchildren and great-grandchildren).

Clara's new master in 1835 was George Brown. He and his family apparently treated Clara kindly although they did not free her until after Brown's death in 1857. A Kentucky law required freed slaves to leave the state, and Clara—now known as "Clara Brown"—made her way to St. Louis where she worked as a domestic servant for a family who had known George Brown. She soon moved with this family to Kansas, and in 1859—when she was nearing sixty years of age—she worked her way to the Colorado gold fields by cooking for members of a wagon train heading west.

Clara Brown settled in the mining town of Auraria near Denver and got a job cooking in a restaurant. Soon, however, she moved about forty miles north of Denver to Mountain City, where she began doing laundry for miners. Her cabin soon became a sort of makeshift clinic as Brown began nursing sick and hurt miners back to health and acting as midwife for some of the pregnant women in the camp.

Like Biddy Mason and Mary Ellen Pleasant in California, Clara Brown invested her money wisely. She used some of it to buy real estate parcels, and she soon owned several mining claims and rental properties. She often loaned money to miners in exchange for a share of any gold they might find. Moreover, she donated quite a bit of her income to several churches that were struggling to become established in various Colorado mining towns. Occasionally, she hosted church groups in her cabin until they could build permanent structures in which to hold services.

In the late 1860s Brown returned to Kentucky and financed the relocation to Colorado of sixteen ex-slaves who wanted to leave the South. A decade later, she visited Kansas and volunteered her nursing and cooking skills to help some of the homesteaders who were struggling to survive there. These kindnesses exhausted the small fortune she had accumulated since becoming free.

In the early 1880s Clara Brown's health began to fail. Because of her generosity to people in Colorado during the twenty-plus years she had lived there, several of her African American and Caucasian friends moved her to Denver and provided her a house where she lived rent-free until her death in October 1885. In 1881, members of the Society of Colorado Pioneers reversed their policy of allowing only white men into the organization and elected Clara Brown to membership in the exclusive group. Such unprecedented action indicates the high esteem in which Brown was held by her fellow westerners—white and black, rich and poor, men and women.[6]

Like Clara Brown, Julia Greeley was born into slavery; she did not, however, know the date and place of her birth. While she was in bondage, one of Greeley's masters became enraged and shot her in the face, disfiguring her and causing her to lose one eye. Sadly, some people ever thereafter referred to her as "One-Eyed Julia." Greeley received her freedom during the Civil War, and went west as the domestic servant of a white woman who—in

1874—married William Gilpin, the first territorial governor of Colorado.

Julia Greeley lived in Denver for the last forty-four years of her life. Mrs. Gilpin, a Catholic, converted her African American servant to that faith. Greeley apparently never married, and she devoted her life to church work and to helping others. After the Gilpins died, she labored for several other wealthy white families and gave away almost all of her money to people in need. One of her more magnanimous gestures occurred when she heard that the body of an elderly African American man was going to be buried in a pauper's grave; at Greeley's insistence, the man was laid to rest in the plot she had purchased for herself. One result of this and other acts of kindness was that many of her fellow Denverites began referring to her as the "Colored Angel of Charity."

Another consequence of her generosity, however, was that she died—in June 1918— without a burial plot. However, her many African American and Caucasian friends—who included some of Colorado's richest and most powerful citizens as well as those on the other end of the social and economic spectrum— bought her a grave site better than the one she had given away. They also furnished her a lavish funeral as a way of paying their respects to a remarkable person who they rightfully believed was deserving of the kind of generosity she had always displayed to others.[7]

Life in the West was often lonely for African American women because so few other members of their race and gender were present on the frontier. As a result, most black women chose to live in urban areas so they could associate with other African American females. Urban black women founded social and literary clubs as well as religious—and sometimes political—societies. These organizations not only allowed them to make friends and to contribute to society, but they also helped them relieve the loneliness and boredom that often characterized life on the frontier.[8]

The lives of two Montana women who resided in small towns where there were few other African American females demonstrate that life in such surroundings could often be lonely and depressing. Although Tish Nevins and Mary Fields were both well-liked by their (mostly Caucasian) acquaintances, one senses that neither was ever truly happy living in the American West. Neither ever married, and both felt a special solitude from having almost no other blacks with whom to associate. Thus,

they never had the opportunity to join clubs and societies, and they rarely got to share personal experiences, hopes, frustrations, or needs with other black women. Still, each made a unique contribution to the western American frontier, attesting to the ability of the human spirit to survive and even thrive under the most adverse of conditions.

Tish Nevins was born a slave in Missouri in 1862. Although freed as a child and reared in the home of a minister for whom her mother worked, she was never sent to school and, consequently, never learned to read or write. When she was twenty-eight years old, Nevins was working as a domestic servant for a white couple. A few days after giving birth to her tenth child, however, Nevins's female employer died rather suddenly. Nevins took it upon herself to become the surrogate mother of the woman's baby and to help the father, Robert Smithey, raise his other children. When Smithey moved his family to Hamilton, Montana, in 1899, Tish Nevins went, too. She lived there for forty-three years, until her death in 1942. For much of that time she operated a boardinghouse that became well-known for its excellent food.

One of only three African Americans in Hamilton, Nevins dedicated herself to her business and to the white children who she thought it was her destiny to raise. She was at once gregarious and humorous around her customers and a strict disciplinarian to the children. Almost all who knew her liked her, and the Smitheys adored her for her devotion to them. But while Nevins was outwardly happy and satisfied that she had found her reasons for existing, she often exhibited a melancholia at not being able to read and at having almost no black people with whom to share her life's experiences.[9]

The life of Mary Fields paralleled, in some respects, that of Tish Nevins. Like Nevins, Fields was born a slave, went west with whites, lived much of her life in a small Montana town, operated a restaurant, and never married (perhaps because almost all of her acquaintances were Caucasians). But Fields was much coarser in manner than Nevins, possibly because she was thirty years older and spent those three decades in slavery in her native Tennessee. Born in 1832, Fields went north after the Civil War and worked in a convent in Ohio for several years. Some of the nuns in the convent decided to move to Montana in 1884 to open a school for Indian girls. Soon thereafter, Fields received word that one of the nuns had taken ill in the West and was near death. Fields went to Montana, nursed the woman back to health, and decided to stay in the West.

One of Mary Fields's jobs at the Montana convent was to drive a wagon into the nearby town of Cascade for supplies. In the winter, the weather made this job especially difficult. Once, she got caught in a blizzard that obscured the road and made further travel impossible. She had to stop the wagon and walk back and forth all night to keep from freezing to death.

Another time, a pack of wolves frightened her horses and overturned the wagon. Fields had to guard her cargo all night to keep the wolves from pillaging it. At dawn, the wolves retreated, Fields righted the wagon, reloaded the supplies, and completed her trip to the convent.

Like all Montana pioneers, Mary Fields had to be tough to survive in the northern plains. And tough she was. She seldom went anywhere without a shotgun or pistol, she smoked cigars constantly, liked to drink, and was always getting into fist fights with the convent's hired men. Once, when she was seventy years old, she knocked a man down who owed her two dollars and refused to pay it.

Ten years after Mary Fields moved to Montana, the area bishop forced her to leave the convent because of her often disruptive behavior. She moved to Cascade where she operated a restaurant and a laundry. The nun she had nursed back to health in 1884 helped her obtain the contract to drive the U.S. mail stagecoach from Cascade to the convent, and she performed this task for eight years. She was well-liked by most people in town and, of course, known by everyone. In her old age she served as the mascot of a local baseball team, and when she died in 1914, local whites raised money to bury her in a cemetery on the road she had driven so often from Cascade to the convent.[10]

The seven women profiled in this article were all unique individuals. Yet in some ways they are representative of other African American female pioneers. They are among those members of their race and gender whose stories have been preserved for history, but they are by no means the only ones who lived on the frontier. Many other black women worked in the West's inhospitable social and physical environment to help settle it. They—and many others like them—contributed to the development of the American West, and they deserve any and all recognition and respect they receive.

ENDNOTES

1. General works on African Americans in the western United States during the late nineteenth and early twentieth centuries include W. Sherman Savage, *Blacks in the West* (Westport, Connecticut: Greenwood Press, 1976); William Loren Katz, *The Black West*, 3rd ed. (Seattle: Open Hand Publishing, Inc., 1987); Kenneth Wiggins Porter, *The Negro on the American Frontier* (New York: Arno Press and the New York Times, 1971); James deT. Abajian, compiler, *Blacks and Their Contributions to the American West: A Bibliography and Union List of Library Holdings Through 1970* (Boston: G.K. Hall and Co., 1974); and Roger D. Hardaway, *A Narrative Bibliography of the African American Frontier: Blacks in the Rocky Mountain West, 1535–1912* (Lewiston, New York: The Edwin Mellen Press, 1995).

2. General works on African American women on the western frontier include Lawrence B. de Graaf, "Race, Sex, and Region: Black Women in the American West, 1850–1920," *Pacific Historical Review* 49 (May 1980): 285–313; and Glenda Riley, "American Daughters: Black Women in the West," *Montana: The Magazine of Western History* 38, no. 2 (Spring 1988): 14–27. See also Anne M. Butler, "Still in Chains: Black Women in Western Prisons, 1865–1910," *Western Historical Quarterly* 20 (1989): 18–35.

3. Henry J. Wolfinger, "A Test of Faith: Jane Elizabeth James and the Origins of the Utah Black Community," in *Social Accommodation in Utah*, ed. Clark Knowlton (Salt Lake City: University of Utah American West Center, 1975): 126–72.

4. Dolores Hayden, "Biddy Mason's Los Angeles, 1856–1891," *California History* 68 (Fall 1989): 86–99, 147–49; and Oscar L. Sims, "Biddy Mason," in *Notable Black American Women*, ed. Jessie Carney Smith (Detroit: Gale Research Inc., 1992): 732–34.

5. Helena Woodard, "Mary Ellen Pleasant, in *Notable Black American Women*: 858–62; W. Sherman Savage, "Pleasant, Mary Ellen," in *Notable American Women, 1607–1950: A Biographical Dictionary*, Vol. 3, ed. Edward T. James (Cambridge, Massachusetts: Belknap Press of Harvard University Press, 1971): 75–77; and Lerone Bennett, Jr., "The Mystery of Mary Ellen Pleasant," *Ebony* 34 (April 1979): 90–92, 94–96; and 34 (May 1979): 71–72, 74, 76, 80, 82, 86. Most historians do not consider Helen Holdredge, *Mammy Pleasant* (New York: Putnam, 1953) to be reliable.

6. Kathleen Bruyn, *"Aunt" Clara Brown: Story of a Black Pioneer* (Boulder, Colorado: Pruett Publishing Co., 1970). The author of this account acknowledges that her book contains fictionalized dialogue but she claims that she has correctly portrayed the basic facts of Clara Brown's life.

7. M. Lilliana Owens, "Julia Greeley, 'Colored Angel of Charity,'" *Colorado Magazine* 20 (1943): 176–78.

8. The two articles that best examine this phenomenon both use the experiences of African American women in Colorado; however, other research shows that black females in other frontier areas acted in similar fashion. See Sue Armitage, Theresa Banfield, and Sarah Jacobus, "Black Women and Their Communities in Colorado," *Frontiers: A Journal of Women's Studies* 2, no. 2 (1977): 45–51; and Lynda F. Dickson, "African American Women's Clubs in Denver, 1890s–1920s," in *Peoples of Color in the American West*, ed. Sucheng Chan, Douglas Henry Daniels, Mario T. Garcia, and Terry P. Wilson (Lexington, Massachusetts: D.C. Heath and Co., 1994): 224–34.

9. Glenn Chaffin, "Aunt Tish: Beloved Gourmet of the Bitter Root," *Montana: The Magazine of Western History* 21, no. 4 (Autumn 1971): 67–69.

10. Gary Cooper, "Stage Coach Mary," *Ebony* 14 (October 1959): 97–100.

"Rights as Well as Duties": The Rhetoric of Leonora O'Reilly

Anne F. Mattina

The following essay provides an analysis of the rhetorical strategies employed by Leonora O'Reilly, a Progressive Era labor reformer. The essay argues that O'Reilly's use of enactment and empowerment are representative of a "feminine style" as defined by Campbell (1989) and extended by Dow and Tonn (1993). As a subject of analysis, O'Reilly's rhetoric provides an opportunity to examine the public voice of a working-class female reformer.

KEY CONCEPTS *Leonora O'Reilly, Women's Trade Union League, True Womanhood, Progressive Era, feminine style, labor reform*

ANNE F. MATTINA *(Ph.D., Ohio State University, 1986) is an Assistant Professor in the Communication Studies Department at Northeastern University, Boston, MA 02115. Material published from the O'Reilly Papers by permission of Schlesinger Library, Radcliffe College, Cambridge, MA. The author wishes to thank the Library for their cooperation in this research project.*

Leonora O'Reilly (1870–1927), a noted Progressive Era labor reformer, was celebrated in her day as an inspirational orator. Born into working class poverty on New York's Lower East Side, she is most remembered for her career as a paid organizer and recruiter for the Women's Trade Union League (WTUL) during the years from 1903 to 1915. She was a tireless advocate for the working class during her life, and along with activism in other areas, most notably suffrage, she remained committed to the cause of labor reform.

O'Reilly is unique as a historical figure for many reasons, not the least of which is her career as a working class female public speaker. Her career came during a time period when women's public roles were still very much proscribed. While the Progressive Era gave rise to the expansion of many aspects of women's lives, public speaking was not seen as a "suitable" career for women. Furthermore, in the early days of "big labor," women were looked upon as expendable to the work force and therefore not worth organizing.

To this point, very little has been published dealing specifically with O'Reilly and her rhetoric. Many historians and women studies scholars have investigated the WTUL, and have noted O'Reilly's importance to the League (Tax, 1980). Most have agreed that she served as the "conscience" of the League during its early years, never wavering in her commitment to the workers, and never letting the upper-class "allies" forget the worker's plight.

O'Reilly's life and rhetoric warrant investigation for several reasons. First, she was a member of the working class operating in a milieu largely dominated by middle- and upper-class educated women. It has been well-documented that those active in the settlement house movement and other causes of the Progressive Era were, for the most part, from the first generations of college educated women in America. O'Reilly left school at the age of eleven, and while she did later complete a course of instruction as an industrial sewing teacher, her formal education was almost non-existent. She worked for pay almost her entire life, an experience not shared by many reformers of this time. Her papers, diaries, and letters provide us with a unique perspective, heretofore largely ignored, of a working woman.

Another rationale for examining O'Reilly's rhetoric is that she was a paid public speaker, a career choice not available to many women before, during or after the Progressive Era. She regularly took to the streets, to meeting halls and even to a Senate committee on suffrage. She was paid for her magazine articles and her opinions solicited by newspapers.

While many women were finding their public voice during this period, they did so risking not only their reputations, but their physical persons as well. Women who spoke publicly risked having their "femininity" questioned, and working women were even more suspect as they had already violated society's ideal by engaging in labor outside of their homes (Campbell, 1989). O'Reilly risked society's censure not only by speaking in public, but by getting paid for her work as well. She was chastised for taking money by upper-class reformers as voluntarism was the only way such behavior was viewed as even semi-respectable (Bulzarik, 1983, p. 71). Her audiences were primarily female, and her message to them to organize, strike, and agitate for the vote was at odds with society's definition of what it meant to be a woman.

Dow and Tonn (1993) call for the revision of "paradigms that view female or feminist rhetorical action simply in terms of its *adaptation* to obstacles posed by patriarchy and more in terms of its attempts to *offer alternatives* to patriarchal modes of thought and reasoning" (original emphasis, p. 299). O'Reilly's significance to rhetorical critics lies in the fact that while she did face the rhetorical challenges posed by gender and class, she did so with a distinct voice. In what follows, I will argue that O'Reilly utilized her expertise as a working woman for the purpose of both enactment and empowerment of her audience, and that these strategies served as a form of "feminine style." As described by Campbell (1989), feminine style is based upon experiences typical of women, historically excluded from the public domain. Discourse resulting from a life primarily centered around home and family reflects the "craft-learning" which occurs there. As Campbell (1989) notes: "Such a discourse will be personal in tone, relying heavily on personal experiences, anecdotes, and other examples" (p. 13). This discourse serves to empower as it validates the experience of both the speaker and the audience, the result of which is "consciousness-raising," which serves to produce "group cohesion and transforms the audience members into 'agents of change'" (Dow and Tonn, 1993, p. 289). Additionally, O'Reilly employed enactment, defined by Campbell as occurring when the speaker is proof of the claim he or she is making (1982, p. 273). Enactment also functions as both proof and a way to present evidence vividly. While O'Reilly may have used the public platform in very similar ways as her male counterparts during the Progressive Era, she did so as a woman, and utilized specific "feminine style" and strategies.

Women's Public Speaking in the Early 20th Century

While the opportunities to speak in public were numerous for female reformers during America's Progressive Era, rhetorical choices were severely constrained. That temperance, suffragist, labor and social welfare advocates were burdened by gender expectations is not a new idea. Since Campbell's (1973) seminal work on the rhetoric of modern women's liberation, scholars have been aware of the oxymoronic nature of being female and being rhetor. In her more recent book, *Man Cannot Speak for Her* (1989), Campbell traces the roots of this oxymoron when she describes the problems faced by earlier advocates of women's rights and reforms.

American women, most particularly white, middle-class women, experienced life under the tenets of "True Womanhood." A "True Woman," according to 19th century societal dictates possessed the characteristics of piety, purity, domes-

ticity and spirituality. As Campbell (1989) explains, these were clearly at odds with the role of rhetor:

> Speakers had to be expert and authoritative; women were submissive. Speakers ventured into the public sphere (the courtroom, the legislature, the pulpit, or the lecture platform); woman's domain was domestic. Speakers called attention to themselves, took stands aggressively, initiated action, affirmed their expertise; "true women" were retiring and modest, their influence was indirect, and they had no expertise or authority. These were viewed as exclusively masculine traits related to man's allegedly lustful, ruthless, competitive, amoral and ambitious nature. Activities requiring such qualities were thought to "unsex" women. (p. 10)

What became known as "woman's sphere" included domestic concerns only. Much research within women's history has shown that the "sphere," while most representative of the privileged classes, held sway over all women regardless of race or class. As Cott (1979) points out in her analysis of the impact of "True Womanhood" during the earlier days of the Industrial Revolution: "It is no accident that the slogan 'women's place is in the home' took on a certain aggressiveness and shrillness precisely at the time when increasing numbers of poorer women left their home to become factory workers" (p. 191). While class distinctions are important to the analysis of a working woman's rhetoric, it should be noted that "the lady and the mill girl" had one thing in common: "they were equally disenfranchised and isolated from the vital centers of power" (Cott, 1979, p. 191).

Despite this, women had publicly agitated for numerous causes during the 19th century, using a variety of rhetorical styles to deal with the tensions engendered by "True Womanhood." Campbell (1989, p. 14) writes of the contradictory nature of the primary arguments made by suffragists and others, that of the tension between argument from justice and argument from expediency. The former argued for women's rights based on their natural rights as citizens, the latter on their special characteristics as women. These themes prevail throughout the next decades of women's rhetoric.

> By the close of the century the spectrum of ideology in the woman (sic) movement had a see-saw quality: at one end, the intention to eliminate sex-specific limitations; at the other, the desire to recognize rather than quash the qualities and habits called female, to protect the interests women had already defined as theirs and give those much greater public scope. (Cott, 1987, p. 19)

One result of this tension was the emergence of a distinct feminine style of rhetoric:

> It will invite audience participation including the process of testing generalizations or principles against the experiences of the audience. Audience members will be addressed as peers, with recognition of authority based on experience, and efforts will be made to create identification with the experience of the audience and those described by the speaker. The goal of such rhetoric is empowerment. (Campbell, 1989, p. 13)

By the first several decades of this century, women's sphere had been somewhat enlarged, particularly for white women of the upper-class who experienced more opportunities for college educations and careers than at any time in the country's history. This led to increased activism among women as a whole. Women of all ages, races, ethnic and economic backgrounds took to the public platform for a myriad of causes, only to feel first hand societal censure for such actions. Most typically, that censure took the form of being labeled "mannish" or "unsexed," labels designed to frighten speakers and audiences of the day. In a time and place where sex-specific behaviors were rigid and unyielding, any hint that a person was not living up to expectations could (and often did) meet with such response as this by William Lee Howard, in the *New York Medical Journal* of 1900:

> The female possessed of masculine ideas of independence, the virago who would sit in the public highways and lift up her pseudo-virile voice, proclaiming her sole right to decide questions of war or religion, or the value of celibacy and the curse of women's impurity, and that disgusting antisocial being, the female sexual pervert, are simply different degrees of the same class-degenerates. (cited in Smith-Rosenberg, 1985, p. 280)

Thus, women in the years between 1900 and the passage of the 19th amendment faced many difficult rhetorical choices. By the very act of public reform they were "unsexing" themselves, and conversely, by arguing for privileges based on gender, they were reinforcing the notion that a separate sphere could/should exist. In this tumultuous rhetorical era, the Women's Trade Union League was formed.

Leonora O'Reilly and the Women's Trade Union League

The WTUL is recognized by many scholars of women's history for its unique configuration of membership. The League was formed by upper-middle class women and men, along with workers in 1903, specifically for the purpose of improving the lives of working class women: "Together these women forged a unique coalition of women workers and wealthy women disenchanted with conventional and philanthropic and reform activities" (Dye, 1980, p. 1). The WTUL was also noted not only for its "cross-class" alliances, but for its ethnic diversity as well, as its membership rolls included Italians, Eastern European Jews, and Irish women along with native born Americans. Recruiting was done in Yiddish and Italian, as well as English. The WTUL was a unique combination of feminine and feminist principles and practices. Teas, socials and elocution lessons were offered by the allies, while more radical workers like O'Reilly helped lead job actions and strikes. Together, workers and allies battled male bosses and male-dominated unions in a concerted effort to organize working women.

O'Reilly had come to labor reform at the very young age of 16, when she joined the Knights of Labor with her mother. In 1897, she organized a women's local of the United Garment Workers of America, and was already in demand as a speaker. Her experience as a worker and labor activist brought her into contact with many upper-class reformers of the period, and she was a charter member of the New York chapter of the WTUL. By 1909, she was a full-time organizer for the group. "There is no doubt of your being the great stump orator!"

wrote League president, Margaret Dreier Robins (cited in James, 1971, p. 652).

O'Reilly's oratory can best be characterized as a rhetoric of dissent. She continually expressed her dissatisfaction with the status quo through agitation, defined as "a persistent and uncompromising statement and restatement of grievances through all available communication channels, with the aim of creating public opinion favorable to a change in some conditions" (Lomas, 1968, p. 2).

Examination of O'Reilly's papers, catalogued within the larger WTUL collection, shows that she skillfully used every opportunity and means to promote labor reform and later in her career, to promote suffrage and peace. Not only did she speak consistently, she contributed to all manner of labor and progressive magazines and newspapers. The annual report issued by the WTUL of New York for the year 1908–09, includes some thirty-two official speeches credited to her alone, and there is evidence that she spoke almost daily during the years 1909–1913. This period saw intense labor unrest throughout the Northeast and Midwest, particularly amongst female workers. "The Great Strikes," as they have come to be known, were led and sustained by the various chapters of the WTUL and its members.

Her personal correspondence alongside League memorabilia provides ample evidence that O'Reilly was tireless in efforts toward reform. "Dear Sister Leonora," wrote Dora Lewis, president of the Pennsylvania Woman Suffrage Association in 1912, "Mrs. Falconer tells me that they were all enchanted with you last week. I am so glad that you were able to deliver your message and cannot understand where you found either voice or thought after the four splendid speeches you made at Independence Square. How *could* you do it?" (original emphasis, O'Reilly papers, reel 6).[1] O'Reilly was also aware of the utility of a public demonstration as her own letters show. "Dear Miss Greenberger," she wrote in 1913,

> Will you help to get out as many girls as you can to walk with us in the Wage Earners Division of the parade Saturday, May 3rd. . . . For the sake of the kiddies in the White Goods Trade those of us who believe in Votes for Women ought to make as big a showing as possible this year to prove to the politicians that the Working Girl has arrived and that she knows that she has rights as well as duties, and means to fight for them. When she isn't fighting she can stand up and be counted at least. So please will you help Mother O'Reilly to put the fear of God if not of Votes in the Politicians hearts. (O'Reilly papers, reel 6)

"The agitator," writes Lomas, is always with us, speaking to whoever will listen" (1968, p. 7). O'Reilly spoke to groups large—an audience of 8,000 in the Hippodrome—and small, often setting up her stump on street corners during the early days of the League. Indeed, she was even invited to testify before Congress on the issue of working women and the vote.

Her message was simultaneously reform and revolution-oriented. On the one hand, her specific programs: a shorter work day, protection of all workers, standardization of wages and suffrage did not necessarily engender an upheaval of the entire system. However, the fact that she was a woman, and a working class woman no less, publicly engaged in these efforts, was so radical as to be considered revolutionary. The public often reacted with outrage to female labor reformers of this period.

Indeed, such outrage occasionally accelerated to violence. The working class women involved in the "Uprising of the 20,000," a major strike in the garment industry in 1909, were physically and verbally abused by police officers and company-financed prostitutes, hired to harass and beat the strikers. (One strike leader suffered 6 broken ribs and numerous stints in jail during the length of the strike.) Once an altercation began, the strikers were immediately hauled off to jail and the prostitutes sent on their way. Before the judge, further harassment was likely to occur. "Magistrate Olmstead," Tax writes, "sentenced another girl with the message: 'You are on strike against God and Nature, whose firm law it is that man shall earn his bread on the sweat of his brow. You are on strike against God' " (1980, pp. 214–220).

O'Reilly herself did not seem deterred by such reaction, however, as the only evidence we have of her slowing down her speaking schedule was in response to health concerns. That she was well aware of the constraints of gender expectations is found in a letter to a friend in 1913:

> This much I believe is true, I am trying to bring harmony out of the chaos we call civilization. Let us all try with hearts as well as heads. This is womans (sic) way, theysay; they used to say further that is woman's weakness. If we succeed we will make of our weakness a lasting strength for mankind. No harm is a good brave try at a thing so splendid. (O'Reilly papers, reel 6)

Feminine Style

As a case study in feminine style, O'Reilly's experience is not easily categorized. She does in fact utilize many of the forms described earlier, yet she was known in her day as an expert both in the areas of labor reform and public speaking. This role of expert would seem at odds with the traditional understanding of the feminine role, and with Campbell's description of feminine style engendering a "peer relationship" between speaker and audience.

In their analysis of Gov. Ann Richards's rhetorical style, Dow and Tonn (1993) face a comparable dilemma. After determining that Richards does not limit her stance to that of a peer, they argue persuasively that her rhetoric "reflects the complicated nature of nurturing persona, in which authority is used for the purpose of fostering growth of the other toward the capacity for independent action. . . . Nurturance is central to the work of empowerment" (pp. 296–297). Like Richards, O'Reilly's rhetorical stance as both an expert and a peer served "to reduce the distance between rhetor and audience and empowers audiences to trust their own perceptions and judgments" (Dow & Tonn, 1993, p. 299).

Bulzarik writes that O'Reilly "based her right to speak for working women on the cumulative experience of herself, her mother and grandmother in the labor force, 'an ancestral and personal experience of daily intercourse of 55 years or more' "(1983, p. 67). This informed her strategic use of enactment. Testifying before the Joint Committee on Suffrage in 1913, O'Reilly begins by stating, "I, too, know whereof I speak"; and concludes her remarks, "You men say to us: 'Go back to the home. Your place is in the home' yet as children we must come out of the home at 11, at 13, and at the age of 15 to earn a living; we have got to make good or starve" (cited in Scott & Scott, 1975, p. 126).

Responding to the publication of Dorothy Richardson's *The Long Day,* a sensationalistic expose of working women, O'Reilly penned a scathing response which she never mailed off. Her papers contain her original manuscript, however, and again we get a sense of her use of enactment:

> No, good Mr. Editor, Mr. Publisher, Mr. Sensational Minister and Lady Bountiful at afternoon teas, you may have paid your money for a *real* working girl sensation but you did not get the *real* thing. No working woman ever wrote like that about her class. . . . I assert positively without fear of contradiction after an experience of over twenty years daily intercourse with them *as one of them*. (original emphasis, O'Reilly papers, reel 9)

In a well-publicized incident during the "Uprising of the 20,000," we get a sense of both O'Reilly's class-consciousness, along with the strategy of enactment. The idea of the WTUL, college and upper-class women "helping the helpless workers" bothered O'Reilly to no end. "The dignity of labor," was a term she used over and over in her speeches and articles. Her class-consciousness led her to a strong embrace of Socialism, much to the dismay of many of the wealthy supporters of the League and those who got involved during the "Uprising." Indeed, Anne Morgan, daughter of industrialist J. P. Morgan, attended a meeting at Carnegie Hall during the strike. On the stage were 370 arrested strikers, and the speakers that night included Leonora O'Reilly and Morris Hillquit, a lawyer for the Socialist Party. The event was cosponsored by the Party and the League. Morgan was so upset by what she heard that night, she felt compelled to call a press conference the next morning:

> I deplore the fanatical statements of Morris Hillquit and Leonora O'Reilly and others at times such as these. . . . In these times of stress, these meetings should be an appeal to reason and sound judgment, and it is extremely dangerous to allow these Socialist appeals to emotionalism. It is very reprehensible for Socialists to take advantage of these poor girls in these times, and when the working people are in such dire straits, to teach their fanatical doctrines. (cited in Tax, 1980, p. 231)

O'Reilly wasted no time in responding, as *The New York Mail* carried this story several days later: *"MISS MORGAN ATTACKED BY STRIKE CHIEF."* The subheads read: "Ignorant of Socialism or Unsympathetic, Says Miss O'Reilly," and "Speech Before Shirtwaist Girls Causes Trouble." O'Reilly immediately identified Morgan's hypocrisy by stating that, "In view of her present attitude, compared with her vaunted interest in the strikers' behalf her charges seem both inconsistent and unkind." O'Reilly continued:

> Perhaps if Miss Morgan had ever been face to face with hunger and eviction for the sake of a principle and that principle the very foundation and watch word of America, 'union', she would understand the way those strikers felt. It communicated itself to me, and I said only what came to me by right of my intimate knowledge of the conditions. (O'Reilly papers, reel 9)

This class-consciousness is also found in O'Reilly's continued efforts towards empowering her audiences. Very early in her career (1896) in her draft of a manuscript of a speech entitled, "Organization," we find strong evidence of this:

> [I]f we do not command respect we will never get it, this same manuf.(acturer) has most respect and consideration for the man who can hold his own with him in the comp.(etitive?) market. So it must be with women. We must show not only our bosses but the world at large that life is a serious matter with us and we want to know its true meaning. We must take up our trades as men do theirs to learn the whole trade . . . we should have our meeting places where we can come together [to] discuss what we think a fair price for our services and then in clear, calm and determined measure present our claims. In this way we must teach our employer that we are workers with them in the industrial world. (O'Reilly papers, reel 9)

She always referred to working women as "thinking women" or "intelligent"—never did she talk down to them, rather she was often inspirational. In a 1910 newspaper column commemorating Labor Day she honors the actions of the strikers, exalting them. She writes:

> Today, then, let us give foremost place to the brave strikers of 1909 and 1910. These men and women who for a principle suffered indignity, imprisonment and hunger while fighting life's hard battle for bread, they risked their lives as surely as any soldier ever did going into battle. Surely these strikers are the vanguard of the intelligent revolt against our present irrational, barbaric, soulless industrial system. (O'Reilly papers, reel 9)

In an essay appearing in the October, 1911 edition of *The Woman Voter* by O'Reilly entitled, "Why the Working Woman Should Vote," the byline reads "By a Labor Leader and Scholar." She begins by posing a series of questions:

> What is this Woman's Movement? How does it affect the Working Woman? Wherefore this world-wide agitation for Votes for Women? Why can't a woman remain content with life as she has always found it?
> Votes for woman; what does this mean? Nothing more than the aspiration of woman to give expression to such intelligence as she possesses through the medium of the ballot box. (O'Reilly papers, reel 9)

Later, in 1912, she wrote an article for the magazine, *Life and Labor,* on "The Story of Kalamazoo," reporting on the striking corset workers in that Michigan city. She noted that the company had gotten a blanket injunction served against the women, to prohibit their public activism. "By this injunc-

tion the corset company expected to silence the women as well as prevent them from picketing the shop. It did neither. The girls told their story to whomsoever would listen." O'Reilly chronicles their resultant time in jail for her readers and concludes with the following admonition:

> Keep in your mind, they are splendid women. They are brave women. It takes this kind of bravery that this land of ours needs to be able to tell unpopular truths to unwilling listeners because you believe the truth is good food for all people. Such is my story! It is a true story! Have you caught its meaning, you of the "Listening Heart?" Can you send word of hope and comfort to those brave girls of Kalamazoo who have dared all for a principle? (O'Reilly papers, reel 9)

In her address to the National Society of Women Workers in 1901, "Women's Opportunities in the Civil Service," O'Reilly recognizes several times that she is speaking "to a very practical body of women," and lists specific benefits to supporting the merit system. She concludes by encouraging her audience to "offer superior qualifications for doing public work." Working women's clubs should study democracy, the Constitution, and Civil Service Reform,

> Take it up, fellow working women, and encourage that intelligence which maintains it to be a duty for us to leave our country in a healthier state than in which we found it. No citizen can do more nor should he do less than that. (cited in Anderson, 1984, p. 126)

O'Reilly's use of the strategies was very important given the nature of the rhetorical constraints she experienced. Gender and class could not only keep a woman from speaking out, but could also keep the rank and file from organizing. The majority of the young women O'Reilly was attempting to reach consisted of three groups: the "Americans" or native-born workers, Eastern European Jewish immigrants, and Italian immigrants. Each group came with its own set of gender and cultural expectations, but all were concerned with propriety. O'Reilly addressed that concern in a "stirring address" before the Men's Club of the People's Home:

> This is so far true that some of the best intentioned people in the world only hinder the progress of woman in the industrial movement through fear that the working-women (sic) may do something "unladylike". The workingwomen have often been induced to leave their braver sisters victims of unscrupulous capitalists, when to revolt would have been nothing but the exercising of the right to seek a higher law. Therefore I say to you: Women, whether you wish it or not, your first step must be to gain equal political rights with men. The next step after that must be "equal pay for equal work." (O'Reilly papers, reel 9)

Later this issue of propriety would anger O'Reilly and cause friction in her relationships within the WTUL. While she did have close friendships with some of the allies (most notably, Margaret Dreier Robins), she was often at odds with many of the upper-class women. She resigned briefly in 1905 because of an "overdose of allies" and as Tax (1980) notes, was the center of controversy because of the attitude exhibited in her speech notes dated 1908, "Contact with the 'lady' does harm in the long run-gives a wrong standard" (p. 114). She warned readers of a Labor Day column, "The woman who labors may have to throw off the cloak of ancient, received opinion from her shoulders" (O'Reilly papers, reel 9).

She sought to empower her audiences, and did so by appealing to them as "thinking women"—having witnessed the condescension of many middle-class reformers, she deliberately chose to exalt the working woman. She spoke their language, and never hesitated to lay claim to her right as a worker to speak to them and for them. She preached a "religion" of labor reform, and while not all may have agreed with her methods, she had their respect. She was very aware of all of the problems both she and her audiences faced each time she ventured forth, and made great efforts to deal with them through her chosen strategies. Clearly, she was aware of the role gender and class played in her life, as well as in those of her audience. Her voice then, was an alternative one in that it was not merely adaptive to the situation she found herself in, but rather one that clearly recognized strength and power in the female role.

Tax (1980) argues persuasively that it was this constant struggle over class that caused O'Reilly to finally leave the League for good in 1915. She found herself increasingly at odds over issues such as the minimum wage—she opposed it, believing it operated as a ceiling for women's wages, rather than a base—and the approach taken by the League toward suffrage. O'Reilly's Wage Earners Suffrage League was linked to the National Woman's Party, seen as the radical wing of the overall movement. O'Reilly stumped for votes in much the same manner she had sought to organize workers, and thus, alienated the more decorous allies.

One of her final public acts took place that year when she was sent as labor's representative to the International Congress of Women at the Hague. With Jane Addams and other American reformers, O'Reilly traveled to Europe to discuss the "principles of a constructive peace." Upon her return, she sought to address the conference at the AFL convention about her experiences but was turned down, as Tax (1980) notes, because the leadership felt there were "sinister influences" behind the peace movement (p. 123).

By late 1915, O'Reilly was physically and emotionally drained. Though still relatively young, she suffered from heart disease, and was forced to curtail her activities. Her life had been spent fighting the good fight for her causes, however the combined strains of physical exhaustion and continued social resistance were overwhelming. An anti-suffrage journal from this period stated plainly that, "Pacifist, socialist, feminist, suffragist are all parts of the same movement—a movement which weakens government, corrupts society and threatens the very existence of our great experiment in democracy" (cited in Cott, 1987, p. 61).

Using an argument that will sound familiar to advocates of modern feminism, the Missouri Anti-Suffrage League asked:

Do you know that there is a close alliance between woman suffrage, Socialism and Feminism: that Feminism advocates non-motherhood, free love, easy divorce, economic independence for all women, and other demoralizing and destructive theories? (cited in Cott, 1987, p. 61)

Such overwhelming resistance, both inside and out of the movement, must have been extremely discouraging to O'Reilly. She spoke again only once, in 1919, at the International Congress of Working Women in Washington. Shortly before she died in 1927, she gave a course on the theory of the labor movement at the New School for Social Research.

O'Reilly's life and rhetoric give us an opportunity to examine the public voice of a working-class female reformer, a voice not frequently included in our discipline's purview. The vast majority of published studies within the area of women's rhetoric have focused upon middle-class women and their concerns. Scholars of women's history have evolved beyond such a monolithic view of American women's lives. If we are to fully understand women's experiences as rhetors, we must begin to validate those voices not privileged by class, race or formal education.

ENDNOTES

1. The Leonora O'Reilly papers are found within the papers of the Women's Trade Union League, microfilm collection, Schlesinger Library, Radcliffe College, Cambridge, MA. The collection includes diaries, correspondence, texts of speeches, newspaper reports of O'Reilly's activities and other miscellaneous items. For a more extensive discussion of her biography, see Mattina 1993.

REFERENCES

Anderson, J. (1984). *Outspoken women*. Dubuque: Kendall Hunt.
Bulzarik, M. J. (1983). The bonds of belonging: Leonora O'Reilly and social reform. *Labor History, 24,* 3–17.
Campbell, K. K. (1973). The rhetoric of women's liberation: an oxymoron. *Quarterly Journal of Speech, 59,* 74–86.
Campbell, K. K. (1982). *The rhetorical act.* Belmont, CA: Wadsworth.
Campbell, K. K. (1989). *Man cannot speak for her.* New York: Praeger.
Cott, N. (1987). *The grounding of modern feminism.* New Haven: Yale University Press.
Cott, N. & Pleck, E. H. (Eds.). (1979). *A heritage of her own.* New York: Simon & Schuster.
Dow, B. & Tonn, M. B. (1993). "Feminine style" and political judgment in the rhetoric of Ann Richards. *Quarterly Journal of Speech, 79,* 286–302.
Dye, N. S. (1980). *As equals and as sisters.* Columbia: University of Missouri Press.
Dye, N. S. (1975). Feminism or unionism? The New York Women's Trade Union League and the labor movement. *Feminist Studies, 3,* 111–125.
Ewen, E. (1989). *Immigrant women in the land of dollars.* New York: Monthly Review Press.
Jacoby, R. M. (1975). *The* Women's Trade Union League and American feminism. *Feminist Studies, 3,* 126–140.
James, E. (Ed.). (1971). *Notable American women.* Cambridge: The Belknap Press of Harvard University Press.
Keneally, J. J. (1973). Women and trade unions 1870–1920: The quandary of the reformer. *Labor History, 14,* 42–55.
Kessler-Harris, A. (1975). Where are the organized women workers? *Feminist Studies, 3,* 92–110.
Lomas, C. (1968). *The agitator in American society.* Englewood Cliffs: Prentice Hall.
Mattina, A. F. (1993). Leonora O'Reilly: working woman orator. In K. K. Campbell (Ed.), *Women public speakers in the United States, 1800–1925: A bio-critical sourcebook, Vol 2.* Westport, CT: Greenwood Press.
O'Reilly Papers. Schlesinger Library, Radcliffe College, Cambridge, MA.
Payne, E. A. (1988). *Reform, labor, and feminism.* Urbana: University of Illinois Press.
Tax, Meredith (1980). *The rising of the women.* New York: Monthly Review Press.

Women, war, and the limits of change.

By Susan M. Hartmann

When World War II called 16 million men out of civilian life, American *women* acquired new responsibilities and unprecedented opportunities. The need to produce enormous amounts of military and civilian goods for the United States and its allies meant that women were allowed—and even encouraged—to do what had previously been reserved for men. Moreover, the war created a moral atmosphere that heightened public sensitivity to injustice, particularly racial discrimination but also discrimination against women.

Equally powerful forces, however, put the brakes on change. Americans acknowledged the critical need for women's contributions to the war effort, but they also cherished conventional gender roles and worried about how women's new activities outside the home would affect male–female relations and family life. Stable family life took on even greater importance as wartime disruptions contributed to rising rates of juvenile delinquency, divorce, and illegitimacy. Women themselves demonstrated their attachment to traditional roles: their employment rose steeply—from 12 million to 19 million—but so did marriage and birth rates. Thus, the World War II era saw increasing tension between women's traditional roles of wife and mother and their growing roles in the world outside the home.

Official policy and propaganda reflected efforts to resolve the conflicting goals of recruiting women to the war effort and preserving women's primary commitments in the home. Policy statements, propaganda, and advertising accentuated gender differences, and appeals to women to assume new responsibilities carried two conditions: they were to do so only for the duration, and they were to retain their primary identities and duties as homemakers and mothers.

Policies on Women in the Military

The emphasis on conventional gender roles accompanied women's entry into one of the last bastions of male exclusivity—the military. For example, leaders of women's organizations advocated military service on the grounds of simple justice—that women, like men, should enjoy the right to participate in all the responsibilities of citizenship. In contrast, military leaders pointed to the requirements of modern, global warfare for a vast and functionally diversified military that included typists, switchboard operators, and nurses as well as combat Soldiers and bombers. They could use women because, according to one Army official, "we have found difficulty in getting enlisted men to perform tedious duties anywhere nearly as well as women will do it."

Gender differences also took center stage in military propaganda aimed at women. Recruitment materials proclaimed that military women retained their "femininity" and even "developed new poise and charm." Advertisements proclaimed that the Army needed women's "delicate hands" for "precision work at which women are so adept" and women for hospital work because "there is a need in a man for comfort and attention that only a woman can fill."

Once in the military, some servicewomen filled jobs generally considered to be men's work, including motor vehicle maintenance and pilot training. In fact, once the WAVES got underway, every Navy combat pilot received some training from a woman. Nonetheless, the vast ma-

Reprinted from *National Forum: The Phi Kappa Phi Journal,* Vol. 75, No. 4, September 1, 1995, pp. 15-20. © 1995 by Susan M. Hartman by permission of the publishers.

jority of 370,000 military women performed jobs similar to those held by women in the civilian economy. In the racially segregated Army, African American women felt even tighter constraints; they were assigned the most menial jobs and confined stateside until 1945.

Women's opportunity for military service survived the end of the war because they had proved worthy and because technology continued to increase the need for support personnel. General Dwight D. Eisenhower, a staunch proponent of women's service, indicated how change would be contained when he testified at congressional hearings: "[A]fter an enlistment or two . . . women will ordinarily—and thank God they will get married." Strict limits on the numbers of women and on their ability to move up in rank also would help keep women attached to traditional gender roles.

Policies and Propaganda on Women in the Labor Force

Mobilization of civilian women for employment reflected similar tensions between change and continuity. Women responded by the millions to the wartime emergency and made possible the production miracle that transformed the American economy. They contributed more than one-third of the labor force during the war, and in 1944 nearly half of all adult women worked at one time or another. Women replaced men in ordnance plants, shipyards, and aircraft factories and filled men's shoes as musicians, airplane pilots, engineers, scientists, college professors, and even Santa Clauses. Although racial discrimination persisted during the war, black women's employment became slightly more diversified as some managed to escape domestic service for commercial service or factory work. Three million women won the benefits of union representation.

The need for female labor produced modest policy changes. In order to control inflation, the government froze wages but encouraged employers to equalize wages between men and women, allowing exceptions to the general freeze to bring women's rates up to those of men.

Government wartime policy also acknowledged women's hardships in trying to combine jobs with traditional family responsibilities. By 1944, nearly one-fourth of married women and 12 percent of women with children under ten were employed. Moreover, the war time scarcity of civilian goods made housekeeping more difficult. Women typically worked 48 hours a week with one day off. Scarcities and rationing made shopping a major problem. Production of labor-saving, household appliances, such as washing machines, refrigerators, and vacuum sweepers, gave way to military imperatives.

Consequently, the government encouraged employers to provide child-care programs, take-home meals, and laundry, repair, and shopping services for their workers. Kaiser shipyards offered an array of assistance, including a 24-hour day-care center, which became a national showcase and won high praise from child development experts. Grocers in New Jersey sent employees to factories to take orders and make deliveries, and some aircraft manufacturers provided shoe repair services or opened department store branches in the plant. But these were exceptions: most women had to juggle on their own the combination of employment and family duties.

Nowhere was the ambivalence and anxiety about changing roles for women more evident than in government policies on day care. Officials discouraged mothers with small children from taking jobs. The Children's Bureau warned that group care for children under two would result in "slower mental development, social ineptness, weakened initiative, and damage to the child's capacity . . . to form satisfactory relationships." FBI Chief J. Edgar Hoover insisted that parental neglect caused "perversion" and "crime," admonishing mothers that their "patriotic duty is not on the factory front. It is on the home front."

Yet officials knew that some mothers needed to work and that employers in areas of severe labor shortages would need to hire mothers. Ultimately the federal government spent around $50 million to match local and state funds for the establishment of 3,000 day-care centers around the country. At peak usage, they accommodated 130,000 children of employed mothers, just a tiny percentage of the children whose mothers worked outside the home.

Like military propaganda, advertising and other media elements emphasized traditional female qualities and roles. For example, a magazine article featuring women workers declared, "You'll like this girl. She does a man's work . . . servicing airplanes, but she hasn't lost any of her feminine sweetness and charm." The theme of femininity pervaded the factory itself where women welders were called "welderettes," and beauty and popularity contests for women workers became routine.

Especially towards the end of the war, another theme joined the theme of femininity—that women's employment was temporary. A vacuum cleaner manufacturer promised that at war's end, "Like you Mrs. America, Eureka will put aside its uniform and return to the ways of peace. . . ." General Electric predicted that women would welcome a return to "their old housekeeping routine," which GE intended to transform with new appliances. In May 1945, the inhouse newspaper at Kaiser Shipyards issued a clear message to its female employees in an article titled, " 'The Kitchen'—Women's Big Post–War Goal."

Women in the Post–War Years

Less than two years after V-J Day, women's share of the labor force had declined from 36 to 28 percent. Those who continued to work were displaced from higher-paying formerly male jobs and bumped back into female jobs. A former welder who became a cashier related her experience: "It kind of hurt . . . you were back to women's wages again . . . practically in half." As women's labor force participation began to rise again, matching the wartime peak by 1950, married women constituted a sizeable portion of the increase. Yet, despite their growing numbers, women made few qualitative gains in employment until the 1970s.

Both official policy and informal practice, of course, favored veterans for jobs. Because men had directly confronted the enemy and had been most responsible for the nation's survival, they enjoyed a host of advantages in the postwar era that were unavailable to most women and that limited the opportunities women enjoyed during the war. The G.I. Bill of Rights (Servicemen's Readjustment Act of 1944) did not set out to discriminate against women, and it benefited women as wives and daughters of veterans. But that law—a natural response to veterans' sacrifices—did inadvertently disadvantage women who could not claim its entitlements.

Educational benefits under the G.I. Bill contributed to the postwar "democratization of higher education," a tremendous growth that extended college education beyond the middle and upper classes. In terms of absolute numbers, female college enrollments grew after the war, but they declined relative to those of men. In fact, by 1950, women's share of undergraduate degrees was lower than it had been before the war, dropping from 41 percent in 1940 to just 24 percent in 1950. As they were discharged from the military, veterans inundated college campuses; at their peak enrollment in 1947, veterans constituted nearly one-half of all college students.

Female veterans also took advantage of the G.I. Bill, but its impact was not gender neutral. Women had comprised less than three percent of all military personnel, so the vast majority of student-veterans were men. Women, in fact, found it more difficult to gain admission to crowded colleges that gave preference to veterans. In some respects the G.I. bill was a forerunner of affirmative action, though in this case men—and their families—benefited. As World War II veterans completed their education, women's share of college degrees rose, but even by 1960, women claimed just one-third of all degrees, still less than their share in 1940. The great postwar expansion of higher education eventually benefited women, but not until the 1960s and 1970s.

While postwar America paid most attention to veterans' economic and educational needs, it did not neglect their emotional needs. Psychiatrists, military doctors, sociologists, and servicemen themselves called attention to the problems returning soldiers would face and assigned women a primary role in ensuring the veterans' satisfactory readjustment to civilian life. Women were told to be sensitive and responsive, to adjust their needs and desires to those of men. One sociologist, for example, advised women to accept "more than the wife's usual responsibility for her marriage," to offer "lavish and undemanding affection," and to "expect no immediate return."

Neither experts nor returning soldiers themselves encouraged the independence and self-confidence women had experienced during the war. When asked what they wanted in a wife, the largest number of veterans responded, "Her specialty must be homemaking," or "a fondness for kids." Fewer than 10 percent wanted a "brainy girl who keeps up with world problems," or a "business girl who could take care of herself." Experts reminded wives that soldiers wanted "feminine" women who would display "tenderness, admiration, or at least submissiveness." Women were advised to give up their jobs if keeping them threatened their marriages. Overall, these experts' advice reinforced the traditional gender roles and behavior that the war had only briefly disrupted.

In an important area—their status under the law— women's advances outlasted the end of the war. Just as World War I had helped to bring about woman suffrage, World War II drew attention to discrimination and energized feminists and women's organizations to press more actively for women's rights. Like civil rights leaders, they pointed to wartime contributions and sacrifices and seized on wartime rhetoric to promote equality at home. Emphasizing the nation's battle for freedom and democracy abroad, one women's rights advocate insisted, "Surely we will not refuse to our own that which we purchase for strangers with the blood of our sons."

With the notorious exception of Japanese-American women whose fundamental rights were stripped away, most women enjoyed modest gains in their legal status. State legislatures removed a number of women's handicaps: some passed laws specifically protecting teachers from salary discrimination; most lifted their bans on married women teachers; and thirteen states made women eligible for jury service, leaving just eight states that barred women from juries. A state judge in North Carolina clearly linked women's war activities to changing attitudes about their rights. Commenting on the state's law excluding women from jury service, he declared, "The disqualification of sex is outmoded. Women are in the Army, Navy and Marine Corps. They work in factories, shops. . . ."

World War II also brought serious attention to the principle of equal pay for equal work for the first time. Although thwarted in Congress, women's organizations and labor unions pushed through equal pay laws in ten states during the 1940s. Moreover, the increased visibility of wage discrimination inspired Women's organizations to keep that issue on their agendas until Congress finally enacted a federal equal pay law in 1963.

Even the proposed equal rights amendment (ERA) gained serious attention for the first time since feminists had made it a goal in 1923. Indeed, in 1946 a majority of the Senate voted for the ERA, but the vote fell short of the required two-thirds majority. Increased public attention to the issue of equal rights spurred supporters of the amendment to continue their efforts, and they kept the ERA alive to become a key rallying point of the revived feminist movement of the 1960s and 1970s.

For American women World War II meant a combination of change and continuity, with continuity proving stronger in the short run. The need for women's contributions to the war effort did promote increasing rights and unprecedented opportunities in the public sphere, but two countervailing forces were even more powerful. First were the firmly entrenched traditional attitudes and historic arrangements that assigned women to the caretaking of the family and defined women primarily by their domestic roles as wives and mothers. Second was the obvious fact of war—men were soldiers, and women, for the most part, were not. Men's roles became even more highly valued, and this increased the disparities in status between women and men. Men were called upon to make the ultimate sacrifice, and they received material and psychological advantages not generally available to women.

Yet World War II set in motion larger changes over the longer run. Its greatest impact on women's status and opportunities was in sowing the seeds of change: a growing acceptance of work outside the home for married women; increased attention to sex discrimination in the workplace; the vast expansion of higher education that at first disadvantaged women in relation to men but eventually opened new doors; and the shot in the arm the war gave to the small and struggling women's rights movement. All of these eventually helped shape a deeper transformation in women's consciousness, ambitions, and opportunities in the 1960s and beyond.

Susan Hartmann is a professor of history and women's studies at Ohio State University and author of The Home Front and Beyond: American Women in the 1940s *and* From Margin to Mainstream: American Women and Politics since 1960. *Her research has been supported with grants and fellowships from the American Council of Learned Societies, the National Endowment for the Humanities, and the Rockefeller Foundation.*

BEYOND GENDER

Sexual Politics Can Advance the Women's Movement for Equality Only So Far

BY BETTY FRIEDAN

In the summer of 1994, I had lunch with a friend near her office in New York City. She happens to be the top woman there and she gets lonesome at lunchtime. The guys at her level all go out together and never have lunch with the women anymore. Is this some new kind of sex discrimination? "Oh no," she says, "It's just that there's so much talk about sexual harassment suits these days. No one knows what it is or isn't, so they figure 'Why risk it?' "

But my friend wasn't looking for feminist advice. Her husband, who was "downsized" at one of our biggest corporations three years earlier, hadn't been able to find a job and had almost stopped looking. "I'm carrying it all," she said. "It's OK, we'll make it. But it's not good at home, the way he feels now. It's as if he's given up. I could get a divorce, I suppose. But he is the father of my children, and I still love him. So that's not an option. But, ambitious as I am, I never figured it would end up like this."

That same week, I saw an item in *The New York Times* which reported that in the previous five years there had been a nearly 20 percent drop in income among college-educated white American men. Not minority, high school educated, or blue-collar men, but white management men in their 40s and early 50s, the masters of the universe. And while women on the whole still do not earn as much money as men, the *Times* noted that college-educated women in the same age group had seen their incomes rise slightly over the same period. Meanwhile, new national studies were indicating that women were now carrying half of the income burden in half of all U.S. families.

Downsizing had not yet hit the headlines in 1994; the "angry white male" had not yet surfaced in that year's election campaign. But my inner Geiger counter had begun to click, the way it does when something foreign to definition, expectation, and accepted truth happens. I

trust that click; it set me on the search that led to the concept of "the feminine mystique," which led to the women's movement for equality. And now, though my and many other women's lives in the 30 years since had been conducted within that liberating frame of reference, I feel again that urgent change is required. My inner Geiger counter does not lie. I sense something that cannot be evaded or handled in the usual feminist terms.

I sense the need for a paradigm shift beyond feminism, beyond sexual politics, beyond identity politics altogether—a new paradigm for women and men. Since then, the more I've thought about this and begun to try to make it happen, the more I realize that many other people from very different political persuasions than mine are moving in the same direction. There's a mounting sense that the crises we are now facing, or denying, cannot be solved in the same terms that we used to conduct our personal, political, business, or family lives. They can no longer be seen in terms of gender. The old paradigm still shaping our thinking may keep us from seeing these problems for what they are, much less solving them.

Competing Paradigms

Before the modern women's movement, every map in every field of endeavor defined women in relation to men. It was a paradigm shift when we began to challenge the rubrics that had been developed only from male experience. This shift opened up every field, as women began to move in great numbers from the 1960s onward into law, medicine, science, business, art, politics, and the humanities. It opened life in complex new directions.

But today I look back and admit anomalies that kept me trying to stretch the box of feminism long before this

This article originally appeared in *The New Democrat*, July/August 1997, pp. 12-14. © 1997 by the Democratic Leadership Council. Reprinted by permission.

crisis. For me, the unwritten, inviolable law against which all thinking about women must be tested is life itself. Does it open or close real life as women live it? Does it permit more choice, autonomy, freedom, and control? Does it empower or restrict?

For those of us who started the modern women's movement, the new paradigm was simply the ethos of American democracy—equality of opportunity, our own voice in the decisions of our destiny, but applied to women in concrete terms as the theory and practice of democracy had never been applied to us before. But for the younger women who came from the 1960s student movement and who had not yet experienced the life that most women led, the paradigm was sexual politics: women as a whole rising up against men as a whole, the oppressed against the oppressors. While seeing women in these terms did open women's lives to new growth and development, I had trouble with this paradigm from the beginning. It didn't fit *life*—life as I and other women had known it, even scientific knowledge about life.

> **Had we weakened ourselves by increasingly organizing over separate, single issues? Did we cloud the vision of the common good by defining our cause in terms of women versus men?**

When I left the presidency of the National Organization for Women in 1970, sexual politics was already dividing our strength. I began putting my energy into teaching, lecturing, and writing again—all of it geared to what I saw as the need for feminist thought to evolve. In my 1981 book *The Second Stage*, I proposed going beyond the impossible dilemmas of the sexual politics paradigm and coming to new terms with family, motherhood, men, and careers. My views were bitterly attacked by the "politically correct" voices of feminism, as if I was betraying the women's movement. Though deeply hurt, I had no desire to mount a divisive counterfeminist movement. I bowed out of feminist organizational politics altogether, except when asked for help.

Women as a "Special Interest"

In the 1980s, when feminist consciousness was supposedly at its apex, women of childbearing years were dividing into two antagonistic camps. They were being forced to make no-win choices that pit motherhood against career. The women's movement for equality was spreading throughout society; women in great numbers were graduating from law, medical, and business schools as well as community colleges and moving into jobs and professions. Yet polls began to show that younger women were reluctant to identify themselves as feminists, though they identified with every item of the women's agenda of equality.

A backlash was growing. Women, blacks, Latinos, gays, the handicapped—all were being labeled "special interests," with a moral claim on society no greater than that of the oil industry or the lumber barons. Women, who constitute 52 percent of the American people, never should have let ourselves be defined this way. Had we weakened ourselves by increasingly organizing over separate, single issues? Did we cloud the vision of the common good by defining our cause in terms of women versus men?

The energy of the leading feminist organizations had been focused on abortion or on sexual politics—rape, date rape, pornography. I have no doubt that the far right has deliberately focused on abortion as symbol and substance of a woman's independence, autonomy, control over her own body, and destiny. But did we somehow let those who opposed our rights, our very personhood as women, box us in and define the terms of our unfinished battle too narrowly?

Year after year we spend all our organizational energy and funds fighting for the right to an abortion, a battle we have already won in Congress and in the courts of law and public opinion. Shouldn't we put at least as much energy into breaking down the remaining barriers to women's advancing to equality with men in our economy? The key to achieving that goal is changing the structures that make it difficult for American women to combine childbearing with advancement in business and the professions.

An Impossible Paradox

In the early 1990s, the Center for Policy Alternatives and the Ms. Foundation conducted a poll to discover the true concerns of women. To the amazement of the politically correct, it revealed that none of the sexual issues ranked among the main problems of women young or old, black or white. For the great majority of the women polled, the main problem was jobs—how to get them, keep them, and get ahead in them; and how to meet the responsibilities of family life while living the equality we'd fought for.

My sense of crisis came in the summer of 1994 as I prepared to come to Washington as a guest scholar at the Woodrow Wilson International Center for Scholars. While packing up my papers, I stumbled across the *Times* article on income losses among middle-aged white male professionals and gains among similarly aged and educated women. Citing the same trend, another article published in *The Economist* posed this question: Have women driven men from the workplace?

At once, I saw the impossible paradox for women: *We are achieving what begins to look like equality because the men are doing worse.* Is their loss really our gain?

Women today enjoy more control over their lives than their mothers ever dreamed of. The great majority have jobs that may not be the greatest, but which give them a life in their 40s and 50s after their kids are off (though the juggling of children and job in their 30s is tough). Many women are doing as well as or better than those downsized men.

> **If jobs, work, and family are the issues that concern women most now, we have to mobilize to protect our children, our families, and ourselves in a new coalition with men.**

Studying the pattern in the news clippings, I sensed a truly serious backlash ahead. I had noticed the court rulings in which divorced women lost custody of a child because they had a demanding job or were pursuing a degree and placed their child in day care for part of the day. The fathers won custody because their new wives or mothers would stay home all day with the child. I also noticed how the religious right marched under the banner of "family values" even as its zealots continued to bomb abortion clinics. Feminist groups have mobilized to defend those clinics. But who is mobilizing to confront the economic inequality and dislocation that threatens the survival and stability of families far more than abortion or pornography?

There has to be a paradigm shift in our thinking about women, not just from sexual politics but from the whole focus of our status vis-a-vis men. If women are winning while men are losing, since most women continue to live with men in families, how long can women really win? If jobs, work, and family are the issues that concern women most now, we have to mobilize to protect our children, our families, and ourselves in a new coalition with men.

Toward a New Vision

Our economy is in need of basic restructuring—one which counters income inequality, confronts the needs of family that can't be ignored in a workplace where women now equal or outnumber men, and insists that more and more men share in the responsibilities of parenting. This restructuring can't be accomplished in terms of women versus men, blacks versus whites, old versus young, conservative versus liberal.

We need a new political movement in America that puts the lives and interests of people first. It can't be done by separate, single-issue movements now, and it has to be political, to protect and translate our new empowerment with a new vision of community, with new structures that open the doors again to real equality of opportunity for the diverse interests of all our children— a new evolution of democracy as we approach the new millennium.

Betty Friedan is an adjunct scholar at the Woodrow Wilson Center for Scholars and the author of several books, including The Feminine Mystique *and* The Fountain of Age.

WOMEN OF THE FUTURE: ALTERNATIVE SCENARIOS

Will women take their newfound power and separate themselves from men? Or will biological technologies allow men and women to become more alike? A futures researcher and political scientist examines five potential scenarios for women.

By Christopher B. Jones

Women's status in Western societies has undergone dramatic changes in the past four decades. The changing status of women is not simply a lifestyle change or a minor alteration of social patterns. It is an unprecedented transformation in our social and cultural reality. And we have only seen the tip of the iceberg.

The historical subordination of women is nearing the threshold of collapse. Social, cultural, political, and technological changes are converging to eat away the structures of male dominance. Over the next millennium, women (and men) are likely to undergo enormous changes, psychologically, culturally, biologically, physiologically, and even genetically. Thus, women in the future may be considerably

different from what they have been in the past.

This author is the wrong gender to describe women's experience, but he has tried to overcome that handicap by studying what women have said and written about their experience and by looking through more objective evidence, such as statistical data.

While women have succeeded in making some inroads into decision-making positions in business and government, they are still expected to perform traditional functions of maintaining a household, taking care of the kids, fixing the meals, and being a good spouse. Not an easy chore. And while the image of superwoman has been featured in both advertising and women's magazines, the image has, of late, come under fire for being

just what it is—superhuman—and not a normal state of activity.

To understand the potential transformational power of the women's movement, we must also understand the growing social and cultural power that comes from the least understood and most maligned part of the women's movement: the radical feminist movement.

Radical feminism was always a strand of the women's movement, even as far back as the nineteenth century, but the radical feminists parted ways with the political feminists sometime during the late 1960s and early 1970s and have continued to follow a different path. Where political feminists want to be equally represented along with men, radical feminists want a totally different power structure. Where political feminists want policies and laws that assist women and families, the radicals want a totally new spiritual paradigm.

Beginning with the premise that the personal is political, radical feminists argue that to adopt traditional political methods would be to play into the hands of male institutions. They seek instead to recreate their own world, their own reality, and give energy to new, female-centered institutions rather than the old male ones. One segment of radical feminists has rediscovered or recreated the pagan practices of the pre-Christian world. They now actively promote Great Goddess worship and paganism or female-oriented aspects of mainstream religions. Mythic remnants of pagan mother-goddess worship can be found in nearly all patriarchal religions: Islam, Judaism, and Christianity. The importance of the Virgin Mary in Catholicism is a classic example.

This trend in women's culture is growing and not easily swept under the rug. While it is not as visible as a female nominee to the Supreme Court, the cultural implications have the potential to be seen in nearly every aspect of life over the next century or two.

Trends Suggest Potential Scenarios

There are at least three mini-trends stemming from radical feminism that could result in dramatically different futures for women—and men. One of those has been called **lesbian separatism**, a tendency for some women to reject men entirely as some sort of evolutionary mistake. This movement has less to do with sexual orientation than with the acceptance of an entirely different paradigm, one that rejects male-influenced values.

At virtually the opposite end of the spectrum is male hatred of women, or misogyny, manifesting itself as a **widespread male backlash** against women. There are already symptoms of this throughout society, and the potential for a reversal in the status of women is a growing possibility. The pressures on men are growing and thus the chances of male backlash may grow. Just as the anti-immigrant movement in Europe has been fueled by loosened immigration laws, so, too, may violence against women grow, if male-dominated society feels truly threatened.

A third mini-trend that has roots in radical feminism is the push toward a **partnership model** of relations between men and women rather than the dominance of either. While the partnership model might suggest a radical redefinition of gender roles and the division of labor in society—even the end of patriarchal religions as we know them—it argues against violence toward either gender and for the growth of healthy relationships between men and women.

One way to make some sense out of these sometimes converging and sometimes conflicting trends is to consider a range of alternative futures for women. These scenarios are suggested in some cases by women's images of the future and in other cases by dominant social, cultural, environmental, and technological trends. These scenarios are intended to show distinct images of how women's social status may evolve.

CLOSING THE GENDER GAP?

Will men and women become more alike in the future, or more different?

Clearly at the biological level there are some differences between the two genders. There is certainly no agreement among feminists on whether these differences are good or bad. Should we strive to obscure the differences between the genders or to heighten them?

Genetically, things will soon be up for grabs. Given what we are learning about the human genetic code—the human genome—males or females could be constructed as similarly or as differently as is genetically possible.

Men and women can also be surgically reconstructed to be more similar or more different. Sex-change operations have become common, so changing gender is a possibility if you decide you were born into the wrong sex. Physiological differences are already narrowing between men and women in advanced countries due to improved health and vitamin use. The most dramatic evidence of this phenomenon is the shrinking gap between men's and women's athletic records.

Culturally, differences between men and women in sharing "nurturing" and "caring" responsibilities for family and the home environment are narrowing somewhat. The terms "house husband" and "parental leave" were unheard of a few decades ago and are indicative of the blurring of domestic gender responsibilities. If my students are an indicator, younger generations may be much more accepting of these changes.

Psychologically, women are increasingly in charge of their own procreation, bodies, financial and political lives, and a burgeoning women's "culture." In this respect, women's growing demand to be independent and more different from men makes them, ironically, more *like* men.

—*Christopher B. Jones*

BOSTON MARATHON

| | **Winning Times** | | | |
	1897	1974	1984	1994
Women	-	2:47:11	2:29:28	2:21:45
Men	2:55:10	2:13:39	2:10:34	2:07:15

Source: *The Universal Almanac 1996* (Andrews and McMeel).

The five scenarios described below are summarized in the chart "Futures of Women."

Scenario #1: Continued Patriarchy

Continued Patriarchy is similar to the "continued growth" or "business-as-usual" image of the future used in futures research. It is the dominant image of the future portrayed on television commercials, in popular magazines, and embodied in business, government, and cultural institutions. This type of future has been characterized as the "future most like the present, 'only more so,' " and championed by futurists such as the late Herman Kahn.

In this scenario, women continue to obtain their rights but at the cost of playing "supermom" and/or becoming more like men.

Women are increasingly accepted in the work force in industrialized countries, but are slow to achieve equal pay for equal work and to break the glass ceiling into management positions. Women in the devel-

> "WOMEN'S RISING STATUS IN SOCIETY REPRESENTS NOTHING LESS THAN A RADICAL TRANSFORMATION OF THE SOCIAL FABRIC."

oping world continue to be exploited and violated more than their sisters in industrialized countries.

The family model in this scenario is still that of the Industrial Age: a mother, father, and two or three children. Levels of spouse and child abuse remain high.

Scenario #2: High-Tech Androgyny

Society experiences a technological transformation that produces basic shifts in the relations between men and women and in most social structures. High-Tech Androgyny is a future of blurred gender roles with clear separation between sexual recreation and human procreation.

In this scenario, work is something one does because one is good at it or because it gives one personal satisfaction. Gender divisions of labor no longer exist. Leisure "work" allows all people to engage in whatever sport, artistic form, handicraft, hobby, or activity they wish. Politics is something women are more equitably involved in due to shifts in child rearing, domestic work, and work outside the home.

Children are "designed" from the best genetic material, gestated in either natural or artificial wombs, and raised in age-cohort groups by robot (and human) nannies. Children are also expected to experiment with sex before puberty. Rites of passage often include gender changes.

FUTURES OF WOMEN

Scenario	Highlights
Continued Patriarchy	Women continue to gain rights, but many are pressured into "supermom" roles. Women are increasingly accepted in the workplace but continue to struggle for equal pay and to break through "glass ceiling." Women tend to be under-represented in political arena. The nuclear family model is the ideal.
High-Tech Androgyny	"Unisex R Us": High technology frees men and women alike from most work, and a leisure society emerges. Gender roles are blurred; sexual recreation is separated from procreation. Children are genetically "designed" and reared by robotic nannies. Children are allowed to experiment with sex and change their genders before puberty.
Separation	Women form a separate society, doing without men both genetically and socially. Men are banned from some communities; some are sent to space colonies. Inter-generational families become the norm, consisting of sisters, daughters, mothers, grandmothers, and aunts. Feminist spirituality emerges in the form of goddess worship, neo-paganism, and witchcraft.
Male Backlash	In a hyper-patriarchy, men reclaim harsh dominance over women. Polygamy is the norm among the wealthy, and harems emerge as a family form. Female infanticide is common. Work is done by female slaves. Fundamentalist male-dominated religions reign supreme, and witch-burning becomes common.
Partnership	Neither males nor females dominate, but work together. Gender-based differences in labor become less pronounced, and women have full political and economic equality. Shared parenting exists in a variety of family forms, including extended, intergenerational groups.

Family roles are totally blurred or nonexistent. Gene and other molecular therapies have markedly increased human longevity.

Scenario #3: Separation

In this future, the insular lesbian movement has ascended, as presaged by the astounding growth of female heads of households in the United States. Many lesbians impregnate themselves, producing "baster babies." Many communities and space settlements are inhabited solely by women; other communities segregate men and women.

The assumption here in the Separation scenario is that men fail to mend their ways, so women decide to do without them. Whether sent to space "on vacation" or otherwise disposed of (perhaps through a genetic epidemic in which only men are victims), men are no longer a problem.

Cloning and artificial insemination are the primary means of procreation in this future. Family structures are extended and intergenerational, including sisters, daughters, aunts, and donors as well as surrogate mothers, grandmothers, and great grandmothers. Families are headed by the oldest matriarchs.

Scenario #4: Backlash

In this future, men have had it with uppity women and put them "back in their place." This could occur after a major global ecological or economic catastrophe, such as depicted in Margaret Atwood's chilling backlash future, *The Handmaid's Tale.*

A Backlash scenario is suggested by some men's increasing frustration with the growing power of women, exemplified by the emergence of a men's movement. While much of the men's movement may be a reasonable exploration of men's traditional and evolving gender roles, there is also a clear misogynist element to it.

Other trends that suggest a reinvigorated hatred of women are the explosive growth of religious (patriarchal) fundamentalism, efforts to end affirmative action, and growing violence against women. Another trend that fits this scenario is the fact that in some countries amniocentesis results in up to 95% of all female fetuses being aborted.

In the Backlash scenario, men reclaim dominance over women, who are considered to be property. Slavery (of women) has returned. Women are expected to chop wood, carry water, and bear children, and they are no longer allowed to learn to read and write. Polygamy becomes common, especially for the wealthy. The number of wives is a sign of wealth. Male children are preferred, and female infanticide is common.

Scenario #5: Partnership

In the Partnership scenario, the basic biological differences between the genders are maintained, but women share power with men equally.

Gender differences are respected, but women and men are treated equally in all spheres of life. Women have extensive involvement, at all levels, equitably with men in the public sphere.

In this scenario, there are fewer gender-based divisions of labor, and parenting is a shared responsibility. Family structures are extended and intergenerational, with tolerance for a wide range of family forms (including non-blood-related). Communities and eco-cities are built around extended family "estates."

Women's Visions

These scenarios of the future are not intended to be a definitive compilation of the rich body of women's and feminist literature. They are only intended as glimpses of alternative possibilities in the next century and beyond. Some of these scenarios may be more probable than others; some, more preferable. In any case, it is important to examine a full range of possibilities, because certain elements of each of these scenarios may be what lies ahead.

There is no question in the author's mind that women's rising status in society represents nothing less than a radical transformation of the social fabric. To assume only "more of the same" in the future is truly an unrealistic expectation.

One message is that women must continue to envision, create, and realize their own futures.

About the Author

Christopher B. Jones is assistant professor of political science at Eastern Oregon State College, School of Administrative Studies, 1410 "L" Avenue, La Grande, Oregon 97850. Telephone 541/962-3385; fax 541/962-3428; e-mail cjones@eosc.osshe.edu. He holds a doctorate and master's in alternative futures from the University of Hawaii at Manoa and has been involved in futures research and education since 1980. He spoke at the Eighth General Assembly in July 1996.

A Farewell to Feminism

Elizabeth Powers

She was intelligent and generous; it was a fine free nature; but what was she going to do with herself? This question was irregular, for with most women one had no occasion to ask it. . . . Isabel's originality was that she gave one an impression of having intentions of her own.
—Henry James, *Portrait of a Lady*

M Y COMING of age in the early 1970's was inextricably linked with what is variously known as feminism, the women's movement, women's liberation. It is a link by which I am much puzzled and troubled. The passing years have brought me a closer look at, so to speak, the fine print, and I shiver now when I observe the evolution that some of my closest friends from that era have undergone, spouting phrases about comparable worth and voicing the most fantastic bureaucratic visions of the future.

But in truth, if I go back to the sources—say, to a *Time* essay by Gloria Steinem in August 1970—I can see that the writing was already on the wall. Steinem, for one, had fully evolved as of that date:

The [feminist] revolution would not take away the option of being a housewife. A woman who prefers to be her husband's housekeeper and/or hostess would receive a percentage of his pay determined by the domestic-relations courts.

ELIZABETH POWERS *teaches humanities at the Manhattan School of Music in New York. She is the author of two novels and co-editor of a forthcoming collection,* Pilgrim Souls: An Anthology of Spiritual Autobiography.

Did I talk like that, advocating state control of private life, with (as Steinem went on) "free nurseries, school lunches, family cafeterias built into every housing complex"? Did I ever stand up in front of people, like the cadres of Red Guards in China, and, parroting the words of Kate Millett in *Sexual Politics* (1970), demand "a permissive single standard of sexual freedom . . . uncorrupted by the crass and exploitative economic bases of traditional sexual alliances"?

As a matter of fact, I do not believe I ever said such things or even contemplated them; nor, I suspect, did most of the women who considered themselves followers of the movement. A dissertation is probably being written which will offer a demographic breakdown of leaders and followers, but my own suspicion is that the leaders were girls whose mothers had been college-educated but became full-time housewives, and so were putatively victimized by what Betty Friedan had defined as the "feminine mystique." The followers, those with backgrounds similar to mine, were not so solidly middle-class or goal-oriented, and had not yet grasped they might be leaders of anything.

We daughters of the working class or the slippery lower reaches of the middle class aspired, by and large, to a greater degree of participation in life outside the home. The shape that participation would take was uncertain. Though a number of highly motivated girls of my generation took advantage of opportunities to enter professional schools, the general affluence of the period allowed those of us who were less motivated or who came from less privileged backgrounds to engage in a lot of shopping around. In my own case, participation did not mean anything practical or even lucrative but rather "fulfillment," a realization of myself in literary and intellectual realms. It was my fortune, as Henry James wrote of Isabel Archer, to care for knowledge that was unfamiliar.

Throughout high school—I grew up in a rather cloistered environment in Kentucky—my aspirations seemed to run in thoroughly conventional directions: I wanted to be a cheerleader and prom queen and, of course, I wanted a boyfriend. But the same thing that kept me from becoming a cheerleader or prom queen also meant I was essentially dateless. I simply did not possess that combination of attributes which, for a brief time, confers unexpected grace on otherwise undeserving teenage girls. When I went to college, in 1965, still desiring to be exceptional in some way, I quickly perceived other possibilities of achievement.

This was a moment when university standards were still sacrosanct and an Ivy League institution was not the only place at which to receive a first-rate education. Though a fair number of women prominent today in public life probably graduated from women's colleges, I suspect the majority went, as I did, to schools like Indiana University (Jane Pauley, my classmate!). It was hard going for me—I was terribly uneducated when I got to college—but for the first time in my life I began to train my mind and came close to perfecting myself in something, namely, a foreign language.

Yet this youthful accomplishment, immeasurably assisted by two years of work and study in Europe, was attended by new challenges, chiefly of a social and sexual nature. Europe produced in me the same feeling that assailed Christopher Newman, the central character of Henry James's novel *The American*, in the presence of Old Master paintings: a vague self-mistrust. Possessing a fair share of Newman's innate American confidence and naturalness, but not his steady moral compass, I found myself entranced by the relaxed cultural habits that had evolved in Europe by the late 1960's. These I could not help contrasting with mid-century America's moral certitudes, centering on sex and the cold war, which now seemed to me to be a caricature of inflexibility.

Not three years before, where I came from, sex had been a matter cloaked in a great deal of mystery. I had been much fascinated by a girl I knew only by sight who became pregnant at fifteen and was married, probably shotgun-style, to her boyfriend of seventeen. Without being able to articulate it, I felt she must have been marked by her experience in a way that ordinary mortals, hewing to the straight and narrow, were not. Transgression may have resulted in shame and social denigration, but through her risk she had become an object of interest. Still, to stand outside the moral order was a fearsome prospect.

My Catholic attitudes were shot through with the fire and brimstone of other American cultural remnants—the sermons of Jonathan Edwards, Hawthorne's *The Scarlet Letter*. In an educated European of the late 1960's, such attitudes provoked only condescending smiles. Europeans, it seemed, got to have the experience minus the soul-scorching. I was ignorant in those days of the social arrangements, mainly an intensive welfare bureaucracy, that cushioned these permissive sentiments and perhaps had even helped bring them into being. Instead, in the presence of mores so different from my own, and influenced as well by superior church architecture and other evidence of cultural tradition, I came to conclude that European attitudes in the matter of sex were wiser than those of Americans. I wanted to be wise like Europeans.

II

"I told you just now I'm very fond of knowledge," Isabel answered.
"Yes, of happy knowledge—of pleasant knowledge. But you haven't suffered, and you're not made to suffer. I hope you'll never see the ghost!"
. . .
"I don't think that's a fault," she answered. "It's not absolutely necessary to suffer; we were not made for that."

THE BIRTH-CONTROL pill, available in Europe in the 1950's, was first approved by the FDA in 1960; the last state ban on contraception was struck down by the Supreme Court in 1965. The pill would seem to have solved the problem for which, historically, the movement for women's emancipation had struggled: freedom from constant reproduction.

Yet the pill was one of those technical achievements, like gunpowder and printing, like the desk-top computer, the effects of which flowed all over the social and political landscape. One of its effects was to alter a perilously achieved historical understanding regarding the responsibility of men to their offspring. With the pill, this responsibility was taken from them overnight. It was at this point, in 1969, returning from Europe, that I entered graduate school at the University of Texas. One of the first things I did after getting an apartment, registering for classes, and picking up my paycheck as a teaching assistant was to go to a doctor and get a prescription—even though I was still a virgin. That knowledge of which Isabel Archer spoke, which could be obtained without difficulty, had suddenly offered itself: all one had to do was take a pill 21 days in a row.

To get at some of the larger confusions engendered by this new dispensation it may be helpful to turn to a prominent book of the early women's movement, Ingrid Bengis's *Combat in the Erogenous Zone* (1972). I wonder if anyone has actually gotten to the end of this exercise in rage and self-pity; despite Bengis's avowed admiration for artists, it seems never to have occurred to *her* to shape her material or give form to her experiences. The book is instead hardly more than an accumulation of horrors, an inventory of the infallible tendency of the nicest-seeming males to take advantage of Ingrid Bengis. The gallery of villains ranges from construction workers whistling at her on the street to the boy she shared a room with who fondled her as she lay blissfully zonked out in her sleeping bag, to the Mexican restaurant owner who gave her a free meal and then demanded sex, to the truck driver who picked her up while hitchhiking and then got upset when she refused to put out.

These were experiences many of us had in the 1970's. In hindsight, the source of Bengis's rage, a rage felt by so many women of our generation, can be discerned as early as the second page of her book, where she speaks of the men (plural) she has loved. The long and the short of it is that, thanks to the pill, young American females of the 1970's were suddenly behaving with the license, but without the sensibility, of jaded aristocrats. We women instinctively knew that what we were conferring was important and had something to do with love, and, like Ingrid Bengis, we used that word when we spoke of sex. Yet the terms of the bargain between men and women had radically changed. The old bargain—sex in exchange for commitment—had issued out of

conditions of what might crassly be called a balance of supply and demand. These conditions were undermined in the 1970's by the flooding of the market with casual sex.

Feminists tend to blame men for their cavalier treatment of women, but, in the realm which Goethe spoke of as *Sittlichkeit* (roughly, morals), men follow the lead of women. Young males, it turns out, will only be protective and caring of females if something is at stake. When women sleep with men they barely know, assuming on their own the responsibility for regulating reproduction, men will be equally casual. A reward not having been fought for or truly earned is not a reward for which any individual will feel more than momentary indebtedness.

No wonder the whistle of construction workers, once a sign of appreciation for rewards not yet earned, and perhaps unattainable, came to sound to us like a hiss of contempt at our availability. The resulting sense of bafflement can be gleaned from where, in her prose, Bengis stamps her foot in emphasis, and where her inimitable ellipses fall:

> *Of course* I was proud to be a woman . . . proud as well of a subtle kind of sexuality. But I was not proud of the way in which that sexuality was systematically abused in the service of something that ultimately cheapened both me and it.

By such displacements outward did rage at men become the fate of an entire generation.

T HE ROLE of the women's movement was to turn this rage into something powerful—sisterhood. As unexpected as it may sound, the experience of becoming a feminist was, for many, akin to a sudden spiritual conversion, a radical turnaround of the kind Tolstoy described in *Confession*, in which "everything that was on the right hand of the journey is now on the left." An essay by Jane O'Reilly, "Click! The Housewife's Moment of Truth" (from the whimsically entitled *The Girl I Left Behind*, 1980), perfectly captures the quality of transformation promised by the movement, and just as perfectly exposes its hollowness.

The essay inhabits a genre the publishing market has long catered to: morality tales in which adolescents learn the deceptiveness of appearances through painful lessons that lead them to maturity and true values. Just so, Jane O'Reilly finally grew up when she encountered women's liberation. Her book is a tale of setting aside the unimportant things, the very things she had once (in the 1950's) perceived that being a woman meant: debutante balls, identification bracelets, popularity, 75 people singing carols on Christmas Eve, drinking cocoa out of Dresden cups, real pearls. The illumination she underwent was to recognize that all these were a snare and a delusion, a cover and a preparation for deferring and submitting to men. Instead, what women needed was to become "equal members of the human society."

O'Reilly's essay contains Erma Bombeck-like hints for negotiating the transition from Cinderella-*cum*-domestic-drone to liberated human being: "(1) Decide what housework needs to be done. Then cut the list in half." In the realm of love, her language is up-to-date, *circa* 1980: "I practiced and practiced taking the sexual initiative"; "I need to get laid." But the subtext is still the same old thing: romance. It turns out Jane O'Reilly truly wanted the flowers, the passionate declarations, and all the rest. For her, too, though perhaps less grimly than for Ingrid Bengis, women's sexual liberation was a bust. The new social arrangements—here is an entry for February 29 from the *Liberated Woman's Appointment Calendar:* "Leap Year Day. Propose to the Person of Your Choice"—failed.

At the end, Jane O'Reilly gives up, though she puts a brave face on it: "I now think love is somehow beside the point." Having sloughed off the demands of boyfriends, husbands, children, parents, in-laws, she is left to craft her own "lifestyle" out of the limp slogans of sisterhood:

> Nontradition has become tradition. My friends are my family, and we will provide for each other. Gathered about the [Christmas] tree will be the intact family from upstairs, the broken family from across the park, an extended family from out of town, my own reconstituted family, and the various inexplicable attachments we have all acquired along the way.

Thus, by 1980, had Kate Millett's turgid and off-putting rhetoric of revolution been refashioned into O'Reilly-style sentimentality. Moreover, this sentimentality had become a staple, peddled in magazines and books, in TV programs and movies. Seldom was it asked whether or how it could actually carry you through long-term illness, financial jeopardy, or personal crises of a truly acute nature.

Instead, as many women went through affair after affair, as they failed with one Mr. Right after another, as they approached forty and saw the possibilities of a family of their own diminishing, as they found themselves living alone, scrambling for an invitation for Christmas dinner, O'Reilly's defeated alternative became more and more a necessary article of faith.

III

"Do you know where you're drifting?" Henrietta pursued [with Isabel], holding out her bonnet delicately.
"No, I haven't the least idea, and I find it very pleasant not to know. A swift carriage, of a dark night, rattling with four horses over roads that one can't see—that's my idea of happiness."

PEOPLE WHO look at my *curriculum vitae* often come up with comments like, "What an interesting life you've led!" By 1988, for instance, when I returned to graduate school to finish my Ph.D., I had lived in Tokyo for several years, working, variously, as a writer of advertising, editor of a travel magazine, and bar girl, with side trips for extended periods to such exotic locales as Bali and Chiang-mai.

My decision in 1974 to take a job in Tokyo was no doubt influenced by my love of things unfamiliar, though the choice was also determined by an impulse today's self-help primers discourage as "geographical escape." Having had so many boyfriends (or been in love with so many, as Ingrid Bengis would have it), I suffered from an intensely unsettled personal life. By this point, I had become diverted from the studious habits of my undergraduate years. With a different perspective on life, so I thought, and perhaps a Japanese boyfriend as well, things would fall into place.

If Henry James's Americans are disabused in their encounters with Europe, so my own love of the unfamiliar was much shaken by Tokyo. As I quickly discovered, not only would I not get to live in a picturesque wooden Japanese house, I was also not going to find a Japanese boyfriend. Japan in 1974 was profoundly conservative, and sexual emancipation was definitely not the order of the day. What was more, Japan must have been the only culture in the world where it was deemed unmanly for a man to display interest in a woman. Overnight I seemed to become invisible.

Within a few days, I felt I had struck a very bad bargain, but I was too stubborn to go back to the U.S. Thrown on my own resources, without multitudinous opportunities for diversion, I finally got down to writing. At first, the pages of my notebooks were filled with little more than Ingrid Bengis-like rantings against the Japanese. Soon, however, I began to write for third- and fourth-rate travel magazines, which in turn led to more substantial opportunities.

It was with a slender stock of writing credentials that I returned in the early 1980's to the U.S., where it soon became clear to me there would be a price to pay for my waywardness. In the few years I had been gone, things in America had changed, and I found I had gotten off the track. In my usual confident way I decided to support myself as a freelance writer and to publish a novel, a task at which I succeeded. But after my first novel a somewhat bleak period followed, as I adhered to my desire to distinguish myself by writing stories and novels that nevertheless went unpublished. I used to meet weekly with a group of writers, all of whom had been published in the field of genre fiction, but they quickly grew impatient with me, giving me little encouragement in my determination to write what they all considered too literary and rightly scorned as unmarketable.

It was about this time, the mid-1980's, that I conceded that the promise of participation and distinction was going to take a long time to realize (I was nothing if not stubborn!). Such a clear-eyed assessment did not result in my entering the job market, however. Instead, in 1988, with my 1970's-based confidence still intact, I returned to graduate school. That I happily contemplated the prospect of teaching at a small liberal-arts college at a time when there was already a glut of Ph.D.'s seems another delusion that only an American woman who came of age in the 1970's could entertain.

IV

Smile not, however, I venture to repeat, at this simple young woman from Albany who debated whether she should accept an English peer before he had offered himself and who was disposed to believe that on the whole she could do better. She was a person of great good faith, and if there was a great deal of folly in her wisdom those who judge her severely may have the satisfaction of finding that, later, she became consistently wise only at the cost of an amount of folly which will constitute almost a direct appeal to charity.

THE WOMEN's movement is usually seen as having grown from the movement for civil rights for blacks, and, to many people, it had to do primarily with equality of economic opportunity. From the late 1960's on, mainstream journalists dutifully trotted out the statistics concerning women's economic and professional disadvantages. Yet feminists agitating about the pay scales of lawyers or accountants were in fact after something else: a change in the very meaning of equality.

For women to be "equal," as Jane O'Reilly dimly perceived ("The point of feminism is not that the world should be the same, but that it should be different"), something more drastic than admission to medical school was required. Female biology itself would have to be interpreted as a humanly limiting condition, established not by nature but by a cabal otherwise known as the patriarchy. There was much at stake, and a 1969 article in the *Nation* spelled it out: the women's movement, intoned the writer, was dedicated "to a total restructuring of society, . . . and is not content simply to integrate women into male-defined goals and values."

This thoroughgoing radicalism, a (relatively) new aspect of the century-old movement for female emancipation, elicited criticism even on the Left. Among the opponents was the socialist and literary critic Irving Howe. In December 1970 Howe published in *Harper's* a long review-essay of Kate Millett's *Sexual Politics*, which a few months earlier had been baptized by *Time* magazine as the *Communist Manifesto* of the women's movement. Howe took the book sharply to task not only for its intellectual and literary failings but also for what he perceived as Millett's dangerous political agenda, which he considered "a parody of the Marxist vision of class struggle." In one of the nastiest literary put-downs of all time, he declared that "the emotions of women toward children don't exactly form an overwhelming preoccupation in *Sexual Politics*: there are times when one feels the book was written by a female impersonator." This was a comment, I recall, that particularly exercised me and my sisters in the movement at the time. That I had not read Millett was beside the point; it was enough that Howe attacked the woman who articulated our rage for us.

Were sexual differences amenable to the kind of social reconfiguration Millett was advocating? Howe, for one, certainly did not think so. To the contrary, he thought they should not be jettisoned on the trash heap of history in the pursuit of some bloodless ideal. In speaking of the struggles of his own parents, toiling as garment workers while raising children in wretched poverty, Howe sounded almost like a conservative. Besides suggesting that the differences between the sexes might in fact contribute to the melioration of our fallen human condition, he also defended the family as being not necessarily oppressive to women:

> That the family . . . has been coextensive with human culture itself and may therefore be supposed to have certain powers of endurance and to yield certain profound satisfactions to human beings other than merely satisfying the dominating impulses of the "master group," hardly causes Miss Millett to skip a phrase. Nor does the thought that in at least some of its aspects the family has protected the interests of women as against those of men.

In retrospect, this may have been the moment when the Left gave way definitively to the New Left. That Howe was fighting a rearguard action is clear from the fact that he soon withdrew from this polemical field—as did Norman Mailer, another leftist stalwart whose lone contribution to the anti-feminist canon was his 1971 *The Prisoner of Sex*. By now, moreover, both the women's movement and the New Left had begun to find a new source of legitimation in a philosophy that had sunk roots in the universities. Call it deconstruction, call it post-structuralism, its intent was to demolish the notion that there could be anything like cultural standards, or agreed-upon truths, or, it went without saying, objective sexual differences.

Today, of course, this relativism-in-the-service-of-a-new-absolutism has contaminated far more than the upper reaches of academia and the fringes of the Modern Language Association. All introductory college courses, be they in literature, sociology, anthropology, religion, etc., have become shot through with the insights of deconstruction, and an afternoon of watching Oprah is enough to demonstrate how they have filtered down into the general culture. The goal of this new orientation is, ostensibly, radical human freedom and equality, without ties to oppressive institutions of any kind, especially not to the patriarchy, that shibboleth of social reconstructionists. But what deconstruction has really done is to banish, as nothing more than a set of arbitrary conventions, the moral promptings that lead people to notice oppression in the first place, and along with them the ability to distinguish true oppression from false.

V

He had told her, the first evening she ever spent at Gardencourt, that if she should live to suffer enough she might some day see the ghost with which the old house was duly provided. She apparently had fulfilled the necessary condition; for the next morning, in the cold, faint dawn, she knew that a spirit was standing by her bed.

THERE IS a cart-before-the-horse quality about feminism. An explosion of economic forces, starting after World War II, sent women into the workplace in large numbers. It was only after this process was in high gear, and when women began directly competing with men in the upper echelons, that feminism came into being. An ideology then arose to justify the unprecedented autonomy on the part of women (and perhaps to assuage some of their felt guilt over the abandonment of hearth and home) and to allocate spoils. A panoply of institutions formed in its turn, to buttress the ideology: women's-studies departments in universities, tax-exempt institutions setting themselves up as lobbyists for "women's issues," a larger and larger government bureaucracy. By now, many women have come to believe that their opportunities stem wholly from the struggles of their feminist forebears and not at all from the steady expansion of the market.

But ideology, as Karl Marx noted long ago, is replete with tensions. These tensions are in abundant evidence in an essay by Diane Johnson in a recent issue of the *New York Review of Books*. Johnson is aware of the distress signals being sent out by contemporary feminism, and she demonstrates that even a liberal like herself can recognize the ridiculousness of academic feminist highjinks:

> . . . endless testimonials, diatribes, and spurious science from people who imagine that their personal experience, the dynamics of their particular family, sexual taste, child-

hood trauma, and personal inclination constitute universals.

Johnson even circles back to the incommensurables of human existence, going so far as to refer to God and original sin. Since she is a novelist, such incommensurables may be on her mind.

Yet on the subject of women and women's issues, she inevitably begins from premises that are at odds with the way individuals struggle to craft their individual solutions to life's demands, a task that, ironically enough, the novel has traditionally taken it as its prerogative to illuminate. Johnson's constant use of the word "class" in connection with women alerts the reader to the nonnovelistic sources of her thinking. Her enumeration of the minimal rights that feminists should urge on everyone is unalloyed bureaucratic boilerplate: personal safety, autonomy in sexual and health matters, equal pay for equal work.

Among my friends who are working women of middle age, there are very few who do not consider themselves feminists. Their attitudes, like Johnson's, are permeated by a belief in the inevitable progress of humanity—from which, they hold, women, prior to the 1960's, were excluded. They remain upbeat concerning the bureaucratic arrangements that will bring about the inevitable progress. Such has been the infiltration of feminist-think that women who 30 years ago would have recoiled from the social engineering extolled by Gloria Steinem now accept the rationale for suspending a six-year-old boy from school for sexual harassment because he has kissed a six-year-old girl.

Johnson herself adduces several sociological studies which purportedly demonstrate that all the parameters are finally lining up and settling into place. She quotes Dr. Daniel J. ("mid-life crisis") Levinson: "Humanity is now in the early phases of a transformation in the meanings of gender and the place of women and men in every society." The same doctor also holds, from the loftiest Archimedean perspective, that such gender transformation (here I am quoting Johnson) "is an irreversible historical trend which will take another century to achieve." And people think Newt Gingrich is a crackpot for spouting Alvin Toffler.

Johnson declines to question whether the "transformation in the meanings of gender" projected by Levinson is a desirable state, whether it is a state any of us would wish to morph into. An irreversible trend, after all, is an irreversible trend. But she compliments France and Scandinavia, "whose governments have committed themselves to large-scale child-care arrangements." These arrangements, like the model farms the Soviets used to allow foreign visitors to see, seem to offer evidence that rational social planning will work and that the awful dislocations and disruptions occurring all around us are only temporary and in any case justified by the march of History.

B**UT MAYBE** Dr. Levinson is on to something. It strikes me that one of the peculiar results of the reign of feminism is that women have actually become unimportant, indeed nonessential. This has come about by feminism's making radically suspect the influence that women, *qua* women, have traditionally exercised on the souls of those with whom they come into contact. The first effective thrust was to deny that any of the endless tasks performed by women within the marriage union contributed in any way to its spiritual wholeness. Housekeeping and childraising were transformed into a purely material operation, consisting of the kind of mindless, mechanical steps that characterize the assembly of an automobile or a computer. It is no surprise that the most ambitious women of my generation fled this scenario of drudgery, and, by extension, also avoided traditional women's occupations as they would the plague. A generation of women who would have been excellent teachers instead became attorneys, in what they were told and seemed to believe would be a net gain for humanity.

This abandonment of the female realm has also led to the production of a class that appears to be in the vanguard of the nanny state: women who "have it all," whose marriages are not so much unions as partnerships of two career paths, and whose children, once assembled and produced, are willingly turned over by them to caretakers. Most of these women have probably not dwelt on the consequences of the Faustian bargain they have struck, but their example says loudly and clearly that children are interchangeable units and that the values they learn can be equally well acquired from a Norwegian au pair and after-school public television as from parents.

Whether such women really do have it all is for them, perhaps, to say. Even so, there remains a lack of synchronicity between the highest levels of feminist achievers and ordinary women. Housework and the raising of children, denigrated by the movement and by so many elite women, is looked upon very differently by my unmarried friends, even those who call themselves feminists. They sense that the struggle to form one's life in conjunction with another—including all those horrible minutiae of daily existence that Jane O'Reilly described as the murder of a woman's soul—is a spiritual enterprise of the highest sort, involving the "discovery," as Midge Decter put it with her habitual precision in *The New Chastity* (1972), "that to be in charge of oneself also requires the courage to recognize the extent of one's frailty and dependence on others." And they sense acutely that, in declining or refusing to make those compromises of daily living-with-another, they have missed out on the greatest of human challenges and have indeed failed in point of courage. They still yearn to meet someone with whom, as the current parlance goes, they can share their life.

The tragic part is the egocentrism of their current existence, the days and years devoted to self-maintenance, with minimal effect on the lives of others. Women now get to fulfill themselves—O'Reilly's passionate wish—but they do so in the most resolute solitude. If there is any validity to what Aristotle said long ago—that one's existence has a goal toward which the soul strives—then the care of one's physical and mental self can only be a subordinate part of a larger existential plan. The women I am talking about do not have such a plan, be it marriage or children or a high-powered career. Instead of caring for the direction of their souls, they tend to their "personal space."

The greatest loss for my friends who have not married is of course the children they never had. Exhortations to self-fulfillment aside, by the time they reached forty many women of my generation were in a desperate race with their bodies. Magazines in the late 1980's began featuring articles on "Mommie Oldest," as women underwent Herculean efforts to get their aging uteruses into shape. *In vitro* fertilization, artificial insemination, hormone shots—if only they could go back and undo all those abortions!

HERE, INDEED, is the great unnameable, the subject that many of us have refused to face squarely in its terrible personal dimension but that, like the purloined letter, has always been there, before our eyes. Childbirth, contraception, abortion: these dividers of women also illuminate the terrible contradictions of feminist ideology, and particularly the contention that women are no different from men.

The divide between the goals of radical, society-transforming feminism and ordinary women is inadvertently captured by Diane Johnson in her criticism of the social thinker Elizabeth Fox-Genovese, whose latest book, *Feminism Is Not the Story of My Life*, dwells precisely on this divide. Fox-Genovese, she writes, "stops just short of saying that feminists will murder infants in their cradles." Even setting partial-birth abortions aside, Johnson's refusal to see what feminism has, in fact, done in this realm is breathtaking. And because she will not acknowledge it, she must also censure Fox-Genovese for speaking of women's sexual decisions as being somehow fraught with special danger. To speak in this way, says Johnson, suggests that women are not up to independent moral choice." But Fox-Genovese does not deny women moral choice; she merely underscores what most women have always known: that sex, for them, *is* fraught with special danger. Ingrid Bengis knew that, though it made her very angry.

I have made my way back to my starting point. Is sex merely a material manifestation, a physical fact and act, a discharge of physical tension? Does it make any difference that the man who caresses a woman's body is a man she met only a few hours before? Or is a woman's experience of sex part of a larger moral, indeed spiritual, equation? Does she require that the man with whom she shares her bed be one whose love has settled unwaveringly and discriminatingly on her? Does she expect him to take responsibility for the child she may conceive? These are the hard questions, ones that many of us have not confronted. But whenever a woman does confront them, and arrives at the latter point of view, you will probably find that she has severed her ties with feminism.

Unit 2

Unit Selections

8. **The Education of Alice and Dorothy: Helping Girls to Thrive in School,** Thomas R. McDaniel
9. **Man's World, Woman's World? Brain Studies Point to Differences,** Gina Kolata
10. **Gay- and Lesbian-Studies Movement Gains Acceptance in Many Areas of Scholarship and Teaching,** Scott Heller
11. **The Trouble with Men,** *The Economist*
12. **The Myth of the Miserable Working Woman,** Rosalind C. Barnett and Caryl Rivers

Key Points to Consider

❖ Why do some educators suggest single-sex schools are better for girls and boys? If this trend catches on, would there still be a need to emphasize fables with female heroines for educating girls or for limiting the Socratic method of instruction for female law students?

❖ What is in store for the future if women in great numbers advance their power and prestige?

❖ Name some bona fide brain differences between the sexes that have been discovered by neuroscientists.

❖ What is the relationship between multiple role demands and stress in the lives of women?

 **Links**   # www.dushkin.com/online/

9. **American Psychoanalytic Association**
   http://www.apsa.org/pubinfo/female.htm
10. **Educational Resources Information Center**
   http://www.aspensys.com/eric/index.html
11. **Sex and Gender**
   http://bioanth.cam.ac.uk/pip4amod3.html
12. **Sexual Assault Information Page**
   http://www.cs.utk.edu/~bartley/saInfoPage.html

These sites are annotated on pages 4 and 5.

Theories on the education of girls and young women have often taken refuge in a biological description that labels women's physiology, social functions, capacities, and orientations as inferior to those of men. It is perhaps for this reason that, sitting in the same classroom, reading the same textbook, and listening to the same teacher, boys and girls receive a very different message that, in turn, affects the education they receive.

The difference in messages to female students does not stop with mandatory schooling. From their freshman years in college through graduate school, female students are more likely to repress their responses. Moreover, teachers often interact with males more frequently, ask them better questions, and give them more precise and helpful feedback. Over the years, this uneven distribution of an instructor's time, energy, attention, and talent—with boys receiving the lion's share of praise and learning stimuli—takes its toll on girls. Since gender bias in general is not overt, most people are unaware of the underlying sexist lessons and quiet losses that women experience in institutions of learning.

Once out of school, females continue to be constantly and everywhere subjected to the unspoken assumption that males are superior. The middle-class white male standard, in particular, has implicitly and explicitly patterned our social basis for education, health, leadership, relationships, and personal autonomy. Whether or not we as individuals accept this standard, we live in a society that organizes itself collectively according to it, and we are, in turn, influenced by it.

Subsequently, Americans expect men to be stronger, more intelligent, more objective, more competent, and more independent than women. Nowhere is this more self-evident than in our education systems where such tacit inequities often chip away at a girls' achievement and self-esteem.

Several articles in this unit explore this dilemma by examining current trends, suggestions, and nontraditional studies for

Education and Psychology

educating women. Also psychological issues, such as the brain's role in dictating differences between men and women, are analyzed. The first article discusses creative ways to educate women. The author, Thomas McDaniel, suggests that teachers should become more involved in helping school girls become more independent and confident. The next article, "Man's World, Woman's World? Brain Studies Point to Differences," by Gina Kolata, reveals some of the miraculous techniques that are used to study the brain. Kolata examines some of the interesting, cognitive, behavioral, and emotional differences in the brain functioning of men and women.

Then Scott Heller discusses the growing popularity of gay and lesbian studies in research and teaching while "The Trouble with Men" describes future power and influence for women because traditional centers of power for men are being phased out.

In the last article in unit 2, Rosalind Barnett and Caryl Rivers, in "The Myth of the Miserable Working Woman," examine the numerous myths about working women. According to the media's portrayal of working women, they are stressed, unhealthy, and unable to cope with both work and family responsibilities. However, recent research indicates that just the opposite is true.

The Education of Alice and Dorothy: Helping Girls to Thrive in School

THOMAS R. McDANIEL

Alice and Dorothy, two schoolgirls, had extraordinary adventures on the way to growing up. Wonderland and Oz were fictional settings for the education of two quite different girls, but what an education these youngsters received! Lewis Carroll and Frank Baum used their fictional worlds to satirize life in their respective societies in the way only good fiction can, and in the process they left enduring lessons. Alice in Wonderland and Dorothy in Oz raise questions about contemporary American education—especially the education of girls.

First, consider poor Alice. Her English world is nicely ordered—with matters of class, values, and proper roles for girls all settled. And then, alas, she falls down the rabbit hole into a place where the world is topsy-turvy. Her order is disrupted, and her notions of the true and proper are called into question. Bizarre characters—from grinning cats to croquet-playing cards—make her rethink her basic values as she seeks her way back home. Recall her encounter with a mischievous, disappearing Cheshire cat:

> "Cheshire-Puss," . . . said Alice, "would you tell me, please, which way I ought to go from here?"
> "That depends a good deal on where you want to get to," said the Cat.
> "I don't much care where—" said Alice.
> "Then it doesn't matter which way you go," said the Cat.
> "—so long as I get somewhere," Alice added as an explanation.
> "Oh, you're sure to do that," said the Cat, "if you only walk long enough."

Thomas R. McDaniel is interim president of Converse College, Spartanburg, South Carolina, and a Clearing House consulting editor.

Do our schools help girls find their special talents? Do they provide the kinds of role models girls need to develop confidence and competence? Do we help schoolgirls look within for the qualities that will lead them to their Emerald Cities?

A wealth of research on education indicates that schools do not serve girls well. *How Schools Shortchange Girls,* a 1992 report from the American Association of University Women, concludes that sexism is pervasive in American schools and includes findings that

- girls get less teacher attention, less praise, and fewer constructive comments than boys;
- when boys call out answers, teachers listen, but when girls call out they are told to raise their hands;
- reports of sexual harassment in schools are increasing;
- girls and women who appear in textbooks are generally sex-role stereotyped; and
- SAT scores under-predict college grades for girls.

We have a way to go in making our schools good places for girls to study and grow. What yellow-brick road shall we provide?

Teachers might begin with an honest assessment of their own attitudes and practices to discover any classroom biases that work against the education of female students. All of us have difficulty seeing our own biases, of course. Test yourself on the table 1 quiz (McDaniel 1989) to determine any tendency you may have toward sexism. This is not a scientific survey but might raise your awareness of certain practices or beliefs. Studies show that teachers, on average, call on boys to answer questions three times as often as they call on girls—but they *believe* that they

From *The Clearing House,* Vol. 67, No. 5, May/June 1994, pp. 288–290. Reprinted with permission of the Helen Dwight Reid Educational Foundation. Published by Heldref Publications, 1319 Eighteenth St. NW, Washington, DC 20036-1802. © 1994.

TABLE 1

Sex-Role Stereotyping Quiz

	Always (10)	Sometimes (5)	Never (0)
1. I call on boys more often than girls.			
2. I think math is more important for boys.			
3. I think girls (women) are poor leaders (bosses).			
4. I think girls are emotional and irrational.			
5. I give girls more assistance on skill activities.			
6. I believe girls are the weaker sex.			
7. I reprimand "sassy" girls but expect boys to be witty.			
8. I think textbooks are free of sex bias.			
9. I make boys defend their answers/opinions in class but don't force girls to explain themselves.			
10. I think girls don't like science.			

Scoring Key: 60-100 . . . Serious sexist; 40-59 . . . Sometimes sexist; below 40 . . . Seldom sexist.

---

call on each group equally. In Caldecott award books for children, boy characters outnumber girls ten to one. We tend not to see such discrepancies in our pedagogy and curriculum.

Then, schools might do more in their parenting programs to pave a yellow-brick road for their daughters. For example, consider these specific suggestions outlined by Silverman (1986) as useful strategies for parents who want gifted daughters to thrive in school:

- hold high expectations for daughters
- encourage high levels of activity
- promote interests in math outside of school
- monitor television programs for sexist stereotypes
- assign chores to boys and girls on a nonsexist basis
- share household duties equally between parents
- encourage siblings to treat each other equitably
- introduce girls to a wide variety of professional women
- encourage girls to take math and science courses

These suggestions to parents could easily apply to girls of all ability levels.

In schools, teachers can also help girls on their way to the Emerald City. Strategies for a successful journey include these:

- design coeducational career development classes
- expose boys and girls to role models of women in professional fields
- discuss nontraditional careers for women
- have girls read biographies of famous women
- provide opportunities for girls to practice math reasoning in many subjects
- discourage sexist remarks and attitudes in the classroom

- discuss sexist messages in the media
- help girls set long-term goals
- challenge girls to defend their answers
- provide equal opportunities for girls to answer questions and lead discussions

Most teachers could use some of these strategies to help girls become more independent and confident.

Finally, as we think about the education of modern-day Alices and Dorothys, we might benefit from a realization that the *equal* treatment of girls and boys does not always mean the *same* treatment. Our object should not be to make girls into the best boys they can be. We are learning more each day about the different ways that girls learn (Belenky et al. 1986), communicate (Tannen 1991), and reach ethical-moral decisions (Gilligan 1987). We are only beginning to answer a question Alice posed early in her adventures: "Who in the world am I? Ah, that's the great puzzle." An educational program that accommodates these differences between boys and girls while challenging both to reach their full potentials can help all our children arrive safely in education's Emerald City. We have a still puzzling and difficult journey ahead in American education. But we are now asking the right questions about the education of girls.

It should not be surprising that women's colleges have been found to be extraordinarily effective in providing a specialized approach to the needs of women learners. Jadwiga Sebrechts, executive director of the Women's College Coalition, reacted to the AAUW report *How Schools Shortchange Girls* this way:

Despite what appears to be political aversion to separation of the sexes, both educational and extracurricular, single sex environments have an enviable track record for nurturing the aspirations of girls and women and for producing the results that are sought through the recommendations of the AAUW report. (1993, informal paper)

She then points out that women's college graduates are two-to-three times more likely to pursue advanced degrees in math and science than graduates of coed colleges and are represented in Fortune 500 companies at six times the rate one would expect given their proportion in the population. What is it about women's colleges that contributes to such accomplishments? Perhaps public school K–12 programs could benefit from a close examination of practices at such colleges.

Those who teach in middle schools and junior highs encounter girls at a critical juncture in their social and educational development: "middlescents" become acutely aware of their sexual nature and identity. As girls enter the teen years, they mysteriously (it seems) develop math anxiety while they also begin making significant decisions about roles, relationships, and careers. They begin wrestling seriously with Alice's existential question—"Who in the world am I?" and they look for answers to that puzzle in the educational programs we provide them. Teachers,

through their awareness as well as their teaching practices, can have a profound impact on the kinds of lives girls have, now and in their futures.

Alice and Dorothy must leave their "real worlds" to encounter the exciting and rewarding experiences that transform their lives. Both girls return home as wise women. Their education tests their abilities, challenges their values, and develops their character. To get "somewhere" still depends on brains, courage, and heart. Are our schools ready and able to provide that kind of education for girls?

References

Belenky, M. et al. 1986. *Women's ways of knowing: The development of self, voice, and mind.* New York: Basic Books.

Gilligan, C. 1987. *In a different voice: Psychological theory and women's development.* Cambridge, Mass.: Harvard University Press.

McDaniel, T. R. 1989. Gender stereotyping. *Teaching for Excellence* 9 (4):2.

Silverman, L. K. 1986. What happens to the gifted girl? In *Critical issues in gifted education,* edited by J. C. Maker, 79–81. Rockville, Md.: Aspen.

Tannen, D. 1991. *You just don't understand: Women and men in conversation.* New York: Ballantine Books.

Man's World, Woman's World? Brain Studies Point to Differences

Gina Kolata

Dr. Ronald Munson, a philosopher of science at the University of Missouri, was elated when Good Housekeeping magazine considered publishing an excerpt from the latest of the novels he writes on the side. The magazine eventually decided not to publish the piece, but Dr. Munson was much consoled by a letter from an editor telling him that she liked the book, which is written from a woman's point of view, and could hardly believe a man had written it.

It is a popular notion: that men and women are so intrinsically different that they literally live in different worlds, unable to understand each other's perspectives fully. There is a male brain and a female brain, a male way of thinking and a female way. But only now are scientists in a position to address whether the notion is true.

The question of brain differences between the sexes is a sensitive and controversial field of inquiry. It has been smirched by unjustifiable interpretations of data, including claims that women are less intelligent because their brains are smaller than those of men. It has been sullied by overinterpretations of data, like the claims that women are genetically less able to do everyday mathematics because men, on average, are slightly better at mentally rotating three dimensional objects in space.

But over the years, with a large body of animal studies and studies of humans that include psychologi-

cal tests, anatomical studies, and increasingly, brain scans, researchers are consistently finding that the brains of the two sexes are subtly but significantly different.

Now researchers have a new non-invasive method, functional magnetic resonance imaging, for studying the live human brain at work. With it, one group recently detected certain apparent differences in the way men's and women's brains function while they are thinking. While stressing extreme caution in drawing conclusions from the data, scientists say nonetheless that the groundwork was being laid for determining what the differences really mean.

"What it means is that we finally have the tools at hand to begin answering these questions," said Dr. Sally Shaywitz, a behavioral scientist at the Yale University School of Medicine. But she cautioned: "We have to be very very careful. It behooves us to understand that we've just begun."

The most striking evidence that the brains of men and women function differently came from a recent study by Dr. Shaywitz and her husband, Dr. Bennett A. Shaywitz, a neurologist, who is also at the Yale medical school. The Shaywitzes and their colleagues used functional magnetic resonance imaging to watch brains in action as 19 men and 19 women read nonsense words and determined whether they rhymed.

In a paper, published in the Feb. 16 issue of Nature, the Shaywitzes

New scanner finds more evidence of how the sexes differ in brain functions.

reported that the subjects did equally well at the task, but the men and women used different areas of their brains. The men used just a small area on the left side of the brain, next to Broca's area, which is near the temple. Broca's area has long been thought to be associated with speech. The women used this area as well as an area on the right side of the brain. This was the first dear evidence that men and women can use their brains differently while they are thinking.

Another recent study by Dr. Ruben C. Gur, the director of the brain behavior laboratory at the University of Pennsylvania School of Medicine, and his colleagues, used magnetic resonance imaging to look at the metabolic activity of the brains of 37 young men and 24 young women when they were at rest, not consciously thinking of anything.

In the study published in the Jan. 27 issue of the journal Science, the investigators found that for the most part, the brains of men and women at rest were indistinguishable from each other. But there was one difference, found in a brain structure called the limbic system that regulates emotions. Men, on average, had higher brain activity in the more ancient and primitive regions of the limbic system, the parts that are more involved with action. Women, on average, had more activity in the newer and more complex parts of the limbic system, which are involved in symbolic actions.

Dr. Gur explained the distinction: "If a dog is angry and jumps and bites, that's an action. If he is angry and bares his fangs and growls, that's more symbolic."

Dr. Sandra Witelson, a neuroscientist at McMaster University in Hamilton, Ontario, has focused on brain anatomy, studying people with terminal cancers that do not involve the brain. The patients have agreed to participate in neurological and psychological tests and then to allow Dr. Witelson and her colleagues to examine their brains after they die, to look for relationships between brain structures and functions. So far she has studied 90 brains.

Men have larger brains; women have more neurons.

Several years ago, Dr. Witelson reported that women have a larger corpus callosum, the tangle of fibers that run down the center of the brain and enable the two hemispheres to communicate. In addition, she said, she found that a region in the right side of the brain that corresponds to the region women used in the reading study by the Shaywitzes was larger in women than in men.

Most recently Dr. Witelson discovered, by painstakingly counting brain cells, that although men have larger brains than women, women have about 11 percent more neurons. These extra nerve cells are densely packed in two of the six layers of the cerebral cortex, the outer shell of the brain, in areas at the level of the temple, behind the eye. These are regions used for understanding language and for recognizing melodies and the

tones in speech. Although the sample was small, five men and four women, "the results are very very clear," Dr. Witelson said.

Going along with the studies of brain anatomy and activity are a large body of psychological studies showing that men and women have different mental abilities. Psychologists have consistently shown that men, on average, are slightly better than women at spatial tasks, like visualizing figures rotated in three dimensions, and women, on average, are slightly better at verbal tasks.

Dr. Gur and his colleagues recently looked at how well men and women can distinguish emotions on someone else's face. Both men and women were equally adept at noticing when someone else was happy, Dr. Gur found. And women had no trouble telling if a man or a woman was sad. But men were different. They were as sensitive as women in deciding if a man's face was sad—giving correct responses 90 percent of the time. But they were correct about 70 percent of the time in deciding if women were sad; the women were correct 90 percent of the time.

"A woman's face had to be really sad for men to see it," Dr. Gur said. "The subtle expressions went right by them."

Studies in laboratory animals also find differences between male and female brains. In rats, for example, male brains are three to seven times larger than female brains in a specific area, the preoptic nucleus, and this difference is controlled by sex hormones that bathe rats when they are fetuses.

"The potential existence of structural sex differences in human brains is almost predicted from the work in other animals," said Dr. Roger Gorski, a professor of anatomy and cell biology at the University of California in Los Angeles. "I think it's a really fundamental concept and I'm sure, without proof, that it applies to our brains."

But the question is, if there are these differences, what do they mean?

Dr. Gorski and others are wary about drawing conclusions. "What happens is that people overinterpret these things," Dr. Gorski said. "The brain is very complicated, and even in animals that we've studied for many years, we don't really know the function of many brain areas."

This is exemplified, Dr. Gorski said, in his own work on differences in rat brains. Fifteen years ago, he and his colleagues discovered that males have a comparatively huge preoptic nucleus and that the area in females is tiny. But Dr. Gorski added: "We've been studying this nucleus for 15 years, and we still don't know what it does. The most likely explanation is that it has to do with sexual behavior, but it is very very difficult to study. These regions are very small and they are interconnected with other things." Moreover, he said, "nothing like it has been shown in humans."

And, with the exception of the work by the Shaywitzes, all other findings of differences in the brains or mental abilities of men and women have also found that there is an amazing degree of overlap. "There is so much overlap that if you take any individual man and woman, they might show differences in the opposite direction" from the statistical findings, Dr. Gorski said.

Dr. Munson, the philosopher of science, said that with the findings so far, "we still can't tell whether the experiences are different" when men and women think. "All we can tell is that the brain processes are different," he said, adding that "there is no Archimedean point on which you can stand, outside of experience, and say the two are the same. It reminds me of the people who show what the world looks like through a multiplicity of lenses and say 'This is what the fly sees.' "But, Dr. Munson added, "We don't know what the fly sees." All we know he explained, is what we see looking through those lenses.

Approaches to Understanding Male-Female Brain Differences

Studies of differences in perception or behavior can suggest how male and female thinking may diverge; studies of structural or metabolic differences can suggest why. But only now are differences in brain organization being studied.

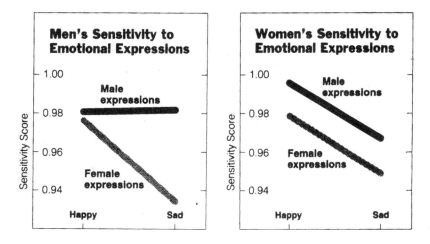

A study compared how well men and women recognized emotions in photos of actors portraying happiness and sadness. Men were equally sensitive to a range of happy and sad faces in men but far less sensitive to sadness in women's faces.

The women in the study were generally more sensitive to happy faces than to sad ones. They were also better able to recognize sadness in a man's face. For both sexes, sensitivity scores reflected the percent of the time the emotion was correctly identified.

Some researchers, however, say that the science is at least showing the way to answering the ancient mind-body problem, as applied to the cognitive worlds of men and women.

Dr. Norman Krasnegor, who directs the human learning and behavior branch at the National Institute of Child Health and Human Development, said the difference that science made was that when philosophers talked about mind, they "always were saying, 'We've got this black box.'" But now he said, "we don't have a black box; now we are beginning to get to its operations."

Dr. Gur said science was the best hope for discovering whether men and women inhabited different worlds. It is not possible to answer that question simply by asking people to describe what they perceive, Dr. Gur said, because "when you talk and ask questions, you are talking to the very small portion of the brain that is capable of talking." If

investigators ask people to tell them what they are thinking, "that may or may not be closely related to what was taking place" in the brain, Dr. Gur said.

On the other hand, he said, scientists have discovered that what primates perceived depends on how their brains function. Some neurons fire only in response to lines that are oriented at particular angles, while others seem to recognize faces. The world may well be what the philosopher Descartes said it was, an embodiment of the workings of the human mind, Dr. Gur said. "Descartes said that we are creating our world," he said. "But there is a world out there that we can't know."

Dr. Gur said that at this point he would hesitate to boldly proclaim that men and women inhabit different worlds. "I'd say that science might be leading us in that direction," he said, but before he commits himself he would like to see more definite differences in the way men's

and women's brains function and to know more about what the differences mean.

Dr. Witelson cautioned that "at this point, it is a very big leap to go from any of the structural or organizational differences that were demonstrated to the cognitive differences that were demonstrated." She explained that "all you have is two sets of differences, and whether one is the basis of the other has not been shown." But she added, "One can speculate."

Dr. Witelson emphasized that in speculating she was "making a very big leap," but she noted that "we all live in our different worlds and our worlds depend on our brains.

"And," she said, "if these sex differences in the brain, with 'if' in big capital letters, do have cognitive consequences, and it would be hard to believe there would be none, then it is possible that there is a genuine difference in the kinds of things that men and women perceive and how these things are integrated. To that extent it may be possible that in some respects there is less of an easy cognitive or emotional communication between the sexes as a group because our brains may be wired differently."

The Shaywitzes said they were reluctant even to speculate from the data at hand. But, they said, they think that the deep philosophical questions about the perceptual worlds of men and women can eventually be resolved by science.

"It is a truism that men and women are different," Dr. Bennett Shaywitz said. "What I think we can do now is to take what is essentially folklore and place it in the context of science. There is a real scientific method available to answer some of these questions."

Dr. Sally Shaywitz added: "I think we've taken a qualitative leap forward in our ability to ask questions." But, she said, "the field is simply too young to have provided more than a very intriguing appetizer."

Gay- and Lesbian-Studies Movement Gains Acceptance in Many Areas of Scholarship and Teaching

At a Harvard U. meeting this week, scholars in the field expect to discuss plans to form an association

By SCOTT HELLER

Martin Duberman faced "vitriolic denunciations" when he first proposed a graduate course in the history of sexuality at the City University of New York in 1978.

Next spring he expects to head up the university's new Center for Lesbian and Gay Studies, which will focus on research, curriculum development, and, eventually, he hopes, offer degrees.

"For the world of academe," says Mr. Duberman, a professor of history at CUNY's Graduate Center and Lehman College, "that's a great deal of progress in a short time."

While courses on lesbian and gay issues have been offered since the 1970's, faculty members report a surge in sophisticated scholarship and blossoming interest on the part of graduate students and undergraduates.

800 Participants, 200 Papers

Some 800 professors, students, writers, and activists are expected at Harvard University this week for the fourth annual Lesbian, Bisexual, and Gay Studies Conference. Two hundred papers will be presented, twice as many as last year. One topic up for discussion is the formation of an official academic association for scholars working in the field.

> **The new work is "an abandonment of the 'great homosexuals in history' scheme in favor of a scheme that charts the proliferation of sexual meanings in a culture."**

"It's exploding; it's incredible the number of academic writing projects being born," says Richard D. Mohr, professor of philosophy at the University of Illinois at Urbana-Champaign. Mr. Mohr is general editor of a new book series from Columbia University Press. Its first three volumes—on gay male theater, homoerotic photography, and lesbian literary theory—will be issued next year.

Last year, the City College of San Francisco created the nation's first department of gay and lesbian studies. Study groups for faculty members and graduate students have been set up at Yale University and the University of California at Santa Cruz.

Why sexuality? And why now?

The growing, vocal presence of lesbian and gay scholars is one reason, says Mr. Mohr. Earlier, professors would establish their reputations before writing their "gay book," he says. Now graduate students are exploring such themes from the start.

The work is closely connected to other developments in the humanities, broadly grouped under the category of cultural studies. Scholars are interested in the experiences of minority groups, in how experiences are shaped by "representation," and in how power is maintained and resisted in society. Looking at the cultural ramifications of AIDS is one heavily researched example.

Literary and Cultural Influences

The influence of various literary and cultural theories—especially feminism and Marxism—is relevant, as well. Lesbian studies, in particular, are deeply related to the growth of women's studies in the last 15 years.

"Gay and lesbian studies can do for sex what feminism did for gender—to set it off as a social and cultural category separate from biology," says David M. Halperin, professor of literature at the Massachusetts Institute of Technology.

A first wave of scholarship came as an outgrowth of the gay-liberation movement of the late 1960's and 1970's. Many of the early works were sociological or historical accounts. They are often described as "essentialist," making the case that homosexuality is biological and has existed basically unchanged throughout history.

'Social Constructionist'

Much of the new scholarship is considered "social constructionist." Scholars attempt to analyze how sexuality has been, and is, "constructed" in various cultures and at various times. They analyze literary, legal, medical, and popular-culture texts.

"It frees us all from the reductive-biological model that dominated since World War II," says Martha Vicinus, professor of English and women's studies at the University of Michigan. "And it frees us from a simplistic Freudian explanation of sexual behavior." Ms. Vicinus is co-editor of *Hidden From History: Reclaiming the Gay and Lesbian Past.*

The new work is "an abandonment of the 'great homosexuals in history' scheme in favor of a scheme that charts the proliferation of sexual meanings in a culture," adds Mr. Halperin.

Worries persist that as work on lesbian and gay issues gets more theoretical—and thus more acceptable to other scholars—it will lose its political edge. Mr. Mohr, who say he is an "old-fashioned essentialist," maintains that much of the new scholarship is imitative, merely "block quoting" the French philosopher Michel Foucault.

This week's meeting at Harvard University, organized under the title "Pleasure/Politics," will span the spectrum, with a particular emphasis on how sexuality relates to race and nationality. Sessions will address AIDS and the politics of fiction; lesbian pornography; homosexual marriages, past, present, and future; and matters of censorship.

Some scholars plan to debate the relationships between the field and women's studies. Other scholars are expected to question what gay studies and lesbian studies do—and don't—have in common.

A Term That Was Once a Slur

Professors affiliated with a gay and lesbian faculty-research group at the University of California at Santa Cruz this year organized a conference titled "Queer Theory." Teresa de Lauretis, a professor of the history of consciousness at Santa Cruz, says the use of the term "queer" is meant to incorporate the experiences of lesbians and gay men, and to give positive meaning to what had been a slur.

The goal, she says, is "to understand homosexuality not as a perversion or an inversion of normal sexual identity but as a sexual behavior and an identity on its own terms—as a cultural form in its own right."

She dismisses the claim that gay and lesbian scholars are inappropriately preaching to their students, arguing that implicit in the typical classroom experience is an endorsement of heterosexuality.

"The point would be to see heterosexuality as a choice, not as a constraint," she says. "But you can only see it as a choice when you allow homosexuality to be a choice as well."

The trouble with men

IT MAY be a man's world now, but "Tomorrow belongs to women" (to borrow the title of a book by Jack Lang, a French politician and sex symbol). No wonder.

Apart from being more violent, more prone to disease, more likely to succumb to drugs, bad diet or suicide—more socially undesirable from almost every point of view, in fact—men, it seems, are also slightly more stupid than women. At any rate, boys are doing less well than girls at school. And since, with each passing year, more brainy word-processing consultants and nursery-school teachers get new jobs while more brawny coal miners and machine-tool operators lose theirs, it seems inevitable that women with their graduate certificates and mothering instincts will soon be doing ever more of the world's work, while men lag further behind. A woman's work is never done; a man is drunk from sun to sun.

Well, does that matter? Biologists might answer: not much. To them, men are useful largely for one thing: supplying genetic products to mothers. Providing half a baby's genes stirs up the gene pool and outwits the bacteria and viruses that prey on the species. Also from a biologist's point of view, a lot of aggressive male behaviour is so much genetic advertising. Having men lock antlers, brag about football and indulge in dangerous virility rituals enables women, in some mysterious way, to pick the best genes to hand on.

But nature's methods seem extremely crude. Why not be a tad more scientific? The next generation does not need the current crop of men to be carrying around their sperm all the time. A clean, well-run sperm bank, regularly topped up, would be just as good—and would dispense with men's unfortunate social side-effects. Sperm banks could provide a wide range of gene services, offering, say, high intelligence, predilection to be a surgeon, blue eyes, long legs and so forth. In America, they already provide a splendid array of choices (and offer insurance in case sperm counts fall even further).

Meanwhile, in terms of cultural evolution, men may well have done their job: they have pretty much set up modern civilisations and technologies; they may not be needed to keep them going. Knowledge-based societies, with their stress on brain not brawn, may be safer in women's hands.

Testosterone and its antidotes

Back to real life. Men have not been humanely phased out. They still have more jobs than women and, on average, earn higher salaries. In the middle and upper income brackets, men are adjusting—albeit slowly—to women's growing economic power. But down at the bottom of the ladder, where men are men and women change the nappies (but also have the jobs), there are troubles of an entirely different order.

Here whole communities are caught in a deadly vice. In areas which used to depend on heavy industry, changes in the nature of work have laid waste the traditional sources of unskilled male employment. Men who used to work in the collieries or shipyards have proved unable (or, which is almost the same thing, unwilling) to do the "women's work" springing up in the industrial ruins. As their jobs have declined, so have their prospects of marriage, for who wants to link their lot with a jobless deadbeat? And as work and marriage have declined together, so everyone has suffered, for these two, since time immemorial, have been the twin responsibilities that have persuaded men to stay with women and children, obey the law and behave as social animals. For women, work and family are often competing spheres; for men, they are linked. When the link is broken, some men, in some places, become loose molecules: uneducated, unskilled, unmarried and unemployed.

Perhaps this will change. Perhaps men will begin to compete more vigorously for "women's work". Perhaps they will find jobs, and, having got them, marry and look after children again. But the evidence so far is against it. At best, men will change

their ways reluctantly and more slowly than the quickening pace of economic change. Meanwhile, the blue-collar problem will grow.

Men learn social behaviour through work and marriage, rather than grasp it by instinct. Nothing can be done to change that. Nothing should be done to turn the clock back—by, for example, discriminating against women at work or keeping open economically pointless factories (which would amount to the same thing, since that would penalise the new jobs women do). The engines of economic change—information technology and globalisation—are, contrary to rumour, benefiting the vast majority of humanity: not just women in the West but millions of men and women everywhere.

So such remedies as are possible must concentrate on the places where the social problems are worst: the inner cities. One reason that boys are falling behind girls at urban primary and secondary schools is that too few male teachers are around for boys to look up to and model their behaviour upon. Attracting more male teachers would help close the gap in educational attainment and improve boys' job prospects. More can and should be done to improve the skills of young men: it is especially worth concentrating on their schooling and vocational education, even though men often pooh-pooh such things. And a lot can be done to alleviate the social evils of areas where employment and marriage rates are lowest. While the source of the trouble may be unemployment, much of the damage that flows from this is connected to the easy availability of guns and drugs. Here, more efficient restrictions are needed, which means, for drugs, decriminalisation and control.

Such a list may seem a piecemeal and partial response to "the trouble with men". Granted, it is only a start. But with all great social changes, there comes a stage, before comprehensive policies can be agreed upon, when what is needed is to recognise that a problem exists and accept that it cannot be left to fester. With men in the ghettos, that stage has arrived.

The Myth of the Miserable Working Woman

She's Tired, She's Stressed Out, She's Unhealthy, She Can't Go Full Speed at Work or Home. Right? Wrong.

Rosalind C. Barnett and Caryl Rivers

Rosalind C. Barnett is a psychologist and a senior research associate at the Wellesley College Center for Research on Women. Caryl Rivers is a professor of journalism at Boston University and the author of More Joy Than Rage: Crossing Generations With the New Feminism.

"You Can't Do Everything," announced a 1989 USA Today *headline on a story suggesting that a slower career track for women might be a good idea. "Mommy Career Track Sets Off a Furor," declaimed the* New York Times *on March 8, 1989, reporting that women cost companies more than men. "Pressed for Success, Women Careerists Are Cheating Themselves," sighed a 1989 headline in the* Washington Post, *going on to cite a book about the "(unhappy personal lives" of women graduates of the Harvard Business School. "Women Discovering They're at Risk for Heart Attacks," Gannett News Service reported with alarm in 1991. "Can Your Career Hurt Your Kids? Yes, Say Many Experts," blared a* Fortune *cover just last May, adding in a chirpy yet soothing fashion, "But smart parents—and flexible companies—won't let it happen."*

If you believe what you read, working women are in big trouble-stressed out, depressed, sick, risking an early death from heart attacks, and so overcome with problems at home that they make inefficient employees at work.

In fact, just the opposite is true. As a research psychologist whose career has focused on women and a journalist-critic who has studied the behavior of the media, we have extensively surveyed the latest data and research and concluded that the public is being engulfed by a tidal wave of disinformation that has serious consequences for the life and health of every American woman. Since large numbers of women began moving into the work force in the 1970s, scores of studies on

their emotional and physical health have painted a very clear picture: Paid employment provides substantial health *benefits* for women. These benefits cut across income and class lines; even women who are working because they have to—not because they want to—share in them.

There is a curious gap, however, between what these studies say and what is generally reported on television, radio, and in newspapers and magazines. The more the research shows work is good for women, the bleaker the media reports seem to become. Whether this bizarre state of affairs is the result of a backlash against women, as *Wall Street Journal* reporter Susan Faludi contends in her new book, *Backlash: The Undeclared War Against American Women,* or of well-meaning ignorance, the effect is the same: Both the shape of national policy and the lives of women are at risk.

Too often, legislation is written and policies are drafted not on the basis of the facts but on the basis of what those in power believe to be the facts. Even the much discussed *Workforce 2000* report, issued by the Department of Labor under the Reagan administration—hardly a hotbed of feminism—admitted that "most current policies were designed for a society in which men worked and women stayed home." If policies are skewed toward solutions that are aimed at reducing women's commitment to work, they will do more than harm women—they will damage companies, managers and the productivity of the American economy.

THE CORONARY THAT WASN'T

One reason the "bad news" about working women jumps to page one is that we're all too willing to believe it. Many adults today grew up at a time when soldiers were returning home from World War II and a way had to be found to get the women who replaced them in industry back into the kitchen. The result was a barrage of propaganda that turned at-home moms into saints and backyard barbecues and station wagons into cultural icons. Many of us still have that outdated postwar map inside our heads, and it leaves us more willing to believe the horror stories than the good news that paid employment is an emotional and medical plus.

In the 19th century it was accepted medical dogma that women should not be educated because the brain and the ovaries could not develop at the same time. Today it's PMS, the wrong math genes or rampaging hormones. Hardly anyone points out the dire predictions that didn't come true.

You may remember the prediction that career women would start having more heart attacks, just like men. But the Framingham Heart Study—a federally funded cardiac project that has been studying 10,000 men and women since 1948—reveals that working women are not having more heart attacks. They're not dying any earlier, either. Not only are women not losing their health advantages; the lifespan gap is actually widening. Only one group of working women suffers more heart attacks than other women: those in low-paying clerical jobs with many demands on them and little control over their work pace, who also have several children and little or no support at home.

As for the recent publicity about women having more problems with heart disease, much of it skims over the important underlying reasons for the increase: namely, that by the time they have a heart attack, women tend to be a good deal older (an average of 67, six years older than the average age for men), and thus frailer, than males who have one. Also, statistics from the National Institutes of Health show that coronary symptoms are treated less aggressively in women—fewer coronary bypasses, for example. In addition, most heart research is done on men, so doctors do not know as much about the causes—and treatment—of heart disease in women. None of these factors have anything to do with work.

But doesn't working put women at greater risk for stress-related illnesses? No. Paid work is actually associated with *reduced* anxiety and depression. In the early 1980s we reported in our book, *Lifeprints* (based on a National Science Foundation-funded study of 300 women), that working women were significantly higher in psychological well-being than those not employed. Working gave them a sense of mastery and control that homemaking didn't provide. More recent studies echo our findings. For example:

• A 1989 report by psychologist Ingrid Waldron and sociologist Jerry Jacobs of Temple University on nationwide surveys of 2,392 white and 892 black women, conducted from 1977 to 1982, found that women who held both work and family roles reported better physical and mental health than homemakers.

• According to sociologists Elaine Wethington of Cornell University and Ronald Kessler of the University of Michigan, data from three years (1985 to 1988) of a continuing federally funded study of 745 married women in Detroit "clearly suggests that employment benefits women emotionally." Women who increase their participation in the labor force report lower levels of psychological distress; those who lessen their commitment to work suffer from higher distress.

• A University of California at Berkeley study published in 1990 followed 140 women for 22 years. At age 43, those who were homemakers had more chronic conditions than the working women and seemed more disillusioned and frustrated. The working mothers were in good health and seemed to be juggling their roles with success.

In sum, paid work offers women heightened self-esteem and enhanced mental and physical health. It's unemployment that's a major risk factor for depression in women.

DOING IT ALL—AND DOING FINE

This isn't true only for affluent women in good jobs; working-class women share the benefits of work, according to psychologists Sandra Scarr and Deborah Phillips of the University of Virginia and Kathleen McCartney of the University of New Hampshire. In reviewing 80 studies on this subject, they reported that working-class women with children say they would not leave work even if they didn't need the money. Work offers not only income but adult companionship, social contact and a connection with the wider world that they cannot get at home.

Doing it all may be tough, but it doesn't wipe out the health benefits of working.

Looking at survey data from around the world, Scarr and Phillips wrote that the lives of mothers who work are not more stressful than the lives of those who are at home. So what about the second shift we've heard so much about? It certainly exists: In industrialized countries, researchers found, fathers work an average of 50 hours a week on the job and doing household chores; mothers work an average of 80 hours. Wethington and Kessler found that in daily "stress diaries" kept by husbands and wives, the women report more stress than the men do. But they also handle it better. In short, doing it all may be tough, but it doesn't wipe out the health benefits of working.

THE ADVANTAGES FOR FAMILIES

What about the kids? Many working parents feel they want more time with their kids, and they say so. But does maternal employment harm children? In 1989 University of Michigan psychologist Lois Hoffman reviewed 50 years of research and found that the expected negative effects never materialized. Most often, children of employed and unemployed mothers didn't differ on measures of child development. But children of both sexes with working mothers have a less sex-stereotyped view of the world because fathers in two-income families tend to do more child care.

However, when mothers work, the quality of non-parental child care is a legitimate worry. Scarr, Phillips and McCartney say there is "near consensus among developmental psychologists and early-childhood experts that child care per se does not constitute a risk factor in children's lives." What causes problems, they report, is poor-quality care and a troubled family life. The need for good child care in this country has been obvious for some time.

What's more, children in two-job families generally don't lose out on one-to-one time with their parents. New studies, such as S. L. Nock and P W. Kingston's *Time with Children: The Impact of Couples' Work-Time Commitments*, show that when both parents of preschoolers are working, they spend as much time in direct interaction with their children as families in which only the fathers work. The difference is that working parents spend more time with their kids on weekends. When only the husband works, parents spend more leisure time with each other. There is a cost to two-income families—the couples lose personal time—but the kids don't seem to pay it.

One question we never used to ask is whether having a working mother could be *good* for children. Hoffman, reflecting on the finding that employed women—both blue-collar and professional—register higher life-satisfaction scores than housewives, thinks it can be. She cites studies involving infants and older children, showing that a mother's satisfaction with her employment status relates positively both to "the quality of the mother-child interaction and to various indexes of the child's adjustment and abilities." For example, psychologists J. Guidubaldi and B. K. Nastasi of Kent State University reported in a 1987 paper that a mother's satisfaction with her job was a good predictor of her child's positive adjustment in school.

Again, this isn't true only for women in high-status jobs. In a 1982 study of sources of stress for children in low-income families, psychologists Cynthia Longfellow and Deborah Belle of the Harvard University School of Education found that employed women were generally less depressed than unemployed women. What's more, their children had fewer behavioral problems.

But the real point about working women and children is that work *isn't* the point at all. There are good mothers and not-so-good mothers, and some work and some don't. When a National Academy of Sciences panel reviewed the previous 50 years of research and dozens of studies in 1982, it found no consistent effects on children from a mother's working. Work is only one of many variables, the panel concluded in *Families That Work*, and not the definitive one.

What is the effect of women's working on their marriages? Having a working wife can increase psychological stress for men, especially older men, who grew up in a world where it was not normal for a wife to work. But men's expectations that they will-and must-be the only provider may be changing. Wethington and Kessler found that a wife's employment could be a significant buffer *against* depression for men born after 1945. Still, the picture of men's psychological well-being is very mixed, and class and expectations clearly play a role. Faludi cites polls showing that young blue-collar men are especially angry at women for invading what they see as their turf as breadwinners, even though a woman with such a job could help protect her husband from economic hardship. But in highly educated, dual-career couples, both partners say the wife's career has enhanced the marriage.

THE FIRST SHIFT: WOMEN AT WORK

While women's own health and the well-being of their families aren't harmed by their working, what effect does this dual role have on their job performance? It's assumed that men can compartmentalize work and home lives but women will bring their home worries with them to work, making them distracted and inefficient employees.

Perhaps the most dangerous myth is that the solution is for women to drop back—or drop out.

The only spillover went in the other direction: The women brought their good feelings about their work home with them and left a bad day at home behind when they came to work. in fact, Wethington and Kessler found that it was the *men* who brought the family stresses with them to work. "Women are able to avoid bringing the contagion of home stress into the workplace," the researchers write, "whereas the inability of men to prevent this kind of contagion is pervasive." The researchers speculate that perhaps women get the message early on that they can handle the home front, while men are taking on chores they aren't trained for and didn't expect.

THE PERILS OF PART-TIME

Perhaps the most dangerous myth is that the solution to most problems women suffer is for them to drop back—or drop out. What studies actually show is a significant connection between a reduced commitment to work and increased psychological stress. In their Detroit study, Wethington and Kessler noted that women who went from being full-time employees to full-time housewives reported increased symptoms of distress, such as depression and anxiety attacks; the longer a woman worked and the more committed she was to the job, the greater her risk for psychological distress when she stopped.

What about part-time work, that oft-touted solution for weary women? Women who work fewer than 20 hours per week, it turns out, do not get the mental-health work benefit, probably because they "operate under the fiction that they can retain full responsibility for child care and home maintenance," wrote Wethington and Kessler. The result: Some part-timers wind up more stressed-out than women working full-time. Part-time employment also provides less money, fewer or no benefits and, often, less interesting work and a more arduous road to promotion.

That doesn't mean that a woman shouldn't cut down on her work hours or arrange a more flexible schedule. But it does mean she should be careful about jumping on a poorly designed mommy track that may make her a second-class citizen at work.

Many women think that when they have a baby, the best thing for their mental health would be to stay home. Wrong once more. According to Wethington and Kessler, having a baby does not increase psychological distress for working women—*unless* the birth results in their dropping out of the labor force. This doesn't mean that any woman who stays home to care for a child is going to be a wreck. But leaving the work force means opting out of the benefits of being in it, and women should be aware of that.

As soon as a woman has any kind of difficulty—emotional, family, medical—the knee-jerk reaction is to get her off the job. No such solution is offered to men, despite the very real correlation for men between job stress and heart attacks.

What the myth of the miserable working woman obscures is the need to focus on how the *quality* of a woman's job affects her health. Media stories warn of the alleged dangers of fast-track jobs. But our *Lifeprints* study found that married women in high-prestige jobs were highest in mental well-being; another study of life stress in women reported that married career women with children suffered the least from stress. Meanwhile, few media tears are shed for the women most at risk: those in the word-processing room who have no control at work, low pay and little support at home.

Women don't need help getting out of the work force; they need help staying in it. As long as much of the media continues to capitalize on national ignorance, that help will have to come from somewhere else. (Not that an occasional letter to the editor isn't useful.) Men need to recognize that they are not just occasional helpers but vital to the success of the family unit. The corporate culture has to be reshaped so that it doesn't run totally according to patterns set by the white male workaholic. This will be good for men *and* women. The government can guarantee parental leave and affordable, available child care. (It did so in the '40s, when women were needed in the factories.) Given that Congress couldn't even get a bill guaranteeing *unpaid* family leave passed last year, this may take some doing. But hey, this is an election year.

Unit 3

13. **Warning: Feminism Is Hazardous to Your Health,** Ruth Conniff
14. **Blocking Women's Health Care,** Melanie Conklin
15. **Women's Health Movements,** Joanne Howes and Amy Allina
16. **Abortion in American History,** Katha Pollitt
17. **Females in Sports: A Book Review,** Mary Jo Festle
18. **Fair Game: Title IX Twenty-Fifth Anniversary,** Janet Lee

Key Points to Consider

❖ Why does the Independent Women's Forum suggest that federal funding for women's diseases is "junk science"?

❖ Why should women look into hospital policies before being admitted?

❖ What conditions have helped women in their quest for health reform?

❖ Give a short history of abortion policies in the United States. Discuss the new debate that centers around the issue of abortion.

❖ Why is it important for women to participate in sports? What are the problems that females continue to encounter 25 years after Title IX?

 **Links**   **www.dushkin.com/online/**

13. **Carnegie Mellon University/Center for the Advancement of Applied Ethics/Philosophy Department**
   http://caae.phil.cmu.edu/caae/Home/Multimedia/Abortion/IssueofAbortion.html
14. **Starting Point: Health**
   http://www.stpt.com/health/health.html
15. **World Health Organization**
   http://www.who.ch/Welcome.html
16. **U.S. National Institutes of Health**
   http://www.nih.gov/

These sites are annotated on pages 4 and 5.

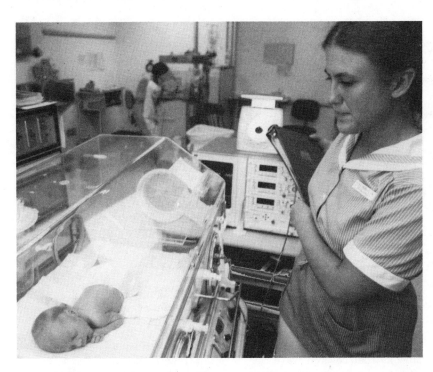

Few public policies advocate major improvements in the general health and well-being of women. Indeed, government policies and priorities that do not overtly account for women's diverse health needs often affect women adversely. This situation becomes obvious when a woman requires health care but cannot afford to pay for it or is unable to identify warning symptoms because she does not know what to look for.

In addition, women's medical needs are often ignored because women are unable to frame the questions that concern their health. This happens when women are underrepresented in medicine and politics, and are, therefore, unfamiliar with the techniques and processes that would win them greater autonomy in policy-making arenas.

In the United States and most other industrial countries, for instance, programs aimed at the prevention and treatment of heart disease, cancer, and AIDS, among other illnesses, have long been neglected because women are unfamiliar with the language describing these illnesses. Meanwhile their efforts to take control of their bodies and reproductive functions have extended from abortion and contraception to include new reproductive technologies like in-vitro fertilization and embryotic implants. Unfortunately, these dramatic advances in biotechnology have made women's bodies more vulnerable to exploitation.

As for women and sports, the legendary Title IX, enacted on June 23, 1972, has been a far-reaching piece of legislation. Before that period, many nontraditional sports, recreational outlets, and academic domains were closed to women. Furthermore, female applicants to universities and colleges were required to have higher Scholastic Aptitude Test scores than males. Besides, there were no athletic scholarships for women, and the widely used Strong Vocational Interest Blank scales had separate scoring systems for males and females—pink tests for girls, emphasizing "female" occupations, and blue tests for boys, dealing with "male" fields such as medicine and science.

Despite challenges to Title IX in the courts, continuing inequities in athletic budgets demonstrate a need for federal policy to ensure that the momentum begun by Title IX continues through the century and beyond.

This unit examines these issues from a variety of perspectives. The first article, "Warning: Feminism Is Hazardous to Your Health," by Ruth Conniff, describes a conservative antifeminist organization that criticizes feminism for its views on plastic surgery and for "feminizing" medical research. In the second article, "Blocking Women's Health Care," Melanie Conklin alerts women to the policies of hospitals that, because of mergers with religious institutions, enforce rules against a variety of reproductive services. Women's health reform is the topic of the third article. In "Women's Health Movements," Joanne Howes and Amy Allina discuss the prominence of reproductive health and women's health care in political debates brought about by the increase of women in positions of influence. An historical overview of abortion policies in the United States is provided in the next article. Katha Pollitt identifies what she refers to as the real debate, which centers on sexual behavior and the subordination of women. The last two articles examine women in sports. In "Females in Sports: A Book Review," Mary Jo Festle discusses sports in terms of a society's culture and mores, while in the last article, Janet Lee examines Title IX historically and finds that inequalities in sport sponsorship still exist after 25 years.

WARNING:
Feminism is hazardous to your health

BY RUTH CONNIFF

Here's some startling news: The latest threat to women's health isn't any of the medical scandals you've been reading about—not unnecessary hysterectomies, not defective birth-control devices, not breast implants, not those medical-research projects that fail to study women. No, the big health risk facing American women today is feminism. So say researchers working with rightwing think tanks, who have isolated a particular strain of radical, deconstructionist feminism now spreading from cultural-studies departments into the general population, distorting medical research, infecting our justice system, and causing mass hysteria.

This frightening trend was the theme of a February conference at the National Press Club in Washington, D.C., called "Women's Health, Law, and the Junking of Science."

The conference, put on by the conservative Independent Women's Forum, presented a series of expert panels to show how a nefarious network of feminist ideologues, public-interest research groups, and trial lawyers are politicizing science and jeopardizing women's health.

"Radical feminist academics and 'fellow travelers' are leading the flight from science and reason," said Noretta Koertge, a professor of the history and philosophy of science from Indiana University. Koertge gave a presentation using overheads that diagramed something she called "menstrual mathematics." This school of thought claims that women are put off by scientific experiments involving hard collisions,

Ruth Conniff is the Washington Editor of The Progressive.

and are more attracted to fluids, she explained. She showed us an e-mail message from a teaching assistant in physics, asking whether there were any textbooks that covered wave theory before quantum mechanics, since that might appeal to women more.

Paul Gross, a professor emeritus of life sciences at the University of Virginia and a visiting scholar at Harvard, followed Koertge. Gross had overheads, too. He flashed a quote from an ecofeminist named Val Plumwood, saying that "rationalism is the key to the linked oppressions of women and nature in the West." He had another one from Jacques Derrida, saying something spurious about reality and the whole Western tradition. He had also downloaded a silly message posted by a graduate student on the Internet, and he had some pictures of New Age magazines touting miracle cures for AIDS and cancer.

All in all, pretty goofy stuff.

"There are questionable and indeed dubious arguments that underlie the study of science," Gross concluded gravely. "Women's studies is particularly fertile ground for the growth of these ideas. The teaching of patent nonsense can't fail to have an impact on the next generation of thinkers and leaders."

But deconstructionist theory, e-mail messages from addled graduate students, and a bunch of loopy New Age magazines hardly add up to an all-out assault on medical science.

Don't be fooled, warned Christina Hoff Sommers, the author of *Who Stole Feminism* and a member of the Independent Women's Forum. "Some of you may think, OK, women's studies departments are anti-rational, but women have other sources of information," she

said. But unfortunately, she explained, the liberal media, influenced by feminists, are "far too eager to portray women as victims of gender bias," and often report distorted "advocacy research" on women's health issues. "Faced with the growing strength of the anti-science-and-reason movement, we can't afford to be passive," Hoff Sommers declared.

During a break in the conference, I chatted with a white-haired man in a tweed jacket sitting next to me—Fredrick Goodwin, the former director of the National Institute of Mental Health, and a professor of psychiatry at George Washington University. Goodwin said he thought the conference was "excellent" and "long overdue."

"I'm interested in victimology," he said. "I treat depression, and I've seen a lot of patients who are products of these women's studies programs. The radical feminist movement is fostering depression in women—fears of the environment, somatization [excessive preoccupation with the body], paranoid thinking. . . . If you took feminism as described here today and applied it to an individual, you'd say that's a person who needs help."

The most riveting presentation of the day was on breast implants. Marcia Ormsby, a very young-looking, blond plastic surgeon from Annapolis, Maryland, showed slides of some of her patients.

"I received hundreds of calls from women across the nation who were ready to consign themselves literally to insane asylums," they were so upset when they heard that breast implants might be linked to serious health problems, she said. "There is a lot of guilt and fear in these patients. Society already is telling them they shouldn't change their bodies," and then the news about implants hit.

Ormsby showed a slide with the words COMMUNICATIONS EFFECTIVENESS, MEDIA, and, underneath, in big capital letters, SENSATIONALISM.

"The implant crisis started with Connie Chung," she said, "and it quickly became headline news." She showed an overhead with the words HEADLINE NEWS.

Women have been unnecessarily terrified by media reports about problems with breast implants, she said. The FDA has even taken implants off the market, pending the results of new research. Yet, said Ormsby, "it seems there's no increase in autoimmune disease. That's fact. That's science."

(Actually, the jury is still out on the relationship between breast implants and autoimmune disease, since the epidemiological studies will take a long time to complete. What's certain is that women have had problems with breast implants that leak and rupture, and many of these patients claim to have become sick from the silicone that spilled into their bodies.)

Silicone is found in such commonplace items as hairspray, Ormsby pointed out, and in other medical devices.

"Where else is silicone found?" she asked. "Penile implants. There is *no* device more fraught with complications than penile implants!" Ormsby said adamantly. "And yet we don't hear about that." I accidentally caught the eye of my new friend the psychiatrist, who was listening intently. "Look at the men who have penile implants," said Ormsby. "They break all the time. Why? Because they're subjected to force. Yet these men have never been brought up on *Face the Nation* with Connie Chung."

Then Ormsby showed a picture of one of her patients with very small breasts. "This woman nursed three children," she said, yet "she looked like a boy scout."

"She was typical of patients I see in her difficulty in dealing with her body image," Ormsby continued. "These are women who are very embarrassed to dress in the gym."

The next slide was the "after" picture. "Here is her result," said Ormsby. Not only did the patient have big, round breasts, she had a terrific tan, interrupted only by the bright white outline of a bikini top, which highlighted the medically relevant region. "You can see she's been wearing her bathing suit and going to the beach," Ormsby pointed out.

My neighbors in the audience and I were duly impressed. The woman next to me looked over and smiled. But then came the bad news:

"What do I have to offer this woman today?" Ormsby asked. "Now my only option is saline implants—for this very, very thin woman—which ripple and hang like a bag of fluid."

I shuddered. The psychiatrist pursed his lips.

If we care about patients such as her, Ormsby said, "we have to learn to empathize and reflect to them what their problems are, because that's the only way we can get to the meat of the problem."

And what is the meat of the problem, exactly? The logical leap from deconstructionist feminist theory to FDA regulations and breast implants was a little hard to follow.

The keynote speaker at the conference was Marcia Angell, executive editor of *The New England Journal of Medicine*, and author of the book *Science on Trial: The Clash of Medical Evidence and the Law in the Breast Implant Case*. Angell had little to say about feminism or the liberal media. But she said she believes that the FDA made the wrong decision when it took silicone breast implants off the market in 1992.

"There was no evidence one way or another about the safety of implants" when the FDA made its decision, she said. Yet, in what Angell called a "backward series of events," in April 1994 women who claimed to be harmed by implants were awarded the largest class-action settlement in history. (The settlement has since fallen apart.) It wasn't until June 1994, Angell said, that the first rigorous, scientific study of implants came out of the Mayo Clinic. It found no link between implants and connective-tissue disease.

(In her book, Angell concedes that the size of the Mayo Clinic study was so small that it did not rule out the possibility of a tripling of the incidence of autoimmune disease among women with implants. Still, she asserts that there is no reason to believe implants cause the disease.)

"This controversy exposes the problem with our runaway tort system," Angell concluded.

Lucinda Finley, another panelist, a law professor from the State University of New York who specializes in product liability and women's health, respectfully disagrees with Angell.

"There are really two competing philosophies here," Finley said. "The

FDA says don't market a product until it is proven safe and effective. The opposing view is that we should go ahead and market a product until it's proven unsafe. I think many consumers prefer the philosophy that we shouldn't market products until we know they're safe."

But most conference participants were not so interested in the fine points of Finley's philosophical debate. They had bigger fish to fry—namely, the feminist, anti-science conspiracy.

"Behind and below the world of scientific evidence is a world of witchcraft: a hard and potent term, but it applies here," said one of the panelists, David Murray, a red-haired, bearded man with a sonorous voice. Murray got his Ph.D. in cultural anthropology from the University of Chicago. He now works for the Statistical Assessment Service, a conservative group "dedicated to improving media coverage of scientific and statistical information."

Murray told us to close our eyes, and began to whisper into the microphone: "Imagine it is a hot, sweltering day. You go to the refrigerator and find that all you have is a single lemon. . . . You cut open the lemon . . . you see the drops of juice glistening on the rind . . . you lift it and squeeze a few drops onto your tongue."

He had us open our eyes. "Many of you may have felt a tingling of the salivary glands as I told that story," he said.

Just as he had managed to induce a physical response in us by talking about the lemon, feminists and the media have managed to persuade people that they are suffering the symptoms of strange diseases, he suggested.

Murray listed some of these imaginary ills: "Gulf War Syndrome, Agent Orange Syndrome, and symptoms experienced by women who happen to have silicone breast implants."

Not only are the ailments suffered by women with breast implants imaginary, "it is a myth that women are second-class citizens in medical research," said Sally Satel, a Washington, D.C., psychiatrist who has written about politics and science for *The Wall Street Journal, The New Republic,* and other publications.

Congress made a big mistake when it ordered the National Institutes of Health (NIH) to include women and minorities in medical trials, Satel said. "Politically correct" medical trials are more expensive, and they dilute research by requiring scientists to split their studies into cumbersome subgroups.

According to Satel, contrary to popular belief and federal decree, women have not been excluded from scientific studies of heart disease and other ailments. In fact, she says, women have for a long time made up at least half of all medical-research subjects. To prove it, Satel displayed a big chart showing that since 1983, there have been approximately the same number of all-male and all-female medical studies, and a much higher number of coed studies. "Here are the 1994 numbers from the NIH," Satel said. "That year there were 1,002,000 subjects under study by NIH-funded researchers and 52 percent were women: 52 percent! Can't get much fairer than that."

During the question-and-answer period, a woman in the audience got up to object to some of Satel's claims. Phyllis Greenberger of the Society for the Advancement of Women's Health Research said that, until Congress pressured the NIH to start counting how many women were in studies, there were no numbers available. "The 52 percent she quoted for 1994 was right, but the fact is we had no data before that. . . ."

Greenberger began to list other objections to Satel's presentation, but Christina Hoff Sommers interrupted: "I'm sorry, but you are not asking a question and no one can hear you."

"Can someone give me a microphone?" Greenberger asked.

"No," said Hoff Sommers.

The audience rebelled. "Let her talk!" a man shouted.

"Give her the microphone!" a woman called out.

"No, I'm not going to give her the microphone," Hoff Sommers snapped. "*They* already have the microphone!"

Hoff Sommers called on Sally Satel to respond.

"How can she respond when there hasn't been a question yet?" a man in the audience demanded.

"All right," Hoff Sommers said testily, turning back to Greenberger. "Can you formulate a question?"

Greenberger did, although it was difficult to hear her. Satel responded that the answer to the question should be clear from her chart.

Afterwards, there was a lot of grumbling. "That really should not have happened," Rickie Silverman, a member of the Independent Women's Forum, said to another Forum member in the buffet line at lunch.

The moderator of the next panel, David Murray, alluded to the scuffle. "Our best service is to encourage open debate," he said. "We've certainly tried to put together the panels that way."

But, in fact, there was almost no debate at the conference. The lone dissenting voice on the final, summary panel was Lucinda Finley's.

Finley defended the FDA's decision to suspend the sale of breast implants, and said it wasn't fair to claim that breast implants don't cause disease, since scientists have not finished studying the problem yet.

The eight other panelists started passing the microphone back and forth, arguing with Finley about whether the scientists who link breast implants to disease are spouting "junk."

As Finley was talking, a tight-lipped Mona Charen, the conservative pundit moderating the final panel, asked, "Can someone get the microphone away from her?"

Finley was dismayed. "I find it ironic," she told me. "They are talking about junk science, and yet they're taking a study that says the question hasn't been answered yet, and using it to claim that the scientific issues about breast implants are completely settled. To me that's bad science."

The irony was not lost on Phyllis Greenberger, either, who talked to me in the hallway briefly after Christina Hoff Sommers shut her up.

"I think what they did to me really showed something," Greenberger said. "If you're justified in your facts, you shouldn't be afraid of hearing the other side. . . . Here they are spending a whole day on 'junk science,' and then they put up a chart you can't see unless you're in the front row, and it's like those charts the politicians use—it looks good, but is it true?"

Greenberger, who is on the Presidential advisory council for HIV/AIDS, hastened to add that her group, the Society for the Advancement of Women's Health Research, is "not a feminist organization in terms of the way they define feminism."

"This stuff at the universities is maybe garbage—they're taking feminism too far," she says. "But there's ample evidence that women haven't been studied enough in medical research. I wouldn't put that in the same category as victimization."

The Independent Women's Forum's whole mission, however, is to point out just how pervasive and damaging feminist ideology and "the politics of victimhood" really are.

For the last few years, the group's members have been busy attacking everything from affirmative action to the Violence Against Women Act to the notion that women have not achieved pay equity with men. The idea that women are not yet equal is itself "victimology," according to the group's press kit, which proclaims: "Since 1992, the Independent Women's Forum has been taking on the old feminist establishment—and winning."

Through opinion pieces in newspapers and magazines, appearances on pundit shows, and conferences like this one, the members of the IWF are out to spread their conservative views.

Denouncing "junk science" is their latest crusade. And they repeat the term so often it becomes a deafening drum beat. Articles about the problem of "junk science"—that is, a broad array of scientific research used by public-interest groups and plaintiffs in product-liability suits—have turned up recently in *The New Republic, Scientific American, ABC News,* and, of course, in newspaper columns by members of the Independent Women's Forum.

"What's starting to happen is that this term, 'junk science,' is being thrown around all the time," Finley says. "People are calling scientists who disagree with them purveyors of 'junk.' But what we're really talking about is a very normal process of scientific disagreement and give-and-take. Calling someone a 'junk scientist' is just a way of shutting them up."

"It's a pejorative term mainly used by industry and its friends to try to trivialize evidence about the risks of medical devices, drugs, and other consumer products," says Sidney Wolfe, director of Public Citizen's Health Research Group. Wolfe has been denounced as a "junk scientist" for promoting the idea that women have been harmed by breast implants. "But the public is right to be concerned about products that have caused harm, or haven't been adequately tested," he says.

By promoting the idea of "junk science," the Independent Women's Forum is doing just what its members accuse the much-maligned "feminist establishment" of doing—trying to silence disagreement and promote an ideological agenda that could warp science and public policy.

But, of course, to accuse them of that would only be the typical, paranoid feminist response.

Blocking Women's Health Care

Your hospital may have a policy you don't know about

BY MELANIE CONKLIN

In the parking lot of a hospital in central California, nurses are handing out plastic bags full of drugs to their patients. The nurses are not dispensing illegal substances. They are handing out the morning-after pill. But in the process, they are disobeying hospital policy.

Though emergency contraception is standard medical protocol in treating rape and incest, this hospital forbids prescribing the high dose of birth-control pills that can flush out a fertilized egg shortly after intercourse.

The hospital is Catholic, and the Roman Catholic Church says birth control is morally wrong.

Such instances where medical personnel are having to offer reproductive health care with a wink and a nod are on the rise as religious hospitals and clinics are merging at an accelerated pace with other health-care providers.

In this era of mergers and managed care, the Roman Catholic Church is having more of a say in all sorts of women's reproductive health-care services. Five of the ten largest hospital corporations are Catholic. (These are: Daughters of Charity National Health System, Catholic Health Initiatives, Catholic Healthcare West, Catholic Health Care Network, and Mercy Health Services.) There are more than 600 Catholic hospitals and 200 health-care centers serving some fifty million patients a year. And as the hospitals merge and affiliate with non-religious facilities, they often close off reproductive health care for women.

"We're seeing a huge increase in the number of hospitals and clinics being purchased by religious hospitals that refuse to offer the full range of reproductive care," says Susan Berke Fogel, legal director at the Women's Law Center in Los Angeles. Fogel tells the story of the nurses in the parking lot but declines to name the hospital or location, saying the nurses could lose their jobs for the stance they are taking.

"It's reprehensible at a time when medical trends are toward integrated health care that we are seeing this competing trend to isolate and marginalize women's health care," she says.

Catholic doctrine opposes abortion, contraception, tubal ligations, vasectomies, and fertility treatments. This doctrine applies not just to Catholics, but to any patient treated in a Catholic facility or even at a hospital or clinic affiliated with a Catholic institution that adheres to this doctrine.

And the number of these affiliated facilities is growing. Catholic Health Association estimates there were more than 100 mergers involving Catholic and secular hospitals in 1994 alone. Although other religious denominations, such as Baptists and Adventists, also run health-care facilities that may limit access to abortion, the biggest threat is from Catholic hospitals. A report by the Johns Hopkins School of Hygiene and Public Health found that 18 percent of all hospital affiliations in the past six years have involved a Catholic facility.

"We're seeing religious viewpoints being imposed in an extremely coercive way on people who don't share those views," says Catherine Weiss, director of the American Civil Liberties Union's Reproductive Freedom Project.

Melanie Conklin is a staff writer at Isthmus, the weekly newspaper of Madison, Wisconsin. This article was underwritten in part by a grant from the Fund for Investigative Journalism, Inc.

Often, the patients are the last to know that a hospital merger has restricted their reproductive health-care options.

Only 27 percent of women understood that being part of a Catholic hospital system could limit their reproductive care, according to a 1995 survey by Catholics for a Free Choice.

Catholics for a Free Choice cites the example of Jenni Zehr, who in 1988 went to Sacred Heart General Hospital, a Catholic hospital in Eugene, Oregon, to give birth. She requested to have a tubal ligation. Her doctors not only did not perform the procedure, they neglected to tell her. She found out when she became pregnant again.

Three years ago, according to the *Oregon Register Guard,* the Oregon Supreme Court ruled that Zehr could sue her doctor for the costs of raising that child.

A nineteen-year-old woman from Troy, New York, had one child and was struggling to put herself through community college. One day, she visited her clinic to get her regular birth-control shot. She didn't know that her clinic had merged with a religious facility.

"She was simply told, 'We don't do that anymore,' and was not referred to any other provider," says Lois Uttley, director of MergerWatch, which is funded by Family Planning Advocates. "She did find a Planned Parenthood clinic, but many poor women in those circumstances might not have transportation or even a phone to help them find another clinic." For patients in smaller communities, there may be no other options.

Then there are the added problems that mergers cause.

Judy Stone is an infectious-disease doctor in Cumberland, Maryland. Two years ago, her employer, Memorial Hospital, affiliated with Sacred Heart, the Catholic hospital. This fall, Memorial decided to become a nursing home and planned to transfer all its hospital business over to Sacred Heart.

"I couldn't sleep at night keeping my mouth shut," says Dr. Stone. "The process was covert, and decisions that should have been being made by the community were hidden."

So at an October 28 city council meeting, Stone gave a speech rapping the hospitals.

"This will be particularly detrimental to the women of the community," she said. "Especially those who are poor and unable to seek reproductive care elsewhere." She claimed it could also overrule living wills and prevent the kind of research Stone does into

new antibiotics or treatment for such conditions as blindness or Parkinson's Disease—all of which use fetal tissue. The merger is still pending.

Other communities are in for some post-merger surprises. Not only can Catholic hospitals refuse to perform certain procedures; they often refuse to refer patients to other clinics.

"In many cases, there are gag rules written into these contracts," says the ACLU's Weiss. "Now you've got a patient who needs hormonal contraception because of problems she would experience if she were to bear children—she's a high-risk patient. Well, they don't tell her that, and they don't refer her for that, and they don't provide it. She says to them, 'What should I do?' And they say, 'I'm sorry, I can't discuss that with you.' She says, 'Where should I go?' And they say, 'I'm sorry, I can't refer you.'"

Some secular health-care companies have policies against abortions, too. Earlier this year, Physicians Plus Medical Group in Madison, Wisconsin, was deciding among four potential merger partners. One was the Nashville-based PhyCor, a management company.

In the process of questioning doctors in other markets who are managed by PhyCor, Physicians Plus doctors discovered that PhyCor has an unpublicized policy against allowing abortions in any clinic that it operates. PhyCor confirms that this is company policy: "In the agreements we enter into with physicians groups, we provide that abortions will not be done in any facility PhyCor owns or leases," says Joe Hutts, the company's president and CEO. He says the physicians—who are partners, not employees—are free to perform abortions as long as they don't do so in any hospital or clinic PhyCor owns. Hutts, who helped found PhyCor ten years ago, says his company will not take any of the profits from abortions. But he stresses that PhyCor, which is publicly traded, is not associated with any denomination.

"We're all Christians," says Hutts. "The idea isn't to impose our beliefs on anybody. We just want to be true to what we believe."

On October 29, PhyCor announced its plan to purchase the nation's other largest medical management company, Medpartners. If the shareholders approve the purchase in February, PhyCor will manage 35,000 physicians and have a presence in all fifty states.

Statistics from the ACLU show that 84 percent of U.S. counties have no available abortion services. With the recent spate of mergers, this percentage is likely to grow.

One problem abortion clinics have is guaranteeing backup in case of a medical emergency. Clinics need this guarantee to stay in business and to provide safe treatment for women. But if the local hospitals have merged with facilities that don't do abortions, these clinics may be out of luck.

They may also be easy marks.

"Abortion has been isolated for a very long time from mainstream medical care," says the ACLU's Weiss. "But this further isolates reproductive-health services in a way that endangers them. An isolated service is particularly vulnerable to anti-choice protest. If you force all these services into physically separate buildings, they are much easier to target. Patients going in and out are much easier to identify and harass."

Pro-choice advocates wonder why the government hasn't treated some of the mergers as violations of anti-trust laws. They also wonder why federal and state laws allow church hospitals to have "conscience clauses" that permit them to opt out of procedures on religious or moral grounds.

"What is essentially happening here is that religious doctrines that govern certain religious denominations are being imposed on everybody else," says Weiss. "I think that's wrong in any setting but it is particularly wrong where the government is involved. What of the separation of church and state?"

That separation is narrowing, as the government is signing more and more contracts with religious health-care providers.

States are pushing poor women on Medicaid into managed-care plans. Some of these plans refuse to supply services like birth control. One example is Fidelis Care New York, an HMO formed by eight Catholic Dioceses. Fidelis serves Medicaid recipients. The HMO will not cover services prohibited by the U.S. Catholic Bishops.

Until recently, Fidelis Care had about 20,000 enrollees. But it tripled its enrollment with its purchase last September of Better Health, an HMO that served 40,000 Medicaid recipients and did offer reproductive health services. Federal law mandates that reproductive services must be covered for Medicaid recipients. In New York, even abortions must be covered. But under a conscience clause, Fidelis is allowed to tell women to go to another provider to access those services.

Annie Keating, who researches health-care mergers for the National Abortion and Reproductive Rights Action League in New York, is worried that many women will sign up with Fidelis unaware that it doesn't cover reproductive health care. Once in the plan, women must stay enrolled for one year.

"The government ought not be able to contract with religious-governed health-care providers who have their services driven by religious doctrine and then impose [that doctrine] on recipients of public assistance," Keating says.

In Ulster and Dutchess counties in New York, two nonsectarian hospitals have announced plans to merge with a third, the Catholic-run Benedictine Hospital. The merger requires all three hospitals to stop performing abortions, tubal ligations, vasectomies, and contraceptive counseling. The two nonsectarian hospitals plan to transfer their abortion services to a separate off-premises women's clinic. Currently, the nonsectarian Kingston Hospital performs about 120 abortions a year, mostly for Medicaid recipients.

But last May, when the three hospitals announced, with much fanfare, the plans to unify, the officials weren't prepared for the outcry from the two communities.

"This is part of a stealth war on reproductive rights," says Caryl Towner,

who founded the group Preserve Medical Secularity to fight the merger. "It's being done under the guise of saving our hospitals, but we don't believe for a minute that this has to be done in a way that imposes all these restrictions on reproductive health care."

Towner's group joined forces with others, including twenty-six doctors at Northern Dutchess Hospital (who voted unanimously against the terms of the merger). They held a rally last July that attracted around 800 people. Since then, merger opponents have sent 2,000 postcards to the hospital officials, gathered 7,000 petition signatures, and repeatedly picketed the hospitals.

MergerWatch's Uttley, who is helping organize the opposition, says community involvement frequently makes the difference in preserving reproductive services. Many times, she says, physicians and representatives of non-Catholic churches end up voicing the strongest opposition.

Take the situation in Gloversville, New York. John A. Nelson, pastor of the First Congregational United Church of Christ, is fighting a proposed joint venture between Feldon County's only hospital, Nathan Littauer, and St. Mary's of Amsterdam, a Catholic subsidiary of St. Louis-based Carondolet. He says some of the more conservative pastors from other congregations are joining him in fighting the merger.

Arthur Brelia, a medical doctor at Nathan Littauer, has also proved a powerful opponent. The seventy-one-year-old obstetrician and gynecologist

resigned from his position as medical chief of staff at Nathan Littauer after the two hospitals' governing boards voted to approve the affiliation. He says he resigned partly so he could have the freedom to criticize without violating any confidentiality requirements.

"I took a public stance and put out a position paper," says Brelia. "The loss of our hospital is not going to help our community. In this deal, the church-dominated hospital has ultimate veto power over any decision."

The hospital has announced it will stop performing abortions, even though it is the only local facility offering the procedure. (Brelia estimates forty to fifty abortions are performed annually at Littauer.) But Brelia says his main concern is that pregnant women will be forced to go far out of their way if they want to be sterilized. "Unless a woman travels forty or fifty miles to the closest urban center, she won't be able to have a postpartum tubal ligation," he says. "That's not a very good choice."

The Reverend Nelson believes it is his religious duty to oppose the potential restrictions on health care. He points out that as the only hospital in a county of 55,000, Nathan Littauer Hospital serves people of many faiths. (There's the added irony that its namesake and benefactor was Nathan Littauer, a prominent Jewish citizen.)

"Theologically it's dangerous to make an idol out of doctrine," says Nelson. "When doctrine and care collide, the only faithful and responsible resolution is for doctrine to retire or change."

Women's Health Movements

Joanne Howes and Amy Allina

Joanne Howes, a long-time activist in the reproductive health and women's movements, is a principal in BASS and HOWES, a Washington, DC-based consulting firm that specializes in political advocacy and public policy concerning issues for women and families.

Amy Allina is a program associate for BASS and HOWES, and a former political organizer for the Maryland affiliate of the National Abortion Rights Action League. She has also worked for the National Women's Health Network.

When Dr. Samuel Broder, director of the National Cancer Institute, went to Capitol Hill in March to testify at a hearing about women's health care in President Clinton's health-care reform plan, he found himself on the defensive. Senator Barbara Mikulski of Maryland was chairing the hearing, and with her looking down on the witness table were four other women Senators: Barbara Boxer, Dianne Feinstein, Carol Moseley-Braun, and Kay Bailey Hutchison. Repeatedly and persistently, the women questioned Dr. Broder about the coverage of mammograms in the President's plan and what it means to the health of women.

His answer—that the studies that have been done so far support the administration's decision to cover mammograms for women over 50, but not women in their forties—did not satisfy the Senators, who were asking questions to which researchers do not yet have answers. When a frustrated Broder started to say, "Let me briefly say, we want to empower women . . . ," he was interrupted by Senator Boxer saying, "*We* are women who *are* empowered, and . . . we want to make sure that we are getting unequivocal science before we throw out the tools that we fought so hard to get."

> *Women are now in positions of power where they can have real influence on the health policies that affect women's lives.*

That exchange, hard to imagine only a few years ago, is indicative of some significant shifts that have taken place around women's health policy. Women had set the agenda for that hearing; women asked the questions; and women demanded answers. Women are now in positions of power where they can have real influence on the health policies that affect women's lives.

Every Senator in attendance that day, even those who oppose the Clinton health-care reform plan, was careful to go on the record proclaiming strong support for women's health. In the 1990s, women's health is an issue with political caché. It is an issue that resonates with voters across economic, racial and partisan lines, and no member of Congress wants to pass up the opportunity to be seen as its champion.

From *Social Policy*, Summer 1994, pp. 6-14. © 1994 by Social Policy Corporation. Reprinted by permission.

This political prominence is the result of years of hard-fought battles. With national attention focused on changing the US healthcare system, women's health advocates now have an uncommon opportunity to use the political power they have built to advance women's health goals. The timing is fortuitous, since women's health advocacy is now at a point of unprecedented strength. From its roots in the self-help, feminist movement of the 1970s, women's health grew to make inroads in electoral politics in the 1980s with abortion rights activism, and in the 1990s has built a mounting campaign against gender inequities in medical and scientific research. But women will achieve nothing without continued organizing, educating, strategizing and the careful exercise of power. When it comes time to make tough decisions about healthcare reform, women's health advocates must draw on the strengths they have built to ensure that legislators make good on their professed support for women's health issues.

What Is Women's Health?

Health care has been a central concern of the women's movement since at least the early 1970s, when women in consciousness-raising groups and other outgrowths of women's liberation began to question the medical establishment. Women who were beginning to have a sense of personal empowerment asked doctors to explain the medical facts of diseases and their treatments, and because they were dissatisfied with the answers, women began to research and discuss the questions among themselves,

The 1970 publication of *Our Bodies, Ourselves* by the Boston Women's Health Book Collective marked the beginning of a new era in women's health—one in which alternative sources of information demystified the medical process and gave women some control over their health and their bodies. In the preface to the first edition of *Our Bodies, Ourselves*, the authors explained that part of their motivation for publishing the book was to "share the knowledge and power" they had gained from their experiences learning about women's bodies and health. Feminist health clinics with similar philosophies sprang up around the country, where lay people and medical staff worked together to teach women how to get and stay healthy. In addition to sharing information with women, the

Women's Health: A Time Line

1970 • Publication of *Our Bodies, Ourselves* • Barbara Seaman documents dangers of high-dose birth control pill • Congress holds hearings • Founding of NARAL

1971 • First feminist health conference • First feminist clinic founded in Los Angeles • Boston gyneocologist reveals that DES, a form of estrogen prescribed for 3 million US women to prevent miscarriage, causes cancer in daughters

1972 • Doris Haire's *The Cultural Warping of Childbirth* indicts US obstetrics for overuse of drugs, forceps, technology

1973 • Southern Poverty Law Center files suit on behalf of women sterilized against their will • *Roe v. Wade*: Supreme Court legalizes abortion

1975 • National Women's Health Network founded • Women injured by Dalkon Shield, an IUD, win first lawsuits against manufacturer

1981 • National Black Women's Health Project founded

1982 • Cesarean Prevention Movement formed to challenge overuse of C-sections • Hysterectomy Educational Resources and Services (HERS) Foundation formed to fight unnecessary hysterectomies

1986 • National Latina Health Organization founded

1988 • Native American Women's Health and Education Resource Center opens on South Dakota reservation

1989 • Supreme Court hands down decision on *Webster v. Reproductive Health Services;* intensification of abortion rights activism

1990 • Society for the Advancement of Women's Health Research founded • NIH creates Office of Research on Women's Health • Official report on NIH procedures with respect to women and clinical research • Congressional Caucus for Women's Issues first introduces the Women's Health Equity Act

1991 • Supreme Court rules companies may not bar possibly pregnant women from jobs

1992 • Congress triples funds for breast cancer research • FDA restricts use of silicone breast implants

1993 • CDC revises definition of AIDS to include symptoms common in women • NIH announces Women's Health Initiative, its largest research study ever

Chart prepared by Flora Davis, author of *Moving the Mountain: The Women's Movement in America since 1960.*

feminist health approach was different from the traditional medical model in that it focused on wellness and health rather than disease and treatment.

At first, the focal issue of the women's health movement was reproductive health. In her history of the women's movement in America, *Moving the Mountain*, Flora Davis describes the early days of the women's health movement: "As health activists organized, the issues that galvanized them tended to involve reproduction. It was there that medical men seemed the most wrong-headed, perhaps because it was, above all, the female ability to bear children that made women seem so alien to many men." The women's health movement mobilized women who wanted the right to make their own reproductive decisions, and who believed that women should have control of their bodies.

Pro-Choice and Self-Help

Because it was under highly politicized attack, abortion was the first women's health issue to have a real impact on the political establishment. After 1980, when Ronald Reagan was elected with a platform that pledged his support to a Human Life Amendment to the Constitution, women started organizing politically to support candidates who would use their elected offices to defend the right to choose. Other health issues, by contrast, did not receive the same kind of attention.

The earliest attacks on access to abortion were directed against young and low-income women, but the abortion rights movement grew enormously after the Supreme Court decision, *Webster* v. *Reproductive Health Services*, in 1989. It was then that people with the power to bring the issue to the political arena realized that they might lose the right to choose. The membership of organizations such as the National Abortion Rights Action League (NARAL) and Planned Parenthood grew by leaps and bounds, with many other organizations created in response to increased interest. By teaching people who were pro-choice how to use the power of their votes, activists were able to increase the political power of the pro-choice movement as well.

At the same time, a new self-help model for women's health was being developed by the Atlanta-based National Black Women's Health Project, founded in 1981. Through the Project, women come together and teach themselves about health issues that affect them and their families and communities. The Project incorporates proven methods of self-help, women's health, and community or-

ganizing to provide women with tools for self-empowerment. Working specifically in African-American communities, the Project's successful approach acknowledges the plurality of women's interests while creating an opportunity for women to identify and understand commonalities. Meeting with fast and widespread success, the Project was quickly followed by the National Latina Health Organization, the Native American Women's Health and Education Resource Center, and other groups modeled on the Project.

By the late 1980s, women who had been fighting battles for political equity and abortion rights began to raise other health issues on the women's rights agenda. As the leaders of the women's liberation movement grew older, they asked questions and challenged doctors' assumptions about menopause and diseases that were more common in older women such as breast cancer and heart disease.

Leaders in the women's community started to use their political organizing skills to focus attention on inequities in health research and other health-care issues where they discovered the same lack of parity with men that they had found in the political and corporate realms.

Gaining National Attention

During this period, women in Congress, both Republicans and Democrats, began to work together to address the new women's health concerns. In 1990, in response to a request from Congresswomen Pat Schroeder and Olympia Snowe and Congressman Henry Waxman, the director of the National Institutes of Health (NIH) appeared before a Congressional subcommittee and was forced to acknowledge that women were not included in most federal research study populations, and that few efforts were being made to analyze study results by gender.

In terms of practical politics, women's health research was a "good issue," since the inequities were so flagrant, and it was easy to explain the problem in television-news-length sound bites. Almost everything that doctors and researchers claimed to know about women's health was based on research that had been conducted on men.

Working side by side with the Congressional Caucus for Women's Issues, the Society for the Advancement of Women's Health Research, founded in 1990, brought together leaders from the fields of medicine and science, public policy, media and government to articulate women's health research needs and

> *By assuming that men and their bodies represented the normal human standard, and that anything that was different was an aberration, the medical community had clearly failed women.*

to advocate for policies that would meet those needs. This effort, and similar advocacy initiatives by other organizations, succeeded in drawing national attention to the problem.

By assuming that men and their bodies represented the normal human standard, and that anything that was different was an aberration, the medical community had clearly failed women. It was obvious to the public, to politicians, and to many members of the medical community that, until they committed resources to examine the development and progression of disease in women, women's health care could not achieve parity with men's. Today, although women's health research is not yet on an equal footing with men's, the increased awareness and commitment of funds are significant.

The public focus on research inequities also brought a new surge of activism to the rest of women's health advocacy. Along with health research, heart disease, breast cancer, and reproductive health, women's health advocates are exploring the health impact of other issues, including violence against women, nutrition and exercise.

Women's health now has tremendous power as a political issue. By asking what it means for women that all the studies of heart disease are done on men or male animals, by asking why women's health is always framed in terms of reproduction, by asking why there is a true early detection method for prostate cancer but not for breast cancer, women in medicine, universities, research laboratories, legislatures, and in the streets have struck a chord.

Both big-picture efforts and targeted campaigns have realized gains: The Campaign for Women's Health—a coalition of close to 100 national, state and grassroots organizations—has built support for broad principles and priorities in women's health. The National Breast Cancer Coalition has achieved stunning successes through its coordination of the advocacy efforts of thousands of breast cancer activists around the country—many of them women living with breast cancer.

Breast cancer activism is an especially powerful example of the enormous potential that political observers believe can be tapped in women's health. Led by breast cancer survivors, advocacy groups have achieved an unforeseen level of success. Public recognition of the problem has skyrocketed in the last five years, and federal appropriations for breast cancer research have increased by 400 percent. Last fall, activists went to the White House to deliver 2.6 million petition signatures in person to President Clinton; soon after, the President and his administration organized and held a National Summit on Breast Cancer at which researchers, doctors, and consumers established a strategy to find a cure for breast cancer.

Women Empowered

With hindsight, it is clear that the timing was just right for the women's health issue. Since the publication of *Our Bodies, Ourselves,* women have made inroads in key professional, academic and political arenas. Enough women's voices in enough different places made it possible to create a chorus of demands that could not be dismissed as marginal. The institutions that had control over health policy—medicine, universities, and Congress—were changing. Women had gained a foothold, and now had the ability to put their issues on the agenda.

The face of medicine, for example, has changed dramatically. In 1970, only seven percent of physicians in this country were women. Today, there are over 100,000 women doctors in the United States, and if this trend continues, by the year 2040 women will make up the majority of physicians.

The impact of this shift on health-care delivery and on the health of women is not yet fully understood, but is being noticed. Last year, the prestigious *New England Journal of Medicine* published a study examining differences between the frequency with which male physicians and female physicians screened their female patients for breast and cervical cancer. The results show that women who see women doctors are significantly more likely to be

Women who see women doctors are significantly more likely to be screened for breast cancer and cervical cancer than those who see male doctors.

screened for those diseases. While there are many possible explanations for these findings, the authors of the study point out that, whatever the reason, "these data suggest that certain aspects of the care rendered by women physicians may be more effective than the care provided by male physicians, at least for women patients." If substantiated in larger and more comprehensive studies, this finding will have far-reaching implications for the future of health-care delivery, professional health education, and management of health-care facilities, as well as for the health of women.

The numbers of women at high levels in government are growing as well. Since 1990, there has been a sharp increase in women elected to Congress. The much heralded Year of the Woman in 1992 built on that trend, and also brought women to influential federal health-policymaking positions as President Clinton appointed Donna Shalala to serve in his cabinet as Secretary of Health and Human Services, Dr. Joycelyn Elders to be Surgeon General, and assigned Hillary Rodham Clinton to oversee the administration's health-care reform initiative. With 48 women in the House and seven in the Senate, the Congressional gender breakdown is still out of balance, but there are now enough women on Capitol Hill to have some impact on legislation and on the legislative agenda.

All the Pieces in Place?

With women allies in positions of power and influence, women activists organized around health issues, and have a number of important successes under their belt. Women's

health advocates are now positioned to play a strong role in the big health-policy question of the day: national health-care reform. This debate will affect not only the health care of every person in the country, but will also set the rules that govern one-seventh of the US economy. We cannot afford to pass up this opportunity.

The national health-care reform debate has not yet focused on issues specific to the health of women. But, like Senator Mikulski, other Congressional committee chairs have held hearings to consider the women's health angle of the proposed plans. Key administration officials and legislative decision makers are well aware of the importance of addressing women's health concerns within the context of this reform effort.

In many ways—as the majority of the uninsured, the majority of health-care consumers, and the majority of health-care decisionmakers in families—women have the most to gain from comprehensive health-care reform. They also, therefore, have the most to lose if this effort fails to achieve real change. So it is not just the questions related directly to insuring women and delivering health care to women that have drawn the attention of women's health advocates.

Practical Politics

The Campaign for Women's Health has formulated an exemplary set of principles for health-care reform. Coalition members have agreed only to support reform plans that assure:

• universal coverage and equal access for all;

• affordable costs;

• mandated comprehensive benefits including preventive and primary care, reproductive health-care services, and long-term care;

• accountability to include participation of women's health advocates in all commissions and regulatory bodies; and

• commitment to protect and advance a women's health-research agenda.

Based on these principles, the Congressional Caucus for Women's Issues also developed a set of criteria by which it is measuring health-care reform plans.

The fact that the Clinton plan incorporates most of these principles is a victory for the women's health advocates who worked closely with the administration task force developing the plan. There are, however, points on which the administration's proposal falls short of the goals set by women's health advocates. The very limited coverage of long-term care and mental health services presents a significant burden to women who are the majority of consumers of such health care, and the cost-sharing proposals built into the Clinton plan are likely to impede women's access to health services. Though the Clinton plan could offer much that is good for women, if it fails to make health-care services economically accessible, little else that it promises will matter for low-income women.

The plans that have been uniformly criticized by women's health advocates both inside and outside of government are those that do not define and mandate a comprehensive benefits package of services that every insurance policy must include. A bipartisan group of 29 women Representatives wrote to the sponsor of one such plan declaring their opposition and explaining that they believe a comprehensive benefits package "is vital to improving women's health care and must be central to any reform effort." The group's commitment, articulated in the letter, not to support any plan that does not "offer explicit coverage of women's health care" attracted significant attention on Capitol Hill and has created some pressure on those attempting to craft compromise legislation.

The abortion question still attracts national attention, and in the health-care reform debate many people have raised the concern that inclusion or exclusion of abortion services in the final plan could scuttle all attempts at reform. But, by supporting the inclusion of a comprehensive benefits package that includes all medically necessary or appropriate services, women's health advocates have staked out a strong position that all women need access to comprehensive reproductive-health services, including abortion. Though this is clearly a controversial issue, it is an essential one for achieving women's health equity. If the new health-care system treats abortion or other reproductive-health services differently from the rest of health care, it will continue the practice of giving women second-class treat-

ment. Further, since two-thirds of typical health-insurance plans routinely cover abortion services, a national health-care package

If the new health-care system treats abortion or other reproductive-health services differently from the rest of health care, it will continue the practice of giving women second-class treatment.

that excludes abortion will mean a step backwards for many women. As a result, women leaders have made it clear that legislators who fail to include abortion coverage will not be considered supporters of women's health.

Learning from 20 Years of Experience

Health-care reform truly puts women's health advocates to the test. The popularity of the issue, the women in positions of power, and the grassroots strength of the movement *could* come together and produce an advance in health policy benefiting women for many generations to come. But that victory will not be possible if advocates do not learn from and build on the lessons of the last 20 years.

Women's health gained its status because it was driven by the real, everyday concerns faced by women in their lives and because it was flexible enough to incorporate the wide range of health issues confronting disparate groups of women and their families. To maintain and mobilize the full strength of this women's health constituency, advocates must keep sight of the plurality of women's interests. To achieve a national commitment to health policies and practices that advance all women's health, women must speak out and tell policy makers that they are watching, that this matters, and that you can't be "for women's health" if you don't support policies that prove it.

Abortion in American History

The year after abortion was legalized in New York State, the maternal-mortality rate there dropped by 45 percent—one reason why legalization can be seen as "a public-health triumph"

by Katha Pollitt

Of all the issues roiling the ongoing culture wars, abortion is both the most intimate and the most common. Almost half of American women have terminated at least one pregnancy, and millions more Americans of both sexes have helped them, as partners, parents, health-care workers, counselors, friends. Collectively, it would seem, Americans have quite a bit of knowledge and experience of abortion. Yet the debate over legal abortion is curiously abstract: we might be discussing brain transplants. My files are crammed with articles assessing the question of when human life begins, the personhood of the fetus and its putative moral and legal status, and acceptable versus deplorable motives for terminating a pregnancy and the philosophical groundings of each one—not to mention the interests of the state, the medical profession, assorted religions, the taxpayer, the infertile, the fetal father, and even the fetal grandparent. Farfetched analogies abound: abortion is like the Holocaust, or slavery; denial of abortion is like forcing a person to spend nine months intravenously hooked up to a medically endangered stranger who happens to be a famous violinist. It sometimes seems that the further abortion is removed from the actual lives and circumstances of real girls and women, the more interesting it becomes to talk

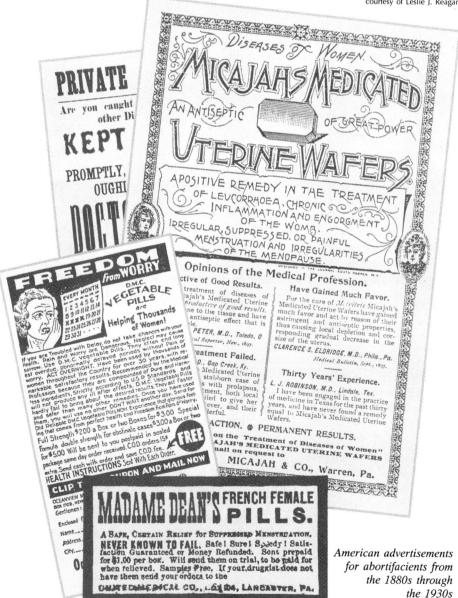

American advertisements for abortifacients from the 1880s through the 1930s

Katha Pollitt is a poet and an essayist and the author of *Reasonable Creatures: Essays on Women and Feminism* (1994).

From *The Atlantic Monthly*, May 1997, pp. 111-115. © 1997 by Katha Pollitt. Reprinted by permission.

WHEN ABORTION WAS A CRIME:

Women, Medicine, and Law in the United States, 1867–1973

by Leslie J. Reagan. University of California

about. The famous-violinist scenario, the invention of the philosopher Judith Jarvis Thomson, has probably inspired as much commentary as any philosophical metaphor since Plato's cave.

Abortion as philosophical puzzle and moral conundrum is all very well, but what about abortion as a real-life social practice? Since the abortion debate is, theoretically at least, aimed at shaping social policy, isn't it important to look at abortion empirically and historically? Opponents often argue as if the widespread use of abortion were a modern innovation, the consequence of some aspect of contemporary life of which they disapprove (feminism, promiscuity, consumerism, Godlessness, permissiveness, individualism), and as if making it illegal would make it go away. What if none of this is true? In *When Abortion Was a Crime,* Leslie J. Reagan demonstrates that abortion has been a common procedure—"part of life"—in America since the eighteenth century, both during the slightly more than half of our history as a nation when it has been legal and during the slightly less than half when it was not. Important and original, vigorously written even down to the footnotes, *When Abortion Was a Crime* manages with apparent ease to combine serious scholarship (it won a President's Book Award from the Social Science History Association) and broad appeal to the general reader.

Some of the story of illegal abortion has been told by other historians: Linda Gordon, Rickie Solinger, James C. Mohr. But Reagan, who is an assistant professor of history, medicine, and women's studies at the University of Illinois, Urbana-Champaign, is the first to span the whole period of criminalization and to cover the subject in such depth. Moving skillfully between a nationwide perspective and a detailed study of Chicago, Reagan draws on a wide variety of primary documents, many never before examined. Using patient records, transcripts of trials and inquests into abortion-related deaths, medical-society proceedings, and reports in the popular press, she reconstructs the complex, shifting network of arrangements and understandings that enabled illegal abortion to persist, and sometimes even to flourish, for more than a hundred years. In doing so she not only brilliantly illuminates a hitherto shadowy aspect of American life but also raises crucial questions about the relationship between official mores and the values by which people—including the promulgators of those official mores—make the decisions that shape their lives.

UNTIL the last third of the nineteenth century, when it was criminalized state by state across the land, abortion was legal before "quickening" (approximately the fourth month of pregnancy). Colonial home medical guides gave recipes for "bringing on the menses" with herbs that could be grown in one's garden or easily found in the woods. By the mid eighteenth century commercial preparations were so widely available that they had inspired their own euphemism ("taking the trade"). Unfortunately, these drugs were often fatal. The first statutes regulating abortion, passed in the 1820s and 1830s, were actually poison-control laws: the sale of commercial abortifacients was banned, but abortion per se was not. The laws made little difference. By the 1840s the abortion business—including the sale of illegal drugs, which were widely advertised in the popular press—was booming. The most famous practitioner, Madame Restell, openly provided abortion services for thirty-five years, with offices in New York, Boston, and Philadelphia and traveling salespeople touting her "Female Monthly Pills."

In one of the many curious twists that mark the history of abortion, the campaign to criminalize it was waged by the same professional group that, a century later, would play an important role in legalization: physicians. The American Medical Association's crusade against abortion was partly a professional move, to establish the supremacy of "regular" physicians over midwives and homeopaths. More broadly, anti-abortion sentiment was connected to nativism, anti-Catholicism, and, as it is today, anti-feminism. Immigration, especially by Catholics and nonwhites, was increasing, while birth rates among white native-born Protestants were declining. (Unlike the typical abortion patient of today, that of the nineteenth century was a middle- or upper-class white married woman.) Would the West "be filled by our own children or by those of aliens?" the physician and anti-abortion leader Horatio R. Storer asked in 1868. "This is a question our women must answer; upon their loins depends the future destiny of the nation." (It should be mentioned that the nineteenth-century women's movement also opposed abortion, having pinned its hopes on "voluntary motherhood"—the right of wives to control the frequency and timing of sex with their husbands.)

Nonetheless, having achieved their legal goal, many doctors—including prominent members of the AMA—went right on providing abortions. Some late-nineteenth-century observers estimated that two million were performed annually (which would mean that in Victorian America the number of abortions per capita was seven or eight times as high as it is today). Reagan argues persuasively that our image of nineteenth-century medicine is too monolithically hierarchical: while medical journals inveighed against abortion (and contraception), women were often able to make doctors listen to their needs and even lower their fees. And because, in the era before the widespread use of hospitals, women chose the doctors who would attend their whole families through many lucrative illnesses, medical men had self-interest as well as compassion for a motive. Thus in an 1888 exposé undercover reporters for the *Chicago Times* obtained an abortion referral from no less a personage than the head of the Chicago Medical Society. (He claimed he was conducting his own investigation.) Unless a woman died, doctors were rarely arrested and even more rarely convicted. Even midwives—whom doctors continued to try to drive out of business by portraying them, unfairly, as dangerous abortion quacks—practiced largely unmolested.

What was the point, then, of making abortion a crime? Reagan argues that its main effect was to expose and humiliate women caught in raids on abortion clinics or brought to the hospital with abortion complications, and thereby send a message to all women about the possible consequences of flouting official gender norms. Publicity—the forced disclosure of sexual secrets before the authorities—was itself the punishment. Reagan's discussion of "dying declarations" makes particularly chilling reading: because the words of the dying are legally admissible in court, women on their deathbeds were informed by police or doctors of their imminent demise and harassed until they admitted to their abortions and named the people connected with them—including, if the woman was unwed, the man responsible for the pregnancy, who could be arrested and even sent to prison. In 1902 the editors of the *Journal of the American Medical Association* endorsed the by then common policy of denying a woman suffering from abortion complications medical care until she "confessed"—a practice that, Reagan shows, kept women from seeking timely treatment, sometimes with fatal results. In the late 1920s some 15,000 women a year died from abortions.

This state of affairs—widespread availability punctuated by law-enforcement crackdowns, popular-press scandals, and fitful attempts at medical self-policing—persisted for decades. Unsurprisingly, the Depression, during which women stood to lose their jobs if they married or had a child, saw a big surge in the abortion rate. Reagan describes clinics complete with doctors, nurses, receptionists, and printed instructions detailing follow-up care, and "birth-control clubs," whose members would pay regularly into a collective fund and draw abortion fees from it as needed. It was only in the 1940s and 1950s that organized medicine and the law combined to force these long-standing operations out of business and to disrupt the networks of communication by which women had found their way to them. Our popular image of illegal abortion as hard to find, extremely dangerous, sordid, and expensive dates from this period, as do the notorious "abortion wards" filled with women suffering from botched operations and attempts at self-abortion (always the most dangerous method). Well-connected white women with private health insurance were sometimes able to obtain "therapeutic" abortions, a never-defined cate-

gory that remained legal throughout the epoch of illegal abortion. But these were rare, and almost never available to non-white or poor women. Even for the privileged, though, access to safe abortion narrowed throughout the fifties, as doctors, fearful of being prosecuted in a repressive political climate for interpreting "therapeutic abortion" too broadly, set up hospital committees to rule on abortion requests. Some committees were more compassionate than others: at Mount Sinai, in New York, suicide attempts were considered an appropriate indication; at other hospitals they were ignored. In one instance of particular callousness, when a teenager tried to kill herself after her request was turned down, the committee decided to hospitalize her for the rest of her pregnancy. (She eventually got her abortion, after her multiple suicide attempts proved too disruptive for the staff.)

The conventional wisdom today considers *Roe* v. *Wade* to be an avant-garde decision, "judicial activism" at either its enlightened best or its high-handed worst. Reagan places the decision in its historical context, showing that it was a logical response to the times. By the sixties the whole jerry-built structure of criminalization was crumbling, along with the ideology of gender and sexuality that lay behind it. Moderate reforms had already been tried: twelve states permitted abortion in instances of rape, incest, danger to physical or mental health, or fetal defect, but since most women, as always, sought abortions for economic, social, or personal reasons, illegal abortion continued to thrive (something to consider for those who advocate once again restricting legal abortion in this way). When New York State decriminalized abortion in 1970 and thousands of well-off women started traveling there to obtain safe abortions while their disadvantaged sisters continued to risk death at home, the inherent unfairness of a legal patchwork was thrown into bold relief (something to ponder for those who want to throw the issue "back to the states"). Far from foisting a radical departure on an unready nation, the Supreme Court was responding to a decade-long buildup of popular sentiment for change. The movement was spearheaded by doctors who saw firsthand the carnage created by illegal abortion (more than 5,000 deaths a year, mostly of black and Hispanic women), and whose hands were now

firmly tied by the hospital committees they themselves had created. They were joined by civil-liberties lawyers, who brought to their briefs a keen understanding of criminalization's discriminatory effects; and by grassroots activists in the reborn women's movement, who by the end of the 1960s were resisting the law, forming such groups as the Society for Humane Abortion, in California, which denounced restrictions as insulting and humiliating to women, and Jane, in Chicago, which began as an abortion-referral service and ended by training its members to perform abortions themselves.

LEGALIZING abortion was a public-health triumph that for pregnant women ranked with the advent of antiseptics and antibiotics. In 1971, the year after decriminalization, the maternal-mortality rate in New York State dropped 45 percent. Today, however, the inequality of access that helped to bring illegality to an end is once again on the increase. More than 80 percent of U.S. counties have no abortion providers, and some whole states have only one or two. The Supreme Court has allowed states to erect barriers to abortion—denial of public funds for poor women's abortions, parental consent and notification requirements, mandatory delays, "counseling sessions." Anti-abortion zealots have committed arson, assault, and murder in their campaign against abortion clinics. A new generation of doctors, who have never seen a woman die from a septic abortion or been haunted by the suicide of a patient denied help, are increasingly reluctant to terminate pregnancies. Only 12 percent of medical schools teach first-trimester abortion as a routine aspect of gynecology. If Reagan is right to correlate anti-abortion activity with periods of high anxiety about feminism and radicalism generally, none of this should come as a surprise. She closes on an ominous note, sketching the possibility of a United States in which not only is abortion once again a crime but anti-abortion fanaticism brings on a Romania-style fetal-police state, complete with government-monitored pregnancies and police investigations of miscarriages.

I came away from the book more sanguine. One of Reagan's noteworthy findings, after all, is that the views of the American people about abortion have remained rather stable over two centuries. Attitudes toward early abortions—in the eighteenth and early nineteenth centuries those before quickening, today those in the first trimester—have always been much more permissive and matter-of-fact than attitudes toward later abortions, just as losing a pregnancy after one or two missed periods, however distressing to a woman who wants to bear a child, has always been seen as a smaller event than miscarrying at six months. Little in the American popular tradition resonates with the "pro-life" doctrine that condemns all abortions alike on the grounds that a fertilized egg is already a baby. Far from being a weird judicial concoction, as its opponents argue, *Roe* v. *Wade*'s trimester system, which gradually extends the right of states to regulate and even ban most abortions as the fetus develops, reflects this folk understanding rather well. Similarly, the general lack of enthusiasm for prosecuting those who perform abortions and the almost total failure to prosecute and jail women for having

them suggest that whatever Americans may consider abortion to be, it isn't baby killing, a crime our courts have always punished quite severely.

When Abortion Was a Crime is rich, thought-provoking, and revelatory on many levels, not least as a triumphant vindication of the somewhat contested disciplines of women's history and social history "from the bottom up." Perhaps its greatest achievement, though, is in a way its simplest: it puts abortion back into the context in which it actually occurs—the lives of obscure and ordinary women. If the abortion debate were really about abortion, Reagan's work would consign many of its terms to the scrap heap: it seems absurd to suggest that the overburdened mothers, desperate young girls, and precariously employed working women who populate these pages risked public humiliation, injury, and death for mere "convenience," much less out of "secular humanism" or a Lockean notion of property rights in

their bodies. It's even more preposterous—not to mention insulting—to see them as standing in relation to their fetuses as a slaveowner to a slave or a Nazi to a Jew.

Reagan suggests that the abortion debate is really an ideological struggle over the position of women. How free should they be to have sexual experiences, in or out of marriage, without paying the price of pregnancy, childbirth, and motherhood? How much right should they have to consult their own needs, interests, and well-being with respect to childbearing or anything else? How subordinate should they be to men, how deeply embedded in the family, how firmly controlled by national or racial objectives? If she is right, and I think she is, a work of history is not going to make much of a dent in the certainties of those who would like to see abortion once again made a crime. The people who need this book the most won't read it. Everyone else, though, will find it enlightening.

Females in Sports

A Book Review

Training the Body for China: Sports in the Moral Order of the People's Republic. By Susan Brownell. Chicago and London: University of Chicago Press, 1995.

Sporting Females: Critical Issues in the History and Sociology of Women's Sports. By Jennifer Hargreaves. London and New York: Routledge, 1994.

The Stronger Women Get, the More Men Love Football: Sexism and the American Culture of Sports. By Mariah Burton Nelson. New York: Avon Books, 1994.

Mary Jo Festle, *Elon College*

The authors of the three books under review share the assumption that sports are not simply games and that, as Susan Brownell puts it, "body culture is embodied culture" (11). They convincingly illustrate how athletics, like other physical practices, serve as windows into a society's interests, habits, values, and power relations.

Although rules fix the structures of international sport, in *Training the Body for China* Brownell argues that those structures can be "emptied" of much of their original Western cultural contents and adapted to each nation's unique circumstances. Gender serves as a good example. Unlike Americans and western Europeans, the Chinese do not regard sports as a traditionally male preserve. In fact, while westerners assume women are biologically weaker than men, the Chinese assume that women have superior capacity to "eat bitterness and endure [the] hard labor" that athletic success requires (Brownell, 228). Socialist ideology, class connotations of sports, and ungendered notions of muscles mean Chinese women have encountered little resistance to athletic participation. Still, Chinese women athletes experience tensions. Torn between the expectations of their families to marry and produce a child and the state to achieve higher sports performances, they project their anxieties onto the bodily fluids associated with reproduction, refusing to train during their menstrual periods. Hopeful that their status as athletes will help them "marry up," they also delay romantic and sexual activities longer than other women.

Brownell's unique perspective (she competed in track both in the United States and in China) makes her well suited to contrast sport systems, but the book does not have a primarily comparative focus. Instead, combining the approaches of Pierre Bourdieu and Victor Turner, she locates her study of sports as daily practice and cultural performance solidly in Chinese history and society. While uneven chapters and heavy theorizing mean the book can be difficult reading, Brownell's observations are reliable and often fascinating. Sports, denounced during the Cultural Revolution, then glorified during the market reform era, obviously have been heavily influenced by state policy. But Brownell resists a simple deterministic interpretation. In the controversy over whether female body builders should be allowed to wear bikinis, she reveals how people took advantage of divisions within the state. When discussing the grassroots movement for "old people's disco," she shows that occasionally change has been initiated by the Chinese people, not the state. Finally, she describes a crucial obstacle for the Chinese government: sports—characterized by individual striving, public display of the body, and a desire for prestige—violate some traditional notions of morality ("face").

In *Sporting Females*, Jennifer Hargreaves scrutinizes the history and sociology of women's sports in Great Britain. She makes her theoretical underpinnings more accessible than Brownell, clearly and concisely critiquing various sociological perspectives. Her approach borrows from cultural Marxism but places gender at center stage, relating it to other structures of power. Thus "hegemony theory" informs her historical narrative. She describes how differences between men and women were accentuated and exaggerated in the nineteenth century and how "scientific" evidence reinforced stereotypes of women as naturally weak and frail. Especially powerful because they were seemingly rooted in the body, these cultural beliefs became common sense, sustained by the practices and attitudes of women themselves. As a result, men came to be associated with and to dominate sports. At the same time, however, oppositional ideas, such as the notion that exercise might be healthy and appropriate for females, slowly germinated. Hargreaves traces in detail both the improvements and the discrimination women experienced in recreation and

sports, relating them to shifts in employment, education, leisure, politics, gender roles, consumerism, ideology, and men's sports. She pays close attention to the ways gender inequalities have been exacerbated by class, ethnicity, sexual orientation, age, and physical disability.

Sports can exploit women, but because they can also be "positive, pleasurable, and empowering," Hargreaves believes women uninvolved or uninterested in sports should be mobilized to participate (289). In one of her most important sections, Hargreaves weighs three alternative strategies from which "sports feminists" must choose. First, women can try to gain equality of opportunity in terms of resources and rewards. This widely accepted liberal approach assumes that integration into male institutions and the male model of sports is both possible and desirable. A second option is a separatist approach in which women bypass male domination and resistance and set up their own institutions. Hargreaves applauds this method for providing greater opportunities as well as a sense of safety, control, confidence, and autonomy for women. However, it can re-create harmful social divisions, absolve sexist institutions of the need to change, and underuse the potential of established sports. The third strategy is for women and men to develop cooperatively new models of sport that minimize its destructive elements, such as sexism, overcompetitiveness, commercialization, homophobia, racism, and nationalism. However appealing, this radical alternative has been attempted only rarely and, given the present distribution of power, faces an uphill challenge. Hargreaves holds back from recommending one approach as best, seeing it as pragmatic for sports feminists to move on all three fronts.

In her passionate indictment of contemporary American sports, Mariah Burton Nelson does not refrain from taking a firm position. She believes that to participate unquestioningly in "manly sports" ignores their harmful, antisocial elements. In a backlash against feminist gains in economics, politics, and social life, Nelson notes, many men have clung to sports such as football as a symbol of men's "natural" superiority. In football, men are in charge and women irrelevant at best. Football venerates male power and male bodies, but football players camouflage their feelings with intramale violence and aggressive heterosexuality. Sexist and homophobic attitudes are prevalent (men ridicule one another as

"..." and "faggots"), and assaults are celebrated, even replayed. Manly sports are rife with images of sexual domination and portray women as objects on which to "score." Repeated incidents of gang rape suggest that sexual aggression accompanies male athletes off the field. There is nonsexual violence against women as well, evidenced not only by prominent cases (e.g., O. J. Simpson, Jose Canseco, Bobby Cox, Moses Malone, etc.) but by the increase in traffic at battered women's shelters after Sunday football games.

This very readable book leaves out theoretical language but is informed by feminist thinking. Two chapters, for example, incisively analyze the media. One contrasts how sportswriters exalt manly sports as exciting and significant, while ignoring, trivializing, and/or sexualizing female athletes. The second describes the sexual dynamics at play when women sportswriters enter the highly gendered space of male locker rooms. The case of Lisa Olson, who found herself surrounded closely by New England Patriots daring her to look at and touch their genitals, is interwoven with other stories of harassment to illustrate how many male athletes and spectators are not only troubled by men's bodies being the subject of the female gaze but also disturbed by the prospect of women *not* looking at them.

In another courageous and noteworthy chapter, Nelson discusses the long-suppressed subject of (mostly male) coaches becoming sexually involved with their young female athletes. Increasingly, men have assumed control of female teams, becoming the "gatekeepers" of female athletic success. Without much difficulty, these coaches can take advantage of their players' dependence, trust, admiration, and desire for approval. While there are some prominent cases of coaches justifying their be-

havior by calling it consensual love and even marrying the athletes, more common are the secretive interactions that leave athletes alone to cope with their feelings of abandonment, hurt, confusion, anger, and shame. Nelson rightfully pulls no punches, labeling the coaches' behavior as abusive. Doctors, ministers, and therapists, she points out, have ethical codes deeming it inappropriate to take sexual advantage of a delicate professional relationship, no matter what the age of the client. Likewise, coaches must not be allowed to exploit an athlete's vulnerability, betray her trust, and deprive her of the nonsexual affection and respect she needs and deserves.

Given the obstacles, why would Nelson not advise women to stay far away from sports? In part, it is because she sees a woman's athletic participation as a feminist act: it is a way for her to experience freedom, gain confidence, repossess her body, improve her chances of health and success, enjoy her physical nature, and find her power. In addition, women's participation as athletes, coaches, athletic directors, and journalists challenges the masculinity and misogyny of sports. If women remain on the sidelines, they are powerless. However difficult it may be, Nelson believes women's gaze, women's insights, and women's voices can help our society begin to "understand and change the manly sports culture in which we all, whether we like it or not, are swimming" (258).

While Brownell's book is quite valuable to those studying non-Western sports or the anthropology of China and Hargreaves's book will be valuable to those interested in British women's sports and the sociology of sports, I recommend Nelson's book as required reading for athletic directors, coaches, and athletes; assign it to your brothers, sisters, spouse, sons, and daughters; and make sure you read it yourself.

FAIR GAME
TITLE IX TWENTY-FIFTH ANNIVERSARY

AFTER 25 YEARS OF TITLE IX, ARE WOMEN REALLY GETTING
AN EQUAL CRACK AT THE BAT? A LOOK AT HOW FAR WE'VE COME
AND HOW FAR WE HAVE LEFT TO GO.

BY JANET LEE

Six years ago, freshmen Kate Lemos and Whitney Post joined Brown University's women's rowing team. At the time, it didn't bother them much that their locker room was the size of a closet or that they didn't have any shower facilities. They didn't really *expect* to have an entire floor to themselves as the men's team did. "It was never a sense of 'This is what we deserve,'" Lemos says. "It was more like, 'This is what we have.' Crew breeds you to tough anything out."

It wasn't until three years later, when Lemos and Post were co-captains of the team, that the facility was renovated and the women got their own locker room with showers and workout space. The university insists the action had nothing to do with the fact that it was embroiled in what has become the highest-profile Title IX lawsuit to date (brought by members of the women's gymnastics team). Post, now a member of the national lightweight rowing team, disagrees. "I'm sure it was a kick in the butt," she says.

Two years after the renovation, the women's rowing team won the national championships. It's a Cinderella story, but with a dark side. The Brown women's rowing team was acknowledged more than 20 years after the enactment of Title IX, the law that in 1971 mandated equal access to educational—and by association, athletic—programs for men and women in schools that receive federal funds.

June 23 is the 25th anniversary of Title IX. The date is an appropriate culmi-nation of a yearlong period that opened with the Olympics and rolled on to see great advances for professional women athletes, particularly in team sports. But how far have women come overall in these 25 years? Athletes are still suing schools over inequities not unlike those the Brown rowers experienced, and defendants are still claiming that women don't deserve equal access because they're not as interested in sports as men are.

FIRST BLUSH OF SUCCESS

"It's a half-full, half-empty story," says Donna Lopiano, Ph.D., executive director of the Women's Sports Foundation. "The downside is it's taken 25 years, and the treatment of athletes is still uneven. The good news is that we've reached a critical mass of the first generation of mothers and fathers who grew up thinking it was fine for their daughters to play sports."

The U.S. women's Olympic soccer, basketball and softball teams, as well as standout performances by numerous other women athletes, are proof of this new generation. The athletes' success stories have propelled them from Atlanta to television commercials and print ads brimming with attitude. These athletes are lending their names to athletic shoes and clothing, and most notably, they're joining pro leagues that have emerged to take advantage of the sudden popu-larity of women's sports.

"It has taken 25 years to make a cham-pion athlete," Lopiano says. "Twenty-five years of access to coaching, competition, scholarships and weight rooms. You're seeing the first blush of what happens when you give women the chance to play."

And it's not only professional women who are fanning the fervor. Although more quietly and with less publicity, the grooming grounds for these star ath-letes—our colleges and universities— are bolstering their women's sports programs with renewed zeal.

Out of fear or a sense of duty—or prob-ably some of each—many schools are serving up women's sports with platters of scholarships and increased funding. The result is often packed sports arenas and, in some cases, women's teams like the Golden or "Lady" Buffs basketball team at the University of Colorado, that are more competitive—and more popular—than the men's teams. "Universities are realizing that that's what they have to do," says Christine Grant, Ph.D., women's athletic director at the University of Iowa. Grant has spent much of the past quarter century making sure Title IX succeeds. She's an expert on the law and has created a Web site (http://www.lib.uiowa.edu/proj/ge/) dedi-cated to the subject. "Universities are re-alizing that it will be less expensive and less damaging to their reputations to be in compliance [with the law]. They may be doing the right thing for the wrong reasons, but at this point, I don't care." In hot pursuit and with an eye toward protecting themselves from costly law-suits in which precedent is against them,

From *Women's Sports and Fitness*, June 1997, pp. 37-40. © 1997 by Women's Sports and Fitness. Reprinted by permission.

entire athletic conferences are devising action plans to get within spitting distance of full compliance in a few years. Some of those blueprints, enacted several years ago, are just now coming to fruition. The Big 10, for example, made a commitment in 1992 that its member schools would try to meet a 60–40 ratio of men's to women's participation by 1997. Five years later only four schools, Iowa, Michigan, Ohio State and Wisconsin, have complied. The law calls for participation ratios to approximate student enrollment ratios—close to 50–50 at most schools—but it's a start.

Some schools have come close to the goal. "We're in the third year of a five-year plan to achieve gender equity," says Bob Frederick, athletic director at the University of Kansas, a member of the Big 12 (formerly the Big 8). "In a number of respects, we've achieved that already." KU added women's soccer and rowing two years ago and plans to fully fund those sports at the end of three more years. At a school where the numbers of men and women students are roughly equal, 49 percent of women and 51 percent of men participate in nine men's sports and 11 women's sports. "I think there's been a tremendous amount of progress made," says Frederick. "In our situation, I've noticed a real change in attitude on the part of the fans and boosters. They realize this is the right thing to do."

The NCAA has made it its mission to ensure that members strive to meet the Title IX mandate. The organization published its second gender-equity study in April (results weren't yet available at press time), and Janet Justus, the NCAA's director of Education Outreach, predicted that participation numbers would be up. "The last time we did the study was in 1990–91. It was the first wake-up call in several years that there was still disparate treatment of men and women in athletics," she says. The NCAA has worked aggressively to reduce the disparities by educating its membership about the law. In addition to forming a gender-equity task force, they regularly offer gender-equity seminars and other educational programs.

In a surprise twist, the Clinton administration stepped in to pave the way for Title IX compliance. The Equity in Athletics Disclosure Act, passed October 1, 1996, makes it easier to find out how well each school is distributing its resources. The act requires coed colleges and universities that receive federal funds to make available to the public information about their sports programs. Schools must disclose statistics about male and female participation, athletic department budgets, scholarship programs, recruiting

expenditures by gender and coach salaries. "Some institutions will be shamed into improving their compliance" is Grant's take on the new legislation.

Even before the equity act, things were looking up. The number of women's athletic teams per school is at an all-time high, according to the study "Women in Intercollegiate Sport," which looked at the 19-year period from 1977 to 1996. The average number of teams per school (divisions I through III) has risen from 5.61 to 7.5. Since 1971, the number of women who participate in collegiate varsity sports has increased by nearly 250 percent, to more than 110,000. (It more than doubled by 1977, only two years after Title IX had been in effect.) And whereas one in 27 girls used to play sports in high school, now it's one in three.

It's not only the participation numbers that are up. In 1972, only $100,000 in college scholarship money was available to women nationwide, says Benita Fitzgerald Mosley, president of the Women's Sports Foundation and director of the ARCO Olympic Training Center in San Diego. That number had risen to $180 million in 1996. Men's programs, which have roughly 78,000 more participants than the women's, award twice that amount.

Sports and Courts

A growing body of legislation consistently supporting the principles of Title IX and the Supreme Court's 1992 ruling that plaintiffs could collect monetary damages in cases of intentional discrimination haven't kept lawsuits out of the courts. The Brown case could be appealed all the way to the Supreme Court, even though the plaintiffs have won all appeals to date. Attorney Deborah Brake, senior counsel at the National Women's Law Center in Washington, D.C., doubts that the high court will hear the case. "We should keep winning," she says. "The law is very strong in the courts." In fact, plaintiffs have not lost any cases to date.

That success rate is bittersweet; after all, a court of law is not the court an athlete wants to be making her play on. A quarter of a century after Title IX, perhaps the main reason only a handful of schools are in compliance is money. "I think the biggest stumbling block is that some schools are using the financial aspect of it as an excuse not to move more quickly," says Frederick. "Everybody—almost everybody—knows it's the right thing to do."

Lopiano agrees. "The existing competitive system in the schools favors

football, basketball and one or two other men's sports," Lopiano says. 'It's like pulling teeth to get them to share [funds]." She blames the leaders of the universities, not just the athletic directors, for this reluctance. "The athletic departments won't [cut high-profile sports' budgets]; they won't put themselves in jeopardy like that."

Athletic directors, on the other hand, claim that cutting those budgets is akin to biting the hand that feeds all programs: Cut the marquee sports' budgets, and you cut revenue for all sports. "When you consider the income from the men's basketball tournament, from our football television contract and the bowl games, there's just a tremendous amount of revenue generated," Frederick counters. "We try to find alternate sources without cutting any sports."

And they have. For example, when the Big 8 expanded to become the Big 12, television revenues poured into members' coffers, money that spilled over into smaller athletic programs at each university. To fill in the gaps, the athletic departments aligned chancellors and athletic boards behind their efforts and ventured off campus to hit up corporate donors and sponsors.

High Hurdles

Without teeth to back it up, legal action can prove largely ineffective. And indeed, enforcement of Title IX has been lacking, critics say. Ensuring compliance with the act falls largely on the Office of Civil Rights (OCR). The Women's Sports Foundation recently released a study of the compliance reviews conducted by the OCR and found the office's performance to be less than acceptable. "The OCR is doing a horrible job," Lopiano says. "It has the ability to notify a school that it is out of compliance, yet they've not found one school out of compliance with Title IX."

But perhaps one of the biggest threats to the law, and one of the main reasons it leaves a nasty taste in the mouths of so many administrators and athletes, is the affirmative action stigma. The perceived similarity to quota rulings means that many assume it to be detrimental to nonrevenue men's sports. Lopiano has made the Women's Sports Foundation's stance on the issue clear, and many schools have followed suit. "We have always said that it is inappropriate for the Title IX solution to bring the level of men's sports down to the women's level," she says.

"There's been a backlash against a lot of the gains we've won," Brake says. "We're seeing the have-nots versus the have-nots. Instead of blaming football and basketball, which continue to hog resources, other men's sports like gymnastics and wrestling are blaming women." When lawyers start tossing out terms like quota and affirmative action, administrators start backpedaling, program plans sputter to a crawl and athletes—male and female—start questioning the fairness of legislating equity. Because of this, Brake thinks, many opponents are hoping that the Brown case will roll back Title IX or at least reveal a much-sought-after loophole. So far neither has happened.

In the end, the primary problem—one that dooms so much well-meaning legislation—is a lack of communication and broad-based commitment. "The biggest threat to Title IX is the unwillingness to sit down and resolve the many problems we have: financial, gender equity and the potential loss of men's minor sports," Grant says. "It will take a national will to do this."

THE FUTURE'S SO BRIGHT

To some administrators, complying with Title IX is a daunting task that requires keeping track of every athlete, changing long-held prejudices and prying dollars out of already tight fists. Others, like Frederick, Grant and Justus, have seen the tide slowly changing and the momentum rising with it. Their jobs will get easier as America grows more used to seeing women as athletes, whether on their local high school field or on national television.

"I think the future is bright," Justus says. "I think the law will be a nontopic in 15 to 20 years." Angie Halbleib, a senior at KU who plays on the women's basketball team, agrees. "I think women's sports will be improving so much we won't have to say we *need* this money."

So there it stands. There will still be lawsuits, certainly, for years to come. There will still be people who think women aren't interested in athletics and don't deserve as many chances to participate in them. But there will also be the girls who idolize Sheryl Swoopes and Mia Hamm, who earn scholarships to play their favorite sports, who wear new uniforms and practice in state-of-the-art facilities. And perhaps ultimately there will be girls who won't need to think about their right to play. They'll just be out there playing.

Then, Title IX will be just another law that's served its purpose, a law that ultimately renders equity a moot point and is, in the end, forgotten.

Unit 4

Unit Selections

Key Points to Consider

❖ Why were records of women's religious roles in Western orders altered?

❖ How was the Goddess myth different from the way we view masculine deties?

❖ How do the religious activites of women in male-led orders differ from the activities of feminist denominations?

 **Links**

www.dushkin.com/online/

These sites are annotated on pages 4 and 5.

The academic study of religion challenges a person's beliefs more than the study of most other academic subjects. Most of you reading this book, for instance, already have strong emotional, reflective opinions about religion. You may also have strong opinions about female philosophy, referred to here as feminism.

Feminism is often disquieting to students whose only exposure is through media stereotypes. The media are seldom accurate in their description of feminist's concerns or they define feminism in radical terms. Moreover, many feminists have philosophical and theoretical perspectives that differ from media stereotypes. However, feminists, regardless of philosophical leaning, are unified in their belief in a better quality of life for women everywhere.

"Religion and Philosophy" was chosen as a major heading for this volume because women often express their deepest concerns, their truest selves, their fears, hopes, and passions during religious activities and through their religious affiliation. In many cultures, for instance, it is within religious domains that women find ways of sanctifying their domestic lives. Elaborate meal preparation for religious holidays has always been an acceptable outlet for frustration with religious subordination.

There are many societies where women lead active dominant religious lives. Yet religious hierarchical orders rarely include women and most key religious philosophies tend to reflect men's, not women's, priorities and life experiences. Perhaps it is for this reason that Elizabeth Cady Stanton decided to author *The Woman's Bible*, still widely read and respected by scholars throughout the world.

The articles selected for this unit explore the many ways that religion has been important to women. The role of Christian women appears most often in this unit because of the long-standing tradition in Western civilization that has consistently excluded women from important positions in the church.

The unit opens with "Women and the Early Church," which examines the significant but scant evidence of women's religious activities that paralleled the treatment of women in other areas of life. A short biography of Mother Theresa follows. The nun, who, dedicated her life to the Catholic order she founded, appears to be almost godlike, especially when compared to the nuns who left their own orders because they could not adjust to modifications in grooming and attire that were initiated in the 1960s. Georgia Hedrich tells their story in "Whatever Happened to Sister Jane?"

Then, Judith S. Antonelli, the author of "The Goddess Myth," alleges that alternatives to male-dominated religions were often abusive, exploitive, and torturous.

Ibn Warraq, in "Islam's Shame: Lifting the Veil of Tears," analyzes women's inferior position in Islamic culture, where Muslim thinkers and Islamic traditions attribute guile, deceit, and treachery to women's intrinsic nature, allowing for a disregard for women's basic rights. After this article is an excerpt from the United Nations Declaration of the Rights of Women, to which the author suggests all Islamic nations refer and use.

The last article in unit 4, by Jung Ha Kim, tells how "churched" Korean American women are both liberated and oppressed by the Christian church and its theology, and what they have done to protect their dignity while leading purposeful lives in America.

Religion and Philosophy

WOMEN AND THE EARLY CHURCH

Brent Shaw offers a forceful reassessment of the women martyrs and heroines whose activities on behalf of the faith provoked unsettled admiration from the church fathers.

Consider a tombstone from late fifth-century southern Italy: 'Leta, the priest (*presbytera*), lived 40 years, 8 months, 9 days. Her husband set this up for her'. Or a Latin inscription from Salona in Dalmatia, dated earlier in the same century: 'I Theodosius purchased this grave plot from the holy priest (*presbytera sancta*) Flavia Vitalia for three gold pieces'. Two notices that would seem to attest the existence of female priests—not unusual in the world of Graeco-Roman antiquity, except that these women were Christians. As late as the fifth and sixth centuries AD women like these were found exercising priestly authority in Christian churches in locales as diverse as the cities of Asia Minor, Greece, Gaul, Sicily and southern Italy. It is also known how very unusual most of these cases were.

The women in Sicily and southern Italy who assumed the power and duties of priests did so in circumstances of considerable local social upheaval where, apparently, few qualified men were available. Their usurpation of male authority was harshly condemned by Pope Gelasius in a letter to the churches of the region (AD 492–96). However significant their mere existence might be for staking out current theological claims, or as ammunition in contemporary ecclesiastical conflict, they are exceptions that prove the rule—that women were gradually, inexorably, and

deliberately excluded from formal positions of authority within the organisation of the Christian Church. A whole series of church councils, between those at Nicaea (325) and at Orange (441), repeatedly issued 'canons' or formal decrees that prohibited women from the ranks of the priesthood and from any involvement in priestly liturgical duties, such as baptism and the eucharist.

Yet the changes in the societies that made up the Roman Empire which were provoked by the new religion of Christianity—ones that transformed the face of what we now somewhat hesitatingly call 'Western Civilization'—must have involved the half of the population who were women. Modern students of that process, however, have advanced much stronger claims than those of mere involvement. They have asserted that women, especially in the ranks of the aristocratic élite, were in the vanguard of the process of conversion and of the evangelisation of the new faith. It has been argued that women were far more influential in the forging of actual early church communities than has been generally recognised in the past. Scholars claim that women once widely performed liturgical roles, including those of baptism and giving the eucharist, later denied to them—a history of early empowerment deliberately obscured, in part, by the later re-editing of church documents. Finally, there are claims

This article first appeared in *History Today*, February 1994, pp. 21–28. © 1994 by History Today, Ltd. Reprinted by permission.

concerning the liberating effects of a Christianity that opened both new avenues of action and formal powers to women from which they had previously been barred. Any attempt to test these claims, and to understand the actual historical experience of women in early Christianity, however, is unendingly blocked by the nature (indeed, the sheer lack) of the surviving historical evidence. There is no doubt that some of the relevant records still exist. More assiduous searching in the last decade or so has brought many previously known but obscure and marginalised documents to the centre of the historian's agenda. But these records are almost entirely written by men. Although they do mention women, debate their roles and behaviour, provide interesting details about their lives, and sometimes even place them at the centre of their accounts, almost none of them were actually written by women themselves—a critical caveat that must constantly be borne in mind in all that follows.

After all, what historians *can* know depends on available records. The production of such records depends on an active literacy that specialises in the writing and the canonisation—the systematic organisation and preservation—of textual materials. What evidence there is clearly suggests a very limited literacy of this type amongst the women of the Roman Empire in which Christianity emerged. Literacy itself was probably restricted to a sizeable, though proportionately small, part of the whole population. Within the sector that might be deemed literate, women's literacy had a rather special character that matched the dominant moral codes of the time. It tended to be passive and consuming rather than active and producing. Women of the aristocratic élite, of whom we know the most, were literate in the sense that they were taught to read—usually, it seems, by their mothers. 'Saint' Jerome, who was especially close to these women, and parasitic on their wealth and social rank, writes at length in one of his letters to a mother how she should cut out little shapes of letters and with them teach her daughter, by this conventional method, to feel and thus to learn her letters. And of reading itself, there are good indications that they did a lot. The fourth-century Roman aristocratic woman Paula knew her scriptures, and certainly her Hebrew, better than her spiritual guru Jerome.

Her contemporary Melania (the Elder) had read 'seven or eight times' the 'three million lines' of the Greek theologian Origen; and, similarly, 250,000 lines of the writings of other Greek 'Fathers' of the church.

When it came to the production of literary texts, however, a whole series of empowerments, conventions, and active restrictions meant that this remained, from the beginning to the end of the antique world in which Christianity evolved, a sphere of activity almost wholly controlled and dominated by men. When women who were literate did advance beyond the passive skills of reading to writing, with certain striking exceptions it was to the private sphere activities of composing letters and of keeping diaries (adjudged by men to be a morally inferior activity). Where active expression was involved, the evidence that we have indicates that it took place in a vast and amorphous world of oral communication labelled talk, conversation, innuendo, and gossip—but not formal public rhetoric. This was a powerful, potentially dangerous, and largely uncontrollable, realm of communication where reputations could be made or destroyed by persons as low as household slaves. But this world is largely, and one fears, permanently, lost to modern-day historians.

The developmental path traversed by Christianity, from the domain of personal to institutionalised power, itself provoked problems of integration. This is true despite the great diversity of structure and belief found in early Christian communities, since the various divergent movements within it, including those labelled schismatic or heretical, developed their own formal organisations or 'churches', and were just as committed to their institutions as any orthodoxy. Donatism—a separate regional variety of Christianity in North Africa from the early fourth century AD—was viewed as dissenting, heretical, schismatic, and dangerous by its orthodox critics, but was every bit as committed to its own texts, hierarchies, church buildings and edifices, readers, deacons, priests, bishops, and elaborate defences of their authority and prerogatives, as were any 'orthodox' Catholics in Italy or elsewhere. The problem is that Christianity, which ended by developing powerful and complex ecclesiastical institutions, had begun life as a quasi-millenarian prophetic 'Jesus movement'

in the region of Palestine. It had spread westward by the dual agencies of individual effort, will and charisma, and the social unit of the household or family. In both eastern and western Mediterranean worlds, therefore, the model or image of the family, so crucial to the spread of early Christianity, became subject to intense ideological scrutiny and regulation. But eventually the family basis of a nascent Christianity soon had to be integrated with, and made subordinate to, formal organisations that embodied values quite different from those of the rebellious expectations of a new personal faith that offered its converts the hope of a substantially changed future.

In Pauline writings, those millennial expectations of the repressed are clearly signalled. Slaves who converted, especially those who were slaves of Christian masters, quickly assumed that the end of time was now at hand and a whole new order was dawning. Since they were just as much the 'brothers' and 'sisters' of their masters and mistresses, and since all were equally the 'sons' and 'daughters' or 'the slaves' of the one God, they reasonably expected that they would be freed from the conventional ties that both bound and ranked them. This misapprehension had to be corrected—as Paul himself made clear in his reply to one Philemon about his escaped slave Onesimus. The case was not an isolated one. The parallel message, and opportunities, broadcast to women of free status no doubt evoked similar expectations and responses. The problem was: how were *they* to be contained? This was not as easily solvable a problem as that of the slaves, many of whom, it must not be forgotten, were women. Slave women who had millennial expectations of more freedom were, no doubt, like slave men, simply ordered (as Paul himself specifically ordained) to get back to their proper place. The larger problem was with free women.

Mediterranean male protocols of both Greek and Roman societies had rather blunt and severe prescriptions on the proper place of women of free status, especially that of wives. What actually happened in the circumstances of daily life was, no doubt, something rather different. The existence of a strong conflict between prescription and reality is indicated by need constantly to restate the protocols themselves in every conceivable form of communication, oral and written, from the high literature of the city-state, in its poetry and drama, to the more mundane extra-canonical technical treatises of doctors and architects. Another indication is that even a male ideologue like Aristotle was forced to concede that although a father and husband's authority over the children and slaves of his own household was 'like that of a king' (the absolute power to command obedience), his relationship to his wife was 'political'. That is to say, the latter relationship was a process of constant negotiation, debate, and arbitration typical of the distribution of power in a democratic polity. The man was always supposed 'to win' this contest, and a specific order within the household, with the man as 'head', was to be maintained.

But any strong millenarian or ecstatic religion, and not just Christianity, that attracted adherents from the 'inferior' elements in the family, by its very nature constituted a threat to family order. In most cases, household heads that faced such systematic threats could be expected to be backed by strong action from their state that would both reaffirm existing norms of the family and the traditional position of women. The so-called Bacchanalian conspiracy in Rome in 186 BC was just such a case. It was a hysterical reaction against the perceived threat of cult cells in Rome and Italy supposedly dedicated to vile secret rituals dedicated to the Greek god Bacchus, groups including free women and slaves that were corrupting young men, and were forming a dangerous and subversive 'state within a state.' Revelations and betrayals led to a systematic repression throughout Italy by the consuls and the Roman senate that prohibited women from such worship and ordered that guilty daughters and wives be handed over to their families for punishment in household courts headed by their fathers and husbands. But early Christian communities did not have this advantage. They had to stabilise the order of the family and household, probably the principal formal container of the new religion down to the end of the first century, while simultaneously facing increasingly hostile local communities that actively courted the violent intervention of officials of the Roman state.

Christian communities responded by restating, with categorical fervour, traditional family relationships in a series of

formal regulations. These are exemplified in the so-called 'Household Tables' found in several of the New Testament books (Ephesians 5.21–6.9; Colossians, 3.18–4.1; 1 Timothy, 2.9–6.2; 1 Peter 2.18–3.12 are the main texts)—tables whose prescriptions were ceaselessly reiterated in the West by the church 'Fathers' from Tertullian to Augustine, and beyond. The imperatives of these texts insisted that all persons—father–husband, mother–wife, children, and, finally, slaves—were to be maintained in a fixed, hierarchical social order, all subordinated to each other and, finally, all were to be subject in fear to God the Father and Lord (dominus meaning 'slave owner') as his children and slaves. This much desired 'proper order' was threatened in numerous structural ways. One of these was that of differential conversion—the main problem here (not necessarily an overwhelming statistical regularity, but rather a perceived problem) being those cases where wives converted to Christianity while their husbands did not. The problem was a long-standing one that characterised the many religious movements into local societies where the new beliefs were not neatly contained as state or civic cults under the supervision and control of the male heads of household who constituted the fully recognised citizens who controlled the levers of government.

As an extension of the rule of order within the household, out of which a good part of the early and formative existence of the church was derived, rules of bodily space and of voice were gradually, but surely, imposed on the architecture of the church itself. Women and girls were seated separately from men and boys—women were ranked: matrons were separated from virgins, widows from those groups, and young girls from all of them. There was also a gradual but finally decisive move to impose head coverings on women (somewhat misrepresented in many modern discussion as 'veils') as a symbol of submission to the 'head' of household and God the Father. These measures had different tempos and regional variations in the Christian communities of the ancient Mediterranean. A recently published sermon of Augustine, for example, attests the new provision of separate entrance doorways for men and women in the main basilica at Carthage—an innovation imposed only in the early 400s

AD. The general tendency of all these measures, however, was in one direction: a purposefully imposed inconspicuousness and silence.

A current meliorist strain in historical interpretation finds it difficult to face the near obvious. Repression can be successful. The vast written records of the early church preserve not one female theologian, even though there is consistent evidence of women's involvement in theological debates and in teaching. Although there might have been some lower order officials, the priesthood and other high offices became closed to women as the church gradually constituted its own 'public sphere' parallel to that of the state. Of course, the process involved constant struggle, and a repression that was never completely closed or finally achieved. Although the church in the west was finally to draw the line at the level of the priesthood, as late as the fifth and sixth centuries women deacons were both ordained and recognised as a formal clerical part of the ecclesiastical hierarchy. In the ritual by which new Christians were created, that of baptism, the 'born again' had to have evil demons driven from their body—a critical function performed by exorcists. Exorcists were just as much a part of the formal hierarchy of church offices as were priests. And women regularly held the office of exorcist—women who were therefore seen to wield considerable spiritual, and secular, power. Moreover, the constant emergence of forms of Christianity that challenged orthodoxy, or of esoteric brands of Christian or 'near-Christian' beliefs and thought, such as those called 'gnostic', produced milieux in which orthodox norms were constantly challenged and questioned. But those who would find 'feminine' emphases in the alternative theodicies of 'gnosticism', must face the unpleasant fact that the feminine principle in this theodicy, however important, was roughly the equivalent of the Devil in 'mainstream' Christian ideology, and that even the 'gnostics' held that the perfected being was going to be male, and that each woman would have to be transformed into a man before achieving that final perfection.

While the church could define and close off specific times and physical spaces that defined its offices and formal powers, it would always have to face challenges that would well up out of the non-ecclesiastically controlled personal behaviours. There were several distinct spheres where the simple actions, experiences or given social positions of individuals bestowed power on them that could not be immediately or directly controlled by the church. These included: transcendent personal experiences such as dreams, prophesies, and ecstatic performance; extraordinary demonstrations of personal bravery and fortitude that even élite Roman men would value as a species of manliness (*virtus*); and the possession of independent status in the secular world outside the direct control of the church—high social rank and wealth. Finally, there were new opportunities offered by the emergence of 'heretical' movements which were, by definition, not under the control of the authorities. In any one of these areas (or better, in combinations of them) women effectively circumvented, and therefore challenged, the continuing efforts of men to monopolise the institutional powers of Christian churches.

A typical phenomenon that exemplifies some of these opportunities, much studied because well-documented cases are so rare, is the movement labelled 'Montanism' (after Montanus, its supposed male head). Emerging from the remote heartlands of Asia Minor in the mid-second century, Montanist adherents exhibited ecstatic experience—dreams, prophetic utterances—with tendencies to separate themselves from the formal churches of the region. Whatever roles and powers 'Montanist' women like the Quintilla, Maximilla, and Priscilla were able to assume, they seem to have had no substantial known impact on the powers of women in the 'orthodox' church. These women may well have been able to denounce their husbands, abandon their marriages, and assume priestly roles (all of this, however, reported in a later hostile rhetoric), but by the time 'Montanism' can be identified in a western Mediterranean context—at Carthage in North Africa at the end of the second century and beginning of the third, it was being effectively tamed to orthodox ends. Women could and, indeed, did prophesy—but, as Tertullian reported of his congregation in Carthage, only at the appropriate time, in church, and the publication of the message was permitted only after the woman had been debriefed by the male presbyters in seclusion after the service. The views of Tertullian (himself labelled a Montanist) on these 'heretical women who dared to teach, exorcise, heal, and baptise' was blunt:

> Women are not permitted to speak in church, to teach, to baptise, to offer eucharist, to undertake any other male duty, or to arrogate to themselves any priestly task whatsoever.

The combined elements of independence from direct male control in the household, personal wealth, and the breakdown of the controls of a single central church could produce opportune circumstances in which a woman could become unusually effective. In AD 312 at Carthage, Lucilla, a wealthy woman of high social standing, refused to apologise for her practice of bestowing a kiss on a holy relic. Caecilian, the priest who dared to reprimand her, suddenly found himself opposed for election to the vacant position of Bishop of Carthage by a male slave from Lucilla's own household. This servant, named Majorinus, was trained, funded and supported by Lucilla and defeated Caecilian in the election. The ensuing battles within the church at Carthage led directly to one of the greatest of the 'schisms' in the history of the church in the West—the emergence of a separate North African or 'Donatist' church. Lucilla, however, was not alone. A century later, Augustine could refer to at least two parallel cases of independent wealthy women who stood at the head of the creation of more schismatic or breakaway movements within the church in North Africa.

The ideology of a church that placed such a high value on virginity was naturally hostile to remarriage and exalted the status of the widow. Because of this, and its prohibitions against divorce, Christianity created a new social group, that of widows, in numbers and with a definition never before seen in the pre-Christian world. But the very existence of a new order of independent women with their own wealth posed a constant threat to the church's desired order. Jerome could condemn a very wealthy woman, a widow, whom he saw ostentatiously distributing alms as a quintessential hypocrisy—but then she had found her place, as much of any of Jerome's highly touted virgins. Reality, however, often confounded the rhetoric. After much sweating and effort, and in hand-wringing despair, Jerome's contemporary, Ambrose, the Bishop of Milan, confessed that there were only twenty known virgins in the large Italian city of Bononia (Bologna). It was not for want of numerous lengthy exhortations to virginity, amongst them Jerome's letter to the noblewoman, Eustochium, that preached the new ascetic ideals. But even Jerome had to admit that his treatise was stoned by the people of Rome.

Indeed, it was the wealthy élite women whom Jerome himself so castigated and fawned upon, 'small women weighed down by sins', who were, in his view, the cause of 'heresies'. But in his own letters we can trace his changed attitudes to a wealthy woman as she shifted status from dependent wife to independent widow. While her husband was still alive, the Spanish noblewoman Theodora merited only perfunctory reference. After her husband's death, she became the object of special attention. She was now one of those widows upon whom Christian ideology bestowed so much prestige. That standing, and her wealth, meant power—and hence the need of incessant instruction from men like Jerome on proper behaviour.

In the critical period of its growth and institutionalisation, and of attacks on it from those who detested and feared Christians, the church could not control the fact that the very process of persecution drew women as well as men into the public arenas of the empire where these matters were finally settled. In their public demonstration of courage, or bodily resistance, of iron-willed and open confrontation with supreme figures of authority—from their own fathers to the Roman governors who put them on trial—women martyrs were perhaps the most difficult case with which the church had to cope. They became central actors in public venues, and active front-line defenders of the faith in a conflict that pitted them against the diabolical forces of the state. Given the prevalent moral codes of that world, the actions of these women meant that great power and glory accrued to their names. So, for example, the pogrom against Christians in the city of Lugdunum (Lyons) in AD 177, highlighted the achievements of a Christian woman who would otherwise have been regarded as 'contemptible' and 'cheap' by the prevalent male values of her world: the slave woman Blandina. But in the words of the man who reported her death, by enduring the almost unspeakable tortures vented on her body, Blandina acquired a fame and renown like that of a 'noble athlete'. She had proven to the population of a major Roman city that she had greater endurance and fortitude than many men. Reports of such achievements by women that confuted the normative values placed on them were subsequently most difficult to explain away.

Much the same could be said of Perpetua, a woman who was executed in the arena at Carthage in AD 203 on the charge of being Christian. The difference in her case is that she was not only a freeborn, wealthy woman of high social standing, but she was also a woman who wrote. It is from her hand that there survives one of the very few, if not only, extensive pieces of narrative prose written by a woman during the whole period of the high Roman Empire. The challenge presented by women like Blandina and Perpetua was to be found in the ideological backwash following their deaths. Their behaviour and achievements in huge public arenas, before crowds of spectators who witnessed their trials, and before tens of thousands who watched their deaths in amphitheatres of the empire, was systematically to refute both assumptions and claims about 'feminine fragility' and 'unworthiness' that underwrote the subordination and silence so insisted upon by Paul and his successors.

The general response to this was to control the very accounts by which persons through time would come to know of the achievement of women martyrs. In most cases, this was easily done because the male ideologues who were the only recorders of the acts of the martyrs, could directly rewrite these women's experiences in a theological form that left only divine interpretations (and explanations) open for their actions. For the most part, this reduced to the truism that they were able to act like men because of the infusion of the spirit of the Christian deity into their bodies. Perpetua's case, however, was more problematic, since she had left a detailed record of her own experiences in her own words. This account then had to be rewritten, reshaped, parodied, mimicked, and preached about till the end of the Roman Empire in the West. Like her bodily martyrdom, her words were an implicit threat to the assumed norms that underwrote the institutional power of the church.

Though signs are notably few in the records that have survived—what else would one expect?—there is nonetheless a myriad of little clues, micro-points of evidence, that point to recurrent resistance to the edifices of male power in ecclesiastical institutions. Such were women in Tertullian's Carthage in the late second and early third century who prophesied, who taught, who told him that he had no business imposing dress codes on them, and still others who insisted on following their modes of worship and actively proselytised for their own beliefs—whose 'silliness', 'madness' and 'unspeakable arrogance' were sufficient to provoke from Tertullian a terrible anger, and a litany of regulatory prose. Despite his efforts, women like these were still present in the Christian congregation of the North African metropolis as late as the fourth and fifth centuries—women who refused to take direction from male priests in the matter of proper behaviour. And in fourth- and fifth-century Rome there were those who, like the noble Marcella, assumed that they could teach the Christian message, and who could hold their own in acrimonious theological debate.

The examples need not be multiplied. They are sufficient to show that, with each generation, there was a continual struggle, a conflict of Aristotle's 'political type', between the men and women who contested the new resource of the church, the new family of Christ. That is why church councils had to keep reiterating those laws that systematically excluded women from its ranks. And that is precisely why the heavy overlay of male ideology (of which the vast bulk of surviving ecclesiastical and theological writings were an important part) had to be restated with every new generation. And why, although those records are indeed 'our history', we must rewrite them.

FOR FURTHER READING:

For original sources see the collections by Ross S. Kraemer, *Maenads, Martyrs, Matrons, Monastics: A Sourcebook on Women's Religions in the Greco-Roman World,* (Fortress, 1988) and by Elizabeth A. Clark, *Women in the Early Church,* (Glazier, 1983); the formative modern critical analysis is that of Elisabeth Schüssler Fiorenza, *In Memory of Her: A Feminist Theological Reconstruction of Christian Origins,* (Crossroad, 1983); on women and 'gnosticism', Elaine Pagels, *The Gnostic Gospels,* (Random House, 1979); replies by Suzanne Heine, *Women and Early Christianity: A Reappraisal,* (Augsburg, 1988); Karen L. King (ed), *Images of the Feminine in Gnosticism,* (Fortress, 1988); on ecclesiastical office, Roger Gryson, *The Ministry of Women in the Early Church,* (Liturgical Press, 1976); Aimé G. Martimort, *Deaconesses: An Historical Study* (Ignatius, 1985); on sexuality, Peter Brown, *The Body and Society: Men, Women, and Sexual Renunciation in Early Christianity,* (Columbia University Press, 1988); on widows, Bonnie B. Thurston, *The Widows: A Women's Ministry in the Early Church,* (Augsburg, 1989); on virgins, Joyce E. Salisbury, *Church Fathers, Independent Virgins,* (Verso, 1991).

***Brent Shaw** is Professor of History at the University of Lethbridge, Alberta, and is author of the article 'The Passion of Perpetua' in* Past and Present, *vol. 139 (1993).*

NO HUMANITARIAN

A portrait of Mother Teresa

Mary Poplin

Last year I spent two months as a volunteer at one of the homes for children operated by the Missionaries of Charity in Calcutta. Like many Western visitors, I initially found the experience disorienting. Despite Mother Teresa's repeated reminders that the order's mission is religious, not social work, most Westerners who visit the homes for sick and handicapped children expect them to look like medical clinics or hospitals. They don't. Most shocking is the absence of hospital-like procedures and equipment. This can be particularly disconcerting for people who have worked in hospital settings in America and Europe. For example, during my stay in Calcutta, a group of European women arrived for a two-week stint as volunteers. They immediately were confronted with a young handicapped girl who had considerable lung congestion. Where, they wondered, was the respiratory therapy machine? Surely, given Mother Teresa's fame, such equipment was available? Informed that the home did not have such equipment, the volunteers began to protest. One health-care professional was so distressed that she left after just a couple of days.

The Missionaries of Charity, one learns, resist owning anything, even medical equipment, that is not widely available to the poor. (Telephones are one of the few exceptions to this rule.) As it turned out, one of the European volunteers managed to locate a portable respiratory machine somewhere in Calcutta. The Missionaries of Charity sisters, as is their practice concerning all gifts intended for the poor, enthusiastically consented to its use. The child recovered quickly; much faster, I fear, than did the volunteers from their annoyance over the primitive medical conditions in which they had to work.

My conversations with the sisters about this incident revealed the enormous gulf between Mother Teresa's work and the everyday assumptions we make in the West about what it means to help the poor. The sisters meekly and patiently listened to the complaints of the volunteers. Rather than respond to criticism about a lack of medical equipment, however, the sisters simply and quietly did their work. "Isn't it wonderful how God provided these volunteers just when this little girl needed them?" they characteristically remarked. Indeed, the sisters' instinctive response was to thank God for one of his many miracles while the European bearers of the miracle became increasingly frustrated by the seeming obliviousness of the nuns.

I began to see the reactions of the sisters and of the Western volunteers as parallel conversations conducted between people who live in the same space and time but in some important sense not in the same world. Two different sets of assumptions and beliefs about reality are at work. I went to Calcutta in an effort to better understand the differences between the way most of us think of our social work (whether it be teaching or helping the poor or sick) and Mother Teresa's radical Christianity in action. I left believing that I had witnessed the Scriptures being lived in a way that I found both humbling and challenging.

Mary Poplin *is a professor of education at The Claremont Graduate University and directs The Institute for Education in Transformation at the Center for Educational Studies. Her work with Mother Teresa began as part of a research project into new approaches to teaching underachieving students in American schools.*

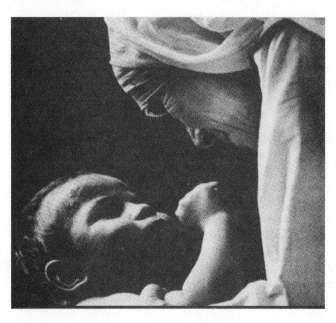

From *Commonweal*, December 19, 1997, pp. 11-14. © 1997 by the Commonweal Foundation. Reprinted by permission.

Mother Teresa was often depicted in the media, especially upon her recent death, as a great humanist, a superior social worker. But she was not humanistic; rather, she was godly. Mother Teresa was in the world but she truly was not of the world. If you stick to just the "facts" about Mother Teresa, you can never fully describe her.

I don't want to present Mother Teresa or the Missionaries as perfect. No one is perfect. The sisters do get cross with one another and other people; they do make mistakes. But you cannot understand Mother Teresa's work unless you fully understand how very differently from our everyday expectations the sisters interpret and respond to what happens in the world around them. The key to understanding the Missionaries of Charity is the sacredness with which they treat all people and the humble and prayerful manner in which all the work is done. The Missionaries of Charity see Jesus in everyone they meet. They see Jesus in a twenty-year-old volunteer from New Jersey searching the Hindu temples and Buddhist ashrams of India for some sense of meaning, in an aged Muslim starved and half-eaten by rats and worms on the street, in a deformed infant just born and found in a garbage heap. They quite literally see Christ in everyone, and especially in the "poorest of the poor." The intent of their community is to treat each human being as they would Christ and to do each task they perform for the benefit of the poor as they would do it for Christ. Thus, it is Jesus' diapers they wash, his meals being prepared, and his body being tended.

> *Things are very different for the Missionaries. A firm acceptance of divine providence sets them apart from our common assumptions about how the world works. They literally believe that God provides all that is needed through prayer.*

Many writers have depicted Mother Teresa as someone who saw the poor and responded sympathetically to their needs. That is not quite the case. Mother Teresa served the poor not because they needed her but because God called her to the work. She was obedient to God's call, not to her social conscience. She often remarked that if God had told her what was to happen after she picked up the first dying person off the Calcutta street, she would never have done it, for she would have been too afraid. Mother Teresa called herself "a pencil in God's hand," and she meant it. One day during morning Mass, as I was sitting on the floor near her, an Indian woman came in and kept bowing to Mother and kissing her hand. Mother kept pointing to the crucifix. Finally, she took the woman's hands and pointed them to the cross and said, firmly, "It is not I, it is him. Give thanks to him."

Because of this absolute belief that it is God who works in and through them, there is no room for pride in the sisters' work. They see themselves as simply accomplishing the work God created them to do with the grace and love he gives them to do it. As a consequence, the sisters manifest both incredible humility and an unshakable sense of hope. Such attitudes are radically different from, and perhaps even at odds with, the motivations behind most social work as we know it. Most of us are drawn to serve the poor out of empathy or pity. Serving the poor is something we decide to do out of our own energy, guilt, or goodness. In this humanistic equation, pride is an ever present temptation.

Things are very different for the Missionaries of Charity. A firm acceptance of divine providence sets them apart from our common assumptions about how the world works. As the sisters' response to the seemingly fortuitous arrival of the respiratory equipment demonstrates, they literally believe that through prayer God provides all that is needed. Many stories of divine providence are told by the Missionaries. There's the day when there was no food and miraculously the schools in Calcutta were closed and all the bread destined for the schools was delivered to the Missionaries. There's the time when answered prayers brought about a cease-fire in Beirut, allowing the sisters to rescue some handicapped children. I myself saw a child who had struggled for months to stay alive evidently healed after a night of prayer. Prayer, not medical or physical work, is the first task of the Missionaries. Prayer is their method, their technology.

A belief that somehow needs will be met as they arise as long as the sisters are doing God's work makes their mission a direct and daily task rather than an indirect and long-term strategy like the antipoverty initiatives we in the West are familiar with. For example, the Missionaries do not question those who come to them for help. A person shows up with an empty pot for her family or just walks in off the street for a plate of food. All are served, for a year or even for every day of their lives. Indeed, those without a pot or plate are fed first. When I was in Calcutta a rumor circulated that some women were reselling the food on the street. While many of the volunteers and paid workers were disturbed by this possibility, the sisters were not. It was God's work, the sisters assured us, he would see to it that all would be well.

In contrast, modern welfare systems use extensive qualification criteria that frequently prevent some from getting the help they need and become a game to get around for others. Rather than directly serving the poor, social workers are often engaged in mounds of paperwork in efforts to monitor and police the aid, and in complying with rules and regulations that actually inhibit meeting the needs of those they seek to serve. These indirect, abstract, and bureaucratic forms of assistance distance the server from the served. They also, I believe, distance the server from his or her own life mission.

To the Missionaries of Charity we are all both worthy and unworthy, and it is only through the grace of God that we have what we have. The sisters literally do not worry about the scarcity of resources, about policing their beneficiaries, and least of all about their own needs. As the Scriptures promise, the sisters believe that the more you give, the more is given to you.

Needless to say, this is contrary to all secular political reasoning. At first glance many of the differences between the work of the Missionaries and that of social workers appear to stem from the fact that the sisters live the lives of the people they serve. They live in the poorest neighborhoods and they know their neighbors. They know the demands of poverty in a way most of us as social workers do not—the time it takes to hand wash clothes on the concrete, to collect water from the spigot, to shop each day for food, to cook over coals, to walk or use poor public transportation. They do not commute to the communities in which they work and return to middle-class lives in the evenings.

Each sister owns no more than what will fit into a small box. Each of them has three saris, one for special occasions, and two which are alternated; one is washed each day while the other is worn. Each of them has a prayer book and song book with covers made out of what appears to be brown paper bags—the books' pages typed on old manual typewriters—a Bible, a cup and dish, a pillow, pillow case and two sheets, a rosary, and a crucifix pin which holds the sari securely. The sisters eat like the poor. And like those they serve, they look forward to ice cream the day after Easter and the day after Christmas.

The destitute families know the sisters understand their plight. Most of the sick infants with whom I worked had to be left with us for an extended period to get well. The parents were not afraid to admit to the sisters that they couldn't care for their children during such illnesses. Sometimes we even had healthy babies whose parents were ill or in crisis. The Missionaries do not judge these parents for their inability to take care of the infants. They do not think of poor parents as the enemies of poor children, as is too often done in this country.

To really comprehend what the sisters are about, however, it is important to understand that they do not embrace this hard life simply to better understand and serve the poor. Rather, they are poor in order to follow Christ, who chose to be poor, to be born in a stable, to live and die with no possessions. Elected poverty is a reparation,

in part, for the materialistic sins of the world. Mother Teresa was firm about the source of poverty; she said, "God does not create poverty, we do, because we do not share." But when asked why she didn't become more involved in the politics of poverty and world hunger, she replied, "that was not my calling, God calls others to this task. Me he just called to tend the poorest of the poor. We must each stay faithful to our own call, be faithful to the things God calls each of us to do and do them with holiness."

Mother Teresa further insisted that the commitments to poverty, chastity, and obedience afford the Missionaries a protection from evil. For example, having embraced radical poverty, there is nothing material that can be used to tempt them. This is the same reason they do not ask for money or devote their energies to procuring the best of modern medical technology. They do not want to be tempted to do things in order to obtain or manage money and thus be drawn away from their primary call "to serve the poorest of the poor with free, whole-hearted service."

In Christopher Hitchens's widely publicized book on Mother Teresa, *The Missionary Position* (Verso), he criticizes her for accepting money and awards from those he considers criminals. Yet just as she asked no questions of the needy, Mother Teresa never considered investigating the lives of those who gave to her. Indeed, she never solicited money. Moreover, the Bible clearly promises that wealth ill-gotten will eventually end up with the poor (Proverbs 13 and 28). As one sister who worked closely with Mother explained to me, "the Missionaries are always happy to accept individual donations as the expression of divine providence. Neither Mother Teresa nor the Missionaries of Charity allows others to raise money in our name. As a matter of fact, whenever we hear of this being done, we take pains to stop it. Mother wants people to give freely and sacrificially, being moved in their hearts by God to do so, rather than just taking part in a social fund-raiser."

Similarly, I have read criticism suggesting that at the end of her life Mother Teresa got the best of health care and the latest technology while the poor around her went without. To the best of my knowledge she got medical attention (not necessarily the best) primarily when she was unconscious and unable to protest. (The children in the order's homes are also taken to the hospital when needed.) In fact, I took with me to Calcutta offers of medical assistance for her. One of the inventors of the latest pacemaker wanted to donate one to Mother as well as the medical services to replace her old one. Through another sister she refused politely, saying she couldn't accept special privileges not given the poor. The sisters are deeply committed to living as close to the poor as possible and anyone who has been to Calcutta for any length of time comes to understand the seriousness and the benefits of this vow.

During my stay I had an opportunity to talk to Mother Teresa about Hitchens's book. "Mother, there are people who write in books that you are one of the wealthiest women in the world, and you don't need any more money," I said. She looked at me, at first quizzically, and then nodded in recognition. "Oh yes, the book. I haven't read it but some of the sisters have. It matters not, he [the author] is forgiven." I laughed and said, "Yes, Mother, in the end of the book, he says he knew you said you forgave him and he's irate because he says he didn't ask you to forgive him and he didn't need it." She looked at me as though I hadn't understood, then gently and confidently instructed me, "Oh, it is not I who forgives, it is God, it is God. God forgives."

Another sister told me how a group of sisters had read the book, then gathered in prayer to discern its meaning. They wanted to know what was God's message to them. "It is a call for us to become more holy," one said. Others agreed. The Missionaries look at such trials and insults as times for self-examination, to build humility and patience, to love their enemies—opportunities to become more holy. Even illness is often interpreted as a way of coming closer to God, as a way of God revealing himself more clearly, and as an opportunity to discern problems in one's own character more profoundly.

We spend a great deal of time in our lives trying to ease and avoid suffering, and when it comes, we do not know what to do with it. Even less do we know how to help others who suffer. We fight it, assign blame to individuals and social systems, and try to protect ourselves. Rarely do any of us consider how suffering might be a gift from God, to call us to become more holy. While we often say that crisis and suffering builds character, we avoid both whenever we can, and expend much effort creating techniques to compensate for, minimize, or overcome the suffering. In fact, much of our secular literature suggests that Mother Teresa and the Missionaries are psychologically flawed in their acceptance of pain and suffering. Having worked alongside them, I think nothing could be further from the truth. We Americans are rarely encouraged to take responsibility for our own suffering. Yet regardless of the situation, each of us, at the very least, has choices to make about how we respond to suffering. To the Missionaries, suffering is not merely a physical experience, but a spiritual encounter, one that encourages them to learn new responses, to seek forgiveness, to turn to God, to think like Christ, and to rejoice that the suffering has produced a good work in them. It is, finally, a spur to action.

Mother Teresa often said, quoting her namesake Thérèse of Lisieux, that while most of us think our lives should be about doing great things, we rather are called to do small things with great love. This is the phrase that best exemplifies the work with the Missionaries of Charity, most of whom will never be known for the millions of little tasks of great love they do in the world. When most of us do such everyday chores, we give them little thought or care. One day, for example, I was helping the sisters with the washing. "Someone should donate a washing machine for all these diapers and clothes," I said. A sister immediately replied, "Oh no, we don't need a washing machine; Jesus helps us wash, love helps us." Washing diapers was never quite the same for me again. The love the sister spoke of is not love that I am used to thinking about or acting on. The Missionaries put real love into the daily tasks of cooking, serving and cleaning up after a meal, washing diapers, smiling at strangers, squashing their own needs and desires, answering the phone, or picking up trash that isn't theirs. When you see such love at work you come to realize how such an ardent love of God enables us to truly love humankind, especially "the poorest of the poor."

It is that love, as Mother Teresa showed us, whose work produces not tiredness but energy. It is not humanistic love drawn from pride and pity, willing to sacrifice goodness for sweetness. It is not a love where anything goes because you are poor or because you are privileged, or where bitterness and anger or indulgence blind the server and the served. It is not tough love. It is not a love where we expect something in return. It is a strong and sacrificial love, the love that allows a sister to pull worms out of the flesh of another human being while being cursed for doing so. It is the love that never gets bitter, that never gives up. It is the love that haunts us when reading Christ's instructions to his disciples, *"What good is it if you love those who love you, do not even the sinners love those who love them?"*

"You fall more in love with Jesus everyday," Mother Teresa told me one day, shaking her finger and looking me right in the eye. She did not know my name or what I do. She had often seen me sitting near her during Mass and adoration, and we had bowed to one another during the kiss of peace. We had spoken directly to one another very little. I now think of her words as a message from the Holy Spirit. Every cell in my body knew what she meant. She was telling me, you cannot do faith in your head. I said, "Yes, Ma'am."

By Judith Antonelli *On The Issues*

THE *Goddess* MYTH

The "golden age" of female divinities was a bad time for women

*O*nce upon a time there was a Great Mother Goddess who was worshipped all over the world. Under Her benevolent care, humans lived in peace with each other and in harmony with nature. Women were honored as Her earthly representatives and served as Her priestesses, enacting Her sacred sexual rites in groves and temples as seasonal festivals. One day a band of male warriors with a violent male god invaded this utopia, destroying the Goddess and installing their god as the "one and only" deity. From that day forward, women were subjugated, nature was exploited, militarism was glorified, and sexual repression became the law. This new order is described in the Hebrew Bible.

The feminist spirituality movement was born two decades ago when women who had rejected the sexist teachings of their traditional religious upbringings discovered they needed some form of spirituality to nourish their souls. A kind, nurturing mother Goddess seemed to fill the void.

Searching for female images of the Divine, they inevitably turned to ancient pagan goddesses such as Isis of Egypt and Ishtar of Babylonia, and, in the process, adopted the romantic notion that the societies that worshipped them held women, sexuality, and nature in high regard. Thus the feminist fairy tale above came into being. Twenty years later, now widely accepted as historical fact, the tale continues to fuel the imaginations of thousands of women looking for an alternative to male-dominated religion.

From *Utne Reader*, November/December 1997, pp. 63-65, 104. Excerpted from *On the Issues,* Summer 1997. © 1997 by On the Issues. Reprinted by permission.

There's just one problem: The fairy tale isn't accurate. It whitewashes the male supremacy and militarism of ancient paganism, falsely attributing the origin of these phenomena to "the Hebrews." In the new goddess myth, Egypt and Babylonia are portrayed as benevolent, peaceful, and matriarchal societies, despite the fact that sexual abuse and exploitation, ritual castration, phallus worship, and even human sacrifice were all integral aspects of their religious traditions. Do women who are enchanted by Isis, for instance, know that worship of her involved the annual drowning of a young virgin girl in the Nile to assure a plentiful harvest? Do devotees of Ishtar realize that many of her priestesses were simply temple slaves who were branded with a star (Ishtar's symbol) just like the animals that were dedicated to her?

In her book *The Battered Woman,* domestic abuse counselor Lenore Walker claims that "prior to the creation of the Bible, women . . . were worshipped as the Goddesses of Life" and, even though she never uses the word *Jew,* implies that the Hebrews invented wife beating. Would she really have us believe that in the older Egyptian and Babylonian societies, men never beat their wives? It is ironic that we must turn to a male author, Pierre Montet, and his book *Everyday Life in Ancient Egypt,* to learn that, in fact, an Egyptian husband had the right to beat his wife, and a brother to beat his sister.

Versions of the feminist fairy tale can be found in magazine articles, best-selling books, and television documentaries on the history of Western religion—a piece of revisionist history that's now believed simply because it's been so often repeated.

The Hebrew Bible tells a different story; but before you can get to it, you've got to forget everything that Christianity has taught you. When Christianity appropriated the Hebrew scriptures as its Old Testament, it ignored centuries of rabbinic commentaries that, in Judaism, are considered essential to understanding any biblical verse. It wasn't Jewish tradition that used the story of Adam and Eve to rationalize the subordination of women, or that equated the forbidden fruit with sexuality (and made the woman a temptress). Nor did the earliest Jews claim that Adam and Eve, by eating the forbidden fruit, stained all of humanity with original sin. These and other concepts now viewed as hostile to women—and often traced to ancient Hebrew thought—actually arose from later readings. Unfortunately, these Christian interpretations now predominate in Western civilization (even in the minds of many Jews).

As for the ancient rabbinic teachings, while many are certainly sexist, many others—some might say most—actually protect the interests of women. The first human was created as a hermaphrodite, for instance, a male and female joined at the back. The "creation of woman" was, more accurately, the separation of the female from the male by cutting them apart at the "side" *(tzela,* a Hebrew word that often gets translated as "rib").

The term *ezer knegdo,* usually translated as "helpmate," has been interpreted to mean that women are to be obedient wives. In actuality, the term means "a help against him": Worthy husbands are to be helped while the unworthy are opposed, thus validating a woman's ability to judge a man accurately and treat him accordingly. As for why the serpent spoke to Eve

alone, Adam was "asleep" (a metaphor, perhaps, for male consciousness).

A passage from Genesis 3:16 calls for a different reading as well: "For your husband you will long, and he will rule you" suggests that (most) women will sexually desire men in spite of the results—acknowledging, perhaps, the discomfort of pregnancy, the pain of childbirth, and the fact that men can be real jerks. (The Hebrew word translated here as "rule," *mashal,* does not mean to rule by domination, but to rule as the sun rules the day and the moon rules the night. From this we can deduce that it refers to a kind of affinity between man and woman.)

While sexism in the Jewish community has kept these interpretations from greatly influencing Jewish education, they do exist in the tradition.

The God of the Hebrew Bible is meant to be an incorporeal (and therefore genderless) Being. Hebrew is a gendered language, however, and the masculine gender, which is the root form, is used in most cases to describe God. There are exceptions: For instance, Moses addresses God as feminine in Numbers 11:15. Also, many Hebrew words can be either masculine or feminine; it is how they are vocalized that determines their gender—and vocalization was determined by men. The "linguistic maleness" of God is exaggerated by translation into nongendered languages such as English. It has been solidified into a physical image of maleness by Christian theology, which has God "impregnating" a woman and "fathering" a son.

In biblical times, the new notion that God was beyond gender had to be radical and potentially very liberating, given the harsh realities of the older Canaanite, Egyptian, and Babylonian religions.

The Canaanite pantheon, for instance, was a product of incest. According to Canaanite epic poetry from the 14th-century B.C.E, the goddess Asherah had 70 children by her brother, the god El—including a son Baal, and a daughter Anat. El also impregnated Baal's daughter. Baal castrated El and then took his mother Asherah sexually. To complete the incestuous circle of this divine dysfunctional family, Baal then had sex with Anat. A symbolic reenactment of the incest between Baal and Asherah formed an essential part of Canaanite fertility rites. The Hebrew Bible found this tradition repugnant and commanded Jews to turn away from such gods and goddesses—a fact that many feminists, rather than applauding, have criticized as patriarchal.

In Egyptian mythology, the universe was created through an act of masturbation by the sun god Atum. When Isis' brother (and husband) Osiris was killed and dismembered, she recovered all his body parts except his penis; the artificial one she proceeded to make for him became a focus of Egyptian worship. At Osiris's bull festival, women carried a genitally explicit replica of him, operated by pulling strings.

In Babylonian mythology, creation is described as a product of the murder of the goddess Tiamat by the god Marduk, who crushed her skull and "split her like a shellfish." He turned half of her body into the sky and the other half into the zenith.

In spite of linguistic maleness, the God of the Hebrew Bible does not commit rape and incest, nor create the universe through masturbation or the murder and mutilation of a female. As the first Hebrews, Abraham and Sarah's radical vision of one genderless God must have been a welcome relief from these pagan gods made in the image of abusive men.

The service of these gods was also primarily sexual, largely exploitive, and sometimes mutilating. The pagan temple was, in effect, the original brothel. The priestess of a goddess lived in the temple and was required to have ritual sex with any man willing to pay the fee. Similarly, the priest of a goddess was a transvestite eunuch who had ritual sex with men. Castration was the means by which these men were "dedicated" to the goddess. The priest of a god was in charge of feeding the god with daily sacrifices and libations and honoring him with song, music, and incense. His was the only type of service that had no sexual component. The priestess of a god, in contrast, was required to have ritual sex at harvest festivals with kings, pharaohs, and emperors.

This, then, is the historical context of the Hebrew Bible. Its laws concerning marriage, divorce, adultery, rape, inheritance, slavery, and conduct in warfare reflect an already existing social reality. There's a difference between what the Bible actually says and what men and women say it says. What appears to be sexism in the Bible is nothing more than a reflection of the sexism that dominated Babylonian, Egyptian, and Canaanite societies in—Isis forgive us—the age of the Great Mother Goddess.

Judith S. Antonelli is a feminist and a religiously observant Jew who lives in Boston. Her book In the Image of God: A Feminist Commentary on the Torah *(Jason Aronson, 1995) was recently released in paperback. Excerpted from* On the Issues *(Summer 1997). Subscriptions: $14.95/yr. (4 issues) from Box 3000, Dept. OTI, Denville, NJ 07834.*

ISLAM AND WOMEN'S RIGHTS

Islam's Shame

Lifting the veil of tears

Ibn Warraq

Islam is deeply anti-woman. Islam is the fundamental cause of the repression of Muslim women and remains the major obstacle to the evolution of their position.[1] Islam has always considered women as creatures inferior in every way: physically, intellectually, and morally. This negative vision is divinely sanctioned in the Koran, corroborated by the *hadiths,* and perpetuated by the commentaries of the theologians, the custodians of Muslim dogma and ignorance.

Far better for these intellectuals to abandon the religious argument, to reject these sacred texts, and have recourse to *reason* alone. They should turn instead to human rights. The Universal Declaration of Human Rights (adopted on December 10, 1948, by the General Assembly of the United Nations in Paris and ratified by most Muslim countries) at no point has recourse to a religious argument. These rights are based on natural rights, which any adult human being capable of choice has. They are rights that human beings have simply because they are human beings. Human reason or rationality is the ultimate arbiter of rights—human rights, the rights of women.

Unfortunately, in practice, in Muslim countries one cannot simply leave the theologians with their narrow, bigoted world view to themselves. One cannot ignore the *ulama,* those learned doctors of Muslim law who by their *fatwas* or decisions in questions touching private or public matters of importance regulate the life of the Muslim community. They still exercise considerable powers of approving or forbidding certain actions. Why the continuing influence of the *mullas*?

The Koran remains for all Muslims, not just "fundamentalists," the uncreated word of God Himself. It is valid for all times and places; its ideas are absolutely true and beyond all criticism. To question it is to question the very word of God, and hence blasphemous. A Muslim's duty is to believe it and obey its divine commands.

Islam is the fundamental cause of the repression of Muslim women and remains the major obstacle to the evolution of their position.

Several other factors contribute to the continuing influence of the *ulama.* Any religion that requires total obedience without thought is not likely to produce people capable of *critical thought,* people capable of free and independent thought. Such a situation is favorable to the development of a powerful "clergy" and is clearly responsible for the intellectual, cultural, and economic stagnation of several centuries. Illiteracy remains high in Muslim countries. Historically, as there never was any separation of state and religion, any criticism of one was seen as a criticism of the other. Inevitably, when many Muslim countries won independence after the Second World War, Islam was unfortunately linked with nationalism, which meant that any criticism of Islam was seen as a betrayal of the newly independent country—an unpatriotic act, an encouragement to colonialism and imperialism. No Muslim country has developed a stable democracy; Muslims are being subjected to every kind of repression possible. Under these conditions healthy criticism of society is not possible, because critical thought and liberty go together.

The above factors explain why Islam in general and the position of women in particular are never criticized, discussed, or subjected to deep scientific or skeptical analysis. All innovations are discouraged in Islam—every problem is seen as a religious problem rather than a social or economic one.

Ibn Warraq, who was raised as a Muslim, now devotes himself to the scholarly examination of the beliefs and practices of Islam. He is the author of Why I Am Not a Muslim *(Prometheus Books, 1995).*

 From *Free Inquiry,* Fall 1997, pp. 30-36. © 1997 by the Council for Secular Humanism. Reprinted by permission.

PROFOUNDLY ANTI-WOMAN

Islam took the legend of Adam and Eve[2] from the Old Testament and adapted it in its own fashion. The creation of mankind from one person is mentioned in the following *suras:*

4.1. O Mankind! Be careful of your duty to your Lord who created you from a single soul and from it created its mate and from them twain hath spread abroad a multiple of men and women.

39.6. He created you from one being, then from that (being) He made its mate.

7.189. He it is who did create you from a single soul and therefrom did make his mate that he might take rest in her.

From these slender sources Muslim theologians have concluded that man was the original creation—womankind was created secondarily for the pleasure and repose of man. The legend was further developed to reinforce the supposed inferiority of women. Finally, the legend was given a sacred character so that to criticize it was to criticize the very words of God, which were immutable and absolute. Here is how Muhammad describes women in general: "Be friendly to women for womankind was created from a rib, but the bent part of the rib, high up, if you try to straighten it you will break it; if you do nothing, she will continue to be bent."

God punishes Adam and Eve for disobeying his orders. But there is nothing in the verses to show that it was Eve (as in the Old Testament) who led Adam astray. And yet Muslim exegetists and jurists have created the myth of Eve the temptress that has since become an integral part of Muslim tradition. Muhammad himself is reputed to have said: "If it had not been for Eve, no woman would have been unfaithful to her husband."

The Islamic tradition also attributes guile and deceit to women and draws its support from the Koran. Modern Muslim commentators interpret certain verses to show that guile, deceit, and treachery are intrinsic to a woman's nature. Not only is she unwilling to change, she is by nature incapable of changing—she has no choice.[3] In attacking the female deities of the

> *Any religion that requires total obedience without thought is not likely to produce people capable of critical thought, people capable of free and independent thought.*

polytheists, the Koran takes the opportunity to malign the female sex further.

4.1 17. They invoke in His stead only females; they pray to none else than Satan, a rebel.

53.21–22. Are yours the males and His the females That indeed were an unfair division!

53.27. Lo! it is those who disbelieve in the Hereafter who name the angels with the names of females.

Other verses from the Koran also seem of a misogynist tendency.

Islamic Mutilation

According to the nineteenth century *Dictionary of Islam* and Richard Burton, female circumcision was widespread in Arabia, where "clitoris cutter" was a legitimate profession practiced by old women, and perhaps most other Islamic countries. According to the Minority Rights Group's Report "Female Genital Mutilation: Proposals for Change," published in 1992, the practice is still followed widely across Western, Saharan, and Eastern Africa, as well as in Yemen and Oman, by Muslims, Christians, Jews, and animists. "Tens of millions of girls are affected every year." Unlike the public nature of the boy's circumcision, female excision is practiced discreetly, and does not have the symbolic significance.

Female excision is not mentioned in the Koran and learned doctors of theology, when they deign to address the matter, spend very little time on it, simply recommending it as a pious act. What exactly does the operation involve? According to Burton,* "in the babe [the clitoris] protrudes beyond the labiae and snipping off the head forms female circumcision." "Excision," continues Burton,

Richard Burton, *The Book of a Thousand Nights and a Night* (London: N.D.) vol. 15.

is universal amongst the negroids of the Upper Nile, the Somal and other adjacent tribes. The operator, an old woman, takes up the instrument, a knife or razor blade fixed into a wooden handle, and with three sweeps cuts off the labia and the head of the clitoris. The parts are then sewn up with a packneedle and a thread of sheepskin; and in Dar-For a tin tube is inserted for the passage of urine. Before marriage the bridegroom trains himself for a month on beef, honey and milk; and if he can open his bride with the natural weapon he is a sworder to whom no women in the tribe can deny herself. If he fails, he tries penetration with his fingers and by way of last resort whips out his whittle and cuts the parts open. The sufferings of the first few nights must be severe.

In modern times little seems to have changed; here is how the *Economist* describes the situation in 1992: "The procedure varies from mildly painful to gruesome, and can involve the removal of the clitoris and other organs with knives, broken glass, and razors—but rarely anesthetic. It can lead to severe problems with menstruation, intercourse and childbirth, psychological disturbances and even death."

—*Ibn Warraq*

2.228. Women who are divorced shall wait, keeping themselves apart, three (monthly) courses. And it is not lawful for them that they should conceal that which Allah hath created in their wombs if they are believers in Allah and the Last Day. And their husbands would be better to take them back in that case if they desire a reconciliation. And they (women) have rights similar to those (of men) over them in kindness, and men are a degree above them. Allah is Mighty, Wise.

2.282. But if he who oweth the debt is of low understanding, or weak or unable himself to dictate, then let the guardian of his interests dictate in (terms of) equity. And call to witness, from among your men, two witnesses. And if two men be not (at hand) then a man and two women, of such as ye approve as witnesses, so that if the one erreth (through forgetfulness) the other will remember.

4.11. Allah chargeth you concerning (the provision for) your children: to the male the equivalent of the portion of two females.

4.34. Men are in charge of women, because Allah hath made the one of them to excel the other, and because they spend of their property (for the support of women). So good women are the obedient, guarding in secret that which Allah hath guarded. As for those from whom ye fear rebellion, admonish them and banish them to beds apart; and scourge (beat) them. Then if they obey you, seek not a way against them Lo! Allah is ever High Exalted, Great.

Equally, in numerous *hadiths* on which are based the Islamic laws, we learn of the woman's role—to stay at home, to be at the beck and call of man to obey him (which is a religious duty), and to assure man a tranquil existence. Here are some examples of these traditions:

• The woman who dies and with whom the husband is satisfied will go to paradise.
• A wife should never refuse herself to her husband even if it is on the saddle of a camel.
• Hellfire appeared to me in a dream and I noticed that it was above all peopled with women who had been ungrateful. "Was it toward God that they were ungrateful?" They had not shown any gratitude toward their husbands for all they had received from them. Even when all your life you have showered a woman with your largesse she will still find something petty to reproach you with one day, saying, "You have never done anything for me."
• If anything presages a bad omen it is: a house, a woman, a horse.
• Never will a people know success if they confide their affairs to a woman.

It will be appropriate to include two quotes from the famous and much revered philosopher al-Ghazali (1058–1111), whom Professor Montgomery Watt describes as the greatest Muslim after Muhammad. In his "The Revival Of The Religious Sciences," Ghazali defines the woman's role:[4]

She should stay at home and get on with her spinning, she should not go out often, she must not be well-informed, nor must she be communicative with her neighbours and only visit them when absolutely necessary; she should take care of her husband and respect him in his presence and his absence and seek to satisfy him in everything; she must not cheat on him nor extort money from him; she must not leave her house without his permission and if given his permission she must leave surreptitiously. She should put on old clothes and take deserted streets and alleys, avoid markets, and make sure that a stranger does not hear her voice or recognize her; she must not speak to a friend of her husband even in need.... Her sole worry should be her virtue, her home as well as her prayers and her fast. If a friend of her husband calls when the latter is absent she must not open the door nor reply to him in order to safeguard her and her husband's honour. She should accept what her husband gives her as sufficient sexual needs at any moment.... She should be clean and ready to satisfy her husband's sexual needs at any moment.

Such are some of the sayings from the putative golden age of Islamic feminism. It was claimed that it was the abandonment of the original teachings of Islam that had led to the present decadence and backwardness of Muslim societies. But

Muslim theologians have concluded that man was the original creation— womankind was created secondarily for the pleasure and repose of man.

there never was an Islamic utopia. To talk of a golden age is only to conform and perpetuate the influence of the clergy, the *mullas,* and their hateful creed that denies humanity to half the inhabitants of this globe, and further retards all serious attempts to liberate Muslim women.

WHAT RIGHTS?

The inequality between men and women[5] in matters of giving testimony or evidence or being a witness is enshrined in the Koran: *sura* 2.282 (quoted above).

How do Muslim apologists justify the above text? Muslim men and women writers point to the putative psychological differences that exist between men and women. The Koran (and hence God) in its sublime wisdom knew that women are sensitive, emotional, sentimental, easily moved, and influenced by their biological rhythm, lacking judgment. But above all they have a shaky memory. In other words, women are psychologically inferior. Such are the dubious arguments used by Muslim intellectuals—male and, astonishingly enough, female intellectuals like Ahmad Jamal, Ms. Zahya Kaddoura, Ms. Ghada al-Kharsa, and Ms. Madiha Khamis. As Ghassan Ascha points out, the absurdity of their arguments are obvious.

By taking the testimony of two beings whose reasoning faculties are faulty we do not obtain the testimony of one complete person with a perfectly functioning rational faculty— such is Islamic arithmetic! By this logic, if the testimony of two women is worth that of one man, then the testimony of four women must be worth that of two men, in which case we can dispense with the testimony of the men. But no! In Islam the rule is not to accept the testimony of women alone in matters to which men theoretically have access. It is said that the Prophet did not accept the testimony of women in matters of marriage, divorce, and *hudud*. *Hudud* are the punishments set down by Muhammad in the Koran and the *hadith* for (1) adultery—stoning to death; (2) fornication—a hundred stripes; (3) false accusation of adultery against a married person—eighty stripes; (4) apostasy—death; (5) drinking wine—eighty stripes; (6) theft—the cutting off of the right hand; (7) simple robbery on the highway—the loss of hands and feet; robbery with murder—death, either by the sword or by crucifixion.

On adultery the Koran 24.4 says: "Those that defame honourable women and cannot produce four witnesses shall be given eighty lashes." Of course, Muslim jurists will only accept four male witnesses. These witnesses must declare that they have "seen the parties in the very act of carnal conjunction." Once an accusation of fornication and adultery has been made, the accuser himself or herself risks punishment if he or she does not furnish the necessary legal proofs. Witnesses are in the same situation. If a man were to break into a woman's dormitory and rape half a dozen women, he would risk nothing since there would be no male witnesses. Indeed the victim of a rape would hesitate before going in front of the law, since she would risk being condemned herself and have little chance of obtaining justice. "If the woman's words were sufficient in such cases," explains Judge Zharoor ul Haq of Pakistan, "then no man would be safe." This iniquitous situation is truly revolting and yet for Muslim law it is a way of avoiding social scandal concerning the all-important sexual taboo. Women found guilty of fornication were literally immured, at first; as the Koran 4.15 says: "Shut them up within their houses till death release them, or God make some way for them." However this was later canceled and stoning substituted for adultery and one hundred lashes for fornication. When a man is to be stoned to death, he is taken to some barren place, where he is stoned first by the witnesses, then the judge, and then the public. When a woman is stoned, a hole to receive her is dug as deep as her waist—the Prophet himself seems to have ordered such procedure. It is lawful for a man to kill his wife and her lover if he catches them in the very act.

In the case where a man suspects his wife of adultery or denies the legitimacy of the offspring, his testimony is worth that of four men. *Sura* 24.6: "If a man accuses his wife but has no witnesses except himself, he shall swear four times by God that his charge is true, calling down upon himself the curse of God if he is lying. But if his wife swears four times by God that his charge is false and calls down His curse upon herself if it be true, she shall receive no punishment." Appearances to the contrary, this is not an example of Koranic justice or equality between the sexes. The woman indeed escapes being stoned to death but she remains rejected and loses her right to the dowry and her right to maintenance, *whatever the outcome of the trial.* A woman does not have the right to charge her husband in a similar manner. Finally, for a Muslim marriage to be valid there must be a multiplicity of witnesses. For Muslim jurists, two men form a multiplicity but not two or three or a thousand women.

In questions of heritage, the Koran tells us that male children should inherit twice the portion of female children:

> 4.11–12. A male shall inherit twice as much as a female. If there be more than two girls, they shall have two-thirds of the inheritance, but if there be one only, she shall inherit the half. Parents shall inherit a sixth each, if the deceased have a child; but if he leave no child and his parents be his heirs, his mother shall have a third. If he have brothers, his mother shall have a sixth after payment of any legacy he may have bequeathed or any debt he may have owed.

To justify this inequality, Muslim authors lean heavily In the fact that a woman receives a dowry and has the right to maintenance from her husband. It is also true that according to Muslim law the mother is not at all obliged to provide for her children, and if she does spend money on her children, it is, to quote Bousquet, "recoverable by her from her husband if he is returned to a better fortune as in the case of any other charitable person. Therefore there is no point in the husband and wife sharing in the taking charge of the household; this weighs upon the husband alone. There is no longer any financial interest between them."[6]

The birth of a girl is still seen as a catastrophe in Islamic societies.

This latter point referred to by Bousquet simply emphasized the negative aspects of a Muslim marriage—that is to say, the total absence of any idea of "association" between "couples" as in Christianity. As to dowry, it is, of course, simply a reconfirmation of the man's claims over the woman in matters of sex and divorce. Furthermore, in reality the woman does not get to use the dowry for herself. The custom is either to use the dowry to furnish the house of the newly married couple or for the wife to offer it to her father. According to the Malekites, the woman can be obliged by law to use the dowry to furnish the house. Muslim law also gives the guardian the right to cancel a marriage—even that of a woman of legal age—if he thinks the dowry is not sufficient. Thus the dowry, instead of being a sign of her independence, turns out once more to be a symbol of her servitude.

The woman has the right to maintenance but this simply emphasizes her total dependence on her husband, with all its attendant sense of insecurity. According to Muslim jurists, the husband is not obliged under Islamic law to pay for her medical expenses in case of illness. Financial independence of the woman would of course be the first step in the liberation of Muslim women and thus it is not surprising that it is seen as a threat to male dominance. Muslim women are now obliged to take equal responsibility for looking after their parents. Article 158 of Syrian law states "The child—male or female—having the necessary means is obliged to take responsibility for his or her poor parents." The birth of a girl is still seen as a catastrophe in Islamic societies. The system of inheritance just adds to her misery and her dependence on the man. If she is an only child she receives only half the legacy of her father; the other half goes to the male members of the father's family. If there are two or more daughters, they inherit two-thirds. This pushes fathers and mothers to prefer male children to female so that they can leave the entirety of their effects or possessions to their own descendants. "Yet when a new-born girl is announced to one of them his countenance darkens and he is filled with gloom" (sura 43.15). The situation is even worse when a woman loses her husband—she only receives a quarter of the legacy. If the deceased leaves more than one wife, all the wives are still obliged to share among themselves a quarter or one-eighth of the legacy.

Muslim jurists[7] are unanimous in their view that men are superior to women in virtue of their reasoning abilities, their knowledge, and their supervisory powers. And since it is the man who assumes financial responsibility for the family, it is

Muslim thinkers continue to confine Muslim women to the house—to leave is against the will of God and the principles of Islam.

argued, it is natural that he should have total power over the woman. These same jurists, of course, totally neglect changing social conditions where a woman may contribute her salary to the upkeep of her family—power over women remains a divine command and "natural" or "in the nature of things." Muslim thinkers continue to confine Muslim women to the house—to leave the house is against the will of God and against the principles of Islam. Confined to their houses, women are then reproached for not having any experience of the outside world!

According to theologians,[8] the husband has the right to administer corporal punishment to his wife if she

1. Refuses to make herself beautiful for him;

2. Refuses to meet his sexual demands;

3. Leaves the house without permission or without any legitimate reason recognized by law; or

4. Neglects her religious duties.

A *hadith* attributes the following saying to the Prophet: "Hang up your whip where your wife can see it." There are a number of other *hadiths* that contradict this one. In those, Muhammad explicitly forbids men to beat their wives—in which case the Prophet himself is contradicting what the Koran, enshrining divine law, permits.

CASE HISTORIES: THE WOMEN OF PAKISTAN

In Pakistan in 1977, General Zia al-Haq took over in a military coup declaring that the process of Islamization was not going fast enough. The *mullas* had finally got someone who was prepared to listen to them.

Zia imposed martial law, total press censorship, and began creating a theocratic state, believing that Pakistan ought to have "the spirit of Islam." He banned women from athletic contests and even enforced the Muslim fast during the month of Ramadan at gunpoint. He openly admitted that there was a contradiction between Islam and democracy. Zia introduced Islamic laws that discriminated against women. The most notorious of these laws were the *Zina* and *Hudud* Ordinances that called for the Islamic punishments of the amputation of hands for stealing and stoning to death for married people found guilty of illicit sex. The term *zina* included adultery, fornication, and rape, and even prostitution. Fornication was punished with a maximum of a hundred lashes administered in public and ten years' imprisonment.

In practice, these laws protect rapists, for a woman who has been raped often finds herself charged with adultery or fornication. To prove *zina*, four Muslim adult males of good repute must be present to testify that sexual penetration has taken place. Furthermore, in keeping with good Islamic practice, these laws value the testimony of men over women. The combined effect of these laws is that it is impossible for a woman to bring a successful charge of rape against a man; instead, she herself, the victim, finds herself charged with illicit sexual intercourse, while the rapist goes free. If the rape results in a pregnancy, this is automatically taken as an admission that adultery or fornication has taken place with the woman's consent rather than that rape has occurred.

Here are some sample cases.[9]

In a town in the northern province of Punjab, a woman and her two daughters were stripped naked, beaten, and gang raped in public, but the police declined to pursue the case.

A thirteen-year-old girl was kidnapped and raped by a "family friend." When her father brought a case against the rapist, it was the girl who was put in prison and charged with *zina*, illegal sexual intercourse. The father managed to secure the child's release by bribing the police. The traumatized child was then severely beaten for disgracing the family honor.

A fifty-year-old widow, Ahmedi Begum,[10] decided to let some rooms in her house in the city of Lahore to two young veiled women. As she was about to show them the rooms, the police burst into the courtyard of the house and arrested the two girls and Ahmedi Begum's nephew, who had simply been standing there. Later that afternoon, Ahmedi Begum went to the police station with her son-in-law to inquire about her nephew and the two girls. The police told Ahmedi they were arresting her too. They confiscated her jewelry and pushed her into another room. While she was waiting, the police officers shoved the two girls, naked and bleeding, into the room and

The United Nations on the Rights of Women

Article 1—Discrimination against women, denying or limiting as it does their equality of rights with men, is fundamentally unjust and constitutes an offence against human dignity.

Article 2—All appropriate measures shall be taken to abolish existing laws, customs, regulations and practices which are discriminatory against women, and to establish adequate legal protection for equal rights of men and women . . .

Article 3—All appropriate measures shall be taken to educate public opinion and to direct national aspirations towards the eradication of prejudice and the abolition of customary and all other practices which are based on the idea of the inferiority of women.

Article 4—All appropriate measures shall be taken to ensure to women on equal terms with men, without any discrimination:
(a) The right to vote in all elections and be eligible for election to all publicly elected bodies;
(b) The right to vote in all public referenda;
(c) The right to hold public office and to exercise all public functions. Such rights shall be guaranteed by legislation.

Article 5—Women shall have the same rights as men to acquire, change or retain their nationality. Marriage to an alien shall not automatically affect the nationality of the wife either by rendering her stateless or by forcing upon her the nationality of her husband.

Article 6—1. Without prejudice to the safeguarding of the unity and the harmony of the family, which remains the basic unit of any society, all appropriate measures, particularly legislative measures, shall be taken to ensure to women, married or unmarried, equal rights with men in the field of civil law. . . .
2. All appropriate measures shall be taken to ensure the principle of equality of status of the husband and wife, and in particular:
(a) Women shall have the same right as men as to free choice of a spouse and to enter into marriage rights with men during marriage and at its dissolution. In all cases the interest of the children shall be paramount. . . .
(c) Parents shall have equal rights and duties in matters relating to their children. In all cases the interest of the children shall be paramount.

3. Child marriage and the betrothal of young girls before puberty shall be prohibited, and effective action, including legislation, shall be taken to specify a minimum age for marriage and to make the registration of marriages in an official registry compulsory.

Article 7—All provisions of penal codes which constitute discrimination against women shall be repealed.

Article 8—All appropriate measures, including legislation, shall be taken to combat all forms of traffic in women and exploitation of prostitution of women.

Article 9—All appropriate measures shall be taken to ensure to girls and women, married or unmarried, equal rights with men in education at all levels. . . .

Article 10—1. All appropriate measures shall be taken to ensure to women, married or unmarried, equal rights with men in the field of economic and social life. . . .
2. In order to prevent discrimination against women on account of marriage or maternity and to ensure their effective right to work, measures shall be taken to prevent their dismissal in the event of marriage or maternity and to provide paid maternity leave, with the guarantee of returning to former employment, and to provide the necessary social services, including child-care facilities.
3. Measures taken to protect women in certain types of work, for reasons inherent in their physical nature, shall not be regarded as discriminatory.

Article 11—1. The principle of equality of rights of men and women demands implementation in all States in accordance with the principles of the Charter of the United Nations and of the Universal Declaration of Human Rights.
2. Governments, non-governmental organizations and individuals are urged, therefore, to do all in their power to promote the implementation of the principles contained in this Declaration. **FI**

Excerpted from the United Nations Declaration on the Rights of Women, adopted November 7, 1967.

---

then proceeded to rape them again in front of the widow. When Ahmedi covered her eyes, the police forced her to watch by pulling her arms to her sides. After suffering various sexual humiliations, Ahmedi herself was stripped and raped by one officer after another. They dragged her outside where she was again beaten. One of the officers forced a policeman's truncheon, covered with chili paste, into her rectum, rupturing it. Ahmedi screamed in horrible agony and fainted, only to wake up in prison, charged with *zina*. Her case was taken up by a human rights lawyer. She was released on bail after three months in prison, but was not acquitted until three years later.

In the meantime, her son-in-law divorced her daughter because of his shame.

Was this an isolated case? Unfortunately no. The Human Rights Commission of Pakistan said in its annual report that one woman is raped every three hours in Pakistan and one in two rape victims is a juvenile. According to Women's Action Forum, a woman's rights organization, 72% of all women in police custody in Pakistan are physically and sexually abused. Furthermore, 75% of all women in jail are there under charges of *zina*. Many of these women remain in jail awaiting trial for years.

In other words, the charge of *zina* is casually applied by any man who wants to get rid of his wife, who is immediately arrested, and kept waiting in prison, sometimes for years. Before the introduction of these laws the total number of women in prison was 70; the present number is more than 3,000. Most of these women have been charged under the *Zina* or *Hudud* Ordinances.[11]

The Western press naively believed that the election of Benazir Bhutto as Pakistan's prime minister in November 1988 would revolutionize women's role not just in Pakistan, but in the entire Islamic world. Under Islamic law of course, women cannot be head of an Islamic state, and Pakistan had become an Islamic republic under the new constitution of 1956. Thus, Benazir Bhutto had defied the *mullas* and won. But her government lasted a bare 20 months, during which period Nawaz Sharif, who was the prime minister briefly in the early 1990s, is said to have encouraged the *mullas* in their opposition to having a woman as the head of an Islamic state. Benazir Bhutto's government was dismissed on charges of corruption, and her husband imprisoned in 1990.

The lot of the Muslim woman was harsh before Benazir's election, and nothing has changed. She has pandered to the religious lobby, the *mullas,* the very people who insist that a woman cannot hold power in an Islamic state, and has repeatedly postponed any positive action on the position of women.

Pakistan shows the same grim picture. Pakistan is one of only four countries in the world where female life expectancy (51 years) is lower than the male (52 years); the average female life expectancy for all poor countries is 61 years. A large number of Pakistani women die in pregnancy or childbirth, six for every 1,000 live births. Despite the fact that contraception has never been banned by orthodox Islam, under Zia the Islamic Idealogy Council of Pakistan declared family planning to be un-Islamic. Various *mullas* condemned family planning as a Western conspiracy to emasculate Islam. As a result, the average fertility rate per woman in Pakistan is 6.9. Pakistan is also among the world's bottom ten countries for female attendance in primary schools. Some people put female literacy in the rural areas as low as 2% (*Economist,* March 5, 1994). As the *Economist* put it, "Some of the blame for all this lies with the attempt of the late President Zia ul Haq to create an Islamic republic. . . . Zia turned the clock back. A 1984 law of his, for instance, gives a woman's legal evidence half the weight of a man's" (*Economist,* January 13, 1990).

Indeed a large part of the blame lies with the attitudes inculcated by Islam, which has always seen woman as inferior to man. The birth of a baby girl is the occasion for mourning. Hundreds of baby girls are abandoned every year in the gutters and dust bins and on the pavements. An organization working in Karachi to save these children has calculated that more than five hundred children are abandoned a year in Karachi alone, and that 99% of them are girls.[12]

Little did Jinnah, the founder of Pakistan, realize how literally true his words were when he said in a 1944 speech:[13] "No nation can rise to the height of glory unless your women are side by side with you. We are victims of evil customs. It is a crime against humanity that our women are shut up within the four walls of the houses as prisoners."

But we do not need to leave with a completely pessimistic picture. Pakistani women have shown themselves to be very courageous, and more and more are fighting for their rights with the help of equally brave organizations such as Women's Action Forum (WAF) and War Against Rape. WAF was formed in 1981 as women came onto the streets to protest against the *Hudud* Ordinances, and to demonstrate their solidarity with a couple who had recently been sentenced to death by stoning for fornication. In 1983, women organized the first demonstrations against martial law.

Notes

1. Ghassan Ascha, *Du Statut Inferieur de la Femme en Islam* (Paris: 1989) p. 11.
2. Ibid., pp. 23f.
3. Ibid., pp. 29f.
4. Ibid., p. 41.
5. Ascha, op. cit., pp. 63f.
6. G. H. Bousquet, *L'Ethique sexuelle de L'Islam* (Paris: 1966) vol. 1, p. 120.
7. Ascha, op. cit. p. 89.
8. Ibid., pp. 108.
9. Kurt Schork, "Pakistan's Women in Despair," *Guardian Weekly,* September 23, 1990.
10. Jan Goodwin, *Price of Honor* (Boston: 1994) p. 49–50.
11. Schork, op. cit.
12. Goodwin, op. cit., p. 64.
13. R. Ahmed, ed., *Sayings of Quaid-i-Azam (Jinnah)* (Karachi: 1986) p. 98.

Whatever Happened to Sister Jane?

Shop. That four-letter word almost single-handedly destroyed religious life as we knew it in the 1950's.

By GEORGIA HEDRICK

REMEMBER HER? Both legion and legend, we called her "Sister." She taught the children of immigrants in parish schools, nursed their sick in hospitals and cared for their orphans in social settlement houses. Remember the outfits? Veils and coifs and capots and cornettes and wimples—an entire medieval array with bell-bottom sleeves, flapping scapulars, billowy capes and floor-length gowns—rosary to the side and cross to the center. She was the past that walked in the present to bring both to the future.

And when she shopped, she never shopped alone. Always she traveled in twos and with a list.

Sisters. Forever sisters.

Then came the 60's. Women religious in the United States peaked to an all-time high of 181,421 and the Second Vatican Council issued the mandate, "Modernize!" She was told to consider health and common sense, not only in what she wore but in how she lived. If she hadn't been female, she might have handled matters differently. But she was a woman, and something strange happens to women when told to shop, to "get a modern look." It doesn't matter that she has dressed the same for hundreds of years. What matters is that she is a woman who has just been told to SHOP.

Shop. That four-letter word almost single-handedly destroyed religious life as we knew it in the 1950's. I know. I was there. I was once a "Sister Jane." I heard the call to shop. I shopped; we shopped. We shopped for essentials in order to dispense with incidentals. We shopped among traditions, to pitch those not germane

GEORGIA HEDRICK, the former Sister Alma Zacharias, D.C., is now a teacher in Reno, Nev.

to the spirit of the order. And we shopped for a lighter weight, more-fit-for-modern-times habit.

The habit I wore had been unchanged for some 300 years. It did not matter that it was not healthy to wear in hot climates or rainy weather; it did not matter that its cost and care were extreme both in time and money. What did matter was tradition! Tradition gave it meaning! It was a banner, a flag, an insignia! It stood for an idea and an ideal.

But in 1963 not too many people remembered what that meaning was.

As a child, I never saw any meaning in nuns' clothing. In fact, I never even saw the woman. All I saw was the habit with a face in front and a form on which it hung. The face never wrinkled but always smiled, never cried, never showed upset or anger—only calm and peace. The face had a voice that spoke with firmness and sureness. That face stood out because it was surrounded by an aura called the habit.

Her veil was to flutter forever, her fingers to fiddle forever with her crucifix, her voice to laugh forever like summer winds. She was to exude goodness to the end of time. This was the meaning of the habit and the woman I called "Sister."

Like thousands of other Catholic teen-age girls of the 50's, I wanted that goodness to rub off on me. When I turned 17 and graduated from high school in June of '57, I entered the Daughters of Charity of St. Vincent de Paul. Back then I thought that to join them would be to be them. The mystery and the magic of this thing called vocation would be mine.

The reality was far different. There was no magic; there was no mystery. There was only tradition. And in a few short years, there wasn't even that. There was only

Vatican II and its command: "Shop around. Find out who you are. Modernize."

Like so many others, I looked like a Sister Jane; I dressed like a Sister Jane; I talked all the right terminology. Yet I knew, I really knew, I wasn't a Sister Jane. That goodness had not rubbed off on me as I thought it would. In fact, a lot of things were not as I thought they would be.

In time, I learned I wasn't alone. There were others, swept along on the idealism of the 50's into the realities of the 60's. In retrospect, I think that many of us entered because the Peace Corps had not been invented and we didn't want to join the armed forces or get married. Curiously, as the recruitment for the Peace Corps went into full swing, women began leaving convents in droves. By 1977 the count of women in religious orders or institutes was down by some 50,000 to 130,804. By 1990 it was 102,504. The 1993 Catholic Almanac reports 97,751 women religious in the United States. Our Sunday Visitor counted women religious at 94,000 as of July 1993. The Tri-Conference Retirement Office for Women Religious in 1993 lists membership in women's religious orders at 92,857. That's a drop of 88,564 in just 27 years, a 48 percent drop in population.

How could such a thing happen? Why?

I attribute it to the stress of shopping. After all, a woman had just been told to shorten her skirt, simplify her headgear, lighten up on the material—plus find reasons for her very religious existence. Stress was inevitable.

In a few short years, Sister Jane had to learn to drive, modify her prayers, get educated in college, understand the problems of John Q. Public and get involved in current moral issues. What had begun as an effort to let a little "fresh air" into a closed and selective church soon became the rush and roar of a mighty wind with the very power of the first Pentecost.

It was a matter of be real or be gone—all tens upon tens of thousands of us. The play was over; we had to turn in our costumes. We former Sister Janes left our convents and novitiates and became our own sort of good woman of the 70's and 80's and 90's. It should be noted that we did this all on our own. There were no halfway houses for former religious in which to learn the social graces expected of career women of the times. There were no support groups telling us we were O.K. There were no farewell parties wishing us good luck. No one said goodbye.

We were just—gone.

Many of us entered because the Peace Corps hadn't been invented and we didn't want to join the armed forces or get married.

We had to endure labels: defections, lost vocations, failures, ex-nuns. These derogatory terms ignored the fact that we were former religious, who, because of irreconcilable differences, had simply gone our own way. All 88,000 and more of us over these past 30 years left our communities, but we did not die. We adjusted—slowly.

I don't know how the others adjusted—but I often wonder. I know I simply pretended and imitated. After all, it worked for me when I was "in"; why not now, when I was "out"? I used to watch television for ideas or strike up conversations in the supermarket line with women who seemed young and single, to get a feel for appropriate behavior. I watched. I learned. Trial and error. Painful. Embarrassing. Often a study in stupidity. But, over time, it worked, and I learned to be "people" enough to pass for a real person. Unless you lived through the readjustment, you simply know not of what I speak. Period.

Some of us term the years we were "in" as the "blackout" years: no radio, television, newspapers, magazines. Everything was limited and censored, even to a controlled circle of friends. In fact, friendship with nuns of other orders had been firmly discouraged. Movies only happened when someone donated a theater in town for "the good sisters," and, like girl scouts on a picnic, we would all go see "Ben Hur" or "The Ten Commandments."

Once we left, what did words like Kent State, Danang, Mr. Ed., Partridge Family, Woodstock, March on Selma, Rosa Parks mean to us? Nothing. They were just words, all of equal value. Just empty words. Yet once out, I was surrounded by people who did use these references, and more. Of one thing only was I sure: I was not 17 anymore. The times had changed.

I had not been on a date for 15 years; I was almost 33. Could it be that you still get asked out to go to a movie and have a Coke afterward? No. Now it was "Your place or mine?" and "How about slipping into something more comfortable?"

I was horrified.

In time, I decided that this was the way it was supposed to be. The rights and wrongs of religious life had no counterpart in the real world. I became a little neon sign saying: available. (For the record, let me say, it was not fun. What I did in the name of being responsive to the needs of the poor was truly pathetic.)

If God, whose special concern is children, fools and former nuns, had not taken pity on me and yanked me by the heart to pay attention, I can only tremble to imagine my future. It happened quite accidentally, which is to say, providentially.

I met a man as I paid my rent one Saturday in February. I looked at him and was stunned by my own thought: This is the one. Instantaneously I believed in him. My faith was total, complete, unquestioning. This was not love, but faith at first sight. I had no reason for it; I didn't even know him. It was a gift. Faith is always a gift.

Was this crazy? Yes. Faith and hope and love are always crazy, as well as inexplicable, and very, very real. They are as real as calm after a storm or rest after tears. There is no why to them—but there is mystery and magic. At last I understood what a vocation was: It wasn't something you get; it is something that gets you.

From that day forward, I kept learning more about vocation. It doesn't stand still; it grows, intensifies and finally falls in love. I had learned this long ago theologically, and it had made no sense. Now I was living it humanly, and it was the most sensible thing I had ever done.

I needed this faith, this love, on any level I could get it. I had thrown away too much when I left. I was unable to make distinctions. Since I couldn't figure out how to apply what I had learned in community to an outside world, I left it all behind.

Leaving one's community was more than a job loss, it was more like a divorce or a death. Mostly it was a radical break with an entire culture, whose values and customs and mores, hundreds of years old and so inextricably intertwined, made me who I was. Leaving it meant leaving everything.

Well, almost. I left religious life, but I learned that it would not leave me. A part of me will be Sister Jane forever. I still think with the words of Saint Vincent de Paul and St. Louise de Marillac when I evaluate matters. In stressful moments, I'll go back to maintaining custody of the eyes, and I'll crawl back inside my head to think. The agony of injustice and discrimination will always tug at me and claim top priority in my focus. It is well nigh impossible to "un-nun" oneself completely.

I just resign myself to being this person, not quite like anyone else my age. And, finally, it's O.K. Finally. After 21 years, finally, it's O.K.

Those first few years out, I had tried so hard to be people. Like Peter, I pretended I "never knew the man!" I avoided going to church; I stayed away from all sorts of churchy people; I tried to live a wild and free life.

Then faith came marching boldly back into my life in the form I least expected: a man. For me, he was the grace of God in human form and I believed. He didn't much believe in himself, let alone God, but I believed. He was the start of my faith growing up all over again.

He was the catalyst that rekindled my faith, tiny spark that it had become. The more I believed in him, the more he believed in himself, and the more we believed in God.

I don't know what worked for my sisters; I only know this is what worked for me.

From that point onward, I learned from my marriage to this man—better than I ever did in community—what religious life was all about. Vocation is a gift given—there is no other reason why someone would live it. A vocation is faith in the value of the life you are now living. There is mystery and magic here: The mystery lies in who gets which gift and the magic is in how it all comes about.

A vocation is a fragile, delicate thing, a tiny spark, needing huffing and puffing to keep it alive. Prayer Service. This is as necessary to make a marriage work as it is to make religious life work. Every vocation lives or dies on the strength of the prayers that support it.

It has taken me 38 years to figure this out. . . .

• • •

Today there are over 88,000 former religious women out and among the rest of the world. Each has been specially trained; each has a memory, which will never quite fade, of having once been a nun; and that memory will make each look at the world uniquely, forever. Each will always be a Sister Jane in some way.

But, where is she, this former Sister Jane? Everywhere.

Just as the former marine is easy to spot, so too is the former nun. The movement of the hands, the look in the eye, the turn of the head, all tell a tale. Sometimes I'll spot one of "us": a teacher, a county official, salesperson, librarian, nurse, new mother. I see the signs. And I wonder: How did she make it? Is she really O.K.? Has the hurt, the sense of failure, the isolation, gone away yet?

Mostly, I wonder: What did she do about all those feelings? In the late 60's and 70's some wrote books, and then that novelty died. But she didn't.

There have been reunions between nuns and former nuns—to get them together and talking. Most orders have had at least one by now. Those who attend are healing, but what about those who do not? Why don't they? Rumor has it that they are still angry, bitter, brooding, even broken.

But larger than the question of where they are is the question of how they are. How is the former Sister Jane?

I know of one who got pregnant and ran to hide—she never has responded to any letter I ever sent, though we went through high school together. I know of another with a drug problem who is now in rehabilitation. I know of several who married alcoholics and abusive men and who are now divorced. One considers herself an atheist. Another tied a plastic bag over her head and went to sleep forever. Many do not live by the faith that once was the foundation of their life. I don't think this pattern is unusual.

Does anyone care?

One group should: the order or institute from which they came. It amazes me that these groups, who were trained never to waste paper or supplies or money given to them, have let whole human lives slip away—lives once labeled "Sister." Surely they did not think the obligation to each other ended when a departure took place. "The community is a good mother" was said to me over and over when I was in. Do good mothers forget their children?

Good communities, like good mothers, ought to check on each of their children from time to time. A sister, like a daughter, is a sister to that family forever. Each ought to feel good about her upbringing; each ought to be able to visit her home and sisters from time to time; each should feel secure that there is always a place at table for her, should she drop by; each should know that should she want a place somewhere in the structure of the order on some level, there is provision for her. Or, should she want nothing but a word of encouragement, there is that, too.

That's not asking too much, is it?

● ● ●

To the present membership of religious women in the United States today, 92,000 and more sisters, I say: We are out here, over 88,000 of your former sisters, who once taught in your schools, or nursed in your hospitals, or served in your social settlement houses or orphanages. We are out and among you and you don't know us. Is not that a reality that begs for closure for justice's sake?

To compound the problem, along come movies like "Sister Act," which ignore this reality and prolong the fantasy of the smiling penguin of the 50's. Movies like "Sister Act" do a grievous injustice to the realities of religious life. They make the world think that nothing has changed. It makes the world forget all about Sister Jane.

"The time has come . . . to speak of many things. . . ." The time has now come to remember, to reach out and to welcome. It is time someone told the former Sister Jane that the world is a better place because of her. It is time for her to be told just how special she is by virtue of her own special background and training. It is time for her to find her very special place in the church.

And, one more thing. It is time that she use *for* her community all the time and training spent on her *by* her community—should she so wish.

My own community—it will always be "my" community—has begun to employ some of its former sisters as salaried lay administrators in its works. Who can understand better the thinking of the community and its orientation? "Sister Act"—fantasy that it is—cannot begin to envision the possibilities of such a joint venture.

Justice demands the correct use of available resources. Peace flows from justice—peace for both former sisters and the communities that watched these sisters go. After all, those dwindling numbers must have raised some questions—as well as gaps—in the works left behind.

Nothing beats the peace that flows from justice—both are the resolution and ultimate solution to all these decades of ignorance.

Again I ask: Whatever happened to Sister Jane? And does anyone care?

Would somebody start, please?

The Labor of Compassion: Voices of "Churched" Korean American Women

JUNG HA KIM

When Chinese come to America, they start laundromats and Chinese restaurants; when Japanese come to America, they start business corporations; when Koreans come to America, they start their churches.

This overgeneralized and ethnocentric remark about Asian Americans actually reveals at least one significant socio-cultural fact about Korean Americans: their church growth.[1] The traditional formula for estimating Korean Americans population in a given area—the number of Korean American churches in the area multipl[ied] by 500[2]—reflects an astonishing and distinct characteristic of the highly "churched" Korean Americans population in the U.S. Sociologists and theologians agree that over 70 percent of Korean Americans are said to be self-claimed Christians compared to only 13 percent of the total population in South Korea in 1982, and 18–21 percent since 1986.[3] Such a dramatic increase of the "churched" population among Korean Americans living in the U.S. may be attributed to the peculiar mission of Korean Americans churches: on the one hand, they offer a vehicle for "Americanization"; and on the other hand, they provide sites for Korean cultural preservation and elaboration.

Conspicuously absent in the thesis of Christianization in either the Americanization or Koreanization process is a focus on Korean

women's participation in the church, even as women constitute a majority of its attendees across states. In fact, the so-called Christianization of Korean Americans is predominantly a feminization of church attendees.

Ironically, the study of "churched" Korean American women has been hindered by their shared membership with more conspicuous "minority" groups, namely Korean American men, with whom they share race-ethnicity, and other women of color, with whom they share gender. As a result, scholars tend to overlook Korean American women's experiences by assuming that their realities are identical to those of Korean American men and/or other women of color.[4] Furthermore, although an increasing number of writers have addressed themselves to the Korean American church—its numerical growth; its schisms; and its multifarious functions—none has focused specifically on women's experiences in a systematic way.[5] No published studies of the Korean American church have even considered the church experience within a gendered context. This initial study addresses the following questions: given that [the] Christian church is both patriarchal and potentially liberatory, and given that the Korean American church is supposed to minister to its members in multiple ways as a racial-ethnic institution within dominant culture(s), how do Korean American women experience their church? In particular, how does patriarchy operate within a Korean American church? How do Korean American women's hyphenated identities become socially and religiously organized? Is it possible to find a sense of "home" in an in-

JUNG HA KIM is a 1.5 generation Korean American woman who teaches at Georgia State University. She is a co-chair of the Asian American consultation at the American Academy of Religion and is a community activist.

From *Amerasia Journal*, Spring 1996, pp. 93-104. © 1996 by the University of California at Los Angeles, Asian American Studies Center. Reprinted by permission.

stitution through inquiry into one's experiences of being a woman within the Korean American church context?

In order to address the foregoing questions I utilized participant observations, in-depth interviews, oral histories and written historical documents. Moreover, these research methods were instrumental for placing "churched" Korean American women's experiences and their own articulations at the center of this exploratory study. As a qualitative attempt to examine the lives of "churched" Korean American women from the perspective of an "outsider within,"[6] a special bilingual sensitivity also fostered women to speak about their own lives and in their own terms. For many "churched" Korean American women suffer from "the cult of 'perfect' language," which is a form of censorship based on racism, sexism, classism and neocolonialism in the U.S.[7]

My work is also significantly influenced by "feminist" methodologies.[8] Feminist research adds an important vantage point to qualitative research by considering gender as a central organizing feature of peoples' lives and thus an important theoretical construct.

Participant observation and interviews were also enhanced by "woman-to-woman talk."[9] Woman-to-woman talk is often qualitatively different from talk in gender-mixed groups for at least two reasons: the woman listener is more likely to listen attentively and seriously and the woman speaker is more likely to use "language in non-standard ways"[10] for naming experiences. Woman-to-woman talk among racially-ethnically similar persons gives speakers an opportunity to describe their worlds with language perhaps not utilized by the dominant group(s) of the society.

The site chosen for the case study is the Kyo-whe,[11] where I was a member and where I have served as a Director of Church Education (DCE) for the past four years.[12] It is situated in an upper-middle class neighborhood of a large city in the Southeast. The history of Kyo-whe formation and of its people are interrelated in that the first migration and immigration of the Korean Americans into the area (and to other parts of the Southern states) occurred after the Immigration Act of 1965. Beginning with a few "pioneers" who came together to form the Kyo-whe in February of 1971 as one of the growing cadre of "new immigrants,"[13] the historical documents of church directories demonstrate its steadily increasing membership: 49 households as of 1985, 68 as of October 1988, 85 as of November 1989 and 101 as of June 1990. The steady growth of the church has not occurred without turmoil, however, especially because of the schismatic tendency among the highly heterogeneous people who are its members. For instance, within the past twenty-four years the church has gone through eleven different pastoral leaders; I recall three different pastors' leadership[14] in my four years of serving the church.

Another difficulty for conducting a study of "living subjects" has to do with the differential alignment of power along lines of age, marital status, class and occupational prestige among adherents of the church and between the researcher and participants. My socio-religious status in the Kyo-whe is: unmarried (which can be translated as "not-yet-an-adult" according to Korean tradition), non-ordained (often seen as "not as holy" as the ordained (male) ministers), relatively young (ageism is one of the powerful and typical ways to establish social relationship in Korean culture), church-related professional woman (DCE). Thus I do not fit easily into the traditionally understood category of church leader. Because of my non-traditional mixture of power and status, women of different status, prestige, and interests relate to me differently. And because of my official position in the church as DCE, I am keenly aware of the possibility that when women are asked to participate in informal interviews, they may be reluctant to deny my request. Questions arise, then, about whether the issue of standard informed consent is sufficiently voluntary. Hence, I was forced to come to terms with the realization that informed consent based on primary relationships is not a single contractual event, but an ongoing process.

In the larger research project I devoted considerable attention to substantiate the claim that the Korean American church is a deeply gendered and racially-ethnically identified institution whose material and ideological arrangements shape, facilitate, reinforce, and sometimes challenge "churched" Korean American women's construction of realities. To say that the church (or any other organization) is gendered means that "advantages and disadvantages, exploitation and control, action and emotion, meaning and identity, are patterned through and in terms of a distinction between male and female, masculine and feminine."[15] Insofar as these patterns systematically advantage males over females, it can be demonstrated that the church is a patriarchal institution.

With regard to material conditions, power structures within the church have typically excluded women from church leadership and religious authority. Woman's ordination controversies;[16] differentiated dress codes and non-inclusive language to define and ritualize various transitional events in human life[17] can be cited as examples of women's exclusion from authority within the church. With regard to symbols and images, the Christian belief system represents a "culture"[18] that defines and justifies its members' gender biased world-view(s). Both the Old and the New Testaments of the Christian Bible are replete with calls for women's subordination (Ephesians 5:24), obedience (I Corinthians 14:33–35) and submission (Leviticus 8, 9, 12:1–5, 15, 18, 21; Ephesians 5:22) to men as the God-ordained (hence, "natural" and unquestionable) order. Thus, on the one hand, the Korean American church places men at the center and behind the pulpit and women in the pews and kitchen-related areas, even as the latter constitute the majority of church attendees in this patriarchal institution. At the same time, the very ethos and functions of the Korean American church are determined by the peculiar characteristics and needs of the hyphenated people, both women and men, as its attendees.

A closer look at church history from a cross-cultural perspective, however, reveals that Christianity has the potential to be both oppressive and liberatory at the same time. That is to say, Christianity has been used as a powerful tool for legitimating the multifaceted oppression of non-Western countries around the world (especially the so-called "third world"), for enslaving millions of African Americans, colonizing (and neo-colonizing) the minds of "minority" groups, and for subordinating women globally. Christianity, however, also has been used as a powerful instrument for social change. With its preferential language for the poor and the oppressed (such as "the sermon on the mount"), the church liberated the lower and outcaste classes from illiteracy in Korea, mobilized the Civil Rights Movement of the late 1960s in the U.S., provided the Biblical roots and language for Latin Americans to articulate their liberation theologies, and empowered women's struggles to transform the patriarchal basis of Christianity. Hence, both the oppressive and liberating potential of the Christian church and its theologies are the context within which "churched" Korean American women find themselves.

At the same time, the Korean American church, as a racial-ethnic religious institution within a dominant culture, is the focal point of socio-cultural integration as well as the center of community life for both its female and its male members. While providing ethnic homogeneity in a highly pluralistic society, the Korean American church not only serves as a "mega church,"[19] with a variety of programs and specific interest groups—such as educating recent arrivals for simple, everyday survival skills like shopping, driving, job hunting, finding an apartment—but also offers psychological and spiritual solace for its members.

In the context of this deeply gendered and highly race-ethnicity-conscious institution, "churched" Korean American women are aware of the fact that their own church renders them to the secondary status and systematically excludes them from gaining public recognition. They are also aware that much of the church work is done by women, yet male church leaders tend to get the credit. As one woman in her mid-fifties aptly commented:

> Is there anything that doesn't require women's work in the church? [We both laughed at this remark.] I really think, all the work that is related to the church is, in fact, women's work. . . . that most of the church work is done by women, but men tend to get all the credit. And I also think that that's just fine, because we women don't work for public recognitions. If there are things that need to be done, then we [women] just do them. That's all.

In short, the Korean American church is a highly contradictory location where a presumably universal "gospel" is preached in a particular tongue, understood by people of hyphenated identities, and experienced through distinct socio-cultural lenses from various life circumstances. By juxtaposing patriarchal readings of the Christian "gospel" while beautifying and abstracting women's (especially, Korean mothers') suffering as the highest form of human love and Christian calling, the Korean American church preaches quasi-Christian messages in the name of religion. To put it differently, the Korean American church as a racial-ethnic institution provides "religious" explanations for its sexism and justifications for the pain experienced and pain endured in the lives of "churched" women. Furthermore, so long as "churched" Korean American women resist thinking of themselves as "100 percent American" and refuse to engage in collective amnesia of the culture they left behind, they are bound to feel an affinity toward the Koreanized Christian messages of women's suffering. "Churched" Korean American women, in turn, are called to sacrifice their interests and concerns as a gender group within their church, in order to reaffirm their sense of loyalty to racial-ethnic identities as a "minority" group within the U.S.

However, by delving into both what "churched" Korean American women say and "listening around" to how they live everyday life in ways that they cannot articulate, I became convinced that they are highly gender-conscious and self-selected survivors. A peculiar set of handed-down folk wisdom and the "hidden transcripts" among women in the context of the Korean American church can demonstrate how they understand and articulate the seemingly oppressive experiences within their church:

Men make rules in the house and in the church and we [women] follow them. [But] Making rules are not as difficult and self-sacrificial as trying to follow them.

Korean men are bossy. They insist that they come first; they speak the last word; and they know better.

Men think that they are the ones who take care of women; but in reality we take care of men. Men don't know anything about women.

God created Korean women very strong. They can survive through anything.

"Churched" Korean American women's handed-down wisdom demonstrate that they use much of what is traditionally known as language of "feminine," "deceptive," and "behind the scene" to their own advantage. Why do "churched" Korean American women adhere to such a seemingly oppressive gender roles and gender language within their church? Are there any advantages for women who insist on traditional understanding of gender? What are the costs? It is by asking these questions as another "churched" Korean American woman, I have encountered the much unexpected and neglected reality: the Korean American church as an important location for both resistance and liberation for woman.

Lipman-Blumen called the utilization of "intelligence, canniness, intuition, interpersonal skills, charm, sexuality, deception, and avoidance"[20] in order to offset the control of those more powerful as "micromanipulation."[21] That is to say, since women historically have had little access to publicly acknowledged power and control, they have learned to use what resources they do have to survive by utilizing informal means of influence.

"Churched" Korean American women also utilize extensive forms of nonverbal daily communication skills in the context of their church: frequent giggles, knowing glances, holding of hands, bitter similes, light hitting on arms and constant eye contact. All these non-verbal forms of communication and articulated wisdom for survival can be seen as instrumental for fostering resistance and self empowerment among "churched" Korean American women. James C. Scott calls both verbal and non-verbal forms of "critique of power spoken behind the back of the dominant" as a "hidden transcript."[22] "For any subordinate groups," Scott argues "there is tremendous desire and will to express publicly what is the hidden transcript, even if that form of expression must use metaphors and allusions in the interest of safety."

Contrary to stereotypes, then, "churched" Korean American women are not all passive and victimized; indeed, they are social agents actively engaged in their own history-making. Racism, sexism, Americanization, Koreanization, Christianization and the process of immigration have not defeated "churched" Korean American women in their ongoing struggle to maintain human dignity and give meanings to their everyday experiences in the U.S. They take special pride in sharing with me how women have developed various strategies of micromanipulation and "hidden transcripts" within their church. "Churched" Korean American women also named their own struggles to be women, Koreans, Americans, and Christians all at the same time as the "labor of compassion." Rather paradoxically, however, in their articulations of "labor of compassion" within their church, women's understanding and experiences of silence is placed at the center for achieving a sense of freedom, resistance and liberation.

For instance, during the Sunday worship service, the predominantly female laity has no formal channel to raise their concerns, except through learned silence as a powerful symbol for both submission and for resistance. I am well aware of the fact that depending on the highly political decision as to how one conducts the study and/or construct the reality, "churched" Korean American women's learned silence may signify internalized submission or self-conscious expression of resistance. Listening to how "churched" Korean American women speak about their own silence, however, has led me to conclude that their learned silence does not necessarily signify passivity or submission, but a form of resistance. For instance, as a woman in her late thirties said, "Sometimes it's better not to verbalize what I really feel and think. In that way [i.e., through silence], I can do whatever I choose to do without unnecessary arguments and headaches." Another woman in her late fifties offered more of a theological grounding for her learned silence: "[e]ven in the doctrine of Trinity, the quiet power of the Holy Spirit plays an essential role of a mediator between God the Father and Christ the Son." Within the context of the Korean American church, then, silence is not to be interpreted solely as manifested subordination. For "silence as a will not to say or a will to unsay and as a language of its own"[23] has been understood and utilized by "churched" Korean American women as a powerful strategy for resistance.

Furthermore, in their seemingly docile silence, "churched" Korean American women nevertheless can learn to speak resistance in their own ways. They can express their deeply felt concerns through controlling their amounts of pledge to the church. Their very attendance at the church can also be utilized politically as a last resort to resist the minister's covert dominance over them. One woman in her mid forties told me: "We [the women in the church] don't have much power in the church. But no one, not even the minister, can take away the power to withdraw from attending the church from us." In short, cultivating learned silence through knowing what not to say and when to keep quiet is often understood as a necessary growing experience for most "churched" Korean American women. One women described what she means by "maturity" and "growing up as a woman" in the church:

Interviewee: "I hate some women in the church when they say 'I can't do this and that because I am a woman.' I think you just waste time asking men to do things for you. As you grow up, as a woman, you just have to know what to do."

Interviewer: "What do you mean? What are the things that women are supposed to know, you think?"

Interviewee: "As women, we are supposed to know when to keep quiet and when not to say anything."

Interviewer: "How do we know when to keep silent?"

Interviewee: (Looking at the interviewer with a puzzling smile) "You know. I'm sure you do. It [i.e., the knowledge] comes to us as naturally as menstruation."

Thus through their explicit display of subjugation by silence and submission, "churched" Korean American women have also learned to hold on the "good" that lies in playing the traditionally expected gender roles. Rather ironically then, through their engineering of learned silence and embracing of traditional gender language and roles, "churched" Korean American women can experience both expected and unexpected rewards in their everyday lives. Furthermore, when "churched" Korean American women have experienced a certain social status and power through relationship to a successful and/or respected man over a good part of their lives, there is little reason for them to give up these traditional roles, especially without alternative avenues for achieving status and power in the U.S. Hence, when all is said and done, the "churched" Korean American women in my study pay little heed to the "women's freedom and liberation" talk of feminism of the dominant culture. In "this reversed world of human relationship in America," to borrow a "churched" woman's expression, the traditional gender roles and role expectations offer "churched" Korean American women alternative ways to be women.

If it is the case that "churched" Korean American women cultivate learned silence not merely as an act of submission, but also as a form of resistance and survival strategy, then the claim that "breaking the silence" by the oppressed as the unquestionable key to liberation needs to be reexamined. The most viable survival and empowerment strategies of "churched" Korean American women must be understood in their own terms rather than through some presumably universal criterion for liberation. Perhaps not all attempts at liberation through micromanipulation are equally empowering, but they first must be understood in their own setting and evaluated within that context. The prominent African American woman author, Alice Walker, writes in her much celebrated book, *The Color Purple*, that "it pisses God off if you walk by the color purple in a field somewhere and don't notice it."[24] And I dare say, I have seen the field of color purple even in the context of the Korean American church.

Within this highly contradictory context of the Korean American church, my search was to elucidate various ways in which "churched" Korean American women find a sense of "home" (if they ever find it at all), in an institution within which their race-ethnicity is valued but their gender is devalued. What I learned from/with other "churched" Korean American women through conducting this study points to a clearly shared reality that they do not readily find a sense of "home" in their church; instead, through constant struggles they make a home for themselves. Together they strive to make a home mainly by utilizing "micromanipulative" survival skills and transmitting "hidden transcripts" from one woman to another, and one generation to the next. By refusing to be paralyzed by various forms of domination in their lives, they struggle to give meaning and names to self-identities and to dream of a better "home" for their U.S. born and raised descendants.

My study also points to the much neglected liberatory aspects of the Korean American church when women's experiences and self-understandings are placed at the center of the inquiry. Hence, the study reminds us about the importance of avoiding either/or construction of reality. Both material and ideological dimensions intersect to produce both gender and racial and ethnic identification. The coercive and voluntaristic aspects of gender/racial-ethnic systems do not function as polar opposites either. Rather, they operate fluidly and complexly along the various intersection of everyday life so that "churched" Korean American women produce their gender, racial-ethnic and religious identities in variable and complex ways from one life circumstance or social situation to another. Furthermore, "churched" Korean American women, as active social agents, have reaffirmed my own speculations about the hyphenated identities which reject neither the culture left behind nor the pressure to conform to the newly transplanted culture. The oppressive and liberatory aspects of participating in the church life do not function as polar opposites for "churched" Korean American women either. Rather they operate intricately and often simultaneously along various dimensions of everyday life. "churched" Korean American women's lives are not

played out as either victims of patriarchy or liberators from various oppressive systems, but as both. The "both-and" focus enables us to comprehend the richness and complexity of situated lives and thereby to do them justice.

Notes

1. This work was first presented at the "Women and Religion" session of the American Academy of Religion in 1992. The larger research project which this article is based on will be published as an Academy Series, "The Bridge-makers and Cross-bearers: Korean American Women and the Church" by the Scholar's Press, 1996 (forthcoming).

2. From the mid-1980s, the formula was revised in order to account for schisms producing a splitting/growing number of Korean Americans churches: the number of Korean Americans churches multiply by 380 or 400 (New York : The Christian Academy of New York, 1988); Y. Kim, "Church Growth: The Development of the Korean Church in America," Ph.D. dissertation, California Graduate School of Theology, 1990.

3. Jong Young Lee, "On Marginality: Toward an Asian American Theology," an unpublished presentation at the 1991 Annual Meetings of the American Academy of Religion in Kansas City, Kansas; Pyong Gap Min, "The Korean American family," in *Ethnic Families in America: Patterns and Variations*, 3rd edition, edited by Charles H. Mindel, et al. (New York: Elasevier, 1983); Eui Hang Shin and Hyun Park, "An Analysis of Causes of Schism in Ethnic Churches: the Case of Korean Americans Churches" *Sociological Analysis: A Journal of the Sociology of Religion* 49:3 (Fall 1988), 234–253.

4. Patricia Bell Scott and Gloria T. Hull, *Black Women in America: Social Science Perspectives* (Chicago: University of Chicago Press, 1989) discussed comparable problems for African American women; when race is discussed, audiences assume male gender, and when women are discussed, audiences assume white women.

5. Kyong-Suk Cho, "Korean Immigrants in Greham, Oregon: Community Life and Social Adjustment," an unpublished master's thesis, University of Oregon, 1963; Bong-youn Cho, "Korean Religions and Cultural Activities in the U.S.," in *Koreans in America* (Chicago: Nelson Hall Press); Dae Gee Kim, *Major Factors Conditioning the Acculturation of Korean Americans with Respect to the Presbyterian in America and Its Ministry*, a Ph.D. in Missionology dissertation, Fuller Theological Seminary, 1985; Ilsoo Kim, *New Urban Immigrants: The Korean Community in New York* (Princeton: Princeton University Press, 1981); Won Moo Hurh, *Korean Immigrants in America: A Structural Analysis of Ethnic Confinement and Adhesive Adaptation* (Teaneck: Fairleigh Dickenson University Press, 1981); Shin and Park, "An Analysis of Causes of Schism in Ethnic Churches: the Case of Korean Americans Churches," *Sociological Analysis: A Journal of the Sociology of Religion* 49:3 (Fall 1988), 234–253; David Kwan-sum Suh, *Korea Kaleidoscope: Oral Histories* (Sierra Mission Area, California: The Korean Oral History Project, United Presbyterian Church, 1983; Paul T. Kim, *Church Growth: The Development of the Korean Church in America*, Ph.D. dissertation, California Graduate School of Theology, 1984); Warren Y. Kim, *Koreans in America*, Seoul: Po Chin Chai, 1971; Euiyoung Yu, "Korean Communities in America: Past, Present and Future," in *Amerasia Journal* 10(1983), 23–52.

6. Patricia Hill Collins, "Learning from the Outsider Within: The Sociological Significance of Black Femi-

nist Thought," in *Social Problems* 33:6 (114–32), December 1986; and ___, *Black Feminist Thought: Knowledge, Consciousness, the Politics of Empowerment*, Perspectives on Gender (Boston: Unwin Hyman, 1990).

7. Mitsuya Yamada, "The Cult of 'Perfect' Language: Censorship by Class, Gender and Race," a paper discussed at the Asian American Women's meeting in Englewood, New Jersey, September 1992.

8. Judith Cook and Mary Margaret Fonow, "Knowledge and Women's Interests: Issues of Epistemology and Methodology in Feminist Sociological Research," *Sociological Inquiry* 56, 1 (Winter 1986), 2–29; ___, eds., *Beyond Methodology: Feminist Scholarship as Lived Research,* (Bloomington: Indianapolis: Indianapolis University Press, 1991); Helen Roberts, ed., *Doing Feminist Research* (London: Routledge & Kegan Paul, 1981); Sarah Matthews, "Rethinking Sociology through a Feminist Perspective," *The American Sociologist* 17 (1982), 29–35.

9. Dale Spencer, *Man Made Language* (London and Boston: Routledge and Kegan Paul, 1985); Marjorie DeVault, "Talking and Listening from Women's Standpoint: Feminist Strategies for Interviewing and Analysis," *Social Problems* 37:1 (February, 1990); Clifford Greetz, *The Interpretation of Culture* (New York: Basic Books Inc., 1973).

10. DeVault, 97.

11. The pseudonym, Kyo-whe, is a Korean word for the church.

12. Prior to making a decision about the research site, I was confronted by several ethical and methodological concerns. Although I did not accept the position of DCE four years ago from the Kyo-whe as an intentional "entree into the field" (see Jorgensen, 1989; especially the section on "Entree Strategies"), I felt that my commitment toward the church and a sense of personal integrity in dealing with various relationships within the church was at stake. I struggled with lingering questions—Would the people perceive me as an opportunist, who uses/abuses human relationships in order to collect "data"? Would my relationships with people change because of my desire to do a case study of them? To what extent should I be overt/covert about the intentions, goals, and analyses of the study with the people? To what degree am I committed to being accountable to the people whom I study? Am I not living off less privileged people in order to gain access to the system of the more powerful? Would this study make any contribution(s) to the people, to the Korean Americans church, and to the larger community as a whole? What about the question of "objectivity" in this study? I decided to pursue the study largely based on two reasons: 1) my stance of "outsider within" (Collins, 1986, 1991) can provide a point of reference for understanding (*Verstehen* in the Weberian sense) the reality that is uncertain and unfamiliar from an outsider's perspective; and 2) most of my relationships with members of the Kyo-whe are built on solidarity from our commonly shared struggles as hyphenated people living in the U.S., and that basic trust between "field-workers and the hosts" (Wax, 1980:281) can enrich qualities of the data.

13. From an "insider's" perspective, perceiving Korean Americans as a "new immigrant" group is problematic. Although the "noticeable" number of Korean immigrants to the U.S. occurred after the 1965 Immigration Act, and the racial-ethnic category of "Korean" appeared for the first time in the U.S. Census in 1970, Korean Americans' history goes back to the year 1903. Hence, Korean Americans who define the U.S. as their "homeland" need to reclaim their sense of "roots" from a distorted American history.

14. According to an article, "Methodists Keep Ministers Moving" in *The Atlanta Constitution,* June 30, 1990, the average stay of a Methodist minister at a church is three to four years.'

15. Joan Acker, "Hierarchies, Jobs, Bodies: a Theory of Gendered Organizations," *Gender and Society* 4:2 (June 1990).

16. Katie G. Cannon, *Black Women Ethics* (Atlanta: Scholars Press, 1988); Mary Daly, *The Church and the Second Sex* (Boston: Beacon Press, 1968); ___, *Beyond God the Father: Toward a Philosophy of Women's Liberation* (Boston: Beacon Press, 1973); Carter Heyward, "The Power of God-with-us," *The Christian Century,* March 14, 1990; Meredith B. McGuirre, *Religion: The Social Context,* (Belmont, California: Wadsworth Publishing Company, 1981).

17. Rosemary Radford Reuther, *Sexism and God-talk: Toward A Feminist Theology* (Boston: Beacon Press, 1983); Pamela Dickey Young, *Feminist Theology/Christian Theology* (Minneapolis: Fortress Press, 1990).

18. Greetz, 89.

19. Robert Wuthnow, *The Reconstruction of American Religion: Society and Faith Since World War II* (Princeton: Princeton University Press, 1988).

20. Jean Lipman-Blueman, *Gender Roles and Power* (Englewood Cliffs: Prentice-Hall, Inc., 1984).

21. Whereas socially legitimate and more visible control by the dominant group(s) is called "macro-manipulation."

22. James C. Scott, *Domination and the Arts of Resistance: Hidden Transcripts* (New Haven and London: Yale University Press, 1990), 164.

23. Trinh, T. Minh-ha, "Commitment from the Mirror-Writing Box," *Making Face, Making Soul: Creative and Critical Perspectives by Women of Color,* Gloria Anzaldua, ed. (San Francisco: an Aunt Lute Foundation Book, 1990), 373.

24. Alice Walker, *The Color Purple* (New York: Washington Square Press, 1982), 178.

Unit 5

Key Points to Consider

❖ Why do you think *Roe v. Wade* is still a heated political topic?

❖ Do you think the charges against Lieutenant Kelly Flinn were enforced because of her gender? Defend your answer.

❖ How can female members of Congress make themselves less vulnerable to gender communication differences?

 **Links** | **www.dushkin.com/online/**

These sites are annotated on pages 4 and 5.

The issues that engage women politically and publicly today belie the notions that women and men experience all issues in the same way, as human ones, or that only domestic issues take up women's political time. Nowhere is this more evident than in issues of public safety, security, and sexuality.

The physical vulnerability and powerlessness of women subjects them to violence and aggression, physical oppression, and exploitation. But what happens in formal public organizations when women voice their concerns over these issues and others regarding reproduction and the political and legal rules of the game? Too often very little happens, in large measure because women are not very numerous in formal public institutions.

Public institutions, regardless of design, often result in the virtual exclusion or marginalization of women from most formal political decision making. The result of this situation is that the area existing between state and family is usually politically gray, thus ignored in conventional discussions and in social science research. Overall, the future of women's public activism—in formal politics and in the politics of everyday life—rests on the construction of the family, civic society, and the economy. Activism very often encounters extremely long odds of winning. When the "fight" is successful, however, women find it gratifying, difficult, surprising, and worthwhile, all at the same time.

This unit is a collection of articles describing women as activists, their achievements and pitfalls, and the laws designed to protect them because they are often physically and mentally vulnerable. The first article in unit 5 examines the most heated political issue today. Carol Sanger, Suzanne Poppema, and Frances Kissling discuss *Roe v. Wade* in terms of its historic significance and efforts to repeal it. The role of women in political activism is featured in "Women's Work" by Stuart Miller, who examines several female environmental activist groups, and "Women in Power: From Tokenism to

Critical Mass," by Jane Jaquette, who discusses the growing participation and representation of women in politics globally. Elizabeth Christiansen, in "Women and War," describes how congresswomen are "faced down" by male language during congressional meetings. Congressmen minimize women's voices in favor of "bigger ideas" involved with war. The last article provides a historical overview of the legal evolution of sexual harassment. Robert Lee Jr. and Paul Greenlaw examine court decisions and guidelines on sexual harassment.

Political Science, Law, and Criminal Justice; Public Policy and Administration

The Future of
ROE V. WADE

TWENTY-FIVE YEARS AGO, on January 22, 1973, in ruling that women have the legal right to end a pregnancy, the United States Supreme Court acknowledged a woman's inalienable right to make decisions about her own body. In the years since then, an increasingly fundamentalist, vocal, and violent antiabortion movement, in the company of a right-leaning Congress, has, brick by brick, law by law, hacked away at this most basic right. Abortion clinics are being bombed, freedoms are being abridged, and women's right to easily accessible, safe, and legal abortion is constantly being undermined. Where are we going? That's the question *Ms.* posed to three women who stand on the front lines of choice.

LEGAL

By Carol Sanger

IN 1973, THE SUPREME COURT **held that a constitutionally protected right of privacy was "broad enough to encompass a woman's decision whether or not to terminate her pregnancy." Those words transformed abortion from a criminal act to a medical procedure. States could no longer arrest doctors for performing abortions or women for receiving them. *Roe* v. *Wade* established that prior to fetal viability, states could regulate the procedure only in the interests of maternal health.**

Twenty-five years and about 35 million legal abortions later, what is the status of a woman's right to choose to end an unwanted pregnancy?

The answer is a complicated mix of law and politics, geography and science, wealth and age. *Roe*, it turned out, was only the starting point, as some states began a ferocious campaign to regulate abortion as close to the permissible line as possible. Many of these regulations, such as spousal consent and mandatory hospitalization, were clearly aimed at deterrence, not health, and were held to be unconstitutional.

But other big restrictions, such as the elimination of Medicaid funding and the requirement of parental consent for pregnant teenagers, were upheld. Each state now gets to decide if abortion will be among the health care services provided to its poorer citizens. And teenagers in many states must go before judges for permission if they can't or won't get their parents' approval. The game plan of abortion opponents was clear: keep the pressure up in state legislatures while waiting for the deaths or resignations of the *Roe* majority on the Court.

By 1992, that shift had occurred. Six of the seven justices who voted for *Roe* were gone, replaced by several justices, including Sandra Day O'Connor, Anthony Kennedy, and David Souter, who had expressed opposition to the reasoning of *Roe* before their appointments. Attention was therefore riveted on *Planned Parenthood of Southeastern Pennsylvania* v. *Casey*. *Casey* was a challenge to Pennsylvania's Abortion Control Act, which required a 24-hour waiting period, propagandistic disclosure materials, and spousal notification before every abortion. But more than selective restrictions were at stake. Many feared the court would take the opportunity to overrule *Roe* altogether. But by a 5-4 vote (the majority included O'Connor, Kennedy, and Souter) it confirmed *Roe*'s essential holding: that a woman's right to choose an abortion before fetal viability is protected by the Constitution.

As important as the ruling was its rationale. As O'Connor, Kennedy, and Souter explained in their joint opinion, while they might not have voted for *Roe* in 1973, they agreed with the long-standing judicial principle that the Court should honor its own previous decisions: "Only the most convincing justi-

For the time being, the basic right to choose an abortion is less precarious than many had feared. That basic right, however, remains a fairly stripped-down model.

fication ... could suffice to demonstrate that a later decision overruling the first was anything but a surrender to political pressure."

The Court found no such justification for overturning *Roe*. On the contrary, it noted the increased significance of the right to abortion: "[F]or two decades of economic and social developments, people have organized intimate relationships and made choices that define their views of themselves and their places in society, in reliance on the availability of abortion in the event that contraception should fail." For the time being, then, the basic right to choose an abortion is less precarious than many had feared.

That basic right, however, remains a fairly stripped-down model. *Casey* allows states to regulate abortion in all sorts of ways so long as the restrictions do not "unduly burden" the decision to abort. Thus, despite their intentionally burdensome practical and psychological effects, Pennsylvania's waiting pe-

riods and mandatory disclosure materials were not considered undue burdens. Only spousal notification was.

Moreover, it is not the survival of the right to abortion—however constrained—but the climate in which abortion decisions are made and implemented that tells the more complete post-*Casey* story. Abortion is not a decision most women take lightly, as they consider the life-altering changes wrought by becoming a mother or by having another child, and confront the moral complexities of terminating a pregnancy. Yet abortion opponents have created a culture of condemnation in which doctors are "killers" and women who seek abortion are labeled murderers, plain and simple.

One of the more diabolical accomplishments of the anti-abortion movement has been to force a quarter-century of our energies into defending *Roe*. This dedication of political, advocacy, and personal resources to securing reproductive freedom has been absolutely necessary. Such freedom is key to women's ability to have and to make choices in all other areas of life.

So, for all its infirmities, *Casey* is a partial reprieve from this long struggle. It buys us some time. This is where politics comes into play. We might think about moving some energies from courts to legislatures, where such wrong-headed—if constitutional—burdens as notification and funding restrictions are enacted. We might also reacquaint our legislators with the many nonprocreative issues that contribute to the quality of women's lives, such as health and child care, pay equity, freedom from workplace discrimination, and so on. Indeed, progress on these economic and social fronts would have a feedback effect and would remove at least some of the factors women take into account when contemplating abortion.

In the end, the abortion question is likely to be decided by medical technology, not judicial commitment to precedent or progressive trends within state legislatures. It is hardly futuristic to imagine that drugs will transform abortion into a private matter between a pregnant woman and her pharmacist. Clinic protesters will just have to pack up.

Until then, vigilance, energy, and compassion are still in order. But perhaps we have at long last begun to row downstream toward the secure waters of choice.

Carol Sanger, a professor of law at Columbia University, specializes in family, gender, and sexual harassment issues.

MEDICAL

By Dr. Suzanne T. Poppema

THIS IS AN EXCITING TIME for practitioners of abortion, even as we face continued threats from antiabortion extremists. Advances in abortion technologies have improved women's health tremendously since *Roe* v. *Wade*.

Before *Roe*, all abortion practice was clandestine, so doctors could get little or no training in how to perform abortions. After legislation, abortion providers, like other health care workers, were able to share information, discuss difficult cases, and help one another perfect techniques to reduce complications and make the procedure less traumatic. New instruments have made it much gentler on the woman's cervix and uterus, and serious complications are exceedingly rare. The risk of death and major injury from abortion has shown a steady and steep decline over the last 25 years.

We are now benefiting from one of the most exciting advances in abortion technology: the use of medications instead of surgery. We are currently using two medications that are very effective in terminating early pregnancies: mifepristone and methotrexate. Mifepristone is a progesterone antagonist that makes the uterus unable to sustain the implanted embryo. When followed in two days with a drug called misoprostol, mifepristone causes the uterus to expel the embryo and pla-

> # Globally, a woman dies every seven minutes from complications of an illegal abortion. If nonsurgical medical abortions were made available to women everywhere, millions of lives would be saved.

centa quickly and efficiently. Methotrexate is equally effective, though the time to completion of the abortion is a little longer.

The use of these drugs has the potential to revolutionize abortion care all over the world. Globally, a woman dies every seven minutes from complications of an illegal abortion. If non-surgical medical abortions were made available to women everywhere, millions of lives would be saved. In the United States, where surgical abortion is safer than carrying a pregnancy to term, the advent of medical abortion may not be a lifesaver, but its potential for improving access to abortion for women is virtually incalculable. There is no need for expensive equipment. The practitioner must be trained in how to recognize the bleeding problems that can arise from an incomplete emptying of the uterus, or from an ectopic pregnancy. With more precautions able to provide abortions, women will have a much greater level of privacy, less need to travel great distances for an abortion, and the opportunity for their primary care practitioner to take care of them.

The advent of ultrasound in clinics has also allowed us to offer a surgical abortion as early as four and a half weeks from the last menstrual period. We have good epidemiological evidence that the risks of abortion procedures rise with the length of gestation, so providing abortions earlier makes medical sense.

The other great "advance" of note is the use of emergency contraception. I use the word advance judiciously, since this technique has been known for the last 20 years, but only recently has it been widely taught. If a woman has unprotected intercourse at a time in her cycle when she is at risk for pregnancy, she can prevent a pregnancy 75 percent of the time by taking birth control pills at high doses within 72 hours of that unprotected intercourse. This regimen is simple, effective, and relatively inexpensive. If everyone at risk knew about this method of contraception, we could reduce unintended pregnancies by 50 percent.

Yet, despite the fact that technologically, we are far ahead of where we were 25 years ago, many of the women who seek abortion services are more frightened and shamed by their decision. Women come to our clinics with the most egregious misinformation fed to them by the antiabortion forces and are surprised that we are competent professionals in clean, well-decorated clinics. They are often shocked that a surgical abortion is not a horrifyingly painful experience. It seems such a travesty that at a time when, from a medical perspective, abortion is easier and safer than ever, women feel worse than ever about needing our service. Most women who have abortions heal well both physically and emotionally, but we must not undervalue the depth of personal soul-searching that a woman typically goes through when faced with an unintended pregnancy.

One of the many tragedies about the possible passage of the so-called partial-birth abortion ban is the chilling effect it may have on the development of new techniques in abortion care. Versions of what is known today as intact D&E have been used for over 100 years. The technique was developed by doctors in order to diminish the potential for damage to the women's uterus by reducing instrumentation. This method also allowed for an intact fetus for the woman to see, if she felt a need to in order to grieve its loss, and it allowed for more accurate genetic studies in some cases. If legislators continue to seek to intrude upon the patient-doctor relationship, our ability and willingness to try new technologies will be diminished.

In 1997 there were more bombings of abortion clinics than in any year since 1984. There were also nine arsons and one attempted murder of an abortion provider. Clinics are finding it impossible to rent space from frightened landlords; service people of all kinds are afraid to come to do work in abortion clinics. Medical schools are reluctant to teach abortion techniques and other reproductive health curricula, and physicians are afraid to provide this service for their patients. As long as the antiabortion movement continues to perpetrate violence against providers, women's access to services will be severely limited.

So while we can enter the next millennium knowing that we have made tremendous advances in improving abortion care for women, our challenge now is to ensure that women can have access to this care, that they have access to the information they need to prevent unintended pregnancies, and that their physicians have the freedom to continue their work.

Dr. Suzanne T. Poppema is the president-elect of the National Abortion Federation, the medical director of Aurora Medical Services in Seattle, and the coauthor of "Why I Am an Abortion Doctor" *(Prometheus Books).*

POLITICAL

By Frances Kissling

WORKING FOR ABORTION RIGHTS 25 years after *Roe* v. *Wade* is nothing if not challenging. While *Roe* was less than perfect, it was still a stunning answer to the long-standing question, when regarding reproduction, of "who decides?" The Court was clear: neither the church nor the state can say whether a pregnancy is to be brought to term or terminated. Making that decision is a right, and it belongs to women. Moreover, the state must have a pretty compelling reason to interfere with that right.

What a difference 25 years make. In those first years after Roe, Medicaid paid for poor women's abortions; adolescents were treated as autonomous persons who got to make their own decisions; abortion providers were worried about too many competitors, not the cost of a bullet-proof vest; antiabortionists were almost all Catholic; and the Moral Majority was not even a glimmer in Jerry Falwell's eye. *Roe* was issued during a liberal, civil rights, affirmative action era. The Pill was generally seen as a good thing, and human sexuality was beginning to be seen as related to pleasure, love, commitment, and relationship—not only or always in marriage or for procreation. The field of bioethics was virtually unknown. The

> The movement and the president spent enormous moral and financial capital on protecting one method of late-term abortion for a few thousand women while hundreds of thousands can't use federal funds for abortions.

first test-tube baby was not yet conceived. Adoption was thought of as a way to find parents for needy children, not children for needy couples.

Now, abortion is still a right, but it can be and is heavily regulated. No one who depends on the federal government for health care can get her abortion paid for, unless her life is in danger or the pregnancy is a result of rape or incest. Not many doctors do or are trained to do abortions. Clinics are invaded by antiabortion crusaders and some are closed down. Adolescents in many states need parental consent, sometimes from both parents. Abortion politics skews all sorts of ethical issues and results in things like a ban, which existed during the Reagan and Bush era, on federally funded research on the use of tissue from aborted fetuses to help cure cancer, Parkinson's disease, and other serious conditions. It seems that most of the gutsy women on TV and the Op-Ed pages are neocons. Congress is decidedly conservative, and so is the mood of the country. The nation debates school uniforms, not schools. A Democratic president ends entitlements for the poor under the banner of "welfare reform." Antiabortionists now claim they want to protect women's health by banning both very early and very late-term abortions. We don't talk about rights, we talk about responsibility.

One thing has not changed. People are still deeply divided about abortion. They want it to be legal, but they want it to be taken seriously. And we, the pro-choice movement, still haven't convinced them that we do. What, I ask myself after 27 years of activism and deep reflection about abortion, is one to do? What in the abortion rights field needs to stay, change, or go? What are the strategies that will sustain us and finally make the best vision of *Roe* a reality? Here are some thoughts.

1. Revitalize the movement. The pro-choice movement needs new leaders. In fact, it needs leaders, period. The movement hasn't been as inclusive as it should be of people of color or of young people. (I will not dignify this failure by naming all the things we all know need to be done to make this a reality.)

2. Move issues of funding and access to the top of our priority list. The movement and the president spent enormous moral and financial capital on protecting one method of late-term abortion for a few thousand women. But when it comes to the hundreds of thousands of women, from Medicaid recipients to women serving in the military, who can't use federal funds for abortions, the president and pro-choice leaders have taken no action.

3. Get outside the Beltway. Part of the reason for #2, above, is that too many of us determine our agenda on the basis of vote counts, not principles. Let's fight for what we believe in, even if we don't think we can win for ten years or so.

4. Keep a feminist core. No need to get extreme. Still, most pro-choice activists got into abortion rights because we believed in feminism. But we've gradually reframed our arguments in terms of reproductive "health" instead of reproductive "rights." In debates over "partial-birth" abortion, we should stop focusing on doctors' rights and put women's rights back at the center of our arguments. Sometimes the Supreme Court justices sound more feminist than we do. In its 1992 decision in *Planned Parenthood* v. *Casey*, for example, the Court affirmed the link between a woman's freedom and her right to reproductive choice. "The ability of women to participate equally in the economic and social life of the Nation has been facilitated by their ability to control their reproductive lives," the justices wrote.

5. Take abortion seriously. It's not just a political issue, it's a moral one. There are a lot of tough questions related to abortion. People want to know what we think and where we stand. Don't be afraid to admit to doubt. Don't be afraid to ask and talk about the tough questions: Does the fetus have value? Are all abortions morally correct decisions? Are late-term abortions different from earlier abortions?

6. Read. Get to know the writing of some of the people who laid the groundwork for a solid pro-choice position. Start with *Our Right to Choose* by Beverly Harrison, *Abortion and a Woman's Choice* by Rosalind Petchesky, and *Abortion and the Politics of Motherhood* by Kristin Luker. It will help clarify your own thinking, and it will help you keep your facts straight.

7. Have and express a vision about the kind of world you want to live in and how abortion fits into it. Abortion is never a single issue. It is a complex tapestry of all the things we believe about race, class, gender, and justice. It is also about sexuality, relationships, and love. If you want people to follow you, give them vision.

Frances Kissling is president of Catholics for a Free Choice.

The long flight home

Women served—and died—in WWII. Now they are remembered

BY ANN DARR

We were at war. The attack had come from a direction we weren't looking. Of course, old Army Gen. Billy Mitchell had predicted back in the 1920s that someday the Japanese would fly over Pearl Harbor and bomb it to smithereens. But nobody believed him. He was even cashiered out of the Army.

My young husband had already signed up to serve in the Navy when he finished his medical training at New

killed in an auto crash when I was 3, I was told I could see her again in heaven. The only way I knew to get there was to fly. The childhood myth followed me and, when the Civilian Pilot Training program course began at the University of Iowa, I applied—one woman in a class of 10. I got my private pilot's license.

It was 1943 before I knew how I could use it to help the war effort. It may surprise some people today, but many of us went into the service for rea-

to try. My college students today have no concept of the uncertainty we lived with in the 1940s. Bulletins from the South Pacific registered loss after loss. We could not take it for granted that we would win World War II.

In 1943, my husband outfitted a destroyer and went to the South Pacific as ship's doc. I was on my way to Sweetwater, Texas, on a train filled with troops, to begin my pilot training with the Women's Air Force Service Pilots, the WASPs.

Again and again I have met people who lived through WWII and didn't know we existed. "Female pilots in WWII? I thought all the women were Riveter Rosies." Or I hear, "So the Army taught you to fly?" No: All the women who went into the flying service had to *know* how to fly. The training was for precision flying in Air Force planes.

Army Air Forces Gen. H. H. "Hap" Arnold encouraged Jacqueline Cochran to go to England to see how the British were using female pilots. Cochran headed the Army Air Forces flying-

ANN DARR   She had flying in her blood, and in 1943 she joined the Women's Air Force Service Pilots. Darr is the author of *Flying the Zuni Mountains* and seven other books.

York's Bellevue Hospital Center. His uncle had been an admiral in WWI. I had a job at NBC Radio writing copy for *The Woman of Tomorrow,* a half-hour daily program on fashion, food, books, and "how to keep your husband happy." More and more, I was using news bulletins about stories of courage and escape in Europe, even movements of the German war machine. We urged women to save sugar, tinfoil, gasoline—anything for the European war effort.

Our show featured a guest interview, often on current events. Once I was filling in on the air and interviewed Clarence Taylor of Taylor-craft Aviation. Growing excited as we talked, I strayed from the written page (all scripts had to be approved by the "continuity department"). I got a throat-cutting gesture from the production booth.

But flying was in my blood. I was raised in Iowa, a prairie child: All we had was the sky. After my mother was

sons both patriotic and humane. Human beings were being destroyed purposely and methodically. Maybe it was naive to think we could make a difference. But somebody had to stop Hitler's march across Europe. It was up to Americans

CATHERINE L. BOWIE   In 1942, she enlisted in the Women's Army Auxiliary Corps. She had divorced her husband and didn't want to go back to live with her father. The armed services were segregated by race, but Bowie never regretted her decision: "In spite of things that people say, I am still an American, and that is what you have to remember. And if you don't feel like you can help protect [your country] and defend it in spite of things, who is going to do it for you?" Bowie spent 22 years in the military, first on KP, cleaning out garbage cans in Fort Des Moines, Iowa. But she went on to duty as an office manager in China and Japan.

From *U.S. News & World Report,* November 17, 1997, pp. 66-69. © November 17, 1997 by U.S. News & World Report. Reprinted by permission.

training program for women pilots with a private license but who had fewer than 500 hours. Sweetwater's Avenger Field was our base. Over the gate was the figure of Fifinella, the flying gremlin, in her red dress, gold helmet, and blue wings, that Walt Disney drew for us—

PEARL V. SPICKNALL
Born in 1899, she was typing letters for the War Department when World War II began. By 1944 she decided to contribute more to the war effort, so she stopped by a local recruitment office to ask how she might be of use. "I wanted to be in the military service like my brother was in World War I—to do something," she says. The Army put her through basic training, then sent her to New Guinea and the Philippines to act as a personal secretary to generals in combat zones. Spicknall is one of 93 female vets living at the U.S. Soldiers' and Airmen's Home in Washington, D.C.

our mascot to ward off gremlins and sabotage. She was the shoulder patch on our flight suits. Avenger, the only all-female base in U.S. history, was fondly called Cochran's Convent.

Twenty-five thousand women applied for the training; 1,830 were accepted after rigorous testing; 1,074 of us won our wings. We flew more than 60 million miles in every type of plane, from P-51 fighters (called pursuits back then) to the B-29 Superfortress. The first women checked out in that huge ship had a specific mission: Male pilots at one base balked at flying because of B-29 "bugs." When a crew of women stepped down from that B-29, the commandant had no more trouble with male pilots. "Even women" could fly it.

"Didn't you hate being used as a guinea pig?" one of the women was asked. "To fly the B-29, I'd be any kind of pig."

At Avenger we were housed in barracks, rose to reveille, marched to the mess hall and flight line, were required to salute Army officers. We needed permission to leave the base and had a strict return time. Taps at 10. We were treated as Air Forces' trainees, with a packed schedule of ground school, phys ed, flight training with civilian instructors—and were checked out at the end of each phase by Army personnel. These were high-stress times. Coming back to our bay in the evening and finding an empty bed was jolting. Wash-out time—a bay-

mate in her civvies, packing her suitcase for home. Or finding an empty cot and the ambulance crash siren still echoing in our ears. One girl whose plane went into an inverted spin survived her jump to learn of the cut rudder cable, leaving just enough for a pilot to get off the ground. Sabotage. By whom?

Graduation from Avenger meant assignments all over the country. Our jobs were aerial dishwashery, as we called them. WASPs ferried thousands of planes from factories to bases or to ports to be shipped overseas. We tested planes, flew simulated strafing and smoking missions, searchlight tracking and mountain mapping. Any flying job that needed doing.

I tested planes at the advanced training base in Stockton, Calif., and once flew with a flock of UC-78s with wind-damaged wings back to the factory in Texas to have them repaired. We flew into the most violent windstorm I have ever tried to avoid.

My next assignment was towing targets at the gunnery school at Las Vegas, flying B-26s while B-17s flew beside us, firing live ammunition at the sleeve

we towed. After a target run, we dropped the sleeve on the desert. The ammo had been dipped in colored wax, and the rim of the holes showed which gunner had hit the target. We used those holey red, blue, green, yellow targets for bedspreads, curtains, whatever.

We understood when we were recruited that Civil Service would provide our pay until the bill in Congress militarizing us was passed. Hap Arnold was on our side and had all the clout needed to get the bill through. Little did we know.

We were even sent to Orlando, Fla., to officers' training school, where we learned military law, military history, how to protect ourselves in military maneuvers. It was there we first heard rumors that we were no longer needed. We knew they were false. How could they do without us?

I will never forget the camaraderie. Friends of my forever. To share the anxieties, aching bones, the effort to do it right. Living close-in, with all the ups and downs.

And I will never forget when a plane crashed in Las Vegas, the male pilot's body was sent home to be buried with honors. The female co-pilot . . . the Army said it was not responsible. The Civil Service said it was not responsible. We took up a collection to send her body home.

Thirty-eight women pilots died serving their country. When Congress took up the bill to militarize WASPs in 1944 we were advised (we heard "ordered") to act like "ladies"—and keep silent. Mistake. Antagonism against women pilots was rampant, fanned by a popular male columnist whose name I have erased. The bill did not pass. The ugly rumors were true. We were to be disbanded.

LORETTA TURNER
She joined the Women's Army Auxiliary Corps in 1944, in part because as a child she'd loved the pilots who flew mail planes over her family's farm, tipping their wings to greet her. She arrived at Wright-Patterson Air Force Base "as green as the grass," but serving as the only woman out of 125 mechanics toughened her up fast. Within five years she became one of the first female air traffic controllers. Her steady nerves during crises led male colleagues to praise her as "one cool SOB."

FRIEDA HELEN SIMON   Born a German Jew, she fled to the United States when Hitler came to power. In 1942, her son, Rudy, joined the Army; she signed up for the Women's Army Auxiliary Corps. He was sent to India, but because she spoke German, Simon was sent to run a hospital kitchen in Battle Creek, Mich., where 100 prisoners of war from Rommel's Army were working. After World War II, the German POWs were sent home, but Simon stayed on at the post until the Korean War ended.

The news arrived in double letters, first one from General Arnold, next from Jacqueline Cochran: Many more soldiers are returning from overseas than had been expected. You have done a fine job, goodbye. On Dec. 20, 1944, before the war was over, we were summarily dismissed. No matter there was still a need for us, doing the flying male pilots scorned or called too dangerous in those worn-out planes. No matter many of us had left jobs we could not go back to. December 20 came and we went. Paying our own way home, of course.

More than 30 years later, when another bill came up in Congress to give us the title of "veteran" retroactively, we ended our silence. WASPs came from all over the country to make our case. Even though the committee chairman said publicly to Bernice Falk Haydu, a former WASP pilot, "I promise you this, young lady, the bill will never leave my committee." When the final vote was taken, we had our place in history. We now had recognition and a burial plot. No GI Bill, no insurance, but we had the name we'd fought for: veteran.

When, in 1987, Brig. Gen. Wilma Vaught began raising funds and hopes for a Women in Military Service for America Memorial, very few dreamed she could do it in 10 years. General Vaught is a determined woman and she vowed to put the memorial in place in time for the remaining WWII veterans to be alive to see it.

She knew, better than we did, I think, what it would mean, how it would feel on this Veterans Day to be remembered—finally. The memorial was dedicated last month in Arlington, Va. Many of us went to the ceremony because we thought we should. What we experienced was a need we didn't know we had. To gather as a bonded group with every body (and soul) there. Flying buddies we hadn't seen for decades. Sons and daughters of mothers who had not lived long enough came to pay their respect, their admiration. More than 30,000 women—and their friends.

We were exhausted physically and emotionally, but we marched across the Potomac from the Lincoln Memorial to *our* memorial with all the energy and flair we could muster. This was our day! This was our night! Recognition for the 1,800,000 women who served or are serving in the military forces of the United States. And when WWI Navy Yeoman Frieda Mae Hardin, now 101, spoke to the crowd, reminding us she couldn't vote when she signed up, saying to the young people, "Go for it!" we were almost ready to serve again.

SEX AND LIES

The strange case of Lieutenant Flinn is over, but in the military the war over women goes on. BY GREGORY L. VISTICA AND EVAN THOMAS

MINOT, N.D., IS A FLAT AND LONELY PLACE. THERE'S not much there, aside from the 150 nuclear-tipped ICBMs buried in the surrounding wheat fields. A young first lieutenant could grow bored and restless, especially if she were the air force's first (and only) female B-52 pilot. Lt. Kelly Flinn believed that dating other pilots would be "unprofessional," so she turned down their advances. Her fellow aviators speculated that the 26-year-old was a lesbian. She drank an occasional beer at Peyton Place, the local pickup bar, but the bartender never saw her there with another man.

She met Marc Zigo at a soccer game. He told her he was a professional soccer player, a navy SEAL and the love of her life. He was none of these; rather, Zigo was a type Kelly Flinn should have recognized from the romance novels she likes to read: an old-fashioned cad. Flinn—who had focused on aeronautical engineering, not boys, after being chosen Outstanding Camper at U.S. Space Camp in Huntsville, Ala., at the age of 12—fell hard. Her affair with Zigo, who happened to be married at the time, might have been forgettable. Bars like Peyton Place fill up every night with servicemen accompanied by women not their wives. Flinn could have been just one more lonely young woman unlucky in love. But she had the misfortune of being a highly visible pilot at a time when the military is cracking down on sex in the ranks.

Technically, Kelly Flinn was charged with adultery—a crime in the military—disobedience and deception. Culturally,

her case became a battle of imagery, with her side casting her as A Woman Wronged. Long profiles in The Washington Post and The New York Times and two interviews on "60 Minutes" made her a heroine, a victim of the loutish male establishment. Flinn warmed to the role. Her family hired a publicist and created a home page on the Internet. By last week, U.S. senators were pressing the air force to "get real," as Republican Majority Leader Trent Lott put it, and grant Flinn an honorable discharge.

At the Pentagon, the generals quietly glowered—but then struck back. "In the end, this is not an issue of adultery," the air force chief of staff, Gen. Ronald Fogleman, lectured a congressional committee. "This is an issue about an officer entrusted to fly nuclear weapons who lied. That's what this is about." Overnight, the newspaper and TV coverage turned ambivalent, pointing out that Flinn had disobeyed orders, a far worse crime in the military than adultery. Watching Fogleman's testimony on C-Span back in Minot, Flinn understood that the game was up. After a few more hours of agonizing, she cut a deal and took a "general discharge," ending the drama.

The trial that America will not see would have been lurid. Criminal investigators had filed reports on Flinn's sexual appetites, helpfully provided by the duplicitous Zigo. But even though there will be no court-martial, Flinn's story is revealing in a different way. It's hard to find a tale that better illustrates the complexities of integrating women into the ranks than the case of Kelly Flinn. Her ordeal exposes the pitfalls of regulating sexual behavior by haphazard enforcement and media-driven morality.

At the U.S. Air Force Academy, from which she graduated in the top 15 percent of her class, Flinn learned not to complain. When a pair of upperclassmen sexually molested her late one night, Flinn, a nice girl from a proper Georgia family, said nothing. She did protest when someone scrawled an obscenity on her dorm-room door—but regretted speaking up after her entire squadron was grounded for the weekend to punish the graffiti artists. Mostly, though, she played along with the establishment. "I was their show girl," she said. With her blond hair bobbed short, she posed for an air force recruiting film. She took air force Secretary Sheila Widnall for a flight, demonstrating the on-board toilet, which had been jokingly modified by her crew with a flowered shower curtain.

She was at once celebrated and resented. Unwilling to date her fellow officers (people of the same rank are allowed to sleep together), she had sex one night with an enlisted man after a wine-and-cheese party at her small bungalow near the base. "Fraternizing" with a superior or a subordinate is forbidden, but the airman Flinn had sex with was not in her chain of command, so her indiscretion seemed relatively minor.

Zigo was different. He was her first real love, the infatuation she had denied herself through years of outmachoing the men and hitting the books. He was handsome and athletic, though he seemed underemployed coaching soccer at the base rec center. He was also married, and even invited Flinn over to dinner with his wife, who is an airman. But he assured Flinn that his marriage was breaking up.

Two weeks after Flinn began seeing Zigo, in July of last year, his wife found some love letters. "I was shocked," Gayla Zigo later wrote. "How could I compete with her? She had power, both as an officer and as an Academy graduate." Gayla Zigo asked her own first sergeant to speak to Flinn. The sergeant, who was also female, warned Flinn that she was risking her career, and advised that she stay away from Airman Zigo's husband.

Flinn says she did—for a little while. But she went back to Zigo, not realizing that the authorities were looking into the romance. The investigation began as a nasty bit of payback. Flinn had encouraged a friend who had been sexually assaulted by another lieutenant to file a complaint. The lieutenant, who was sentenced to nine months in prison for various sexual offenses, got even by telling investigators about Flinn and Zigo. Questioned at the end of November, Flinn lied twice—under oath. She said her relationship with Zigo was "platonic." She believed she had a pact with Zigo to keep their affair secret.

She didn't know Zigo was telling the air force everything. In vivid detail, he described her sexual preferences and method of birth control. He even drew a map of her bedroom, labeled "Kelly's Where It Happened," so the gumshoes could precisely envision the scene of the crime. In December, after his wife confronted him for hitting on yet another woman, Zigo tried to commit suicide by swallowing sleeping pills. Abandoned by his wife, he washed up on Flinn's doorstep. She took him in.

Putting Adultery on Trial

Though Flinn's case brought the issue to the fore, the numbers of prosecutions for adultery in the ranks show that men are more likely to face charges.

	NUMBER OF PERSONNEL	COURTS-MARTIAL INCLUDING ADULTERY	COURTS-MARTIAL INCLUD. ADULTERY, PER 100,000
Army			
men	417,507	79	19
women	69,623	2	2.9
Navy			
men	357,833	15	4.2
women	54,692	0	0
Air-Force			
men	320,182	60	19
women	64,814	7	11

SOURCE: THE PENTAGON, 1996 FIGURES

Flinn knew she was jeopardizing her career. She went to see her commanding officer, Col. Theodore LaPlante. In another time—and perhaps if she had been a man—Flinn might have quietly resolved her problems. Adultery is prohibited in the military because it can create jealousies that undermine unit morale. In the relatively few cases where marital cheating is exposed, commanders have traditionally meted out some punishment—a small fine, say, or a letter of reprimand. Even when the adultery is accompanied by lying or an attempted cover-up, the penalty has commonly stopped short of a full-scale court-martial and dismissal from the service.

Lately, however, the air force has been more strict. Tailhook sent a shock through all branches of the service. In the air force, the number of courts-martial for adultery, while still small, grew from 36 in 1990 to 67 (60 men, 7 women) in 1996. A commander who goes by the book has less freedom these days to handle adultery cases informally.

By all accounts, LaPlante, then the commander of the 23d Bomb Squadron, is a by-the-book officer. A top-rate flier, he is less comfortable handling personnel problems. He was stiff and severe with Flinn when he met her in his office in mid-December. "Don't tell me too much," LaPlante said. "I might be the ultimate hammer." A couple of days later, Flinn was back in his office. This time she was read her rights and received a direct order: stay at least 100 feet away from Marc Zigo. (The air force can't confirm that the first meeting took place.)

Instead, incredibly, she took Zigo home to Georgia to meet her parents. She might have been able to rescue her career if she had obeyed the order, though she would surely have faced some kind of discipline for the adultery and the lies. But as she later said, "I guess I gave up. I figured at least I'd salvage my relationship with Marc."

In late January she discovered she was sleeping with the enemy. Flinn's lawyer discovered that Zigo had ratted to air force investigators back in December. A serious row broke out between the lovers. Zigo, who was on probation in Washington state for assaulting his wife in 1995, became abusive, according to Flinn. She finally called base security to get an MP to escort Zigo from her home.

Flinn's superiors were enraged by her insubordination. The base was buzzing with gossip about her ill-concealed adultery with the husband of an enlisted woman. (Flinn had begun picking up Zigo from work every night at the rec center.) The "hammer" fell on Jan. 28: Flinn was formally charged with adultery (with Zigo), fraternization (with the airman), lying and disobeying an order. If convicted, she faced nine and a half years in prison.

Flinn's family rallied behind her. They hired a top lawyer, Frank Spinner, who had handled many sex cases in military courts, most recently the court-martial of Delmar Simpson, one of the Aberdeen drill sergeants convicted of raping recruits. In turn, Spinner hired a psychologist to produce a sympathetic profile of Flinn. She had been so busy achieving, the psychologist contended, that she had never made time for love. A closet romantic—she is fond of inspirational sayings and books about chivalry—Flinn is also a patriot. Or so she was engagingly described by the reporters for major publications invited to interview her. The Washington Post ended its 3,000-word profile with the scene of her stopping her jeep out of respect when the loudspeakers along Bomber Boulevard at the base crackled with "The Star-Spangled Banner" at evening retreat, the ceremonial lowering of the flag.

The Flinn family insists that it didn't begin the PR wars: the air force had put out a press release detailing the charges against her before the court-martial papers were even filed. But in any case, the Flinns were clearly winning for most of April and May. Senators spoke out. "It's a case of the punishment being greatly disproportionate to the crime," said Sen. Slade Gorton of Washington on the "Today" show.

Flinn's real target in Washington was Sheila Widnall, the first-ever female secretary of the air force. In early May the Flinns thought (mistakenly, it turned out) that Widnall was signaling—through an article in The New York Times—that Flinn should ask for an honorable discharge. Her active-duty career would be over, but she would at least be able to fly for the National Guard or the Air Force Reserve.

Widnall, a former MIT professor, is an expert in weapons systems, not human relations. She was under considerable pressure from the uniformed brass to let the case go forward to trial and its most likely outcome: a dishonorable discharge. Interestingly, the hard-liners included most women in uniform. It is almost unheard of for an officer facing a court-martial to be given an honorable discharge. Making an exception for Flinn, the women argued, would create an uproar over favoritism and seriously set back the cause of women in the ranks.

Reeling from Flinn's PR blitz, the generals counterattacked. Last week Zigo's wife suddenly surfaced with a letter portraying Flinn as an arrogant husband stealer. The letter, released by the air force, disputed Flinn's claim that she believed Zigo was separated. "Less than a week after we arrived on base, Lt. Flinn was in bed with my husband having sex," Gayla Zigo wrote. "On several occasions, I came home from work and found her at my house with Marc... She was always in her flight suit flaunting the fact that she was an Academy graduate and the first female bomber pilot. She told me once that she wanted to settle down with someone. I didn't know *that* somebody was my husband."

General Fogleman, the top-ranked officer in the air force, weighed in the same day on Capitol Hill. When Sen. Tom Harkin accused the air force of looking "ridiculous," an irritated Fogleman cut him off. The stakes were far more serious than adultery, the general said. The air force couldn't afford to have insubordinate liars flying planes full of nuclear weapons. Sitting beside Fogleman was Secretary Widnall. Her silence spoke volumes to Flinn's team, watching C-Span back in Minot.

By 7 o'clock that night, the air force had told Flinn that she would be denied an honorable discharge. Huddled with her parents and two brothers, Flinn tearfully insisted that she wanted to go forward with the trial. But her family and her lawyer knew better. Her sex life would become even more of a public spectacle. Finally, at about 3 a.m., Flinn decided to give up the fight. She would ask instead for a lesser "general discharge," given to soldiers whose negative record outweighs their contributions, but who have not disgraced the uniform.

A Depressing String of Scandals

From the service academies to the front lines, a series of high-profile cases of sexual misconduct has raised serious questions. A sampling:

Annapolis: In 1990, Midshipman Gwen Dreyer reported being handcuffed to a urinal by male classmates. She resigned.

Tailhook: Lt. Paula Coughlin and more than 80 other women charged that they were sexually attacked by naval aviators at the 1991 Tailhook convention—an imbroglio that led to the resignations of high-ranking officers.

Love Boat: During the gulf war 36 female sailors on the navy supply ship Acadia returned home pregnant.

Adm. Richard Macke: In 1995, after U.S. servicemen raped a 12-year-old Japanese girl in a car, he said: "For the price they paid to rent the car they could have had a girl." He was forced to resign.

Aberdeen: In 1996, 19 women trainees filed rape and assault complaints against 20 drill sergeants. Drill Sgt. Delmar Simpson was sentenced to 25 years and dishonorably discharged.

Lt. Col. Karen Tew: Dismissed from the air force for having an affair with an enlisted man, she committed suicide in March.

Army Sgt. Maj. Gene McKinney: The army's senior enlisted man was charged with sexual misconduct by a former aide. He denies the allegations, and is currently suspended with pay.

FIGHTING THE NEXT WAR

A former top female Pentagon official on how to head off future sex scandals.
BY BARBARA SPYRIDON POPE

KELLY FLINN MAY BE packing her bags in Minot, N.D., but the military can't really leave her behind: it must answer the questions about women in the ranks that her case raised. It's going to be very hard. I know, because I've been through military sex scandals—I was assistant secretary of the navy during Tailhook, the case where aviators groped and abused women, including fellow officers, at a Las Vegas convention in 1991. I have some bad news: there are no easy answers. Women are in the military to stay, and you can't reverse human nature with orders from on high. Still, there are basic principles that can help the Pentagon avoid double standards—and more Flinn-like embarrassments:

Don't automatically think of sex cases as gender cases. Yes, it's important to ask if Lieutenant Flinn was singled out just because she was a woman. But it's most important to see that the rules are consistently applied to everyone, male and female. My father was a navy veteran, and my parents taught me to believe that the higher the seniority, the greater the responsibility. But too often enlisted personnel and junior officers get hammered while senior officers slide by. A double standard of any kind undermines leadership, which in turn weakens the readiness to fight and win wars. If soldiers see their superiors getting away with something, they start to question all rules. How can we be sure these soldiers will obey orders in combat?

Don't let politics decide the case. The services should listen to lawmakers, because they represent the people—and fund the military. But it's a mistake to reflexively cave in to politicians. I think of the case of Adm. Stanley Arthur, a Vietnam veteran who was denied a much-deserved promotion in 1994 to be head of U.S. forces in the Pacific. One issue was Arthur's refusal to reinstate a female helicopter pilot who had failed flight school. The woman complained to Congress that her failing grade was retribution for a sexual-harassment complaint she had filed against a superior; the brass in the Pentagon bowed to the pressure from the Hill. Only later did it become clear that Arthur had been right—that though navy officials agreed she had been harassed, she would have washed out as a pilot anyway. But by then it was too late to save Arthur.

Be clear what the rules are. Ethics are hard to regulate. There are many shades of gray, not the bright lines the military prefers. But sexual jealousy can ruin the essential bonds between soldiers. Certainly, fraternization—the military's unwieldy term for having sex with a fellow warrior in the same chain of command—should be banned. Adultery is a harder question. In most cases, sex with civilians probably won't influence readiness. But what if a pilot is sleeping with his navigator's wife? The military needs to draw sharper distinctions to make the rules meaningful—and avoid more cases like Flinn's. And that is certainly in everybody's interest.

POPE *was the first female assistant secretary of the navy, 1989 to 1993.*

Even a general discharge was not a sure bet, however. Many of the uniformed brass also wanted to press ahead to trial. Widnall was torn. She was not unsympathetic to Flinn; she thought the pilot was the victim of a cad. Yet she wanted to support her top officers. Looking weary and stressed, Widnall opted for compromise and offered Flinn a deal. She would have to pay back $20,000 in tuition to the Air Force Academy, which requires its graduates to serve for five full years (Flinn has served four). And it's unlikely that she will ever fly in the National Guard. Still, she can probably get a job as a commercial-airline pilot.

Exhausted, Kelly Flinn slept while her lawyer and family discussed the terms on CNN, and her benighted lover, Marc Zigo, appeared before the cameras to sneer that "at no time was a gun [put] to Lieutenant Flinn's head" to have sex. On Friday her family released her letter of resignation to Widnall. The thought of losing her wings, Flinn wrote, "is the cause of my relentless tears." Even as she resigned, she asked "for a second chance." Life may give her one, but not the U.S. Air Force.

With JOHN BARRY *in Washington and* KATHLEEN DILL *in Minot*

Women's Work

By Stuart Miller

It's as basic as keeping the air we breathe clean and the water we drink pure, and it's as politically knotty as halting construction of incinerators in the inner city and reducing population growth in developing nations. Environmental activism comes in may guises but shares one common trait—it has increasingly become women's work.

"Women are now taking their place side by side and equal to men," says Barbara Bramble, the National Wildlife Federation's (NWF) international office director.

The environmental glass ceiling has chipped and splintered in the last 15 years; where the top slots were once completely dominated by men, women now hold key policymaking positions at organizations like Greenpeace, the Sierra Club, the National Audubon Society, NWF, The Wilderness Society, INFORM, the Humane Society of the U.S. (HSUS) and the League of Conservation Voters (LCV).

"The number of women in leadership roles reflects the fact that women care about these issues and are attracted to this kind of work in the first place," says Patricia Forkan, executive vice president of HSUS. "Cause-related organizations demand teamwork, which is how women tend to manage."

Women have not just entered the halls of power, they are achieving significant successes there. In Congress,

The Leadership of the Environmental Movement—and the Grassroots Rank-and-File—Are No Longer Male Preserves

Senator Barbara Boxer (D-California) strengthened the Safe Drinking Water Act. Before retiring last year, Representative Pat Schroeder (D-Colorado) wrote legislation transforming a military Superfund site into a wildlife refuge.

Since Kathryn Fuller became president of the World Wildlife Fund (WWF) seven years ago, the organization has doubled its revenue and membership, helped secure an ivory ban, promoted the debt-for-nature swaps in Asia and Latin America, and developed an environmental educational program called "Windows on the Wild" which is currently being introduced into middle school curricula around the country.

Greenpeace USA was falling apart financially in the early 1990s, but since Barbara Dudley became executive director four years ago, she has helped stabilize the organization's finances. Additionally, Greenpeace under Dudley has earned crucial environmental victories: By educating small-time fishermen about sustainable fishing and working to change the focus of its fisheries campaign from "jobs versus the environment" to "jobs and the environment," Greenpeace was able to help defeat the Individual Transferable Quotas (ITQs) favored by corporate fisheries. "We even got a decent fisheries management bill," says Dudley, who adds that the bill was co-sponsored by Republican Don Young of Alaska, chairman of the House Resources Committee. (Normally notoriously anti-environment, Young listened to the local fishermen galvanized by Greenpeace.)

Greenpeace under Dudley has also started making inroads in its battle to ban chlorine, a dangerous toxin backed by a wealthy industry. Humanizing a complex issue by raising heath issues— like the 1993 report linking chlorine to breast cancer—Greenpeace gained support from women's groups and organizations like the American Public Health Association.

At the Sierra Club, Debbie Sease was the primary lobbyist on the California Desert Protection Act, and as legislative director, she has been the chief strategist in the battle against the war on the environment waged by the Republican leadership in recent years. Sease can also be found brainstorming with the other female power players in the environmental movement at a networking luncheon held in Washington, D.C. every six weeks. Started during the Clinton administration by several women,

including Carol Browner, head of the Environmental Protection Agency (EPA), the lunches attract women like Sease and Dudley from major organizations as well as government officials like Katie McGinty, senior environmental advisor to President Clinton and chair of the President's Council on Environmental Quality.

The animal rights movement also includes many women leaders like Ingrid Newkirk of the People for the Ethical Treatment of Animals (PETA). HSUS' Forkan oversees the leading national group's whole domestic operations, which include everything from humane legislation to wildlife and farm animal protection.

The Movement Evolves

While part of the power shift is easily attributable to the women's movement and society's overall breakthrough in the last quarter-century, Bramble says a major reason for this flourishing has been the evolution of the environmental movement. A generation ago, concerns about conservation held the spotlight—it was all about outdoor activities, hunting, fishing and hiking . . . very male activities—but in the last quarter century, the light has shined equally bright on health and urban issues like clean air and safe drinking water. Not surprisingly, many female environmentalists say, it was a woman, Rachel Carson, who sparked this shift in priorities.

"As the environmental movement has come to include an environmental health movement, it has come to include women in leadership," says Greenpeace's Dudley. There is, however, much enduring chauvinism and the pace of advancement is excruciatingly slow, she adds. Many men are reluctant to share power and, equally significant, to adopt the approach to environmentalism and negotiating generally favored by women. Still, progress is undeniable and has inspired even more women to become involved, paving the way for greater change.

While there are definitely women involved in traditional male activities, Bramble says, it is still not the norm and most women join causes because of concerns over health-related and community-related problems (which have traditionally been neglected by men). When chemicals in the atmosphere af-

fect fertility issues, she explains, "that strikes a personal chord."

A Grassroots Force

The changes are coming from the ground up. At the grassroots level, where women have long been an active force, the last generation witnessed a surge of new involvement. When Lois Marie Gibbs formed the Citizens Clearinghouse for Hazardous Waste (CCHW) 15 years ago, the organization had 3,000 names around the country (most were women), but they were largely working alone or in small groups. Today, CCHW works with 8,000 grassroots organizations nationwide, and 80 percent are headed by women. "The movement is now extremely powerful at the local level," Gibbs says, which has helped propel women to statewide and even national prominence.

As media coverage brought the pervasive nature of industrial pollutants— from hazardous waste dumps to polluted rivers and wells—into American living rooms, Gibbs says women began saying, "Wait a minute, that's my backyard. Maybe that's why my kids are sick."

At the grassroots level, where middle-class women have long been environmental activists, the last decade has also seen an influx of minority and working-class women, says Charlene Spretnak, author of Green Politics. Spretnak says these women—many of whom don't associate themselves with the "green" movement and perceive themselves more as community activists than environmentalists—have flocked to one of the hottest new niches: environmental justice—working to prevent placement of incinerators and toxic waste dumps in poor areas.

The traditional role of nurturing the family prompts women to put the greater good over economic self-interest in their activism, says Karen Steuer, a legislative staffer on the House's Committee on Resources, adding that in Congress, it is easier to find men willing to dismantle environmental laws than it is women. Steuer, like everyone else interviewed for this story, stressed that her comments were broad generalizations— there are certainly many compassionate, committed male environmentalists, they say. But they add that they had witnessed these patterns too often to discount them as unfair stereotypes.

VISIONARY THINKING

Women Shape the Environmental Movement's Theoretical Base

Women's contributions to the environmental movement have and continue to take many forms. Women serve as frontline leaders at grassroots actions around the world. They hold management positions at the largest—and the smallest—environmental groups and foundations. They contribute amply to the thinking that guides the movement's agenda. Modern environmentalism rests on a philosophical base that women have had a firm hand in shaping.

One such movement mentor is British-born futurist Hazel Henderson, who's spent 30 years pointing the way towards a more sustainable economic model. Since co-founding New York's Citizens for Clean Air in 1964, Henderson, through her writing, lecturing and constant activism, has worked to reform world financial institutions like the International Monetary Fund (IMF) and the World Bank, helped build support for the United Nations, and argued for corporate social responsibility and a tax policy that recognizes environmental factors as part of the real cost of doing business. Henderson's latest book is Building a Win-Win World: Life Beyond Global Economic Warfare (Berrett Koehler).

"Environmentalists have finally begun to realize that we have to go global," Henderson said in a recent interview. "It's a matter of looking at the global commons and all the commercial uses that we make of it. Our environmental impact is not really included in the cost of doing business or calculating the gross national product. Social and environmental costs have traditionally been externalized, which is why the industrial economies have gone so far off course. Nineteenth century economic textbooks are not going to get us to 21st century economies. Fortunately, now almost everyone in the economics profession agrees on the need for full-cost accounting."

Henderson brings a healthy skepticism to the study of economics. Unlike most males in her profession, she's not held in thrall by the sheer magnitude of the international financial flow, referring to it instead as "the global casino." Governments—and economists—tend to get overwhelmed, she says, by "that $1.3 trillion in currencies that sloshes around the planet every 24 hours." Henderson also holds considerable misgivings

about international trade treaties such as the North American Free Trade Agreement (NAFTA) and the General Agreement on Tariffs and Trade (GATT), which she says "are very narrowly conceived, and tend to hold ecological cooperation hostage."

But Henderson does have a few kind words for the World Bank and its Wealth Index, which considers environmental factors in its development decisions. "They're finally going in the right direction," she says. "It takes a lot of pushing to get these big institutions turned around."

Turning around big institutions is something Dr. Theo Colborn knows about. The co-author of the bestselling Our Stolen Future (which is based on her research into chemical fertility-threatening "endocrine disruptors"), faced considerable hostility from industry.

A role as a modern-day Rachel Carson is hardly something Colborn's previous life had prepared her for. The former Colorado resident had been a pharmacist, sheep rancher and grandmother until, at age 50, she went back to school and earned a Ph.D. in zoology.

Colborn's involvement in the environment began with local Colorado issues, specifically water quality, which was threatened by mining development. "I got involved in starting the Western Slope Energy Research Center, which fought against air and water pollution," Colborn says. "And I began to realize that even though I may have known more about water than many of the people in the opposition, I didn't have the credentials."

After earning her degree, Colborn, who had seen the harmful effects of chemicals like the pregnancy drug DES (which caused sterility in many women) during her work as a pharmacist, began the research that led to Our Stolen Future. She is now at work on research papers—to be published in scientific journals—that describe how endocrine disruptors affect the developing human brain and alter sexual reproduction in fish.

Colborn, who is a senior scientist with the World Wildlife Fund in Washington, D.C. was surprised to learn how many environmental groups are headed by women (see main story). "Maybe we have a better feel for systems," she says. "We look at things more holisti-

cally. The literature claims women have more intuition than men, which broadens our scope of thinking and leaves us with more open minds. Women have more feeling for how things interrelate than men."

Dr. Helen Caldicott, the Australian physician who's probably done more than anyone else to alert the world to the dangers of nuclear war, sees women—particularly American women—as a great, unorganized force. In her new autobiography, A Desperate Passion (Norton), she describes how her group Women's Action for New Directions (WAND) developed the motto "200 women in Congress by the year 2000." She writes, "Although women number 53 percent of the American population, they comprise only two percent of the congressional delegation. This has to change."

Women, Caldicott said in an interview, "are a tremendous force—if you empower them. They're as difficult to organize as doctors, but once you get them going they're unstoppable. Women are much more open with their feelings and the truth, and they're one of the golden keys to the salvation of this planet."

Like Caldicott, Dartmouth professor Donella Meadows deserves credit for alerting the American people to looming environmental disaster. Her 1972 book The Limits of Growth was a wakeup call, based on computer projections, about the consequences of continued development and population growth. In the 1992 Beyond the Limits, she concluded that the point of sustainability had been passed. "All through The Limits to Growth, we assumed the Limits were up ahead somewhere," she says. "Now we believe they're behind us." And like many of the women who lead the environmental movement, she can personalize what to some is an abstract concept. "I've heard many people talk about trying to take their grandchildren to places they loved as children, and they're gone, or the water is polluted or the trees have been cut down," she says.

CONTACTS: Women's Action for New Directions, 691 Massachusetts Avenue, Boston, MA 02258/(617)643-6740.

—JIM MOTAVALLI

"Men are out in front on property rights and self-interest issues; more men are convinced that if you do the right thing economically, everything else follows," Steuer says. "Women think about their families and the environment. They worry, 'If I take my kids to the beach, can they swim or will they be wading around in oil spills?' "

McGinty adds that men tend to be "technological optimists," confident we are "one machine away from delinking ourselves from nature," while women humbly intuit the "fundamental connection" between humans and nature.

As bearers of children, women have an innate emotional bond to the Earth, says Theodore Roszak, director of the Ecopsychology Institute, which studies the relationships between individuals and nature. While men traditionally viewed Mother Nature "as a devious female to be put in her place, to be tamed" by technology (just as they historically viewed marriage in terms of domination and submission), women have shifted the emphasis from using science to subjugate nature to finding ways to accommodate nature.

"Seeing the Earth as a female subject to ruthless domination has made women

Wormser spent each summer in college as a forester in Haiti. "I was looking for a truth to base my life's work on and my first truth was that soil erosion is bad, so I went to Haiti and started planting trees," Wormser says. When poor, rural Haitians let their goats eat the trees, Wormser learned a greater truth: "Environmental problems are not just logistical but also societal."

Wormser realized that solving environmental dilemmas involves exploring all sides of a subject and bringing everyone together to find a feasible solution. She co-founded both the Boston Coalition on Population and Development, which brought together groups concerned with overpopulation and world development issues, and the Environmental Roundtable, which coalesced 40 local groups and chapters of major organizations like the Sierra Club and Audubon to battle the Republicans' Contract With America. Much of Wormser's work has not been about the scientific details of environmentalism—she doesn't have to know the minutia of every environmental bill. Instead, she tries to find a way to get representatives from different groups like the Wildlands Project and the Riverways Program to

croloans [to start their own businesses]." When that happens, she says, "birth rates go down."

Vicki Robin, president of the New Road Map Foundation, an all-volunteer group that teaches low-consumption lifestyles, says lowering consumption and planning a sustainable future are equally crucial for society. Robin, co-author of the book *Your Money or Your Life,* lives happily on about $7,000 a year. New Road Map is staffed primarily by women (although her co-author is a man) and Robin has discovered through the years that women are "more able to go through a transformative process and really re-examine who they are and take on a different way of thinking. Women are more fluid, men are more solid. Men are very often defined by their jobs and their roles. They have a stronger ego identity."

Cathy Carlson, legislative representative for the National Wildlife Federation, says the fact that "women bring less of an ego to the table" is essential to her success as a lobbyist. In delicate negotiations with the government and industry leaders on the adverse impact of mining and livestock grazing on water resources and wildlife habitat, Carlson has seen firsthand how she can be effective at breaking the gridlock on environmental issues. Women are better at "finding ways to move an idea forward so that everyone's values are met and the goals are accomplished. Men feel the need to stand by their position—they get their ego involved, and they act like two bulls in a pasture—you can't get past the headbutting."

In meetings where dialogue becomes impossible because "the testosterone levels in the room are too high," Carlson sometimes finds herself chiding men, saying "Fred, you're not listening to Harry," the way one might encourage children in the sandbox to play nice. "As a mother I see a lot of parallels," she says. "You have to negotiate things out with a five-year-old and the same principles apply."

On topics that "strike at the heart of traditional male values of independence," such as restricting where on the plains men can roam with their livestock, a woman's sensitivity is crucial, says Carlson. She's constantly dealing with "cowboys who want to be at one with the land. They are caught up in the myth of the Western man." Yet she says while women environmentalists can

> *Women have not just entered the halls of power, they are achieving significant successes there.*

relate better emotionally to the cause," Roszak says. "Women in the environmental movement have always had the sense of being on Earth's side."

The Forest and the Trees

Bramble says one critical factor in the emergence of women as key players in the environmental movement has been the shift in the last decade toward holistic environmental thinking—an understanding that you have to see the forest *and* the trees.

Like many of these women, Julie Wormser, now a regional associate at The Wilderness Society, first grasped this holistic concept out in the field.

put aside their individual agendas and work together to convince politicians of the urgency of their cause.

Women have also brought new ideas to old issues, such as population control and consumption. Roszak says that "often, the basic barrier is male psychology, their insisting on women's role in life. Men are not aware that the root of the population problem is that women are left with only one thing to do: mother children. It is not just about contraceptives."

Spretnak agrees, saying it has been women who have replaced the strategy of lowering birth rates in developing countries by shipping contraceptives with offering women "access to education, access to health care and mi-

GREEN AT THE GRASSROOTS

Women Form the Frontlines of Local Environmental Activism

Kim Phillips is an accidental environmentalist. While most women now attaining national clout in the environmental arena spent years studying the issues and building their careers, the grassroots movement is led by former housewives like Phillips who knew little about environmental issues until one hit close to home.

Phillips, now the environmental chairperson of the Texas Parents-Teachers Association and a leader of Citizens to Save Lake Waco, says if someone had told her in 1990 she'd become an environmental activist, "I would have thought they were crazy. I didn't know what the environment was." But in 1991, when Waco proposed a landfill expansion next to South Bosque Elementary School, when she was PTA president, Phillips learned fast. "You get so angry when you find out the government is not protecting you" that you decide to do it on your own, she says. (The landfill wasn't stopped, but the PTA won limits on access times for garbage trucks, better liners for the landfill and monthly meetings with the mayor. Phillips has since persuaded the state legislature to toughen laws about dump site locations.)

Phillips is not alone. Issues of environmental justice and health have captured the nation's attention in the last 15 years, sparked by the explosion of grassroots organizations. While women in national environmental organizations and governments are slowly gaining power, there's no denying their leadership roles out on the frontlines.

In Pensacola, Florida, Margaret Williams heads Citizens Against Toxic Exposure, a group formed in 1991 to battle the Environmental Protection Agency's digging on a toxic site near her home. "As with most people, environmental issues had never crossed my mind," she says. But when residents—

most of them elderly and not well-off financially—began suffering eye and skin irritations and breathing problems, Williams quickly learned about the poisonous effects of dioxin. Although her group lost the battle to stop the digging, it recently persuaded the federal government to pay for the relocation of all 358 families.

"Women are leading the charge," says Terri Swearingen, who achieved national recognition for her attempts to stop development of a hazardous waste incinerator in East Liverpool, Ohio. Most of these women aren't media-savvy and aren't polished public speakers; Phillips says that everything she knows about organizing, "I learned through the PTA." But Swearingen says ignorance is actually "a great asset—I didn't know the obstacles that would be in the way, so I didn't see them. I just forged onward." The incinerator went up anyway, but Swearingen's dogged protests, and willingness to get arrested for the cause, gained enough attention to prompt Ohio Governor George Voinovich to halt future incinerator construction, and the Clinton administration to strengthen its regulations.

Most environmental justice protests arise out of poor, often minority communities, and usually it's women who become involved at the grassroots level "because they are concerned about their children and about their health problems," says Hazel Johnson, executive director of People for Community Recovery (PCR) in Chicago. Johnson only became an environmentalist when she learned about her neighborhood's disproportionately high rates of cancer, asthma and bronchitis—all traced to waste dumps and plants near the projects.

Swearingen adds that men expend their energy at work, "then they come home and see their family—it's totally

separate. They don't want to know about problems." (Phillips adds that she's seen many women give up environmental activism because their husbands felt threatened by it.)

Johnson says that men working at the grassroots level focus too much on establishing their power. Despite her title, she remains devoted to the concept of teamwork. "I don't consider myself the leader," she says, even though PCR—which she formed in 1978 to help tenants at her housing project get repairs done—has removed asbestos, shut down hazardous waste incinerators and stopped a new landfill project. Johnson was given a President's Environmental and Conservation Challenge Medal in 1992. "I'm a person who likes to have action," she says, "and I'll do whatever it takes to get it done."

Getting things done is often made more challenging because the media and industry frequently treat a female activist as "a hysterical housewife," Swearingen says. "So what if you're just a mom." Phillips adds, however, that a mom "is the best thing in the world to be." She says a Waco city official once asked her, "Where are the cookies? The PTA is supposed to bring cookies," and then didn't bother deposing her in the case he was working on, though she was an expert witness. "It's the idiot bimbo-head syndrome, but I love it— it's always good to be underestimated," Phillips says. "When people make comments like that, it just makes me dig in."

CONTACTS: Citizens Against Toxic Exposure, 6400 Marianna Drive, Pensacola, FL 32504/(904)494-2601; Citizens To Save Lake Waco, 324 Blue Bonnet Circle, McGregor, TX 76657/(817)848-5472; People for Community Recovery, 13116 South Ellis Avenue, Chicago, IL 60627/(312)468-1645.

—*S.M.*

"look past the boots and the hats to focus on environmental damage," they must achieve their goals without challenging the underlying values or shattering the male myth that the West is an open frontier, where nobody will tell them what they can or cannot do.

Finding Common Ground

Lisa Creasman, state director for The Nature Conservancy in Louisiana, also sees herself as a facilitator, using leadership to create partnerships that safeguard the land. Creasman often discusses

acquiring land for the Conservancy with private owners and negotiates partnerships with businesses. The Conservancy "also interjects itself into confrontational situations between landowners and government agencies," she says. "I look at everybody's needs and try to be

> *The changes are coming from the ground up. At the grassroots level, where women have long been an active force, the last generation witnessed a surge of new involvement.*

considerate of the other side. We have to find common ground." The Army, looking for extra space for training ground adjacent to Fort Polk, covets the Forest Service's Vernon District woodlands, which Creasman says is "biologically unique." So the Conservancy has studied both pieces of land and the Army's training plans in an effort to provide a compromise.

Creasman also says progress for women in the South is excruciatingly slow—she is often the only woman in meetings. "In the South, women are just little ladies," she says. She may be the ranking official, but many men make eye contact exclusively with her male colleagues and she is often addressed, "Hey, cutie." Creasman handles these slights by ignoring them, concentrating on "the issues and the facts," she says. "Maybe they don't respect me afterwards, but they understand the issue better."

Because Southerners, particularly wealthy oil-and-gas men along the coast, can be dismissive of businesswomen, Creasman occasionally brings a male staffer along to close a deal on a land purchase or request a donation. "I don't feel like I'm sacrificing anything," she says. "I keep focused on what I want to accomplish."

There has, however, been an evolution of sorts, Gibbs says. "We used to have a male organizing director and people would often talk just to him even if we were sitting at the same table. At one meeting, I was arguing that risk assessment doesn't work, and a man leaned around to my science director—who was male—and said, 'Please explain to Lois what this means. Sometimes it's hard for women to understand.'"

Dudley is appalled that the "Green Group"—the CEOs of the national environmental organizations that are recognized most often by the press as the "environmental movement"—is almost entirely male, although she believes the group is making itself "less and less relevant" by not including women like Gibbs. However, she adds that it isn't just male environmentalists who are behind the times—"when the press wants a quote from the environmental movement, they quote a man" the vast majority of the time.

Gibbs says that is slowly changing but that reporters still quote men for data, policy and intellectual ideas and women environmentalists "for the human interest side"—even if both the man and woman give the same quotes. On the other hand, Gibbs says, "at least they call us—that part of it has changed."

As more and more women establish themselves as experts and power players, they are finally becoming more difficult to ignore—even in fields that were traditionally the man's domain. In her early days as a lobbyist, Carlson says men listened more attentively to other men than to her. Now, however, she says, "People know I can deliver on [threats and promises], so they know they have to pay attention."

So ultimately, perhaps, the environmental movement will adapt to the point where men are comfortable sharing their power with women and even following their lead in an effort to support a common cause.

CONTACTS: Women's Environment and Development Organization, 355 Lexington Avenue, 3rd floor, New York, NY 10017/(212)973-0325; Women's International Network, 187 Grant Street, Lexington, MA 02173/(617)862-9431.

STUART MILLER is a freelance writer based in New York and author of The Other Islands of New York City: A Historical Companion.

Women and War

How "Power-Over" Politics Silenced U.S. Congresswomen in the Persian Gulf War

by Adrienne Elizabeth Christiansen

Recent tensions between the United States and Iraq over U.N. weapons inspections recall a period seven years ago this January when the U.S. Congress spent three days intensely debating several resolutions that would have either curtailed or authorized the use of military force in Iraq.

Ultimately, Congress did authorize military force, and the Persian Gulf War ensued. One noteworthy aspect of the congressional debate is that there were almost no expressions of concern about women as a class, either as soldiers, civilians, or war casualties. This near silence on the "women and war" question is remarkable given that the presence of 32,000 female soldiers in the Persian Gulf prompted several reporters to dub the conflict a "mommy's war." In addition, the 102nd Congress had more female members (thirty) than at any other time in U.S. history. Nearly half of these members had identified themselves as feminists or as strong supporters of women's interests.

The eight female legislators who were active environmentalists were similarly silent on how a Middle East war would affect the ecosystem. Of the more than fifty speeches given by women during the debate, only Representative Nancy Pelosi of California raised the subject of the Persian Gulf War's possible effect on the environment. The scenarios she outlined seem eerily prescient given the catastrophe that ensued. Even though she merely described some of the devastation that would occur if Saddam Hussein fulfilled his public threat to blow up Kuwaiti oil fields, her speech prompted ridicule from her colleagues.

I believe that this situation demonstrates the difficulty of raising feminist and environmental issues during times of heightened military activity, even when the consequences for women and the environment are enormous.

The three-day televised debate in Congress provides a fascinating case study in the variety of communication barriers with which female legislators contend—barriers that are even more onerous when women must deal with the topics of war and peace. It also provides an opportunity to make a case for the important yet often overlooked relationship between rape and other forms of sexual assault, militarism, and environmental degradation.

The Gulf War Debates

If there ever is a time when the free and open exchange of argument and persuasion contribute to the health of a democracy, it is in deciding whether to wage war. Unfortunately, U.S. history is riddled with wars that were never declared (for example, the Vietnam War and the Panamanian War); this made the 1991 congressional debate a rare and extraordinary opportunity to deliberate over the reasons for war or peace. For three days, Americans heard and watched their elected representatives somberly claim never to have voted on a more important resolution. The importance of their decision, it was repeated, necessitated an exploration of all the possible ramifications of a vote to go to war. There was much talk about "saving face," "having egg on our faces," the crisis being a "defining moment in history," "sending a message" to Saddam Hussein, the need to "stand firm with resolve and unity," and the upcoming war as the "last, best hope for peace."

From *The Humanist,* January/February 1998, pp. 12-19. Adapted from "Rhetoric, Rape, and Ecowarfare in the Persian Gulf" in *Ecofeminism: Women, Culture, Nature* (edited by Karen J. Warren). © 1997 by Indiana University Press.

Many members of the House spoke briefly about the potential deaths of U.S. soldiers, but in general the debate was more a discussion of the economic, political, and geostrategic ramifications of a war with Iraq.

In contrast to the lengthy speeches on how a Persian Gulf War might affect Middle Eastern stability, U.S. military might, the world economy, and the new world order, Representative Barbara Boxer of California was the only female legislator to discuss any aspect of women and war. Her comments on this topic were limited to two very brief statements, one in which she noted that female soldiers in Saudi Arabia were treated differently than their male comrades and one in which she decried the military's practice of sending single parents or both parents to the Gulf. Unfortunately, Boxer's examples of how the female soldiers were treated ultimately served to belittle their capabilities. She said:

> They are working very hard and they are explaining to us how it feels to have to go into the back door to use the gymnasium because the Saudis do not want them to come in the front door. They have to fight to get to have the use of the gymnasium, and then, once they are in there, being subjected to literature trying to convert them [to Islam]. It is tough for them to take. . . . In the rules our service people are told that women are not allowed to drive in Saudi Arabia. If they are in their military vehicle and in their military uniforms, it is OK. However, I was informed that if they do that and they attempt to drive into town in their military car and in their uniforms, they are run off the road by the Saudis.

The problem with Boxer's statement is that it was not linked to any broader discussion of the justification for or against going to war. She did not use these stories to raise her colleagues' consciousness about the morality of sending female soldiers to a war to reestablish nondemocratic monarchies, to defend societies where women's rights and movements are severely curtailed, or to talk about the environmental effects of war on women and other humans. By failing to link these anecdotes to a broader examination of the war's purpose, Boxer inadvertently reinforced the image of female soldiers as weak and incapable of enduring the rigors of war. Who would argue that the discomfort of going through back doors and having religious literature thrust upon them is in any way comparable to the discomfort of being on the "front line" in a desert combat zone?

Ironically, Boxer did not discuss other issues about women and war that are serious and pervasive. Neither she nor her female colleagues discussed the likelihood of U.S., Iraqi, Kuwaiti, and Saudi Arabian women being raped and sexually assaulted during the war. None of the women discussed the deleterious health effects of war on female munitions workers, especially those in the electronics industry. No one addressed the limitations on U.S. military women's pay and career advancement due to congressional restrictions on women in combat positions.

Only Boxer mentioned the problem of minor children being left in the United States when parents were shipped to Saudi Arabia. To raise these issues, of course, would have held up the legislators to ridicule for paying attention to such picayune details when the important issues were about national humiliation, geopolitical strategy, and what George Bush called "a big idea—a new world order where diverse nations are drawn together in common cause to

> No one discussed the likelihood of women soldiers being raped and sexually assaulted, the deleterious health effects of war on female munitions workers, or the limitations on their pay and career advancement by congressional restrictions.

achieve the universal aspirations of mankind: peace and security, freedom and the rule of law."

Just as the female legislators did not raise issues typically thought of as important to women, most of them failed to articulate how a Middle East war might affect the environment. A claim of ignorance on the part of the legislators would be hard to sustain, given that prior to the congressional debate Saddam Hussein had threatened to blow up the oil wells if he were attacked by coalition forces. He had already demonstrated his willingness to engage in ecowarfare when he blew up wells and dumped oil in the Persian Gulf in 1983 during the Iran-Iraq War. These actions were widely reported in the mass media and well known to the U.S. government. In addition, the devastating effects of war on the environment have been a serious concern to scientists and environmentalists for at least fifteen years. The Stockholm International Peace Research Institute has been a leader in sponsoring extensive research on this topic. While it is unrealistic to expect legislators to be aware of scientific research studies on the subject of war and the environment, the mass media published a number of articles on this subject, specifically relating to a Persian Gulf War, prior to congressional debate.

Pelosi tried to warn her colleagues of the impending ecocatastrophe. Her remarks (January 12, 1991) were brief, vivid, and uncannily accurate:

> The war cloud that would result from exploding oil fields and large-scale bombing of Kuwait, Iraq, Saudi Arabia, and other countries in the Middle East would doom the environment for many years to come. . . . Let us focus on these images: Fires raging for weeks, or perhaps months, sending tons of smoke and debris into the Earth's atmosphere. Oil equal to a dozen Exxon *Valdez* spills coursing

through Gulf waters. Millions of dolphins, fish, sea birds, and other marine life washed onto Gulf shores. Smoke and debris blocking sunlight, causing temperatures to drop and altering crop seasons which would result in widespread famine. Toxic plumes ascending to the upper atmosphere and falling as acid rain. Chemical contamination of air, water, and vegetation.

She urged the legislators to pay attention to concerns that would "affect human life and all of life on earth." In many ways, Pelosi had to contend with the opposite rhetorical problem that Boxer faced. Whereas Boxer failed to link her concerns about the treatment of U.S. female soldiers to any broader argument about why we should not go to war, Pelosi used many examples and linked them to worldwide harm as reasons why we should refrain from a war. Where Boxer's examples seemed so minor that they could be shrugged off as irrelevant, Pelosi's case was so extensive that it apparently seemed fantastic and could be shrugged off as grandiose.

I would not expect elected representatives to be concerned with mangrove trees, cormorants, coral reefs, desert vegetation, or fish when U.S. troops and allies were about to face "weapons of mass destruction." Nevertheless, going to war to ensure the continuing flow of Middle Eastern oil had serious environmental consequences specific to the United States in the form of energy dependency, air pollution, and acid rain. Even on this myopic, self-entered point, only two female legislators spoke up.

Representatives Marcy Kaptur and Mary Rose Oakar both made long, logical, well-supported cases in trying to dissuade their colleagues from voting for war. They described the "immorality" of going to war to protect a Middle East oil supply when we had had nearly twenty years since the 1973 OPEC oil embargo to fundamentally change our energy use. As Kaptur said, "America saw this crisis coming. This is not news to us." Both women strongly criticized the Bush administration for its failure to provide an energy plan as required by the 1977 Energy Organization Act. Unlike Pelosi, who focused on environmental degradation, Kaptur and Oakar approached the subject as an issue of political independence from Middle East countries. Their solution was for us to develop new energy technologies. According to Oakar, the United States has "centuries of unmined coal, shale oil, solar energy, synthetic fuel, unexcavated oil." Kaptur concurred: "Let's spend those billions of dollars being wasted in the desert, let's spend them here in America to develop our clean coal technologies, our agriculture and alcohol fuels, hydrogen and solar power." Neither woman named continued or increased pollution or environmental damage to the United States and its citizens as a reason to stay out of a war with Iraq, even though both women clearly believed that our energy use must change and that future energy technologies must be environmentally sound.

Why was it that during deliberations of the gravest importance to humans and to nonhuman nature our legislators barely considered the environmental ramifications of our actions for ourselves, our allies, and our adversaries? Why did Pelosi's speech meet with derision? Was the near silence on the part of the legislators an example of "selling out" politically or part of some larger dynamic? The almost total lack of discussion about the environment during the congressional debate belies both an arrogance about the importance of humans over other kinds of nature and a remarkable shortsightedness about how the ecosystem and the earth's resources sustain human life. I believe that the sparse discussion of how the war would affect women and the environment was a result of their integral connection. To demonstrate this connection necessitates an examination of the rhetorical situation faced by the female legislators.

Rhetorical Obstacles

Social attitudes and beliefs that men and women are fundamentally different create the most entrenched rhetorical obstacles that limit a woman's ability to discuss women and the environment in congressional debates about war. For centuries, women have been depicted as constitutionally peace-loving where men are war-loving. Men fight one another at the war's front, but women are supposed to be passive, supportive observers on the home front. Women are supposed to abhor war because our procreative abilities make us "closer to nature." Since men cannot give birth to another human being, they are said to be "closer to culture," which includes the development of munitions and other technological advances.

In contrast to human procreation, men "give birth" to new social orders by creating and using sophisticated instruments of death and destruction. As William J. Broyles put it in a 1984 *Esquire* article entitled "Why Men Love War": "At some terrible level [it] is the closest thing to what childbirth is for women: the initiation into the power of life and death." Carol Cohn also found a strong relationship between "giving birth" and creating atomic bombs in the language of the defense intellectuals she studied. In the summer 1987 *Signs,* a leading journal of women and culture in society, Cohn writes:

> The entire history of the bomb project, in fact, seems permeated with imagery that confounds humanity's overwhelming technological power to destroy nature with the power to create: imagery that converts men's destruction into their rebirth. Lawrence wrote of the Trinity test of the first atomic bomb: "One felt as though he had been privileged to witness the Birth of the World." In a 1985 interview, General Bruce K. Holloway, the commander in chief of the Strategic Air Command from 1968 to 1972, described a nuclear war as involving "a big bang, like the start of the universe."

In addition to having to deal with the illogic that equates human birth with wartime death and destruction, female members of Congress have little authority to speak about war—given longstanding attitudes that women are to be passive and silent during these times. Women's primary roles are restricted to being patriotic supporters, grief-stricken widows or family members, civilian casualties, or rape victims/war booty. In her 1987 book *Women and War*, Jean Bethke Elshtain observes that the expectation that women are to fill passive roles during times of war even extends to passivity in articulating their concerns about war:

> In the matter of women and war [women] are invited to turn away. War is men's: men are the historic authors of organized violence. Yes, women have been drawn in—and they have been required to observe, suffer, cope, mourn, honor, adore, witness, work. But men have done the describing and defining of war, and the women are "affected" by it: they mostly react.

Another limitation on women's ability to speak authentically about war occurs because of their historic exclusion from military service and their continuing exclusion from combat positions. Since the earliest days of this country's existence, a powerful conceptual relationship has existed between military service and ideas about citizenship. This relationship is not unique to the United States and can be traced back to the beliefs and writings of the ancient Greeks.

Women's political ambitions have been thwarted by their inability to serve in military combat positions, resulting in obvious difficulties in speaking about war. The women who do get elected are unquestionably handicapped when their male colleagues use military service as an authorizing device for their political arguments. As cited in her book *Women, Militarism, and War*, Sheila Tobias has established through historical example that, during times when heroism in warfare and leadership in politics are strongly linked, women experience great difficulties getting elected to public office. When military service is claimed to be a necessary precursor to public service, women lose out.

This was certainly the case during the 1988 presidential election between George Bush and Michael Dukakis. Bush repeatedly pointed to his military service as a navy pilot to bolster his credentials for the presidency. He ridiculed Dukakis' well-known ride in an army tank. Bush's derision stemmed not merely from the fact that the ride was an election-time publicity stunt but that it was obscene for Dukakis to take on the mantle and perquisites of soldiering when he had no previous military service. During the Persian Gulf War debates, female members of Congress were negatively affected by the attitude that prior military service was the only legitimate precursor for discussing war. Whereas their male counterparts repeatedly referred to their own military service and sacrifice, the women had to draw upon their connections to other people in the service. For example, several congresswomen mentioned their male family members who were servicemen or their congressional employees who were connected to the military. For some of the female representatives, their connection to the military was only that they were there to speak *on behalf* of their constituents who were in the Gulf or had family members in the Gulf.

Had they wanted to discuss issues of women and the environment, the female members of Congress also would have faced other restrictive obstacles—attitudes about the impropriety of women speaking in public. Prohibitions against women speaking in public have a long and well-documented history. Saint Paul's biblical edict for women to "remain silent" in church has been taken to mean that women should remain silent in *all* public spaces. By the

> In addition to having to deal with the illogic that equates human birth with wartime death and destruction, women's political ambitions have been thwarted by their inability to serve in military combat positions, resulting in obvious difficulties in speaking about war.

very act of standing and addressing a group of people, a female speaker claims to have ideas worthy of an audience. She literally asserts her own authority and legitimacy. In part because of this powerful self-validating and self-authorizing action, women in the nineteenth century endured sanctions that included being criticized from the pulpit by clergy, suffering ridicule in editorials and cartoons, being refused their requests to rent auditoriums, having to defend themselves from claims that they were sexual deviants and monsters, having to face angry mobs, and being repeatedly threatened with bodily harm. Clearly, contemporary female members of Congress did not face these social sanctions when speaking during the Gulf War debates. However, each woman had to contend with the belief (reflected in numbers of women elected to the House) that the public sphere of government "belongs" to men and that she was usurping her socially defined position.

Similarly, each woman had to face a prejudiced assumption that she was ignorant or incompetent about war simply because this culture defines war as a quintessentially masculine activity. Like contemporary female soldiers who are accused of being lesbians because they have violated assigned sex roles and have asserted their competence in military matters, female members of Congress risked having their qualifications as women called into question. Having to demonstrate their competence and authority while reassuring audiences that they are feminine women is an age-old dichotomy for female speakers. Current examples of this phenomenon are provided by

Geraldine Ferraro's unsuccessful run for the vice-presidency, the round of criticism Attorney General Janet Reno received when she was nominated for her cabinet post, and the ongoing, vitriolic criticism of Hillary Clinton's public policy roles.

The rhetorical obstacles to legitimacy that female members of Congress face as public speakers are quite daunting by themselves. When the subject is as significant and deadly as going to war, the rhetorical obstacles loom even larger for women. It is as if, in our fear and awe, we resort to our most ancient and entrenched beliefs about sex roles. In these times, female members of Congress face their greatest rhetorical challenges.

Counterproductive Responses

The female members of Congress who spoke during the Persian Gulf War debates faced a rhetorical situation where masculine, gender-marked language and argument ruled the day. Male members of Congress especially knew the political price they would pay if they were perceived to be "weak," "soft," or "appeasers." There was perhaps no better moment in recent congressional history where a situation was so thoroughly tied to maintaining images of traditional sex roles. Unfortunately, the "sexualized" and "gendered" nature of the war discussion put all congresswomen in an untenable rhetorical situation. If they used those strategies that demonstrated their traditional femininity, their arguments would be highly personal, singular, and particular. Their arguments would not be able to "engage," let alone challenge, the sweeping political, economic, and geostrategic arguments that dominated the discussion. If the congresswomen adopted deductive, abstract, and general arguments about whether to go to war, they risked sounding like most of their male colleagues and appearing to violate sex roles at a time when sex roles were being strongly enforced.

My analysis of the group of speeches given by the female members of Congress illuminates an interesting division. Those representatives who supported the resolution authorizing the use of military force against Iraq utilized militaristic jargon and "talking points" suggested by the Bush administration. They are practically indistinguishable from the vast majority of speeches in favor of the war. For example, many in this group of speeches reasoned deductively—principles were laid out and the specific case of Iraq was judged by it. Remarks by Representative Olympia Snowe of Maine provides a good illustration:

> Tomorrow, I will vote to support the U.N. resolution and preserve all our options against Iraq. I will do so not because the military option is inevitable but in order not to undermine the President's efforts to achieve a peaceful outcome to this crisis—efforts which require that a credible military threat be maintained against a brutal aggressor who only understands the language of force. A credible threat is necessary against a man who has raised one of the world's largest armies, used chemical weapons against

his own people, invaded two neighbors and is developing nuclear and biological capabilities. We are hardly dealing with a man of peace in Saddam Hussein.

In another respect, the language of the war's supporters was often abstract and generalized. References to American soldiers were almost always in terms of "American forces" or the "fine men and women of the military."

In contrast, references to soldiers on the part of the war's opponents were couched in possessive terms like *our* and highlighted the soldiers' youth and vulnerability. Barbara Boxer repeatedly referred to soldiers as "our children" or "our kids." The war, she said, was "not about egg on our faces; it is about blood on our kids." Representative Patsy Mink of Hawaii also made a speech quite typical of this approach:

> Before we commit our children to this violence, I ask that Congress tell our children why declaring war against Iraq is necessary for peace in the world, and that Congress advise our children that they go to war because their Government has exhausted all other avenues to peace. I can say neither to my children nor to your children, and so I must vote no against war, and yes for a greater effort for peace.

This quotation aptly demonstrates the personal tone of the speaker. She invites audience members to consider their own offspring and to focus on themselves and their own families rather than generalized abstractions like the new world order.

The quality of abstraction versus concrete specificity is the single most defining difference between the speeches by the war's supporters and opponents. The female opponents tried to reduce the "distance" between war as a concept and war as a bloody reality. Utilizing what Karilyn Kohrs Campbell, a leading scholar of women and rhetoric, calls the "feminine style," they took four rhetorical paths: they discussed the potential war in familiar, highly personal terms; they argued that the abstract logic used by the war's supporters was inappropriate; they vividly depicted the war's violent outcome on human bodies and body parts; and they tried to assert the primacy of domestic issues over foreign policy issues. A speech by Marcy Kaptur illustrates the personal tone taken by many of the war's opponents:

> Let me speak as one of the members of Congress who grew up during the Vietnam era, whose friends fought and died in that battle. . . . I speak on behalf of every mother, every wife, every father, every husband and relative who has a loved one serving our Nation in the U.S. military.

Other representatives tried to deny the abstract logic of war that they heard during the debates. Boxer quipped that "this is not about . . . saving face. It is about saving lives. Peace through war makes about as much sense as health through sickness." Representative Cardiss Collins of Illinois made a similar argument when she noted that "there is not yet any reason good enough to die for. America should not be in the business of wasting our young lives for the sake of some oblique geopolitical strategy contrived on some chalkboard."

Whereas the war's supporters talked mostly about the political, economic, and strategic ramifications of going to war, several of the war's opponents reminded the country that Americans would not just be "lost" in battle but would be killing other people as well. The opponents stressed that war takes its toll on humans, especially human bodies. Representative Jolene Unsoeld of Washington utilized this technique when she argued that

> war is not a simple righting of wrongs. It is about tears and pain. It is about lost arms and legs. It is about paralyzed bodies lying inert in already overwhelmed veteran hospitals. It is about shattered dreams and shattered families and children losing their mothers and fathers. It is about sending America's children to kill and be killed.

In similar fashion, Boxer drew upon the lyrics of a song popularized by Bette Midler called "From a Distance" in order to chastise the war's supporters. Although Boxer was roundly ridiculed for employing such an unlikely and "inappropriate" source, the lyrics supported the point of her argument:

> From a distance we all have enough, and no one is in need, and there are no guns, no bombs, and no disease, no hungry mouths to feed. From a distance you look like my friend, even though we are at war. From a distance I just can't comprehend what all this fighting is for. . . . Have you ever seen a body that is shot apart? Have you ever seen it up close? From a distance, from very far away, it may look still and peaceful. But up close you see the violence, the pain, the suffering, the horror.

The final way that women who opposed the war dealt with the rhetorical obstacles they faced was by comparing foreign and domestic policy. In doing this, they attempted to speak about subjects that were properly thought of as belonging to women's "sphere." A number of female representatives made analogies between the expenses of running Operation Desert Storm and what that money might be used for in the United States. Representative Barbara-Rose Collins of Michigan, who had been sworn in only a week earlier, questioned why the Bush administration was willing to spend so much money on a foreign monarchy "in a time of limited resources to rebuild our cities, feed and house our homeless, and educate our young." Mary Rose Oakar noted that the monthly price tag of more than $2 billion "has led us into a recession which has seen a loss of almost a million jobs in the past five months." Representative Louise Slaughter of New York asked a series of rhetorical questions about the costs of the war, including "What will be the cost, for example, of caring for a new generation of disabled veterans, who will require a lifetime of medical care as a result of the Persian Gulf War?" Finally, Boxer said in a very impassioned statement:

> A robbery is taking place right here, right now. Billions of dollars out the door to pay for an operation called the World vs. Saddam Hussein. But the world does not pay. We do—Uncle Sugar Daddy. . . . We have spent more on Desert Shield so far than we spend in one year on Head Start, cancer research, AIDS research, Alzheimer's, heart research, and childhood immunization, all combined.

Traditionally, the use of the "feminine style" of rhetoric is a helpful and appropriate way to deal with the competing demands that a female speaker be simultaneously logical and feminine. In this case, however, I believe that the rhetoric strategies that usually assuage an audience about a rhetor's femininity undermined the arguments that the women made in opposing the war. By discussing the effects of war on human bodies, the women reinforced stereotypes that women cannot "reason" about war beyond the purely physical, emotional, and specific level. Those women who avoided the "feminine style" and spoke in an acceptably warriorlike language did not make themselves seem unfeminine as much as they made themselves invisible as women. They did not bring a "woman's perspective" to the debate. I leave other writers the task of determining whether there are unique, "essential" female qualities. But in a warlike context where pressures to conform to the most rigid sex roles are in force, the breadth and diversity of human experience with war ought to be considered and discussed.

"Power-Over" Politics

Short of a direct challenge to the underlying assumptions of the war discourse, no amount of rhetorical adaptation would have benefited the women. It is a vivid example of what Jean Bethke Elshtain called the "incommensurable universes" between the language of military warriors and war victims. In addition, I believe that, by failing to illuminate and attack the war's premise of "power-over" politics, no woman would have been able to credibly raise concerns about the war's effect on women and the environment.

The fundamental truth of war is that individuals are supposed to kill other human beings. To do otherwise is to not be engaged in war. Killing another human being is an act that relies on the highest form of abstract thinking—the mental transformation of oneself as a superior being whose lethal violence is justified and the transformation of one's enemy into a lesser "other" whose death is not only acceptable but morally inconsequential. The entire practice of war is predicated on the abstract concept of "exchangeability of human beings," including those in one's own military forces. By using this phrase, I mean to highlight the mental transformation that one must endure to continuously ignore one's ability to sense unending variations among people. Even among one's own troops, one tries to replace or exchange one fallen soldier with another, as if they were identical entities. The use of regulation haircuts, physical qualities, and military uniforms are all designed to reinforce the perception that one soldier is indistinguishable from another and therefore replaceable. The most important abstraction, however, is the one that transforms "equally created men" into superior and inferior men and thereby the justification for militarily dominating the inferiors. This form of thinking has been referred to as *"power-over" politics.*

Beliefs in the justification of "power-over" politics served as the core assumption by both Iraq and the United States before and during the Persian Gulf War. Saddam Hussein obviously believed that it was appropriate for his troops to invade Kuwait, oppress the people through rapes, torture, and killing, and take the country's material goods. George Bush characterized the Iraqi actions as "naked aggression," and indeed they were. Nevertheless, Bush's actions were predicated on the exact same set of operating assumptions that Saddam Hussein used—power over.

The speeches given by the female opponents of the Gulf War were materially, argumentatively, and rhetorically ineffective because they did nothing to challenge power-over politics, or the use of force to make one's will manifest. No female legislator asked whether the United States had any right to compel another country to do its bidding, either through economic embargoes, United Nations sanctions, or military aggression. In fact, many of the women affirmed that the United States "could not allow" Saddam Hussein's troops to stay in Kuwait. Thus the main question discussed during the congressional debate was not *if* the United States should force Iraq to do its will but *how best* to force Iraq to do its will. In agreeing that the United States could force its will on Iraq, the female legislators ended up granting both the premise of power-over politics and the underlying justification for going to war.

When they accepted the underlying premise of the war—power-over—the congresswomen ensured that their arguments opposing the war would be unconvincing. In their speeches, Representatives Pelosi and Boxer attempted to make the concerns of women and the environment count in a context where domination of women and the ecosystem is part and parcel of power-over thinking. The rape of women by soldiers and the environmental degradation are an accepted reality (even perquisite) of war; they also symbolically represent the internal dynamic of war. During these times, women are not only secondary but also play a "background" role for the political and military action. We are supposed to eagerly support military aggression by laboring in munitions factories, raising children on our own, and providing "support services" to the men near the "front," as well as providing moral support, comfort, sexual release, and a rapt, listening audience for war stories when the fighting is over. The role of

being a supportive backdrop is similar to the role played by the ecosystem during a war. The environment is perceived to be unimportant because it serves as background for the use and support of military action. It is supposed to easily give up its resources to the fighting forces without fail. Its well-being must not supplant the military objective.

Being Heard

An analysis of the speeches given by female members of Congress during the Gulf War debates demonstrates that their relative silence about the war's effect on women and the environment was a product of social forces that narrowed the range of "acceptable" topics to military, economic, and geostrategic prudence. Their silence reflects the inability to make women and the environment "count" when the real issue of the debate was how best to overpower Iraq. The power-over politics that justified our involvement in the Persian Gulf War is the same dynamic that justifies using women as sexual war booty, destroying the environment in war, and denigrating women's concerns as unimportant in congressional debates.

The conceptual framework which connects rhetoric, rape, and ecowarfare is typified by several faulty beliefs: that humankind is independent of, not reliant upon, the nonhuman environment; that the needs of nations and individuals are independent of the needs of other nations and individuals; that our primary concerns are immediate rather than long-term, and instant gratification best solves our problems and meets our needs; and that our independence from one another also makes us better than one another. Thus to meet our own immediate needs or desires we may engage in any form of behavior, including oppression, dominance, and destruction of those we identify as "other," even when in the process we destroy our own long-term self-interest and sustenance.

The actions of both the United States and Iraq during the Persian Gulf War demonstrate that each country adheres to this patriarchal conceptual framework. Until concerned women and men are able to directly challenge the underlying assumptions of power-over politics and this conceptual framework, wars will continue to be fought and the effect on women and the environment will continue to seem irrelevant.

Adrienne Elizabeth Christiansen is an associate professor of communication studies at Macalester College in Saint Paul, Minnesota. This article is adapted from Christiansen's "Rhetoric, Rape, and Eco-warfare in the Persian Gulf" in Ecofeminism: Women, Culture, Nature *(edited by Karen J. Warren and published by Indiana University Press, 1997; available at bookstores or by calling 800-842-6796).*

Women in Power: From Tokenism to Critical Mass

by Jane S. Jaquette

ever before have so many women held so
much power. The growing participation
and representation of woman in politics is
one of the most remarkable developments of
the late twentieth century. For the first time,
women in all countries and social classes are
becoming politically active, achieving dramatic gains in the number and kind of offices
they hold. Why is political power, off limits
for so long, suddenly becoming accessible to
women? And what are the implications of this
trend for domestic and foreign policy?

Women have been gaining the right to vote
and run for office since New Zealand became
the first country to authorize women's suffrage in 1893. By 1920, the year the United
States amended the Constitution to allow
women to vote, 10 countries had already
granted women the franchise. Yet many European countries did not allow women to vote
until after World War II, including France,
Greece, Italy, and Switzerland. In Latin America, Ecuador was the first to recognize
women's political rights, in 1929; but women
could not vote in Mexico until 1953. In Asia,
women voted first in Mongolia, in 1923; then,
with the U.S. occupation after 1945, women
secured the right to vote in Japan and South
Korea. The former European colonies in Africa and Asia enfranchised women when they

gained independence, from the late 1940s into
the 1970s.

Historically, women began to demand the
right to vote by claiming their equality: If all
men are created equal, why not women? The
American and British suffrage movements inspired "women's emancipation" efforts among
educated female (and sometimes male) élites
worldwide, and most contemporary feminist
movements trace their roots to these stirrings
at the turn of the century. The nineteenth-
century European movements had a strong
influence on the thinking of Friedrich Engels,
who made gender equality a central tenet of
socialist doctrine. A similar movement among
the Russian intelligentsia ensured that the
equality of women in political and economic
life would be an important goal of the Soviet
state—and subsequently of its Central and
Eastern European satellites.

> *Historically, a country's level of economic development has not been a reliable indicator of women's representation.*

But if the logic existed to support women's
claims to political equality, the facts on the
ground did not. As educated women mobilized to demand the right to vote, men in all
countries largely resisted, with the result that
most of the world's women gained this basic

JANE S. JAQUETTE *is chair of the department of diplo-
macy and world affairs and B. H. Orr professor of liberal
arts at Occidental College. Her latest book* Trying Democracy: Women in Post–Authoritarian Politics in
Latin America and Central and Eastern Europe *will
be published by The Johns Hopkins University Press
soon.*

right of citizenship only in the last 50 years. Before women could vote, they organized to influence legislation, from the marriage and property rights acts of the mid-nineteenth century to the early twentieth century wave of Progressive legislation in the United States and Western Europe's generous maternal and protective labor laws.

However, the vote itself did not bring women into politics. On the contrary, some countries gave women the right to vote but not to run for office. In virtually every nation, women who tried to enter politics were subject to popular ridicule. Political parties routinely excluded women from decision-making positions, resisted nominating them as candidates, and denied their female candidates adequate campaign support.

Cultural factors partially explain the varying degrees of women's representation from region to region and country to country. Predictably, women in the Nordic and northern European countries, with long traditions of gender equality, have been the most successful in breaking through traditional resistance and increasing their representation. In contrast, those in Arab countries, with curbs against women in public life and contemporary pressures to abandon secular laws for religious rules, have consistently registered the lowest levels of female participation (and the lowest levels of democratization).

But "culture" does not fully explain why women in the United States and Great Britain, which rank high on various measures of gender equality, accounted for less than 7 percent

of all parliamentarians as late as 1987. Nor have women been excluded from politics in all Islamic nations. The legislatures of Syria and Indonesia, while decidedly undemocratic, are composed of 10 to 12 percent women. Former prime ministers Benazir Bhutto of Pakistan and Khaleda Zia of Bangladesh have wielded major power in Muslim societies.

Historically, a country's level of development has not been a reliable indicator of women's representation. Of the 32 most developed countries that reported electoral data in 1975, 19 had fewer than 10 percent female legislators and 11 had fewer than 5 percent. In France, Greece, and Japan—all developed, industrialized countries—female members accounted for 2 percent or less of their legislatures.

Although more women than ever are working for wages, even an increase in female participation in the work force does not necessarily translate into greater political clout for women. In recent years, for example, much of the growth in participation has been in low-wage labor. And although women's managerial participation has increased dramatically in many countries, from New Zealand to Peru, women are still rarely found at the highest levels of corporate management and ownership. Their underrepresentation in top management limits the number of private sector women invited to enter government as high-level appointees; women's lower salaries, in turn, restrict an important source of financial support for female candidates.

One can, however, discern significant worldwide increases in female representation

Percent of Women in National Legislatures, by region, 1975–97			
	1975	1987	1997*
Arab States	3.5	2.8	3.3
Asia (Asia excluding China, Mongolia, N. Korea, Vietnam)†	8.4 (3.8)	9.7 (6.2)	13.4 (6.3)
Central and Eastern Europe and Former Soviet Union	23.3	23.1	11.5
Developed countries (excluding East Asia)	5.1	9.6	14.7
Latin America and the Caribbean	6.0	6.9	10.5
Nordic Countries	16.1	28.8	36.4

* 1997 statistics for lower houses and single house systems. (Mongolia excluded.)
† women's representation under party control

Sources: *Democracy Still in the Making: A World Comparative Study* (Geneva: Inter-Parliamentary Union, 1997) and *The World's Women, 1970–1990: Trends and Statistics* (New York: United Nations, 1991).

beginning in 1975, the year in which the United Nations held its first international women's conference. From 1975 to 1995, the number of women legislators doubled in the developed West; the global average rose from 7.4 percent to nearly 11 percent.

Between 1987 and 1995 in particular, women's representation registered a dramatic increase in the developed countries, Africa, and Latin America. Of the 32 women who have served as presidents or prime ministers during the twentieth century, 24 were in power in the 1990s. In the United States, women now make up 11.2 percent of Congress, about one-third the proportion in Nordic countries, but substantially higher than the 5 percent in 1987. And although only 23 women won seats in the Diet in Japan's 1996 elections, an unprecedented 153 women ran for office. In 1997, the Inter-Parliamentary Union reported only nine countries with no women in their legislatures. From 1987 to 1995, the number of countries without any women ministers dropped from 93 to 47, and 10 countries reported that women held more than 20 percent of all ministerial-level positions, although generally in "female" portfolios like health, education, and environment rather than the "power ministries" like finance and defense.

The only exception to the global acceleration in women's representation during the past decade is in the New Independent States of the former Soviet Union and the former members of the Eastern bloc. Here, representation has dropped from earlier highs under communist rule of 25 to 35 percent women (although they exercised little real power) to around 8 to 15 percent today, and numbers are lower in the largely Muslim states of Central Asia. Where women's representation is still under Communist Party control, as in China, North Korea, and Vietnam, women still account for about 20 percent of the national legislators.

THE GLOBALIZATION OF THE WOMEN'S MOVEMENT

Why the surge in women officeholders in the last 10 years?

Three interconnected reasons seem to stand out: First, the rise of women's movements worldwide has heightened women's awareness of their political potential and developed new issues for which women are ready to mobilize. Second, a new willingness by political

parties and states to ease the constraints on women's access to politics, from increasing their recruitment pools to modifying electoral systems and adopting quotas. And third, as social issues supplant security concerns in the post–Cold War political environment, opportunities have opened for new styles of leadership and have reordered political priorities.

The recent wave of female mobilization is a response to a series of political and economic crises—and opportunities—over the last two decades. On the political front, women's groups like the Madres de la Plaza de Mayo (Argentine mothers who demonstrated on behalf of their "disappeared" husbands and children) helped to inspire the defense of human rights in Latin America and beyond. Women were also recognized as valued participants in the opposition to authoritarian rule in the former Soviet bloc, where they

Women on Women

"A man, who during the course of his life has never been elected anywhere, and who is named prime minister (it was the case with George Pompidou and Raymond Barre, who had never been elected to any position)—everyone found that absolutely normal. A woman who has been elected for 10 years at the National Assembly . . . at the regional level, who is the mayor of a city, it is as if she were coming out of nowhere."
—Edith Cresson, former prime minister of France

"I really do think that women are more cautious in adopting . . . decisions [to go to war]. . . . But I don't think that the woman will ever sacrifice the interests of the nation or the interest of the state due to . . . weakness."
—Kazimiera Prunskiene, former prime minister of Lithuania

"The traditional issues we were steered into—child care, health care, and education—have now become the sexy issues of the decade."
—Nancy K. Kopp, former speaker pro tem. of the Maryland House of Delegates

"Women cannot lead without men, but men have to this day considered themselves capable of leading without women. Women would always take men into consideration. That's the difference."
—Vigdis Finnbogadóttir, former president of Iceland

"Do I have an option?"
—Patricia Schroeder, former U.S. representative, when asked by the press if she was "running as a woman."

Sources: Laura Liswood, Women World Leaders (London: HarperCollins, 1994); Linda Witt, Karen M. Paget, & Glenna Matthews, Running as a Woman: Gender and Power in American Politics (New York: Free Press, 1994).

took up the cause of human rights when their husbands and sons were arrested—dissident Andrei Sakharov's wife, Yelena Bonner, is just one example. In Africa and Asia, women are increasingly regarded as important opposition figures. In South Africa, for example, women were among prominent anti-apartheid leaders and have helped to lead the new government-sponsored effort to develop a women's charter for the post–apartheid period. In Iran, women have played an important role in defining electoral outcomes, despite the conventional wisdom that they are powerless.

The Old Girls Network

Historically, one of the greatest barriers to elected office for women has been inadequate financial support. Often lacking incumbent status or access to financial networks, they have had to build their own fund-raising networks from scratch.

One of the most successful such groups has been EMILY's List (EMILY stands for Early Money is Like Yeast), the first partisan organization set up to fund women candidates in the United States. Ironically for an organization that is now America's largest political action committee (PAC), its roots lie in a political defeat. In 1982, Harriet Woods won the Democratic primary for a Senate seat in Missouri but then received only token financial backing from her party. She called on Washington, D.C., philanthropist Ellen Malcolm for help. But the money proved to be too little and too late to counter her male opponent's negative advertising campaign. Stung by this defeat, Malcolm went on to found EMILY's List in 1985 to raise money for Democratic women candidates who support abortion rights (a.k.a., "pro-choice").

EMILY's List received a major boost in 1992, when the all-male Senate Judiciary Committee confirmed Clarence Thomas to the U.S. Supreme Court despite law professor Anita Hill's accusations of sexual harassment. A torrent of female outrage turned into a record flood of financial support for female candidates in that year's elections. EMILY's List grew from 3,000 to 23,000 members and raised $6 million. It also inspired several state-level imitators, including May's List in Washington State and the Minnesota $$ Million. And EMILY's List now has a number of Republican competitors, including WISH (Women in the Senate and House), which supports pro-choice female candidates, and the Women's Leadership Fund.

According to Rutgers University's Center for the American Woman and Politics, 11 national and 47 state or local PACs and donor networks now either give money predominantly to women or receive most of their contributions from women. Organizations to fund women candidates have been established in several other nations as well. In 1993, Britain's Labour Party launched EMILY's List U.K. In 1995, the Australian Labor Party decided to form its own version of EMILY's List to meet its target of a 35 percent female Parliament by 2002.

On the economic front, the widespread adoption of market-oriented reforms, often accompanied by austerity programs, has had a severe impact on many women, who in turn have organized against price rises and the loss of health care and other public services. Women created communal kitchens in Chile and Peru to help feed their communities. Other small-scale, self-help programs like the Grameen Bank in Bangladesh and the Self-Employed Women's Association in India were developed to meet women's needs for credit. The war in Bosnia put an international spotlight on rape as a weapon of war and led to the demand that "women's rights" be considered "human rights" rather than some different or lesser category of concern.

These efforts were reinforced by international connections, many of which were created by the U.N. Decade for Women (1976–85). Three times during the decade (in 1975, 1980, and 1985) and again in 1995, the United Nations convened official delegations from member countries to report on the status of women and to commit governments to remedy women's lack of access to political, economic, and educational resources. Not only did these conferences encourage a flurry of local and national organizing, but they produced parallel meetings of nongovernmental organizations (NGOS), including the nearly 30,000 women who participated in the NGO conference in Beijing in 1995.

The Decade for Women originally meant that women's issues were geared to the U.N. agenda, which in the 1970s focused on the creation of a "new international economic order" and a more equitable sharing of resources between North and South. By the mid-1980s, however, attention had shifted from integrating women into world development efforts to enhancing roles for women in the promotion of market economics and democracy. The turn toward democracy made it easier for women to seek explicitly political goals, and the footdragging by the U.N. and its member countries on implementing their international pledges helped to stimulate women's interest in increasing their political power.

BREAKING THE POLITICAL GLASS CEILING

Since some of the public policies holding women back from greater political power—particularly women's access to education—

have been easing rapidly, attention has turned to other barriers. Chief among them have been the constraints on the pool of women available to run for office. Although women constitute a growing proportion of the rank and file in political parties, unions, and civil services, they still account for only a small proportion of the higher echelons that provide a springboard to higher political office.

Although women participate more actively in local government than they do at the national level, many more men make the jump from local to national leadership. One problem has been a lack of campaign funds. In the United States, women began to address that obstacle in the 1980s through innovative fundraising strategies. In other countries, women have organized voting blocs to support female candidates. Yet there is only one women's political party, in Iceland, that has succeeded over time in electing women to office. By the mid-1990s, the European-based Inter-Parliamentary Union was holding meetings twice a year for female parliamentarians aimed at improving their electoral skills as well as their abilities to perform more effectively in office. In another innovative effort, a group called Women of Russia organized to stem the decline in women's representation under the new democratic electoral rules. Women of Russia surprised everyone by gathering over 100,000 signatures and winning 8 percent of the vote in the 1993 Duma elections, but in the 1995 elections they failed to maintain the minimum level of support necessary under Russian electoral rules. As a result of Women in Russia's initial success, however, other Russian parties are nominating more women.

Research has shown that different kinds of voting systems can dramatically affect women's chances of election. The widely accepted explanation for the relatively low numbers of female legislators in the United States and Britain is their "single-member district" electoral systems. When each district elects only one candidate, minority votes are lost. Significantly more women are elected in countries with electoral systems based on proportional representation (in which candidates are elected from party lists according to the percentage of total votes the party receives) or on at-large districts ("multi-member constituencies"). Several countries have experimented with different electoral systems, including mixed single-member and multi-member district systems, to improve the partici-

pation of underrepresented groups, particularly women.

The surest way to achieve an increased number of women in national legislatures is to adopt a quota system that requires a certain percentage of women to be nominated or elected. Although the issue of quotas is scarcely open to debate in the United States—where Lani Guinier's nomination for U.S. attorney general in 1993 was torpedoed by detractors' interpretations of essays she had written in support of "group" representation—many political parties (especially on the Left) and national legislatures around the world are experimenting with gender quotas. Quotas account for the high levels of female representation in the Nordic countries and for the recent doubling (to 18 percent) of the number of women in the House of Commons in Britain when the Labour Party swept the election. A quota law in Argentina increased the women in its house of representatives from 4 percent in 1991 to over 16 percent in 1993 and 28 percent in 1995. In Brazil, when quotas were used in the 1997 congressional elections, the number of women legislators increased by nearly 40 percent since the last elections.

Quotas are used in Taiwan, by some of the political parties in Chile, and are under active discussion in Costa Rica, Ecuador, Paraguay, South Korea, and several other countries. The Indian constitution now mandates that one-third of the seats in local government bodies be "reserved" for women, and Pakistan is debating a similar measure. In Mexico, the Institutional Revolutionary Party (PRI) and its leftist opposition have adopted quotas, while the right-of-center party accepts the goal but maintains that it can promote women as effectively without them. Japan has adopted measures to ensure that more women are appointed to ministerial posts, and Bangladesh, among other countries, is experimenting with quotas for top civil service jobs.

It is obvious that quotas increase the number of women officeholders, but why are they being adopted now? Even where quotas are not seen to violate fundamental notions of democracy, as they appear to be in the United States, there are powerful arguments against them. Some insist that they will ghettoize women legislators and their issues. Others object that quotas lead to "proxy" representation, where women legislators run as "fronts" for their husbands or other male interests. In India, for example, there are many anecdotal cases of this phenomenon, and in

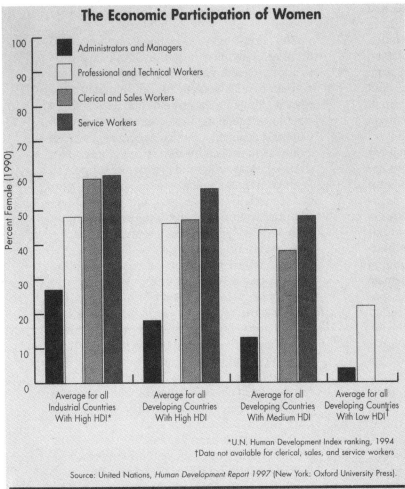

The Economic Participation of Women

Percent Female (1990)

- Administrators and Managers
- Professional and Technical Workers
- Clerical and Sales Workers
- Service Workers

Average for all Industrial Countries With High HDI*

Average for all Developing Countries With High HDI

Average for all Developing Countries With Medium HDI

Average for all Developing Countries With Low HDI†

*U.N. Human Development Index ranking, 1994
†Data not available for clerical, sales, and service workers

Source: United Nations, *Human Development Report 1997* (New York: Oxford University Press).

WHAT DO WOMEN WANT?

The post–Cold War shift in national priorities from defense and security concerns to social and environmental issues also plays to women's strong suits. So do the negative impacts of economic globalization and structural adjustment policies, which have put the need for effective social safety nets high on domestic agendas. Many observers argue that the rejection of "unbridled capitalism" and the desire to retain social welfare policies explain the victories of the Labour Party in Britain, the socialists in France, and the electoral loss of the PRI in Mexico last July. Rightly or wrongly, many voters also associate market reforms with a rise in corruption. Despite accusations of corruption against leaders such as Pakistan's Bhutto and Tansu Ciller in Turkey, women's perceived "purity" and their status as outsiders, once considered political weaknesses, are now seen as strengths. In the last 10 years, it is not so much the case that women have come to politics; rather, politics has come to women.

If the trend continues, quotas will soon produce a quantum leap in women's political power. For the first time, women will form a "critical mass" of legislators in many countries, able to set new agendas and perhaps create new styles of leadership. How will women use their growing political influence?

One way to predict the direction of change is to look at how the political attitudes of women differ from those of men. Surveys show that one of the most persistent gender differences regards attitudes toward peace and war: Women are more pacifistic than men, less likely to favor defense spending, or to support aggressive policies abroad. Recent interviews of women heads of state show that most believe that they are more committed to peace than their male counterparts. Historically and today, women and women leaders are more interested in the so-called "soft" issues, including the environment and social welfare. On some measures, women are more conservative than men: They are less likely to vote for the parties on the Left, and rather than pursue their own self-interests, they

Argentina there are complaints that many of the women nominated by the majority Peronist Party (which pushed through the quota law) have been chosen because of their unquestioning loyalty to President Carlos Saul Menem rather than because of their qualifications as candidates—as if only women could be considered party hacks.

Despite the controversy quotas raise, they have become popular not only because women have organized to push for them, but—importantly—because more men have become convinced that quotas serve useful political goals in a more democratic environment. A sea change in attitudes about women in public office is occurring at a time when the number of countries under some form of democratic governance is expanding rapidly, giving new salience to the question of whether national legislatures are truly representative of pluralistic societies. Adequate representation of all groups could strengthen the consolidation of democracies that are open and responsive—and thus make them more durable.

more often mobilize for defensive reasons—namely to protect the interests of the family. As a result, these tendencies will probably place more focus on policies to support the family and to strengthen local communities.

But women are far from conservative in one important sense: Women are more likely than men to support state regulation of business to protect the consumer and the environment and to assure that the needs of society's weakest members are addressed. Because women are often more skeptical than men about the effectiveness of market reforms, the election of more women may signal a softening of some of reform's harsher aspects. The market's continued dominance in global politics will reinforce women s efforts to improve their access to the resources that count, from education and credit to the ownership of land and housing.

Women who find themselves experiencing real power for the first time may decide to try out blanket initiatives in areas that they believe male leaders have traditionally neglected: declarations banning war and legislation on children's rights and social or political morality.

However, radical change is unlikely. Predictions that women will act as a bloc have never been borne out in the past. Like their male counterparts, female officeholders come from all parts of the ideological spectrum and depend on the support of diverse and often divided constituencies. Women leaders are not necessarily pacificists or environmentally oriented. While former prime minister Gro Harlem Brundtland of Norway or Ireland's president Mary Robinson may support the "soft" issues, Indira Gandhi or Margaret Thatcher is capable of using force to achieve her ends.

Further, few of the initiatives on those social issues mobilizing women today directly confront male power. Global support for efforts to stem violence against women is an important exception. Antidiscrimination legislation has been developed at the international level through the U.N. Convention on the Elimination of All Forms of Discrimination Against Women—which has been ratified by 160 countries, but not the United States. The implementation of the instrument by signatories, however, lags far behind. And women leaders themselves disagree on many of the issues affecting women most, from reproductive rights and family law to genital mutilation.

Today, women are recruited aggressively into politics not to right past inequities or to recognize their equal citizenship—but to bring a different, explicitly female perspective to the political arena and to appeal to the women's vote. Whether the rationale for increasing female representation is equality or difference, women will have an unprecedented opportunity to put their stamp on politics and to increase the range of alternatives available to policymakers across the globe.

WANT TO KNOW MORE?

Merilee Karl's compendium *Women and Empowerment: Participation and Decision-Making* (London: Zed Books, 1995) discusses women's participation in a range of institutional settings from an activist perspective. A rich and thoughtful treatment of women's political participation covering a variety of cases is *Women and Politics Worldwide*, Barbara Nelson & Najma Chowdhury, eds. (New Haven: Yale University Press, 1994). Laura Liswood interviews 15 female politicians in *Women World Leaders* (London: Pandora, 1994). For information on the impact of electoral systems, consult Wilma Rule & Joseph F. Zimmerman's *Electoral Systems in Comparative Perspective: Their Impact on Women and Minorities* (Westport, Connecticut: Greenwood Press, 1994). The story of women's ascent into U.S. politics is found in Linda Witt, Karen M. Paget, & Clenna Matthews' *Running as a Woman: Gender and Power in American Politics* (New York: The Free Press, 1994). Nancy Adler & Dafna Izraeli, on the other hand, present notable research on women in the private sector in *Competitive Frontiers: Women Managers in a Global Economy* (Cambridge: Blackwell, 1994).

A key source for data on women in power is the United Nations' *Human Development Report 1995* (New York: Oxford University Press, 1995), which is dedicated to gender comparisons. For some historical statistics, see *The World's Women, 1970–1990: Trends and Statistics* (New York: United Nations, 1991). Updates and special studies on women's political participation are available through the Inter-Parliamentary Union's Web page. Access this site and others on women in political and economic power through **www.foreignpolicy.com.**

The Legal Evolution of Sexual Harassment

Robert D. Lee, Jr., Penn State University, University Park

Paul S. Greenlaw, Penn State University, University Park

What is the legal status of sexual harassment policy? A coordinated policy against sexual harassment, a primary concern of employment discrimination in the 1990s, is emerging as a result of judicial decisions and executive-branch actions. This has included definitions of what constitutes quid-pro-quo and hostile-environment harassment, as well as a policy that encompasses gender harassment and seemingly the standard of the reasonable woman. Both public and private employers can be held responsible for acts of their supervisors, co-workers, and even nonemployees. The greater protections afforded public employees perhaps place a more significant responsibility on public sector employers. Several legal questions remain unanswered, and pending before Congress is legislation that would clarify the definition of harassment and impose additional requirements on employers.

Editors note: Since this article was accepted for publication, the EEOC has withdrawn the proposed guidelines reviewed here. The discussion, however, remains relevant in light of the Supreme Court's reliance on the proposed guidelines in its Harris *decision and the insights that the withdrawn regulations offer about the EEOC's views.*

In this article, we examine the legal evolution of sexual harassment in the workplace. The U.S. Supreme Court's 1993 unanimous decision in *Harris* v. *Forklift Systems, Inc.,* clarified some aspects of law. Here, a lower court ruling was overturned that would have restricted the chances of persons successfully bringing sexual harassment suits. Just prior to the handing down of this decision, the Equal Employment Opportunity Commission (EEOC) issued proposed guidelines intended to clarify what constitutes harassment and what obligations employers have in preventing and eliminating harassment. The guidelines apply broadly to "harassment based on race, color, religion, *gender,* national origin, age, or disability" (emphasis added). The Supreme Court regarded the proposed regulations sufficiently authoritative to discuss them in the *Harris* decision. As will be seen, the judicial and executive branches of the government have begun developing a coordinated approach to combatting sexual harassment in the workplace.

The discussion here, as the title of this article suggests, is primarily legal in nature. A thorough review of the literature is forgone for an examination and analysis of *primary* legal sources. These sources include decisions made by the federal courts and guidelines issued by the Equal Employment Opportunity Commission. Major emphasis is given to what is known as hostile-environment harassment, since the subject has been the main focus of attention in sexual harassment court cases.

Sex Discrimination, Sexual Harassment, and the *Harris* Case

The existence of sex discrimination in employment is well documented. Women's salaries are typically lower than those of men (Lee, 1989; Willoughby, 1991), and discrimination often presents a glass ceiling that thwarts women in advancing their careers (Bullard and Wright, 1993; Guy, 1993; Kelly, *et al.,* 1991; Merit Systems Protection Board, 1992). Those who are sexually harassed can experience severe harm in terms of their careers, personal finances, and mental health (Kreps, 1993; McCann and McGinn, 1992; Wagner, 1992). Discrimination can lead to lower overall productivity of an organization's work force.

A wide assortment of laws has addressed sex discrimination. The Equal Pay Act of 1963 required equal pay for equal work between the sexes (*Aldrich* v. *Randolph Central School District,* 1992; Greenlaw and Lee, 1993). Title VII of the Civil Rights Act of 1964 prohibited sex discrimination with respect to terms, conditions, and privileges of employment (such as in hiring, promoting, and firing employees). An amendment to Title VII, the Pregnancy Discrimination Act of 1978 prohibited discrimination based on pregnancy, childbirth, or related medical conditions (*Gedulig* v. *Aiello,* 1974; *General Electric* v. *Gilbert,* 1976). The U.S. Supreme Court in two Title VII-based cases banned sex discrimination with respect to retirement plan contributions and benefits (*City of Los Angeles, Department of Water and Power* v. *Manhart,* 1978; *Arizona Governing Committee for Tax Deferred Annuity and Deferred Compensation Plans* v. *Norris,* 1983). Special protections against various forms of sex discrimination are available to government workers through the due process clause of the Fifth and Fourteenth Amendments, and the equal protection clause of the Fourteenth Amendment. In addition, state and local cases may be filed using the Civil Rights Act of 1871. The cases are known as Section 1983 suits, since the 1871 legislation is codified at 42 U.S.C. 1983.

The topic of sexual harassment is of increasing importance as women—the usual subjects of harassment—have come to constitute a greater proportion of the work force. In a study of federal workers, 42 percent of the women reported being sexually harassed within a two-year period (Merit Systems Protection Board, 1988; 2). Half or more of working women can expect to be sexually harassed during their careers (National Council for Research on Women, 1991; 9). In 1989–1990, sexual harassment cases accounted for 5.4 percent of all cases filed before the EEOC and state human rights commissions; that number increased to 8.0 percent in 1992–1993. In this time period, the number of cases rose from 6,127 cases to 11,908, nearly a doubling of complaints (unpublished data from EEOC). All too often the investigation of complaints seems excessively slow, and those filing the complaints report they become the subjects of reprisals (General Accounting Office, 1993).

The nation's attention has been fixed on harassment charges in several recent high-profile situations. Highly publicized cases include the 1991 Clarence Thomas nomination hearings for the Supreme Court, the Navy's 1991 Tailhook convention in Las Vegas, the 1994 investigation of Senator Bob Packwood (R. OR), and the 1994 suit filed against President Clinton for allegedly engaging in sexual harassment while governor of Arkansas. Clearly, sexual harassment is one of the most prominent employment issues of the 1990s.

Sexual harassment, particularly the hostile-environment type, which will be fully explained later, has had a stormy legal history. In 1980, the EEOC issued guidelines declaring sexual harassment to be a form of sex discrimination and in violation of Title VII of the Civil Rights Act. Not until 1986— 22 years after passage of the Civil Rights Act and 6 years after the issuance of EEOC's guidelines—did the Supreme Court rule that sexual harassment violated the prohibition against sex discrimination. However, the Court's 1986 decision in *Meritor Savings Bank* v. *Vinson* did not resolve such issues as what form of behavior constituted harassment and what degree of proof must be provided in order to prevail in court. By 1993, the circuit courts were in disarray concerning the degree of severity which had to underlie hostile environment claims for the plaintiff to prevail. The *Harris* case involved a woman who worked for an equipment rental company and alleged repeated abuses by the company's president. The specific question in the *Harris* case was whether the hostile environment had to be so intense that it caused grave psychological harm. As will be seen, the Supreme Court took a middle ground between the positions of the circuits. The outcome of the case applies to all employers, including the federal, state, and local governments.

Types of Sexual Harassment

Sex was of comparatively minor concern in drafting the Civil Rights Act of 1964, and legislative intent regarding sex discrimination was unspecified in the law, and left largely unspecified in hearings and the like. Over time, the Title VII ban against sex discrimination has been interpreted to include sexual harassment, of which there are two basic types—quid pro quo and the hostile (or abusive) work environment.

Quid Pro Quo

Quid-pro-quo harassment involves tangible aspects of an employee's job. "Here the plaintiff attempts to prove that the harasser has denied job benefits, such as a promotion, [or] salary increase . . . because sexual favors were not granted; or the harasser has taken away job benefits (e.g., discharge or demotion) because sexual favors on the part of the employee were not forthcoming" (Greenlaw and Kohl, 1992; 164–165). Quid-pro-quo sexual harassment is also sometimes referred to as sexual extortion.

Not until ten years after the passage of the Civil Rights Act did a quid-pro-quo sexual harassment case reach the federal courts. Then a federal employee claimed to have been discharged for refusing to have an affair with her supervisor (*Barnes* v. *Train,* 1974). The court, however, ruled that this was "not the type of discrimination purposed by the Act and found no basis for the suit" (Woerner and Oswald, 1990; 786). In 1976, a turning point was reached when a district court ruled quid-pro-quo harassment was actionable under Title VII; the case involved employees in the Department of Justice (*Williams* v. *Saxbe,* 1976). Quid-pro-quo cases continue to the present. Current and former employees of the District of Columbia Department of Corrections filed suit in 1994 alleging "supervisors demanded sex from their female subordinates, made threats against employees who refused their advances, and retaliated against employees who complained"

(*Neal* v. *Ridley,* 1994; also see *Karibian* v. *Columbia University,* 1994).

Quid-pro-quo actions, unlike those involving a hostile environment, have *never* been heard by the Supreme Court. This is probably because the issues involved are fairly straightforward as opposed to the difficulty of defining "hostile environment."

In 1980, the EEOC adopted *Guidelines on Discrimination Because of Sex,* which covered both types of sexual harassment. The guidelines define sexual harassment as follows:

Unwelcome sexual advances, requests for sexual favors, and other verbal or physical conduct of a sexual nature constitute harassment when (1) submission to such conduct is made either explicitly or implicitly a term or condition of an individual's employment, (2) submission to or rejection of such conduct by an individual is used as the basis for employment decisions affecting such individual, or (3) such conduct has the purpose or effect of unreasonably interfering with an individual's work performance or *creating an intimidating, hostile, or offensive working environment* (emphasis added) (Equal Employment Opportunity Commission, 1980).

The first two items listed are of the quid-pro-quo form of harassment and the third is of the hostile-environment type, which is discussed shortly.

Sexual harassment was deemed to be a form of sex discrimination in the landmark Supreme Court decision of *Meritor Savings Bank, FSB* v. *Vinson* (1986). The Court's opinion strongly endorsed the EEOC 1980 guidelines, pointing out that although they were not controlling on the courts, the guidelines did represent a body of experience and judgment which the courts could use. The Court relied upon a circuit court decision involving discrimination against an Hispanic person (*Rogers* v. *Equal Employment Opportunity Commission,* 1971), noting this was "the first case to recognize a cause of action based upon a discriminatory work environment." The Court stated that subsequent to *Rogers,* courts had applied the law to harassment involving race, religion, and national origin and concluded that it was appropriate to extend the law to sexual harassment.

Hostile-Environment Harassment

In order to prevail in a claim of hostile-environment sexual harassment, one must show five conditions: "(1) she belongs to a protected group, (2) she was subject to unwelcome sexual harassment, (3) the harassment was based on sex, (4) the harassment affected a term, condition or privilege of employment, and (5) [the employer] knew or should have known of the harassment and failed to take proper remedial action" (*Burns* v. *McGregor Electronic Industries, Inc.,* 1992; 564; also see *Stafford* v. *Missouri,* 1993, involving the Missouri Department of Corrections).

The EEOC's proposed 1993 guidelines classify harassing behavior into two categories. The first refers to "epithets, slurs, negative stereotyping, or threatening, intimidating, or hostile acts" (EEOC, 1993). In the *Meritor Savings* case, a female employee alleged she was fondled by her supervisor, followed into the women's lavatory, and was forcibly raped. In the 1993

Supreme Court case of *Harris* v. *Forklift Systems, Inc.,* a woman employee was expected to obtain coins from her supervisors front pants pockets and was told that the two of them should go to a local motel to negotiate her pay raise. Sexual harassment can occur in a variety of circumstances, including after the dissolution of a mutually consenting relationship; a male supervisor might decide to harass a female subordinate after their sexual partnership ends, as apparently happened in *Babcock* v. *Frank (1992)* involving two Postal Service workers.

According to the proposed EEOC guidelines, employees are protected even when the harassing behavior "is not targeted specifically at them." For instance, a woman could file a sexual harassment charge if she repeatedly witnesses a male supervisor openly harassing another female employee. However, the courts have ruled that such third parties are not necessarily protected when mutually consenting relationships exist and sexual conduct occurs off the job. For example, a woman working for a county government failed in a hostile environment suit when she alleged a co-worker had romantic liaisons with various supervisors during nonbusiness hours; she contended these liaisons created a sexually charged work environment (*Candelore* v. *Clark County Sanitation District,* 1992).

The second category under the EEOC guidelines consists of "written or graphic material that denigrates or shows hostility or aversion toward an individual or group . . . and that is placed on walls, bulletin boards, or elsewhere on the employer's premises or circulated in the workplace" (EEOC, 1993). Instances can include posters showing people explicitly engaged in sexual acts, E-mail messages of a sexual nature broadcast to employees, and employee clothing, such as tee shirts, with sexual drawings or slogans.

Special Facets of Hostile-Environment Harassment

Several specific issues have emerged regarding hostile-environment harassment. Topics include gender-based discrimination, the severity and pervasiveness of discrimination, the reasonableness of a harassment complaint, and harassment's effects on employment.

Gender and Sex

Hostile-environment sexual harassment can be nonsexual. In other words, the environment can be negatively focused against a gender without reference to sexual behavior. In the eyes of the courts, Title VII bars "any harassment or other unequal treatment of an employee . . . that would not occur but for the sex of the employee" (*McKinney* v. *Dole,* 1985; 1138). In a case of women flag personnel at road construction sites, the use of vulgar names and less overtly sexual behavior (such as a man urinating in a woman's water bottle and men using surveying equipment to watch women urinating in ditches) was considered gender-based harassment (*Hall* v. *Gus Construction Co., Inc.,* 1985). Slapping a woman on the buttocks and making references to women as being intellectually inferior to men is prohibited behavior (*Campbell* v. *Board of Regents of the State of Kansas*, 1991; *Campbell* v. *Kansas State University*, 1991).

The 1993 *Harris* case included important gender-harassment behavior as well as behavior of a sexual nature. On several occasions, the woman employee, in the presence of other employees, was told by her supervisor "You're a woman, what do you know." She was told "We need a man as the rental manager" and was called "a dumb ass woman." Comments such as these are sex based but not sexual in content.

In its 1993 proposed harassment guidelines, the EEOC specifically notes that "sex harassment is not limited to harassment that is sexual in nature, but also includes harassment due to gender-based animus" (*Equal Employment Opportunity Commission*, 1993; 51267). The commission went on to note that these proposed broad guidelines dealing with race, age, and other forms of harassment as well as sexual harassment would not replace the existing guidelines on sexual harassment, since the latter "raises issues about human interaction that are to some extent unique in comparison to other harassment" (*Equal Employment Opportunity Commission*, 1993; 51267). Both the EEOC and the Supreme Court are adopting virtually identical stances regarding gender harassment.

At least two key questions are raised in this regard. First, is there really a single continuum of harassment ranging from highly explicit sexual behavior to somewhat overtly sexual to gender-motivated behavior or are there two different continua, with one for sex and one for gender? Second, will problems arise with sexual harassment being treated in two separate, albeit closely related regulations, and would one set of guidelines on sexual harassment be preferable to two? For the moment, the two sets of regulations appear well meshed, but whether gaps between the two will emerge in litigation is, of course, to be Determined.

Severity and Pervasiveness

In order to establish the existence of a hostile environment, the plaintiff must show that the environment was "sufficiently severe or pervasive" (*Meritor Savings*, 1986). One must show that severe sexually harassing behavior existed and/or that sexually harassing behavior existed over time and pervaded the work setting. A few harassing events over a short period fail to constitute a hostile environment (*Babcock* v. *Frank*, 1992), such as a supervisor simply uttering an epithet (*Fazzi* v. *City of Northlake*, 1994). In the case mentioned above about a woman being slapped on the buttocks, that action by itself might not have established a hostile environment but the supervisor's repeated threats to slap her did. Once the supervisor carried out this threat, the employee appropriately was continually concerned that the behavior would be repeated. In another case, a male supervisor and female subordinate met socially after work, he "rubbed his hand along her upper thigh" and kissed her; a few weeks later, they walked together during the lunch period, and he "lurched" at her from behind some bushes. This behavior, while inappropriate and warranting employer intervention, was not found to be "so pervasive or de-

bilitating as to be considered hostile" (*Saxton* v. *American Telephone and Telegraph*, 1993).

Given the vast array of human behavior that is possible, setting an explicit standard for when a hostile environment exists may be impossible, and therefore, the EEOC has a policy of treating situations on a case-by-case basis. According to the guidelines adopted in 1980, "The Commission will look at the record as a whole and at the totality of the circumstances, such as the nature of the sexual advances and the context in which the alleged incidents occurred" (EEOC, 1980). This same position is taken in the proposed 1993 guidelines.

Similarly, the Supreme Court in *Meritor Savings* held that "the record as a whole" must be examined to consider the "totality of circumstances." The Court further enunciated this standard in its 1993 *Harris* decision: "Whether an environment is 'hostile' or 'abusive' can be determined only by looking at all the circumstances. These may include the frequency of the discriminatory conduct; its severity; whether it is physically threatening or humiliating, or a mere offensive utterance; and whether it unreasonably interferes with an employee's work performance" (371).

Reasonableness and the Reasonable Woman

The proposed harassment guidelines of the EEOC provide that conduct will be judged using a "reasonable person" standard, namely what is regarded as socially acceptable behavior. The use of the term "reasonable person" goes back at least to 1988 in sexual harassment cases (*Bennett* v. *Corron & Black Corp.*, 1988). One immediate problem in applying such a standard is that behavior considered to be acceptable in some work sites, and therefore might be regarded as "reasonable," might well be considered unreasonable to others. For example, the construction industry has been notoriously sexist, often condoning behavior that would be intolerable elsewhere.

Further complicating the situation is that which may seem reasonable to men is not necessarily reasonable to women (Thacker and Gohmann, 1993). *Ellison* v. *Brady* (1991), a circuit court of appeals case involving a complaint by a U.S. Treasury Department employee, formally recognized the standard of the "reasonable woman." The alleged harassment entailed a male coworker giving a woman handwritten notes. This correspondence was largely nonlascivious but more expressive of strong affection: "I know that you are worth knowing with or without sex. . . . Leaving aside the hassles and disasters of recent weeks [sic]. I have enjoyed you so much over these past few months. Watching you. Experiencing you from O so far away. Admiring your style and elan . . ." (874). While the man might have thought the correspondence was innocent, the woman thought he was "crazy," and the court ruled that a reasonable woman would be frightened by such behavior.

Recognition of the "reasonable woman" doctrine in *Ellison* was not without controversy. Circuit Judge Stephens, in his dissent in the case, strongly criticized the "reasonable woman" concept and supported the "reasonable man" term "as it is used in the law of torts" referring to the "average adult person" (884).

Judge Stephens added, "Title VII presupposes the use of a legal term that can apply to all persons" (884).

Since the *Ellison* decision and despite the Stephens dissent, the standard of the reasonable woman has gained major acceptance. In a nonemployment case, the reasonable woman standard was used in considering the practice of male prison guards searching fully dressed female prisoners (*Jordan* v. *Gardner,* 1993). The proposed EEOC harassment guidelines state, "The 'reasonable person' standard includes consideration of the perspective of persons of the alleged victim's race, color, religion, gender, national origin, age, or disability" (EEOC, 1993).

Of particular significance, the reasonable woman standard was integral to the Supreme Court's 1993 *Harris* decision. The Court quoted at length from the district court opinion which noted that the behavior involved was harmful to women whereas it probably would have been only offensive to men but not so severe as to affect work performance. While not specifically supporting the reasonable woman standard, the Court gave the impression of supporting it; certainly, the case could have been used as an occasion for striking down the standard, had it so wished. One can anticipate the reasonable woman standard cutting in two directions in future cases. Hostile environments will be recognized where men saw no harm but women did. Also, some women may lose cases in which it is ruled that they were too easily offended and that a reasonable woman would not have been.

In concurring with the *Harris* decision, Justice Scalia expressed concern that reasonableness may provide little real guidance in determining what is a hostile work environment. He also expressed concern that the Court had used the term "abusive" apparently as a synonym for "hostile" in the context of a work environment. The lack of definition of these terms, in his opinion, allows "virtually unguided juries [to] decide whether sex-related conduct engaged in (or permitted by) an, employer is egregious enough to warrant an award of damages" (372). However, the justice admitted to having no alternative substitute that would clarify the situation.

Harassment's Effects on Employment

In order to prevail in a hostile-environment case, a plaintiff often attempts to show the severity of the harassment by indicating its effects on employment. Issues have arisen whether harassment has resulted in reduced work performance, economic or other tangible loss, psychological harm, and loss of employment due to dismissal, forced resignation, or what is known as constructive discharge.

While quid-pro-quo discrimination typically affects economic aspects of a job, such as being denied a promotion or threatened with firing if not complying with sexual advances, hostile environment harassment has no such requirement. The Supreme Court ruled in the 1986 *Meritor Savings* case that economic or tangible discrimination need not be shown and that non-economic injury could violate Title VII. In the road construction case, the women employees were convincing in identifying an extensive series of events that forced them to resign (*Hall* v. *Gus Construction Co., Inc.,* 1988). Circuit

courts will overturn district courts, finding that a set of circumstances was insufficient to result in constructive discharge (*Burns* v. *McGregor Electronic Industries, Inc.,* 1993), but also will vacate jury awards of damages when the jury is found not to have been "reasonable" and to have concluded that an employee was forced to resign because of harassment (*Stafford* v. *Missouri,* 1993). In a 1994 district court case involving "full body hugs" and "sexual innuendos, sexual advances, sexual talk, and admitted unwelcome touching," the court found that any reasonable person, male or female, would have had little choice but to resign (*Currie* v. *Kowalewski,* 1994).

One line of argument that plaintiffs have used is that the environment was so intensely hostile that it caused grave psychological harm. The circuit courts were in disagreement on this matter, sometimes ruling that the offensive conduct had to be "sufficiently severe and persistent to affect seriously the psychological well-being of an employee," as in the case of alleged harassment in the Federal Aviation Administration (*Downes* v. *FAA,* 1985; 292). Another court ruled that the environment would have to "seriously [affect] the psychological well-being of a reasonable employee" to be deemed hostile (*Rabidue* v. *Osceola Refining Co.,* 1986; 620; also see *Vance* v. *Southern Bell Telephone and Telegraph Co.,* 1989). In contrast, the important case of *Ellison* v. *Brady,* discussed above regarding the reasonable woman standard, concluded, "Surely, employees need not endure sexual harassment until their psychological well-being is seriously affected to the extent that they suffer anxiety and debilitation" (878).

The Supreme Court's 1993 *Harris* decision is important in this regard. The Court said it was taking a "middle path between making actionable any conduct that is merely offensive and requiring the conduct to cause a tangible psychological injury." In other words, a person might allege such injury to document the severity of the harassment but is not obligated to show psychological injury. In the words of the Court,

> Title VII comes into play before the harassing conduct leads to a nervous breakdown. A discriminatorily abusive work environment, even one that does not seriously affect employees' psychological well-being, can and often will detract from employees' job performance, discourage employees from remaining on the job, or keep them from advancing in their careers (370–371).

In a case subsequent to the *Harris* decision, a district court found that a female FBI employee who had suffered a mental breakdown had not linked that condition with her employment, despite a lengthy list of events on the job that supposedly had caused her illness. In referring to *Harris,* the district court held that "abnormal sensitivity" could not be the basis for a charge of sexual harassment (*Sudtelgte* v. *Reno,* 1994). Similarly, another district court found against a plaintiif, who alleged a hostile environment had resulted in "suffering from depression, inability to concentrate, sleeplessness, high blood pressure, and chest pains" but failed to offer "any evidence of sexual advances, sexual or gender-based comments, or any demeaning references to women" (*Laird* v. *Cragin Federal Bank,* 1994; 7–9, 12).

Employer Responsibilities

The 1980 EEOC guidelines indicate that an employer is responsible for the acts of its "agents and supervisory employees." In addition, the employer can be responsible for sexual harassment between fellow employees and by nonemployees.

Supervisors, Co-Workers, and Nonemployees

The Supreme Court in its 1986 *Meritor Savings* opinion left ambiguous the extent of employer responsibility.

> Congress' decision to define "employer" to include any "agent" of an employer . . . surely evinces an intent to place some limits on the acts of employees for which employers under Title VII are to be held responsible. For this reason, . . . employers are [not] always automatically liable for sexual harassment by their supervisors. . . . For the same reason, absence of notice to an employer does not necessarily insulate that employer from liability (*Meritor Savings,* 1986; 72).

The courts have attempted to resolve the seeming incongruence between the guidelines, which hold employers responsible for harassment, and *Meritor Savings,* which provides an escape hatch for employers. The prevailing trend of case law "seems to hold that employers are liable for failing to remedy or prevent a hostile or offensive work environment of which management level employees knew, or in the exercise of reasonable care should have known" (*Equal Employment Opportunity Commission* v. *Hacienda Hotel* 1989; 1515–1516). "Knew" can be read here as having received notice, while "should have known" refers to harassment which is so pervasive that management "could not have helped knowing about it" (Greenlaw and Kohl, 1992; 169).

The guidelines proposed by the EEOC provide greater detail regarding employer responsibility. An employer is responsible for the acts of its supervisors if (1) the employer "knew or should have known of the conduct and failed to take immediate and appropriate corrective action" or (2) independent of the previous condition, the supervisors were "acting in an 'agency capacity.'" This condition is met when supervisors act with "apparent authority" and (a) the employer does not have "an explicit policy against harassment" or (b) the employer does not have "a reasonably accessible procedure by which victims of harassment can make their complaints known to appropriate officials" who can take corrective action.

Meritor Savings held that simply having an antidiscrimination policy and a grievance procedure was not necessarily sufficient for protecting an employer from liability. The proposed guidelines emphasize the point that both harassment policy and grievance procedure must be in place and that they must be treated seriously by the employer. As the EEOC explains in its draft regulations, without these two conditions "employees could reasonably believe that a harassing supervisor's actions will be ignored, tolerated, or even condoned by the employer."

With regard to co-workers and harassment, employers are liable when supervisors "knew or should have known of the conduct" and did not correct the situation. An employer in a 1994 district court case was found not liable for acts of co-workers because the behavior was not reported to supervisors; a woman was allegedly hugged and kissed by a co-worker and was raped by an unknown attacker (*Doe and Doe* v. *Donnelley & Sons,* 1994).

Employers may be responsible for the acts of nonemployees when supervisors "knew or should have known of the conduct" and had some control over the nonemployees. The latter situation might involve harassment by welfare recipients, unemployment insurance clients, and others.

Types of Employers

While Title VII and the ban on hostile environment sex harassment apply to all forms of employers, other legal provisions complicate the situation. As a result, the law pertaining to hostile environment harassment varies among private employers, state and local governments, and the federal government.

With regard to private employers, not only may the company be liable but so may other parties. For example, the individual supervisor or foreman may be named in the suit (*Hall* v. *Gus Construction Co., Inc.,* 1988), and the owner of a professional corporation being the "alter ego" of the firm can be named as an individual (*Janopoulos* v. *Harvey L. Walner & Associates, Ltd.,* 1993).

State and local governments not only must comply with Title VII but they also can be liable under the equal protection clause of the Fourteenth Amendment. Moreover, state officials may be sued as individuals under Section 1983, and local governments and local officials also may be sued under Section 1983. In these cases, the plaintiffs claim their civil rights as guaranteed under 42 U.S.C. §1983 were denied them "under color of law" (*Campbell* v. *Board of Regents of State of Kansas,* 1991). The courts have held that when both Section 1983 and Title VII claims are treated together, the Title VII verdict must be consistent with the jury's decision in the Section 1983 portion of the case (*Ways* v. *City of Lincoln,* 1989; *Stafford* v. *Missouri,* 1993). (The due process clause of the Fourteenth Amendment is also a possible avenue, in which a plaintiff would claim a property right—his or her job—was denied without due process of law.)

Federal cases can become extremely complicated due to several laws possibly applying to a given situation. Besides Title VII applying, other laws include the Federal Tort Claims Act of 1946, the Federal Employees Liability Reform and Tort Compensation Act of 1988 (the Westfall Act; see *Westfall* v. *Erwin,* 1988), and appropriate state tort laws (*Mitchell* v. *Carlson,* 1990; *Bartlett* v. *United States,* 1993; *Jamison* v. *Wiley,* 1994).

Corrective and Preventive Actions by Employers

Employers must not only have a procedure by which employees can complain of harassment but that procedure must lead to corrective action. When an employee complains about being harassed by her supervisor, that complaint should not be followed by even more numerous and "intense" sexual advances (*Davis* v. *Tri-State Mack Distributors, Inc.,* 1992). In a Postal Service case, the agency was found to have taken corrective action each time a woman employee complained of sexual harassment (*Babcock* v. *Frank*, 1992). Additionally, the employer is obligated to take sufficiently strong measures to prevent the recurrence of harassment. An example of insufficient action involved a woman employee of the Veterans Administration having been harassed by a co-worker. The agency responded by having the co-worker undergo counseling, and subsequent harassment only resulted in further counseling, which failed to halt the worker's harassing behavior (*Intlekofer* v. *Turnage*, 1992; also see Butler, 1994).

Preventing sexual harassment, of course, is preferable to taking remedial action once harassment has occurred. This is the position of both the EEOC 1980 guidelines and the proposed harassment guidelines. The 1980 guidelines call for "affirmatively raising the subject, expressing strong disapproval, developing appropriate sanctions, informing employees of their rights to raise and how to raise the issue of harassment under Title VII, and developing methods to sensitize all concerned" (EEOC, 1980). The proposed guidelines recommend "an explicit policy against harassment that is clearly and regularly communicated to employees, explaining sanctions for harassment, developing methods to sensitize all supervisory and non-supervisory employees on issues of harassment, and informing employees of their right to raise, and the procedures for raising, the issue of harassment under Title VII" (EEOC, 1993). The Supreme Court's 1993 *Harris* decision, which rejected the notion that an employee would need to show psychological harm resulting from a hostile environment, is seen as underscoring the need for employers to prevent abuse, because plaintiffs are more likely to be successful in the post-*Harris* era.

Ignorance of the law is unavailable as a defense for employers. Employers are expected to comply with statutes, EEOC guidelines, and court decisions. Information is available from EEOC to help employers learn what is expected of them, including policy guidance that interprets pertinent court decisions (Equal Employment Opportunity Commission, 1990).

As an example of what can be done, Minneapolis recently replaced its existing sexual harassment policy with a more definitive one, with supervisors being held to a higher standard than other workers. To dramatize the seriousness with which the city views sexual harassment, the new policy requires that within one day of the filing of a complaint, an investigation must be begun. A supervisor who fails to enforce the policy will receive a final warning (i.e., not an initial warning) or will be discharged on the first offense of failing to enforce the policy ("New Minneapolis Sexual Harassment Policy," 1994).

Conclusion

Harris v. *Forklift Systems, Inc.* (1993) marks the second time that the Supreme Court has dealt with the hostile environment arm of sexual harassment (the other case being *Meritor Savings*, 1986). The subject perhaps has demanded the attention of the court because of the greater ambiguity associated with this form of harassment than the quid-pro-quo form. The *Harris* case reiterated earlier findings that the entire circumstances of a situation need to be reviewed in determining whether a hostile environment exists. The Court clarified the matter somewhat by offering examples of what factors to consider such as the frequency of events and whether conditions were humiliating. Importantly, the Court resolved a conflict among the circuits by ruling that plaintiffs need not show psychological injury stemming from harassment, a factor that may lead to more suits against employers and more victories. The Court for the first time acknowledged the standard of the reasonable woman but did not explicitly endorse it.

The proposed guidelines of the Equal Employment Opportunity Commission cover "gender harassment" as distinguished from the possibly more narrowly defined "sexual harassment," although the courts have found that sexual harassment only needs to be sex based and not of a sexual nature. The proposed guidelines mesh well with the *Harris* decision on such important matters as considering what behavior is reasonable, including from the perspective of the victim of harassment, and as not requiring psychological injury be shown. The guidelines place strong emphasis upon the responsibilities of employers to prevent harassment and to correct it. Federal agencies and state and local governments can be held responsible for their supervisory personnel, workers, and even nonemployees. Preventing harassment is the first line of defense, while the second is taking sufficiently strong action when harassment occurs to insure it will not recur.

Numerous ambiguities remain. As Justice Scalia noted, what the word "hostile" means is still unresolved, and the concept of "reasonableness" may provide little guidance to a jury. While the Supreme Court has recognized the existence of the reasonable woman standard, the Court has avoided explicitly endorsing it. Public employers can anticipate suits involving situations that may seem nonoffensive or reasonable to most of their men workers but not to their women workers. Cases involving public employment can be considerably more complex than private sector cases, because public workers may enlist rights beyond those guaranteed by Title VII.

Finally, legislative action may be forthcoming. Senator Patty Murray (D, Wash.) and Representative George Miller (D, Calif.) have introduced bills in Congress that would provide a definition of sexual harassment and would require employers to notify employees about their rights and how to file complaints with the Equal Employment Opportunity Commission.

■ ■ ■

Robert D. Lee, Jr., is a professor of public administration and professor of hotel, restaurant, and recreation management at The Pennsylvania State University, University Park. He is coauthor of *Public Budgeting Systems,* 5th ed. (Aspen Publishers, 1994) and author of *Public Personnel Systems,* 3rd ed. (Aspen Publishers, 1993).

Paul S. Greenlaw received his Ph.D. from the Maxwell School of Citizenship and Public Affairs, Syracuse University. He has taught American government at Duke University and worked in the personnel field in industry. He is a professor of management at Penn State where he specializes in computer educational simulation and equal employment opportunity law. He is the author or coauthor of 12 books and over 50 articles.

References

Aldrich v. *Randolph Central School District, 963* F.2d 520 (2nd Cir. 1992); cert. denied 113 S. Ct. 440 (1992).

Arizona Governing Committee for Tax Deferred Annuity and Deferred Compensation Plans v. *Norris,* 463 U.S. 1073 (1983).

Babcock v. *Frank,* 783 F. Supp. 800 (S.D.N.Y. 1992).

Barnes v. *Train,* 13 FEP 123 (D.C.D.C. 1974).

Bartlett v. *United States,* 835 F. Supp. 1246 (E.D.Wash. 1993).

Bennett v. *Corron & Black Corp.,* 845 F.2d 105(5th Cir. 1988).

Bullard, Angela M. and Deil S. Wright, 1993. "Circumventing the Glass Ceiling: Women Executives in American State Governments." *Public Administration Review,* vol. 53 (May/June), 189–202.

Burns v. *McGregor Electronic Industries, Inc.,* 955 F. 2d 559 (8th Cir. 1993a); 989 F. 2d 959 (8th Cir. 1993).

Butler, Suzanne R., 1994. "Sexual Harassment: Winning the War, but Losing the Peace." *Journal of Individual Employment Rights,* vol. 2 (4), 339–362.

Campbell v. *Board of Regents of State of Kansas,* 770 F. Supp. 1479 (D.Kan. 1991).

Campbell v. *Kansas State University,* 780 F. Supp 755 (D.Kan. 1991).

Candelore v. *Clark County Sanitation District,* 975 F. 2d 588 (9th Cir. 1992).

City of Los Angeles, Department of Water and Power v. *Manhart,* 435 U.S. 702 (1978).

Civil Rights Act, ch.22, 17 Stat. 13, 42 U.S.C. 1983 (1871).

Civil Rights Act, P.L. 88-352, 78 Stat. 241, Title VII, 42 U.S.C. 2000e 2(a) (1964).

Currie v. *Kowalewski,* U.S. Dist. Lexis 909 (N.D.N.Y. 1994).

Davis v. *Tri-State Mack Distributors, Inc.,* 981 F. 2d 340 (8th Cir. 1992).

Doe and Doe v. *Donnelley and Sons,* U.S. Dist. Lexis 1561 (S.D.Ind. 1994).

Downes v. *Federal Aviation Administration,* 775 F.2d 288 (Fed. Cir. 1985).

Ellison v. *Brady,* 924 F.2d 872 (9th Cir. 1991).

Equal Employment Opportunity Commission v. *Hacienda Hotel* 881 F.2d 1504 (9th Cir. 1989).

Equal Employment Opportunity Commission (EEOC), 1980. *Guidelines on Discrimination Because of Sex.* 29 C.F.R. 1604.11.

_____, 1990. *Policy Guidance on Current Issues of Sexual Harassment,* N-915-050.

_____, 1993. *Guidelines on Harassment Based on Race, Color, Religion, Gender, National Origin, Age or Disability.* 58 Fed. Reg. 51,266; Proposed to be codified at 29 C.F.R. 1609.

Fazzi v. *City of Northlake,* U.S. Dist. Lexis 610 (N.D.Ill. 1994).

Federal Employees Liability Reform and Tort Compensation Act (Westfall Act), PL 100-694, 102 Stat. 4563 (1988).

Federal Tort Claims Act, ch. 753, Title IV, 60 Stat. 842 (1946).

Gedulig v. *Aiello,* 417 U.S. 484 (1974).

General Accounting Office, 1993. *Federal Employment: Sexual Harassment at the Department of Veterans Affairs.* Washington: U.S. Government Printing Office.

General Electric v. *Gilbert,* 429 U.S. 125 (1976).

Greenlaw, Paul S. and John P. Kohl, 1992. "Proving Title VII Sexual Harassment." *Labor Law Journal,* vol. 43 (March), 164–171.

Greenlaw, Paul S. and Robert D. Lee, Jr., 1993. "Three Decades of Experience with the Equal Pay Act." *Review of Public Personnel Administration,* vol. 13 (Fall), 43–57.

Guy, Mary E., 1993. "Three Steps Forward, Two Steps Backward: The Status of Women's Integration in Public Management." *Public Administration Review,* vol. 53 (July/August), 285–292.

Hall v. *Gus Construction Co.,* 842 F.2d 1010 (8th Cir. 1988).

Harris v. *Forklift Systems, Inc.,* 114 S. Ct. 367 (1993).

Intlekofer v. *Turnage,* 973 F. 2d 773 (9th Cir. 1992).

Jamison v. *Wiley,* U.S. App. Lexis 558 (4th Cir. 1994).

Janopoulos v. *Harvey L. Walner & Associates, Ltd.,* 835 F. Supp. 459 (N.D.Ill. 1993).

Jordon v. *Gardner,* 986 F. 2d 1521(9th Cir. 1993).

Karibian v. *Columbia University,* 14 F.3d 773 (2nd Cir. 1994).

Kelly, Rita Mae et al., 1991. "Public Managers in the States: A Comparison of Career Advancement by Sex." *Public Administration Review,* vol. 51 (September/October), 402–412.

Kreps, Gary L., ed., 1993. *Sexual Harassment: Communication Implications.* Cresskill, NJ: Hampton Press.

Laird v. *Cragin Federal Bank,* U.S. Dist. Lexis 339 (N.D.Ill. 1994).

Lee, Yong S., 1989. "Shaping Judicial Response to Gender Discrimination in Employment Compensation." *Public Administration Review, vol. 49* (September/October), 420–430.

McCann, Nancy Dodd and Thomas A. McGinn, 1992. *Harassed: 100 Women Define Inappropriate Behavior in the Workplace.* Homewood, IL: Business One Irwin.

McKinney v. *Dole,* 765 F.2d 1129 (D.C. Cir. 1985).

Merit Systems Protection Board, 1988. *Sexual Harassment in the Federal Government: An Update.* Washington: U.S. Government Printing Office.

_____, 1992. *A Question of Equity: Women and the Glass Ceiling in the Federal Government.* Washington: U.S. Government Printing Office.

Meritor Savings Bank, FSB v. *Vinson,* 477 U.S. 57 (1986).

Mitchell v. *Carlson,* 896 F. 2d 128 (5th Cir. 1990).

National Council for Research on Women, 1991. *Sexual Harassment: Research and Resources.* New York: National Council for Research on Women.

Neal v. *Ridley,* No. 93-2420, filed 1/5/94, 32 GERR 76 (D.C.D.C. 1994).

"New Minneapolis Sexual Harassment Policy Specifies Conduct, Penalties" (1994). 32 GERR 13–14.

Pregnancy Discrimination Act, P.L. 95-955, 92 Stat. 2076 (1978).

Rabidue v. *Osceola Refining Co.,* 805 F.2d 611(6th Cir. 1986).

Rogers v. *Equal Employment Opportunity Commission,* 454 F. 2d 234 (5th Cir. 1971); cert. denied 406 U.S. 957 (1972).

Saxton v. *American Telephone and Telegraph Company,* 10 F. 3d 526 (7th Cir. 1993).

Stafford v. *Missouri,* 835 F. Supp. 1136 (W.D.Mo. 1993).

Sudtelgte v. *Reno,* U.S. Dist. Lexis 82 (W.D.Mo. 1994).

Thacker, Rebecca A. and Stephen F. Gohmann, 1993. "Male/Female Differences in Perceptions and Effects of Hostile Environment Sexual Harassment: 'Reasonable' Assumptions?" *Public Personnel Management,* vol. 22 (Fall), 461–472.

Vance v. *Southern Bell Telephone and Telegraph Co.,* 863 F.2d 1503 (11th Cir. 1989).

Wagner, Ellen J., 1992. *Sexual Harassment in the Workplace.* New York: AMACOM.

Ways v. *City of Lincoln,* 871 F. 2d 750 (8th Cir. 1989).

Westfall v. *Erwin,* 484 U.S. 292 (1988).

Williams v. *Saxbe,* 413 F. Supp. 654 (D.C.D.C. 1976).

Willoughby, Katherine, 1991. "Gender-Based Wage Gap: The Case of the State Budget Analyst." *Review of Public Personnel Administration,* vol. 12 (September/December),33–46.

Woerner, W. and S. Oswald, 1990. "Sexual Harassment in the Workplace: A View Through the Eyes of the Courts." *Labor Law Journal* vol. 40 (November), 786–793.

Unit 6

Unit Selections

Key Points to Consider

❖ Why did women agree to work in male-dominated occupations during the war?

❖ Why are gender networks and mentors important to the successful building of their careers by women?

❖ Describe the business style differences between male and female entrepreneurs. The similarities.

 **Links** ## www.dushkin.com/online/

These sites are annotated on pages 4 and 5.

The capitalist-industrial economy has been overwhelmingly a male creation, operating on principles established by men and, therefore, reflecting a male style of relationship. But increasingly a place has had to be made in it for women, whether or not men wanted it. Today between 50 to 75 percent of the labor force in industrialized countries around the world consists of women.

Yet women have always shared the burden of providing for their families. Alongside their spouses, they helped to provide shelter and clothing. Women also ran the family business which, early on, was farming. Not only did women manage the household; they constructed material for clothing from raw flax and cotton while nursing and caring for their children; they also helped sow crops used for consumption by the family or sold for profit.

With the coming of the industrial revolution and the need for labor outside the home, women and children transferred their labor from the farm to the factory. The industrial revolution, thus, moved basic textile construction out of the home and into large mass-production mills. This familiarity with factory work eased the later transfer of women into war industries, while husbands and loved ones fought overseas.

Women made great strides during World War II, moving into more skilled and higher-paying jobs. As servicemen returned, however, women were rolled back to their lower status, unskilled positions. They were also encouraged by television programming and government propaganda to assume their previous role—housewife.

Today, increasing numbers of women are entering traditionally male-dominated professions. Thirty-five years ago there were few women engineers, dentists, attorneys, or physicians. In the early 1990s, women have entered these fields in substantial numbers. Yet women's earnings remain in the range of 50–60 percent of men's on average. This earnings gap is most visible among middle-aged women. The earnings of young women are almost equivalent to those of men of the same age, but, to achieve comparable earnings, women need more education than men.

The existence of the earnings gap between men and women is an argument used by proponents of *comparable worth*. Comparable worth advocates the use of job evaluation systems to compare dissimilar jobs and their relative values to an organization in monetary terms. Also envisioned is legislation that will ensure equal results in addition to the equal access already guaranteed by antidiscrimination laws. Yet all benefits have costs, and comparable worth has the serious potential to damage not only

the economy, but also those people for whom it promises higher income.

Another impediment to women in the workforce is the glass ceiling. The glass ceiling is a transparent barrier that keeps women from rising above a certain level in corporations. It is not simply a barrier for a particular individual, based on that persons's inability to handle a higher level job. Rather, the glass ceiling applies to women as a group, who are kept from advancing because they are women. This barrier has been broken by very few women, and is discouraging to those who advance within its reach.

This unit begins by describing lady brakemen of the Pennsylvania railroad during World War II. Although the women were not always treated as equals with male workers, they were passionate about their patriotism for their country. In the second article, Susan M. Schor describes how successful women advance their careers through gender networks and assistance by mentors. The use of mentors is the equivalent to the "old boy network" from which women are excluded. The third article discusses federal laws regarding pregnancy and the workforce. Amy Oakes suggests that managers take care to avoid discriminatory pitfalls. The last article, "Female Entrepreneurs: How Far Have They Come?" is a case study of North American businesswomen. E. Holly Buttner discusses the differences between and similarities of men and women business owners and sex-role stereotypes in female entrepreneurship.

CONSIGNED TO THE
Pennsylvania Railroad's
"Garbage Run," they fought
their own war on the
home front, and they
helped shape a victory
as surely as their brothers
and husbands did overseas

THE LADY BRAKEMEN

BY JOCELYN W. KNOWLES

ALL THE NEW LADY BRAKEMEN ON THE PENNSYLVANIA Railroad were put to work on what was officially known as the Jersey Coast Extra List. The crew dispatchers referred to it as the Women's List, and the male brakemen, who had been consigned to it before the women were hired, called it the Garbage Run. It was also known as the meat—as opposed to the gravy, the cushy sit-down jobs on the main line Washington Express, which paid three times as much for about one-tenth the work. There were thirty-two stops on the Jersey Coast run, and it took three hours to make it, often in old cattle cars converted for commuter use. But in the beginning the women, not knowing better, loved it.

It was 1944, we were all fired up with wartime patriotism, and the notion of doing "a man's job" was in those days thrilling. Besides, the want ad that appeared in The New York Times promised $7.11 a day for unskilled, pleasant railroad work that required no prior experience. That was far more than typing or clerking paid or any of the other jobs for "girls." Forty young women, most in their early twenties, were hired. We were chosen, so far as I could tell, for eagerness, proper subservience, clean fingernails, neat hair, and sufficient evidence of ability to memorize and obey railroad rules. I myself had a gut sense that it would not do to confess that I was motivated by a romantic conception of railroads acquired from movies and novels. A literature major at Columbia University, I got most of my notions and very little from living. I said instead that I had a brother overseas and wanted to do my share. That was true; most of us new hires had relatives in the war, and that fact for some reason seemed to guarantee that we could be relied on to leave the railroad when the war was over. So I quit my job—my first since graduating—as a receptionist at 20th Century-Fox, which by comparison was neither wild nor daring and certainly didn't pay as well.

IT TOOK US A REMARKABLY LONG TIME to learn that while we were indeed earning $7.11 a day for hopping on and off station platforms sixty-four times in three hours going down the coast and sixty-four times again coming back, some men were collecting $21 a day for just sitting down four hours each way to and from Washington in plush, clean cars pulled by diesel engines. For one thing, information about the way things worked on the railroad was hard to come by. It wasn't merely that the men were so curiously hostile and reticent but that the running of the road was such a complex affair that even old-timers didn't always comprehend why things happened the way they did and couldn't explain a lot of it even if they were willing. Many of the men assumed, as we did, that things happened that way because it was the only way they could. There were hundreds of rules, written down in thick books, governing every aspect of the operations, and they had to be memorized unquestioningly. The very thing that was most seductive about the road—the movement—was what had to be absolutely controlled. No move could be plotted that might violate any one of those seemingly endless and often conflicting regulations—federal, state, interstate, safety, labor, intra-union, insurance, and rules of other railroads sharing the same tracks: a staggeringly dense lot of logistics. And then the condition of the road, the equipment, the switching problems, the location of an extra car to be brought from a distant yard to make up a full train, and, of course, economy

all had to be considered in making up and scheduling every train that went out. It's not surprising that passengers were often regarded by railroaders as a superfluous nuisance. Ordering a crew was possibly the simplest part of that whole complicated system, but there were so many considerations governing hours, working conditions, and pay that what might seem the most obvious way might turn out to be the most expensive. The crews were entitled to different wage rates depending upon which terminal they originated at, how many miles they worked, how many hours they laid over, their rail time, and more.

So it was no wonder that it took us a little while to begin questioning the way things were ordered for us. Yet even after we understood that it was because we were women that we had been assigned the run where you worked the hardest and made the least money, we still loved being on the railroad. Nevertheless, the questions began to fester.

"Well, you know, you girls don't do the work the fellows do—"

"They *sit* all the way to Washington! Once they've got the tickets out of Newark, there's nothing for them to do!"

"Well, that's true enough on those Washington expresses, but they're ready to do things you girls just can't do."

"Like what?"

"Well, you don't move baggage, do you?"

"No."

"Or carry the markers down to the trains?"

"No."

"Or throw switches?"

"No."

"Well, you see, you aren't real brakemen at all. You're just ticket takers."

"We hired on as brakemen. The trainmaster says we're brakemen."

"But you just admitted yourself you don't do all the jobs a real brakeman does, so how can you expect—"

"But nobody asked us to. We were in training for two weeks, and nobody even told us we were *supposed* to do those things."

"Probably figured you couldn't do 'em, so what was the use of asking? Af-

ter all, you girls are ladies, don't forget that. You wouldn't *want* to do such things, would you?"

"I don't know. It's something to think about."

"Well now, don't think about it too much. No use bothering your head and fussing. After all, you girls won't be here very long anyway. War'll be over pretty soon, and you know when the fellows come back, you'll be giving them back their jobs. You know that, don't you?"

"Yes."

"You girls just don't have any seniority, you see. Around here you gotta have seniority; the railroad's no place for women. Now don't take offense. I'm not saying you girls aren't doing a damn fine job, because you are! Better than ninety percent of these no-good young sprats around here."

That was the sort of discussion you could have with a "neutral" conductor, while you sat and counted tickets in the switching yard at the end of the run. It was the damnedest, most circular piece of reasoning I ever heard, and all the other girls got the same sort of jabber from every man who was willing to discuss the matter: The reason we averaged two-thirds less pay than the men and were limited to the Garbage Run was that we weren't required to do all the work the men sometimes did. We were neither required nor permitted to do that work because it was assumed that we couldn't or wouldn't do it, yet if we did do it, we still couldn't have the same chance at all the jobs because we were only temporary workers without seniority. But we could not have seniority because the railroad was no place for women.

Men who hired on after us—and before long there were about five hundred of them, all rejected by the Army—did have seniority, so that when the servicemen returned from the war and took their jobs, they eventually could get them back when there was more work. The forty girls never could.

Unavoidably, the trouble was that we were women. Until then almost every one of us had had the impression that men didn't hold it against women for being women, so it was a surprise. But if the men had had better manners, or better arguments, most of us would have let the whole thing go, for not one of us was anxious to work a baggage car, carry markers, or throw switches.

One day I was working with a girl named Claire Fredericks who talked a conductor into letting us throw a switch. It was pure serendipity, for Mr. Keefer was about the only conductor on the Bay Head run who would have permitted it, Little Claire was the only one who could have asked, and I was one of the few girls, at first, who were willing to try.

Mr. Keefer was close to retirement and, because of that, didn't care much one way or the other whether the women stayed on the road.

CLAIRE WAS THE ONLY ONE OF US whom the men honored with a real railroad sobriquet. They called her Little Smokey as a kind of grudging tribute to her stamina and her capacity for work. "Big Smokey" was a legend of the New York Division, famous for his ability to work while sleeping, or vice versa. We used to see him sitting on the bench in the crew dispatcher's office, sleeping with his eyes open, waiting for someone to fail to show up for a job and hoping to get it at the last minute when the dispatcher got desperate. He would already have completed his daily maximum sixteen hours of rail time and not be legally entitled to another second. But if no one else was around, he'd get it anyway.

Little Smokey would sit there on the bench beside him. He never talked to her; he had no energy to waste. She was a very little girl, but she was strong and could work from one end of the day to the next, without sleep, and when the dispatcher wanted to shop her, she wheedled him into another day's work. She was not pretty, but she was chipper, always freshly made up and ready to go. She kept two clean shirts in her locker at all times and changed automatically every eight hours. She was chronically good-humored and laughed off insults in a friendly way, and she settled herself on the bench beside Big Smokey and waited cheerfully and confidently for the dispatcher to give her the same illegal handouts he gave to Big Smokey. At first, of course, he wouldn't.

"G'wan home, girlie, you're shopped," he would tell her. "You've had your sixteen hours." It was a serious violation of a federal safety statute to work more than sixteen hours without eight hours of sleep, and the brakeman who got caught doing it was just as much in

trouble as the dispatcher who permitted him to.

Eventually the dispatcher mellowed and treated her as near to equal with Big Smokey as he could, considering that he could not send her on the big main liners or assign her to flagging or moving baggage. She had one goal in mind: money. She did not care for the adventure or the fun of the railroad, nor was she there out of any patriotic motive. She did not care whether the men liked her or didn't, so long as she had a chance to make money. She was not rude or angry. She just wanted money. She had been a cosmetics demonstrator at Woolworth's, and without doubt she had worked just as hard and determinedly there as she did on the railroad. But the store closed after eight hours, and the railroad went on and on, gloriously, forever, and she strung herself out as long as she could wheedle a job—twenty-four or even forty-eight hours without going home, napping on benches, on station platforms, or in deadhead cars.

WELL, WHEN THE TRAIN pulled into Bay Head Junction that day, it stopped as usual at the station to let off passengers and then it pulled into the yard, where it was switched to a siding for what my grandmother would have called "a lick and a spit" to ready it for the return journey.

The engineer stopped the train a short distance before the first switch. Mr. Keefer stood on the steps of the head car and watched us. The engineer, to our surprise, gave us a V sign as we walked past his cab. Smokey, on her stilt heels, teetered along three inches below my shoulder level. It was a big, heavy switch, and it was rusty. I tried to pull it up. Smokey tried. We tried pulling it together, my hands over hers. Then Smokey bent down and grabbed the switch with both hands, and I stood behind her and grabbed her at the waist. I pulled her, and she pulled the switch. We both fell over backward onto the track, but the switch had moved! A fraction. We went to the other side of the switch and tried kicking it up. I attempted to use my backside as a lever. It moved an inch. All the while we were groaning and grunting. Smokey lost her cap. I tore the shoulder seam of my jacket. Smokey took off her shoes. At last, kicking and pushing and pulling, we got the switch halfway up, then over

the halfway mark. Smokey jumped on it. We both bounced on it. The switch went down, and we waited while the engineer moved the train ahead to the next one. He was grinning as he passed us. Mr. Keefer sent the flagman to throw the next switch. We were humiliated. We were surprised at how difficult it had been and were well aware that no one was going to let us throw switches like that as a regular thing.

"Why don't they oil those switches?" I asked Mr. Keefer. "If they weren't so rusty, we could throw them."

Mr. Keefer nodded agreeably. "Could be," he said. "That could be." But that was as far as he wanted to go with the matter.

"You'd think the men would want them oiled," I said to Little Smokey as we counted our tickets.

"Not them," she said good-humoredly. "They're proud of their hernias. You got to have a hernia to be a real railroad man."

There were two lady brakemen in the crew dispatcher's shack. They had watched our moment of glory but were not impressed. "What do you think you're doing anyway?" said one of them. "Next thing you know, we'll all be working baggage! Who wants to throw switches anyway?"

Nevertheless, Little Smokey and I each bought a pocket-size can of 3-in-1 oil for the next opportunity—if it ever came.

The next day Peggy Sigafoos was waiting in the locker room at Penn Station. The railroad grapevine moves fast. Peggy was the trainmaster's appointed lady's rep. The men had union representation, but we were not permitted to join the union. We considered Peggy a gumshoe.

"Hear you and Smokey were having some fun at the junction," she said, dimpling at me when I came in. She was fair-haired and square-jawed. She had a horseshoe-shaped mouth I did not like.

"Yes, it was fun."

"What's up?"

"How do you mean?"

"You girls after something in particular?"

"They want to get to work the Washington trains," said someone in the locker room who did not.

"That's what it sounded like to me," said Peggy. "But you know it can't be done, don't you?"

"Why not, if we can do the work?"

"You're not allowed, that's why. You're only here temporarily. The men had a choice between working with Negroes and working with women, and they chose us. But they don't want us here, and we can't stay on indefinitely. That's the way it is. Don't rock the boat. I'm telling it to you straight: There's nothing you can do about it, and you'll get yourselves in trouble if you try. So quit throwing switches, got it?" She sucked in her dimples and looked older than her twenty-three years.

I've conveniently forgotten my reply. It wasn't anything memorable; my best retorts always arrive the next morning, between sleep and waking. But until she made that statement, we were all merely offended and exasperated women, each in her own way. The switch throwing had been an unplanned and aimless act. We did, indeed, wish for a chance at the Washington jobs, but the situation seemed so complex that not one of the forty of us had a notion how to change it.

Now it occurred to me that if in truth there had been a choice offered the men between blacks and women, the situation was even worse than we thought. It was not merely a matter of throwing switches, carrying markers, and working baggage cars. It was simple bigotry. And we were not being used to fill a labor shortage at all but to permit men to profit from it. If black men had been hired instead of white women, refusing them seniority and recall rights might have caused a scandal. It was true we weren't anxious to do the heavy work, but this wasn't the crux of the matter. If the switches were oiled, we could throw them; if the eight-pound aluminum markers used on other railroads replaced the forty-pound markers the Pennsy flagmen struggled with, we could carry them; and adequate assistance for men in the baggage car would be adequate for us too. Somehow the men appeared to take pride in doing work that injured them. It seemed to me it would be more to their advantage to improve matters for themselves than to insist that we do as they did. That seemed purely stupid.

The effect of Peggy's disclosure, however, was to so outrage everyone that it united the women, and at least temporarily we were suddenly all out to get to Washington or bust.

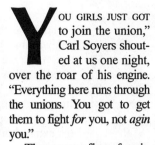
Pulling a track wrench to tighten a rail joint.

YOU GIRLS JUST GOT to join the union," Carl Soyers shouted at us one night, over the roar of his engine. "Everything here runs through the unions. You got to get them to fight *for* you, not *agin* you."

There were five of us in his cab. He was giving us a ride back to New York. It was after midnight, and we would otherwise have had to lay over at the junction until the next morning to deadhead home. There really was space in the cab only for one person besides the engineer and the fireman. With five of us, it was terrifying. We clutched one another and the grab irons as the locomotive took the curves at ninety. One inch this way and we could fall to the tracks; one inch that way and we'd be in the firebox. It was a very cold night; our faces froze, and our backs, against the fire, burned. Above the metal screech of wheels on rail Carl shouted his advice, not so much out of friendship for us as contempt for the passenger crews. He hated their starched collars and their gold watches. Engineers thought of themselves as the elite of the road. Carl himself was always so meticulous about his appearance that he did indeed look regal. His overalls had a special cut, and with them he always wore a natty black scarf around his neck. He carried a little black leather satchel full of tools, which he kept like jewels, cleaning and oiling them as he sat in the dispatcher's shack at the junction.

"The union won't let us in!" Little Smokey cried.

"You tried?"

"They said we weren't allowed to join."

"You didn't apply."

"It's a waste of time."

"If you were members, they'd have to represent you, don't you see? Besides, you'd be doing them a favor. They can't go giving away seniority like this! It's all those dumbbells have got to hang onto themselves. Join the union, girls!"

In their previous lives most of the women had been casual nonunion labor—manicurists, nursemaids, typists, file clerks. One had been a nun. The fact is that we regarded ourselves as society

did; we were transients, not serious breadwinners, people who might eventually be supported by men. We felt ourselves to be temporary in any work force, although most of us knew we'd be working at one thing or another all our lives. Still, we accepted these contradictory notions and did not feel indentured anywhere. We could always do something else, and there was always the chance that the Rider on the White Horse would come out of the mists and take us away from all silly, trivial employments. Feeling separate and outside the mainstream of the work world, isolated from the realities of social organization, why *should* we choose the underdog role? I think this is why we had not seriously tried to join the union.

But now, on our first try, all our applications for membership in the local lodge of the Brotherhood of Railroad Trainmen were unanimously blackballed.

"We shouldn't be downhearted," said Little Smokey when we heard the news. "There are plenty of men out there who think we're terrific. They sympathize with us. They'd help us."

"Where are they?" Men who liked Smokey didn't necessarily care about the rest of us.

"Well," she said, putting a little spit on a run in her stocking, "I meet a lot of fellas from St. Louis—"

"*St. Louis?*"

"Deadheading," she said primly.

"What good are fellows from St. Louis going to do us?" There were no lady brakemen on that division.

"You'd be surprised."

Sometimes Little Smokey did not seem very bright.

"I *would* be surprised."

"One of them told me we should start up a petition. *They'd* sign it!"

It was an inspired idea. The railroad was a perfect place for a petition. You could give a friendly conductor the piece of paper in the morning, and by evening, when you got it back from him, it could have been all over the property from New York to St. Louis, from Jersey City to Harrisburg. Men who had never seen a lady brakeman and who didn't feel threatened by one could calmly consider the issues.

IT CAUGHT ON FAST. EVEN THE GIRLS who didn't want to throw switches or carry markers or work baggage cars took at least two petitions to pass around. Everyone preferred to ask the men's help rather than fight them. And even those men who hated having women on the railroad were enlivened by the activity. There was a great buzz and stir all up and down the road. Arguments went on for days, so that by the time management and the union both forbade us to pass out any more petitions, our goal had been pretty well achieved; we had hundreds of signatures advocating membership for women in the union.

But the lodge would not acknowledge the petitions, which went into the wastebasket. "That ain't the way you do business on the railroad," explained one well-meaning conductor. "You got to do things the right way, go through channels." But the channels seemed closed to us.

I WENT TO SEE MIKE QUILL, PRESIDENT of the fledgling CIO's Transport Workers Union, which was making heavy inroads into craft unions like the Brotherhood of Railroad Trainmen (BRT). Railroad workers were separated into dozens of different unions according to craft, and they were often weakened in their struggles with management by intramural antagonisms, like the engineers and firemen despising the trainmen. The CIO sought to organize all workers in a trade into the same union to present a united bargaining unit. Quill's union, which had a reputation for militancy, was then organizing furiously for all transportation workers. There were no color or sex bars to membership, and I imagined that the plight of the lady brakemen would appeal to him. He was charmed and astounded to meet a genuine lady brakeman from the Pennsy, and he invited me at once for a drink in a dark bar and listened to my tale. But even as I talked, he was shaking his head. He explained in his good Irish brogue how he wished he could help, but the fact was that he was interested, d'ye see, darrling, in organizing the railroad men, if he could get a lever, but it was plain as day that forty women were not that lever, given the men's antagonism. It was plain as day. I understood what he meant. He wished us good luck.

At this juncture the trainmaster himself entered the picture. His road had government contracts, moved government troops and supplies, and could not

Learning to oil an engine in Long Island.

afford a scandal. The scandal was that the critical wartime labor shortage that we had been hired to relieve continued on the main line, where troops and supplies were often held up while all the extra labor—the women—waited for work on the Jersey Coast runs. It's possible that the trainmaster regretted having gone along with the union on the women's working conditions, but I suppose at the time it all had seemed reasonable enough. The trainmaster was subject to the same influences as the rest of the men on the road. He was insular. He had lived with the unions, the conditions, the book of rules, the awkward bulk of outdated federal regulations governing railroad operations for his entire life. He came from a railroad family. His sons were on the road. Changes in the outside world filtered in only dimly. He sat at his big rolltop desk in a highceilinged, high-windowed, oak-paneled office and was subject to the same fantasies and prides as the men he supervised, and he ran his office as trainmasters always had, with feudal authority. He would not have liked his daughter on the road, and he did not respect the women who had come there.

THE TRAINMASTER NOW CALLED A meeting, and the Women's List was shut down. We all buzzed and stewed with excitement. What could be happening? Perhaps we had won something after all. But that was not the case. He sat there on the platform in the speaker's chair, pale-eyed, thin-lipped, and austere, but he did not address us directly. He merely lent his presence while Peggy, through whom he spoke, translated his wishes. He would make sotto voce comments, which she repeated to the audience, as though being a man, he thought his language might be different from ours. The subject of the meeting was not working conditions. He wanted us to know that he had been thinking about the issue of pants versus skirts, and he was now ready to grant permission for pants. But once the decision was taken, everyone must abide by it. There would then be no more skirts.

No one had mentioned this matter of pants versus skirts since we'd arrived on the road, but it was still a lively issue. In retrospect it's hard to explain how such a matter could successfully split the ranks of a group of women on the verge of winning historic rights in a male stronghold. But this is what happened.

A SPECIAL DESIGNER HAD BEEN hired to make an acceptable uniform for the women. No airline-stewardess chic, however. The object was to disguise the female anatomy and de-flatter what could not be concealed. The jacket was long enough to cover the hips and shaped to flatten the breasts. A man's shirt with a stiffly starched male collar and a black necktie were worn under it, while a man's hat—the trainman's own peaked cap with the inscription "Trainman" in gold braid across the peak—sat deep on the forehead, covered the ears, and made a mess of any woman's hair. Short hair stuck out like Raggedy Ann fringes; long hair looked grotesque and in any case was not permitted. Some girls stuffed all their hair under the cap so that they did, in fact, look like men in skirts, for although the uniform was meant to make us as unprovocative as possible, we had to wear skirts because they were ladylike. They blew up in the draft as we walked between cars or stood in the spring breeze on the platform. Our legs froze in winter, and in the rain and snow all the pleating came undone. Sensible, comfortable shoes looked terrible with those skirts, but high heels were impractical—that is, for anyone but Smokey. Even so, after an initial plea for pants had been refused, we put up with the skirts; by now many of the Uncle Toms among us were devoted to them. They were ladies, as we were so often reminded, and they didn't want to be indistinguishable from the men.

After a moment of stupefaction a torrent of argument broke loose, and Peggy, with her square-jawed, dimpled smile, gaveled for order.

It was a great ploy. Women who had been sore at the men were now sore at one another. There was a split between those who regarded themselves as "ladies" and those who regarded themselves as "women." Those who wanted to be ladies and thought that throwing switches was unladylike did want to keep the skirts, but there were also many among them who wanted equal work and equal rights who thought their hips or thighs were too heavy and did not want to wear pants; they fought with the girls who had good legs and did want pants, even though they, too, were for seniority rights. It was a mess.

The trainmaster, with his pale eyes, watched with satisfaction. The issue was not then resolved, and for a long time it divided our attention and consumed energy and heat that had been directed at other matters.

ONE SUMMER EVENING, RETURNing to the locker room after a murderously busy weekend job, I saw Smokey standing outside talking to two big fellows with cigars and powdered jowls. She wore her fresh shirt and fresh makeup. Her cap sat precariously, as usual, atop her upswept hairdo. She was chuckling and batting her eyes, as was her habit with men. She grabbed my elbow as I made for the locker-room door.

"I want you to meet some *friends*," she said, so meaningfully that both men laughed. I myself was feeling slow, if not altogether numb, after twenty-two hours of rail time.

"These two gentlemen," Smokey went on, "are from the Grand Lodge of the Brotherhood of Railroad Trainmen; they are *vice presidents*. The *president* sent them to find out what's going on down here, and they want to talk to *us*."

The two men—Joe Cahill and Boyce Eidson—had rooms in the hotel across from the station. We went to Cahill's room, where Smokey promptly made herself comfortable on one of the twin beds. The men were visibly affected by this. Cahill quietly opened the hotel-room door and wedged a doorstop under it, which only created even more of a feeling of embarrassment. I myself sat primly on a straight-backed chair, but only because if I'd relaxed at all, I'd have collapsed. Cahill called room service and ordered a couple of bottles of whiskey and soda, catching Eidson's eye as he did so.

"That what you girls drink?" he barked. He was a barker and a grumbler, a chunky, florid, silver-haired gent with ruddy face and stubby fingers. His face looked scrubbed, polished, massaged, and powdered, and there was an expression in it—impetuous and boyish—that I found attractive. His suit was of the silkiest worsted, beautifully tailored and of a shade that matched his tousled silver hair. Boyce Eidson—much less color-

ful—called him Little Snake. Since there was nothing snaky in his appearance, I assumed it referred to his character, although he looked to me entirely forthright. He sounded rough and tough; he hustled and made other displays of vigor, but his eyes were intelligent, grave, and even soft behind steel-rimmed spectacles. Much later I discovered that the trainmen's union people referred to the switchmen's union people as snakes, and once in the long ago Cahill had been one of them.

"Sweet Tom Collins for me," said Smokey. "Two cherries please." She chuckled at him. He glared toward me.

"Wine," I said. "Red, please."

"*Wine*?" He seemed paralyzed at the idea.

"Give the orders, Little Snake," said Eidson, puffing at his cigar.

Cahill did so. "Well," he said, turning to Smokey, not me, "let's get on with this thing. What's troubling you girls?"

Smokey giggled, stretched herself out on the bed. "We want some of that there senior-ority thing, Mr. Cahill, and brother, we *need* it!"

"We want to join the brotherhood," I told him. "They blackballed all of us."

"You girls knew when you hired on what the score was."

"No. It's true we signed a paper, but we didn't understand it at all. We didn't know its significance. We didn't know anything about railroads. We didn't understand how important seniority was."

"That so?" Cahill was very tough.

We were silent. Then Smokey pulled what she thought was our ace in the hole. "The men want us to be in the union."

"That so?"

"You tell him." She turned to me. "She can talk better."

The truth is, I could not talk. I forgot the beginning of a sentence before I got to the end. I got flustered, hemmed, hawed, worried about appearing intelligent, having been taught that men needed to feel superior and that if I wished to be loved, I had to be a simpleton. That was all coming a bit undone on the railroad. There they didn't love us even as simpletons.

I related the details, as best I could, of how we worked, what we were paid, how we were treated, and how, finally, "some of us" had even talked to Mike Quill when the New York lodge blackballed our membership applications. Cahill perked up at that. I didn't say how

many "some of us" was or that Mike Quill had been plainly uninterested.

"Well, you girls can't ask no favors," Cahill said. "If you want equal rights, you got to do equal work, and if you want to join the union, you got to go through channels like everybody else. You don't go making no revolutions at the drop of a hat."

"We went through channels, Mr. Cahill," said Smokey, sitting up to spear a cherry in her drink. "Didn't you hear? They blackballed us."

"Try again."

"What's the use? It's just wasting our time."

"Thought you said the men was all dying for you to be in the union."

"Well," said Smokey, "men we don't know, men who work on other divisions, want us. The men we work with *hate* us!"

Cahill and his friend laughed. "Now you do what I say! I'm going to have me a little talk with ol' Doc Sites."

DOC SITES WAS THE GRIEVANCE chairman for the Eastern Division of the Pennsylvania Railroad, a most powerful job in the union hierarchy. It was under his jurisdiction that our working arrangements had been invented.

We did as Cahill suggested. Soon thereafter we each received a letter from Doc Sites advising us that the Philadelphia lodge of the BRT would be pleased to accept us as "Special Members" for the duration of our employment. Evidently the New York lodge, where we belonged, was intransigent.

"It's not what you'd call an unqualified win," Smokey said.

But twenty-seven of us rode down to Philadelphia for the first meeting. It was a busy night on the road, and the crew dispatcher had threatened to turn us all in for doing so, but we went anyway.

The meeting room was in an old fraternal building, the Elks or the Lions or the Masons. It reminded me of the trainmaster's office—the same vintage and ambience. Musty, high-ceilinged, oak-paneled, dimly lit male rooms. Outside the door the sergeant at arms sat at a little table, checking credentials. Beside him stood Doc Sites himself, ostensibly to make a courteous show of welcome to the women, but more likely to keep the men from mayhem. They were not overjoyed to have us; they had simply been ordered to take us in. It was all the sergeant at arms could do to nod civilly as the twenty-seven of us breached the door. We were still in uniforms, looking as much like men-in-skirts as possible.

WE OCCUPIED two rows of seats near the front of the room and waited for the men to assemble. No one sat within a row of us. Everyone waited in silence. By nearly an hour after the scheduled meeting time, only seventeen men had come; it was their idea of a protest against our presence. But as it dawned on us that we outnumbered them at the meeting, we offered two resolutions at once: that the lodge go on record in favor of calling for a revision of the constitution of the BRT to delete the "male white" requirement for membership forever and that BRT representatives meet immediately with management to abrogate all discriminatory agreements governing the women's work conditions and rights.

The motion passed twenty-seven to seventeen, with no discussion whatever. It was glorious, but it was too easy. At the next meeting the men got some sense and turned out in droves to overturn both motions on a point of order.

One day one of the ladiest of the lady brakemen—a girl who loved her skirt and didn't want to throw switches or join a union or work to Washington—fell off the train and broke her back. She had been standing, against the rules, on the platform between cars, counting her tickets as her train took the big curve at Asbury Park. The doors were open. She lost her footing and fell to the tracks. A company representative was Johnny-on-the-spot when she came to in the hospital, and she and her grateful, befuddled parents were persuaded to accept twelve thousand dollars for her injuries. As it turned out, she was going to be paralyzed for the rest of her life. She had no insurance coverage. Nobody realized, however, until Carl Soyer told us, that if she had had union insurance, she would have had all her bills paid. We didn't comprehend until then that no matter how many safety rules we memorized, we were as vulnerable as the men to the railroad's traditional dangers and

A powerful Washington, D.C., railroader.

that no commercial insurance company would underwrite the risks.

The sudden fear of terrible accidents gave us a burst of renewed support right when the BRT's president decided to look into the troubles of the women on the Pennsylvania Railroad and ordered a hearing. It was the eve of a threatened wartime strike on the railroads, and the union needed no extraneous bad publicity. Furthermore, there was always lurking in the minds of these old-time unionists the fear of the CIO and its militant attractions for disaffected members.

A. F. Whitney, the president, was a square-shaped, imperious old man, an absolute autocrat who strove to be enlightened yet, like the trainmaster, maintained a feudal relationship with those around him. He arrived for the hearing in New York accompanied by various aides, sycophants, messengers, and vice presidents. It was a Roman procession.

In the conference room a subdued and respectful Cahill sat at Whitney's right hand, and Doc Sites sat in exile, far down at the farthest end of the table. We had prepared a proper brief, and I was delegated to write and present it. It was modeled on the Emancipation Proclamation and said many of the same things. How could they be better said? No union (nation) could foster (exist) discrimination (half slave) against any group of workers within its jurisdiction without harming itself and its own members (half free). I was rather carried away by it myself. But it also discussed more mundane matters, like work-saving innovations that would be profitable to men and women alike: oiling switches, using aluminum markers, and so on. We tried to put the problem where it really did belong: improved working conditions for all. Finally we offered a long list of main-line trains and dates—which all of us had been collecting—that had left their terminals undermanned while the lady brakemen on the Bay Head Extra List waited for job assignments, sometimes going two or three days without work.

At the conclusion one of the grievance chairmen turned to Cahill and said within my hearing, "What are they, some kind of Commies? Did you ever hear a natural woman talk like that?"

I was admitted to a brief audience with Whitney. In a regal gesture he extended his square hand. One knuckle was missing, lost in a long-ago switching accident.

"I want to assure you," he said, "that we will give your case the consideration it deserves. Meanwhile, and regardless of what our final decision will be, I am sending out an order today, as a sign of my own personal distaste for discrimination against you ladies, that hereafter you shall be addressed as 'brothers.' I understand," he said meaningfully, "that in Mike Quill's union they discriminate against women by addressing them as 'sisters.' "

Fortunately the rulings that came down were more what we had in mind: The constitution of the brotherhood was to be amended to delete the "white male" requirement for membership, opening the way for the employment of blacks as trainmen. Women were to have equal rights of recall, to hold regular jobs, and to receive equal pay for equal work. Smokey and I, along with two other women who had been vocal, were rewarded amid much fuss and fanfare with jobs as the first women organizers in the history of the BRT. It was surely meant to signal to intransigent men, perhaps tempted by the CIO, that the old slumberous brotherhood was taking on a new look. But that's another story.

WHEN THE WAR WAS OVER, many of the women left the railroad, but they left of their own accord, not out of necessity. Others stayed on. Fifty years have gone by, and women brakemen on the railroads across the country are no longer a novelty. The queer thing is that women brakemen to whom I have talked, some of them now holding jobs in freight as well as in passenger service, have no idea of the seriocomic struggle that mothered their current rights. There having been no written history of it, it has passed into an oblivion shared with the earliest invention of the wheel.

Jocelyn W. Knowles is a writer in Sarasota, Florida.

Separate And Unequal: The Nature of Women's And Men's Career-Building Relationships

Susan M. Schor

Share a joke with the guys in the locker room after a lunchtime racquetball game. Take your wife to the CEO's cocktail party. Call your ex-fraternity buddy to alert him to a possible new sales contact. These are all time-proven ways in which men have cultivated relationships at work to tighten their grasp on the higher rungs of the executive ladder. But do women executives also have to be like one of the boys to get to the top? The answer, according to my research, is no.

During the past 20 years, scholars and practitioners have been scrutinizing the challenges women face as they attempt to climb the corporate ladder. Executive positions in U.S. corporations are still overwhelmingly dominated by men. As of 1996, reports Townsend (1996), fewer than 5 percent of top management positions were held by women. But while other researchers were documenting the many women bumping into the now infamous glass ceiling, another critical question begged to be addressed: How do those few women who are at the top become successful in spite of the obstacles?

Both women and men who have risen into the rarefied ranks of senior management credit the nature and quality of their relationships with other people as key elements. They see the most beneficial relationships as those they have with their mentors and with people in informal networks. The importance and nature of both have been well developed in the literature. Kram (1985) identified two types of functions of mentor-

> From mentoring to networks, from the home front to the links, successful men and women executives tend to take quite different paths to the top.

protégé relationships: career assistance and psychosocial support. Career development assistance includes sponsoring, coaching, advising on career moves, and ensuring visibility and access to important social networks, resources, and assignments. Psychosocial functions consist of role modeling, feedback, counseling, and social support. In addition to these, executives' networks provide information, organizational and career advice, access to power, social support, and friendship. And Burke and McKeen (1990) suggest that family members may also play significant roles in career advancement, though as yet this has received little attention.

Most of the research on the glass ceiling phenomenon, mentors, and networks has focused on entry-

Reprinted from *Business Horizons,* September/October 1997, pp. 51-58. © 1997 by the Foundation for the School of Business at Indiana University. Used with permission.

and middle-level managers. But although this has shed light on early career issues, the findings are not necessarily applicable to those who have neared the pinnacle of the hierarchy. Because so few people—especially women—advance to senior levels, we must turn there. Mainiero (1994) and Morrison, White, and Van Velsor (1987) interviewed executive women regarding their advancement strategies. I interviewed both men and women and was able to compare their respective experiences.

I began my exploration of career advancement experiences by locating ten women presidents and vice-presidents in large insurance corporations in the Northeast, then matching them demographically with ten men in similar positions. I first interviewed these 20 people over the telephone, then met with each for a two-hour, tape-recorded interview using an identical set of questions for each. During the interviews I asked the respondents to reflect on their career journeys. Thematic and conceptual analysis of their answers and observations revealed that the interpersonal relationships these successful women drew upon for advancement in their careers differed greatly from those of the men. Because the number of people interviewed was neither very large nor randomly selected, I was unable to generalize definitively from their expe-

riences. But the differences between the men's and women's experiences in this sample were so sharp that larger-scale studies are certainly warranted.

The career-enhancing relationships of both the men and the women fell into three broad categories: mentors, informal networks of colleagues, and their spouses. Most prior research was conducted under the assumption that these relationships are similar in quantity, quality, and character for both men and women—an assumption my research found to be untrue for those with whom I spoke.

WOMEN'S MENTORS: MORE OF THEM AND MORE HIGHLY PLACED

More executive women than executive men had mentors. On the average, they also had more mentors than did the men. Following convention, I have defined a mentor-protégé relationship as one in which both are aware of the relationship and intend that its primary purpose should be to advance the career of the protégé. All the women reported having from one to four mentors in their careers, but only half of the men reported having had any at all. Those who did had only one or two.

Eighty percent of the women's mentors were male; all of the men's mentors were male. Women's relationships with their mentors averaged five years in length, while men's averaged two years. A concise summary of these differences is provided in **Figure 1.**

It is surprising that mentors were ubiquitous in these women's careers, given findings that women in lower and middle management often have difficulty in obtaining mentors. Although previous research reports that mentors have been important in the advancement of all senior managers, they may in fact be much more crucial for women as they move up the hall toward the big corner office. Half the men achieved executive status without them, whereas none of the women did. Whether having a mentor is an absolute necessity for women, then, remains a question for future studies.

Figure 1

Differences In Relationship With Mentors By Gender

CHARACTERISTIC	WOMEN	MEN
Those having at least one mentor	100%	50%
Average number of mentors per executive	2.3	1.0
Range of mentors per executive	1–4	0–2
Average length of relationship	5 years	2 years
Percentage of male mentors	80%	100%
Percentage of female mentors	20%	0%
Usual organizational position of mentor	Highest levels throughout org.	Immediate boss
Mentor's relationship functions	Many	Few
Most frequent relationship function(s)	Advisor, teacher, path paver, career guide	Role model

Upon reflection, it does not seem especially remarkable that both the men's and women's mentors were predominantly male. To begin with, there are many more men than women in upper-level positions, thus giving more of them the potential to become mentors. Second, the ratio of potential protégés to mentors is much greater for the few women top executives, who might choose to mentor a junior man instead of a junior woman. And the executive women otherwise in a position to mentor sometimes face obstacles that make the formation and maintenance of such a relationship problematic. They may have less available time, or they may not feel as qualified to be mentors as some male counterparts.

Suitable mentors generally have been thought to be of the same sex as their protégés, so men have the advantage of the same sex role models *and* the benefit of access to the male-dominant culture. Men form relationships with influential others in the organization who are like themselves and who are part of the same culture. A woman usually has to choose one or the other. If she has a male mentor who offers her the power as well as the transition into the male culture, she has to forgo the advantages of being with women colleagues. If she wants to be mentored by someone most like herself (that is, a woman), she often has to forgo the access to power in the organization. It is quite possible, though, that the women in this study sought both power and critical role modeling by having both male and female mentors.

The Organizational Positions Of Mentors
The women typically developed mentoring relationships with people several levels above them in the hierarchy and in "influential" positions. The men's mentors were closer to home, typically consisting of their immediate bosses. The higher-level mentors gave the women the sponsorship, visibility, and access to the dominant, mostly-male group in upper management that an immediate boss was not able to provide.

The men, we can speculate, may not have needed as much advocacy from above because they fit more easily into the dominant group and did not need the additional leverage a highly-placed mentor provided. Another possible explanation of why the women's immediate (male) bosses were less likely to be their mentors is that even *rumors* of sexual involvement can create resentful coworkers and damage the careers of both the mentor and subordinate.

One way to explain the difference in the length of the mentoring relationships is by considering the relative positions of the mentors in the firm. The subordinate-boss relationship is typically a short one, dissolved upon the promotion or transfer of either party. In contrast, mentor-protégé relationships across the organization are not limited by the same structural constraints and can last until they are no longer needed.

The Differing Functions Of Mentors
Mentors typically function in two broad categories, "general mentoring" and "career advancement." A general mentor acts as a sounding board, advisor, teacher, provider of support and encouragement, and role model—a person to emulate or from whom one can "pick up pieces along the way." A career advancer paves paths, offers occupational guidance, and procures appointments to talent-highlighting projects and committees. Though both women and men reported the presence of most of these functions, all were prominent for the women's mentor relationships except that of "role model." By contrast, men primarily described their mentors as role models. They did not perceive them as advisors, teachers, path pavers, or career guides.

Most of the women described their mentors as "sounding boards." One informant defined her mentor as "someone to discuss your thoughts and ideas with, someone you can relate to." Only women reported that their mentors were advisors to them, someone "you would go to for advice about what to do and what not to do in certain situations."

Nine of the women but only two of the men described their mentors as teachers of managerial and political skills. As one woman said,

> He was a superb politician and he was very good about tutoring me on all kinds of things—where the bodies were buried, what kind of memo you did or didn't send out, and lots of things like that.

Three men and ten women reported that their mentors were very supportive and encouraging. One woman believed she owed her success to her male mentor's continually saying, "You can do it. You've got it." Nine of the women and two of the men reported receiving career guidance from their mentors. They were given advice and direction about the timing and positioning of job changes. One woman described it this way:

> I [had] lunch with him one day. We agreed it was time for me to move into another job. I should look around and we should let personnel know that it was time to move me. They should come up with some jobs that I should be a candidate for. After I had interviewed for three of them I had lunch with him again.

All of the women reported that their mentors enhanced their careers by securing for them appointments on task forces, company-wide committees, and special assignments that gave them broad exposure. Only four men reported getting these appointments from their mentors.

Mentors who function as a sponsor tell influential others in the firm about the protégé's strengths and potential and often recommend or endorse the protégé for a promotion or a particular position. All the women and only three men reported that their mentors served as their sponsors. Every man acknowledged he had a sponsor, but seven of them did not identify their sponsors as mentors. In fact, the men were not certain they actually had a sponsor, but merely assumed it. As one of them said, explaining his rapid advancement, "There must have been someone who was sponsoring me."

Each female executive interviewed gave at least one example of a higher-level mentor who worked hard to move her up in her organization. One woman described the contribution of her path paver, saying, "He was actually instrumental in moving me into the job. I'm not sure this company would have taken that risk had it not been for him. He made a compelling case."

"Path pavers" typically go to much greater efforts to advance their protégés than do sponsors. Unlike the men's assumption that some anonymous benefactor must have been sponsoring them, each female senior manager knew for certain that her path paver had gone to great effort or had taken risks for her. Each described those efforts as multifaceted: openly lauding her capacities to the organization generally, as well as lobbying behind the scenes to move her into a specific position.

Six of the male executives reported that they benefited by adopting older, more senior executives as role models. But "role models" need not even be aware of being emulated to be effective, let alone actively par-

ticipate in the relationship. Indeed, more men claimed to have a role model than a mentor. One explanation for this is that men's relationships with their mentors tend to be shorter. Leaving aside the issue of whether they have the inclination, they may not have the opportunity to develop the breadth and emotional depth of the longer-term relationship typical of the women and their mentors.

WOMEN'S NETWORKS: MORE "WORK" THAN "NET"

Women and men alike reported involvement with informal networks, which were viewed as essential to their career advancement (see **Figure 2**). As one vice president explained,

> Nobody, absolutely nobody, in a company can advance without good informal networks because of the fact that if people don't like you, there are a hundred thousand ways they can screw you and you'll never know it.

All of the women reported being part of a women's network, a subgroup of their broader range of career-related connections.

Developing Networks
The men said they networked "automatically" and "unconsciously" and usually felt readily included when they reached out to others. The women reported that for them, networking was likely to be much more "work" than "net"; they expended greater effort in building and maintaining their networks. Many women commented on the difficulties of gaining access. Said one,

> I rarely felt included in networks. I usually had to initiate my own contacts and did not experience others coming to me, even though I was in a very high position in my organization. I really had to do it myself, almost all of the time.

Women initiated more work-based relationships, went to more work-related functions, and invited more co-workers to lunch than did men. The latter, on the other hand, spent more time developing their networks outside the immediate work setting in such activities as golf and tennis as well as in socializing with their colleagues and wives. Most of the women said they never socialized with their informal networks outside of work.

Figure 2

Differences in Network Characteristics by Sex

Network Characteristics	WOMEN	MEN
Types of networks	Women-only network; informal networks	Informal networks
Ease of access	Difficult	Easy
Effort expended	Extraordinary	Minimal
Timing	During work day	Outside of work
Range of functions	Wide	Moderate
Most frequent functions	Visibility, advice, information, support	Career advancement contacts

The contrast between women building and developing their networks on company time and men building their networks outside of work is perhaps not surprising. Fostering networks on the golf course or by playing other sports has been a tradition for corporate males. These activities strengthen ties between them and provide opportunities to gain information and build political allies. It is an aspect of the "old boys' network" from which the women in this study said they had been excluded.

Women, on the other hand, generally carry most of the home and child care responsibilities, constraining their time outside of working hours more than their male counterparts. This constraint results in a double whammy for them: They must work harder during the work day to maintain their informal contacts, then find themselves cut out of potentially valuable business-related contacts formed after work.

The difficulty women experience in gaining access to informal networks has been attributed to several other factors as well, including lack of fit with the dominant coalition, discrimination, systemic barriers and homophily (the near universal preference for interaction with others of the same sex). When I asked these particular women how they managed to gain the access they did, they were clear in their answers: their mentor.

Functions Of Networks
Networking served six functions for the executives I studied: improving job performance, providing visibility, enhancing reputations, providing information, giving advice and support, and aiding career advancement. Although both the men and the women said their networks helped improve job performance and provided visibility, they differed on other points. Most women, but few men, said networking enhanced their reputations and provided valuable information, advice, support, and encouragement.

According to the women, networks served as "vehicles for positive press" and provided "a lot of prestige" and "clout." They found it especially helpful when supporters in their networks stood up for them when they were being considered for promotion. As one woman reported,

> When someone speaks up for you, saying yes, she can do the job, the fact that you're in a good relationship with a bunch of people in that room is probably more important because there will be more doubt in people's minds about whether a woman can do the job better than a man. When they know you, they can speak in your behalf.

All the women described their networks as valuable sources of organizational information; in contrast, only one man said he viewed it that way. Nine women, but only two men, reported that their networks provided them with advice on how to deal

with situations and often received feedback from them. One woman said that a network "covers up my mistakes and lets me know when something's not going well before I find out otherwise." Eight women and one man derived support and encouragement from their networks. One woman described some people in her network as "that cushion that you had when you needed one."

Men and women alike affirmed the value of networks in getting promoted into senior management. However, the actual role networks played in this respect for each group differed in this study. Only women reported having gone to people in their networks for help in handling job changes, seeking information about position openings, and discussing strategies for getting the jobs. As one said, "I would go sit in someone's office and just talk about my desire to move up and people I should go talk to to let them know I'm very interested." Only men reported that others in their networks had contacted them (without being asked) to offer them a job. One comment was, "He knew me when I was at [another firm]. Then he moved here and when an opening was available in his area, he contacted me and asked me to come over and meet some people."

This notion that people in the men's networks sought them out to tell them of job change possibilities while women had to locate openings for themselves is a potentially disturbing one. One might speculate that those who are sought for positions are apt to have a better chance at getting them than those who are not.

SPOUSES: PILLOW TALK HELPS

In this study, the two groups differed greatly in both the kind and degree of career support they received from their spouses (see **Figure 3**). The women had to manage complex home-related responsibilities and dual-career tensions while their husbands worked outside the home. In contrast, about half of the executive men's wives did so. Each of those men maintained that he saw his wife's exclusive assumption of child and home care responsibilities as helpful to his career. Speaking of his wife, one senior manager said,

> She recognizes that I've got to spend a lot of time doing this and I think she agrees that that's important. I think her support is important. But I think that probably the family may have gotten the short end of the stick in terms of the amount of my time.

The female executives said they could count on their husbands' active advice on career-related matters. One woman told me,

Figure 3

Relationships with Spouse

Marital Situations	WOMEN	MEN
Spouses' employment Assistance from spouse	All employed Job and career advice	50% employed Home care

He is a wonderful person to talk to about what is going on here and get a really objective appraisal about it because he knows me and he knows my strengths and weaknesses, and he's a loving critic and he can really say, "This is what really happened in that situation and this is what you were doing."

But the executive men did not look to their wives for that kind of assistance. This could be explained by considering that when both spouses work full time they have more work-related issues in common. Executive women may also seek specific advice from their husbands to help them function better in a predominantly male upper-management environment. It is also plausible that women may simply be more active advice-and-support seekers than men and, therefore, may add their spouses to their list of available and valued advisors.

WHAT WOMEN SHOULD DO TO GET WHAT THEY WANT

Is there a "man's way" and a "woman's way" of advancing to senior management? According to my findings, the short answer is "yes." With mentors, colleagues, and spouses, women executives worked harder at maintaining richer, broader relationships around work issues than the men did. They were actively involved in building multiple relationships that meet the variety of career needs they perceive they have. The men were considerably less active in doing this, as illustrated by one man's comment about career-facilitating relationships:

I don't have a lot of people. I don't feel the need to have a lot of people. I know myself and I know what I have to do. I don't have a lot of time. You have to spend time to do that, and I tend to not make the time for that.

Differences between executive women's and men's relationships in organizations parallels what psychologists have been reporting about male and female development. For men, the emphasis has been on autonomy and individuation; for women, on a process of growth within relationships. Men's identity has been defined by separateness, women's by attachment to others. In considering this, we can better understand how career-building relationships in this study differ at their very core.

The men and women of the corporation can, as individuals, take some comfort in knowing they do not necessarily have to change. Men's modes of career advancement have worked for years. Women can actively engage their relationship-building strengths by seeking development through mentoring, initiating and maintaining informal networks, building alliances, and seeking support from friends and family.

I do presume, however, that people of both sexes can benefit by learning from the modes of the other, greatly expanding their repertoire of career-building skills and activities. The interpersonal communication skills of active listening, self-disclosure, giving and receiving feedback, assertiveness, and managing conflict are all critical for sustaining the mentoring relationships that build careers. These skills can be learned through practice in experiential on-the-job training workshops or off-site college courses.

Implications for CEOs and Managers

CEOs and managers of human resources, training, and organization development can also use these findings to focus their cultural change, succession planning, and training efforts in specific directions. The most effective action can come from CEOs and others at the highest organizational levels in fostering a culture that encourages—or at least does not discourage—mentor-protégé relationships.

This will likely prove difficult. Large corporations are, for the most part, rigidly hierarchical. Although people typically believe it is "legitimate" for subordinates to seek career advice from their immediate supervisors and for managers to foster the career advancement of their direct reports, the mentor-protégé relationship is often well outside the "chain of command." Because this relationship develops much as friendships do, out of complex interpersonal attractions, it is not likely to be advanced by clumsy organizational attempts at matchmaking. Formal mentoring programs, in which individuals are assigned to be a mentor or protégé on the basis of arguably dubious criteria, are likely to yield fair to poor results. Some people, for a variety of good and bad reasons, are simply unable to make good use of the mentor to whom they are assigned, while those ordered to mentor may lack the time, inclination, interpersonal skills, or particular knowledge their assigned protégé may require.

Given our currently limited ability to "legislate" mutually fulfilling friendships of any sort, let alone that of mentor-protégé, organizations can probably best help by greatly improving the opportunities for less experienced managers to rub shoulders with the more experienced ones at both formal and informal times and places. Arranging formal "mixer" activities and informal work-flow patterns (consider where you put the water cooler; take the locks off the "executive" washroom) could result in many worthwhile relationships.

Succession planning efforts can benefit from any attention paid to the mentor-protégé relationship. Senior executives could be rewarded for the time and effort they spend seeking out and developing executive talent in others, no matter where they find them in the organization. Senior executives might be encouraged to invite their protégés at least to witness upper-level decision-making meetings, or be funded to participate with their mentor in off-site conferences, meetings, and workshops. These and similar initiatives expand the opportunities for both mentors and potential protégés to "see and be seen."

For the design and delivery of training programs, the possibilities abound. HR managers can provide management development sessions for men and women (separately and in mixed groups) that might be labeled "How to Be a Good Mentor" and "How to Be a Good Protégé." In these sessions, participants could engage in discussions of the several valuable functions of mentor-protégé relationships, beyond that of mere "role model," and their positive effects on career advancement. Specific attention should be paid to encouraging participants to share and openly discuss worries that are usually not talked about. These could include ways to maintain the relationship over the long term and work through issues that may arise, such as one-sided or mutual sexual attraction, misunderstandings that might lead to sexual harassment charges, and coping with office gossip.

What can we ultimately conclude from the success stories of the executive women and men in this study? It seems obvious to state that business hierarchies have only a few positions at the top, for men *or* women. This truism reminds us that there are plenty of people of both sexes who will do all the right things and, because of luck, fate, or circumstance, still won't make it. The men in my study who made it to the top did so by managing their relationships "like one of the guys," among other things. But what is fascinating is that all of the women executives I studied made it to the top by managing their relationships "like one of the women."

Perhaps, then, the important message that can be taken from these findings is that women can facilitate their advancement to executive ranks by continuing to do what they do very well: forming close, lasting relationships with others—both men and women—who will reciprocate.

References

D. J. Brass, "Men's and Women's Networks: A Study on Interaction Patterns and Influence in an Organization," *Academy of Management Journal*, 28, 2 (1985): 327–343.

D. D. Bowen, "Were Men Meant to Mentor Women?" *Training and Development Journal*, 39, 2 (1985): 31–34.

R. J. Burke and C. A. McKeen, "Mentoring in Organizations: Implications for Women," *Journal of Business Ethics*, April–May 1990, pp. 317–332.

R. J. Burke, C. A. McKeen and C. McKenna, "Benefits of Mentoring in Organizations: The Mentor's Perspective," *Journal of Managerial Psychology*, May 1994, pp. 23–32.

R. S. Burt, *Structural Holes: The Social Structure of Competition* (Cambridge, MA: Harvard University Press, 1992).

N. Chodorow, *The Reproduction of Mothering* (Berkeley: University of California Press, 1978).

J. G. Clawson and K. E. Kram. "Managing Cross-Gender Mentoring," *Business Horizons*, May–June 1984, pp. 22–32.

G. F. Dreher and R. A. Ash, "A Comparative Study of Mentoring among Men and Women in Managerial, Professional, and Technical Positions," *Journal of Applied Psychology*, October 1990, pp. 539–546.

G. F. Dreher and T. H. Cox, "Race, Gender, and Opportunity: A Study of Compensation Attainment and the Establishment of Mentoring Relationships," *Journal of Applied Psychology*, 81, 3 (1996): 297–308.

E. A. Fagenson, "The Mentor Advantage: Perceived Career/Job Experiences of Protégés Versus Non-Protégés," *Journal of Organizational Behavior*, 10, 4 (1989): 309–320.

C. J. Fombrun, "Strategies for Network Research in Organizations," *Academy of Management Review*, 7, 2 (1982): 280–291.

C. Gilligan, *In A Different Voice* (Cambridge, MA: Harvard University Press, 1982).

B. Glaser and A. Strauss, *The Discovery of Grounded Theory* (Chicago: Aldine, 1967).

D. M. Hunt and C. Michael, "Mentorship: A Career Training and Development Tool," *Academy of Management Review*, 8, 3 (1983): 475–485.

H. Ibarra, "Homophily and Differential Returns: Sex Differences in Network Structure and Access in an Advertising Firm," *Administrative Science Quarterly*, 37 (1992): 422–447.

H. Ibarra, "Personal Networks of Women and Minorities in Management: A Conceptual Framework," *Academy of Management Review*, January 1993, pp. 56–87.

R. M. Kanter, *Men and Women of The Corporation* (New York: Basic Books, 1977).

R. Keele, "Mentoring or Networking? Strong and Weak Ties in Career Development," in L. L. Moore (ed.), *Not As Far As You Think* (Lexington, MA: Lexington Books, 1986), pp. 53–68.

D. Krackhardt, "The Strength of Strong Ties: The Importance of Philos in Organizations," in N. Nohria and R. G. Eccles (eds.), *Networks and Organizations: Structure, Form, and Action* (Cambridge, MA: Harvard Business School Press, 1995).

K. E. Kram, *Mentoring at Work: Developmental Relationships in Organizational Life.* (Glenview. IL: Scott, Foresman, 1985).

D. J. Levinson, C. N. Darrow, E. B. Klein, M. H. Levinson, and B. McKee, *Seasons of a Man's Life* (Englewood Cliffs, NJ: Prentice-Hall, 1978).

J. R. Lincoln and J. Miller, "Work and Friendship Ties in Organizations: A Comparative Analysis of Relational Networks," *Administrative Science Quarterly*, June 1979, pp. 181–199.

L. Mainiero, "Getting Anointed for Advancement: The Case of Executive Women," *Academy of Management Executive*, May 1994, pp. 53–67.

A. M. Morrison and M. A. Von Glinow, "Women and Minorities in Management," *American Psychologist*, February 1990, pp. 200–208.

A. Morrison, R. White, and Van Velsor, *Breaking The Glass Ceiling* (Reading, MA: Addison-Wesley, 1987).

S. Morse, "A Comparative Study of The Advancement Experiences and Career-Facilitating Relationships of Male and Female Senior Managers," unpublished Ph.D. dissertation, University of Massachusetts, 1989.

R. A. Noe, "Women and Mentoring: A Review and Research Agenda," *Academy of Management Review, 13*, 1 (1988): 65–78.

V. A. Parker and K. E. Kram, "Women Mentoring Women: Creating Conditions for Connection," *Business Horizons*, March–April 1993, pp. 42–51.

B. R. Ragins, "Barriers to Mentoring: The Female Manager's Dilemma," *Human Relations, 42*, 1 (1989): 1–22.

B. R. Ragins and J. L. Cotton, "Easier Said Than Done: Gender Differences in Perceived Barriers to Gaining a Mentor," *Academy of Management Journal*, December 1991, pp. 939–951.

B. R. Ragins and J. L. Cotton, "Gender and Willingness To Mentor in Organizations," *Journal of Management*, Spring 1993, pp. 97–111.

B. R. Ragins and D. B. McFarlin, "Perceptions of Mentor Roles in Cross-Gender Mentoring Relationships," *Journal of Vocational Behavior, 37*, 3 (1990): 321–339.

B. R. Ragins and E. Sundstrom, "Gender and Power in Organizations: A Longitudinal Perspective," *Psychological Bulletin*, January 1989, pp. 51–88.

T. A. Scandura, "Mentorship and Career Mobility: An Empirical Investigation," *Journal of Organizational Behavior*, March 1992, pp. 169–174.

E. C. Shapiro, F. P. Haseltine, and M. P. Rowe, "Moving Up: Role Models, Mentors, and The Patron System," *Sloan Management Review*, Spring 1978, pp. 51–58.

E. E. Solomon, R. C. Bishop, and R. K. Bresser, "Organizational Moderators of Gender Differences in Career Development: A Facet Classification," *Journal of Vocational Behavior, 29*, 1 (1986): 27–41.

A. Strauss, *Qualitative Analysis for Social Scientists* (New York: Cambridge University Press, 1987).

J. Surrey, "Self-in-Relation: A Theory of Women's Development," paper presented at Stone Center Colloquium Series, Wellesley College, Wellesley, Massachusetts, 1984.

B. Townsend, "Room at the Top for Women," *American Demographics*, July 1996, pp. 28–35.

D. Wallace, "How Women Can Link Up on the Links," *Business Week*, February 29, 1994, p. 114.

W. Whitely, T. W. Dougherty, and G. F. Dreher, "Relationship of Career Mentoring and Socioeconomic Origin To Managers' and Professionals' Early Career Success," *Academy of Management Journal, 34*, 2 (1991): 331–351.

Susan M. Schor is an associate professor of management at the Lubin School of Business, Pace University, White Plains, New York. She wishes to thank Michael Sabiers for his valuable comments and suggestions during the preparation of this article.

Managing Pregnancy In The Workplace

Amy Oakes Wren, Roland E. Kidwell Jr., and Linda Achey Kidwell

Two months into her first pregnancy, Angela Anderson was called into the office of the president of a major Louisiana bank. The president was very complimentary of Angela's work in one of the bank's branch offices, where she had served as a teller for almost two years. As a result, he told her, he had decided to promote her. She would become his personal assistant, a position sought by many of the bank's employees.

In her excitement, Angela told him that the promotion was the second most exciting thing to happen to her that week. When her boss asked about the first exciting event, Angela said she had just discovered she was going to have a baby. The president's demeanor suddenly changed. He said he did not think he could rely on a pregnant personal assistant, and he was withdrawing the promotion. Devastated, Angela left the office and returned to her position as teller.

When working women become working mothers-to-be, a manager's ignorance can prove costly.

Although many managers and employees might be amazed at this blatant bias against Angela, her case is a fairly typical example of pregnancy discrimination. Most such actions toward pregnant women result from outdated beliefs that pregnant women are unproductive, sickly, and delicate. Yet these mistakes have cost employers millions of dollars because pregnancy discrimination violates federal laws.

Despite the laws designed to protect workers who become pregnant, female employees increasingly believe they are unfairly denied promotions, proper medical leave, and even their jobs because they have become pregnant, or because they *might* become pregnant. In fact, the Equal Employment Opportunity Commission reported that pregnancy discrimination complaints nationwide have increased 40 percent in the first half of this decade, from 3,000 in 1991 to 4,191 in 1995.

The issue of pregnancy discrimination has become even more focused as women of child-bearing age enter the work force at higher rates and corporate downsizing forces many managers to seek higher levels of productivity among remaining employees. Unfortunately, some managers have taken unlawful actions against pregnant workers because they perceive them as less productive, absent more often, or unable to perform their jobs. With two-thirds of the net additions to the U.S. work force in the remainder of the 1990s

Reprinted from *Business Horizons,* November/December 1996, pp. 61-67. © 1996 by the Foundation for the School of Business at Indiana University. Used with permission.

projected to be female, the treatment of women at work is a crucial issue for organizations.

FEDERAL LAWS RELATED TO PREGNANCY DISCRIMINATION

Three federal laws designed to protect workers relate to pregnancy: Title VII of the 1964 Civil Rights Act, the Pregnancy Discrimination Act of 1978, and the Family and Medical Leave Act of 1993. In addition, the Americans With Disabilities Act, or ADA, may provide some protection for pregnant employees.

The 1964 Civil Rights Act. Title VII of the 1964 Civil Rights Act prohibits employers of 15 or more employees from refusing to hire or discharge any person or otherwise discriminate in terms, conditions, or privileges of employment based on an individual's sex. Originally, the U.S. Supreme Court held in *General Electric v. Gilbert* that discrimination based on pregnancy was not the same as discrimination based on sex. In the Gilbert case, decided in 1976, GE provided a disability plan to all employees disabled because of sickness or accident, but excluded all disabilities from pregnancy.

The reasoning used in not finding discrimination was that the plan provided benefits to both men and non-pregnant women. The Court stated the disability plan was simply an insurance policy that covered some risks and not others. Pregnancy was a condition that was not covered. In addition, the Court said, "There is no risk from which men are protected and women are not. Likewise, there is no risk from which women are protected and men are not."

Pregnancy Discrimination Act Of 1978. In the aftermath of the Gilbert case and others like it, Congress amended Title VII of the 1964 Civil Rights Act by passing the Pregnancy Discrimination Act (PDA) of 1978. This act essentially overruled the Gilbert decision by making it clear that all employers must treat pregnant and non-pregnant employees in the same manner. As a result, pregnant women must be given the same benefits as men and non-pregnant women. The act states that:

> The terms "because of sex" or "on the basis of sex" include, but are not limited to, because of or on the basis of pregnancy, childbirth, or related medical condition; and women affected by pregnancy, childbirth, or related medical condition, shall be treated the same for all employment-related purposes, including the receipt of benefits under fringe benefit programs, as other persons not so affected but similar in their ability or inability to work.

The Family And Medical Leave Act. The Family and Medical Leave Act (FMLA), which became law in 1993, is one of the most important federal laws dealing with pregnancy, childbirth, adoption, and placement for foster care for both men and women. Under the FMLA, men and women can take 12 weeks of unpaid leave per year for the birth or adoption of a child, placement for foster care, the care of a sick child, or chronic illnesses such as morning sickness. To be covered, the person must work for a company that employs at least 50 people within a 75-mile radius and must have worked there for at least 12 months or 1,250 hours. The employee must give 30 days' notice of an intent to

---

Figure 1

Practices That Could Lead To A Pregnancy Discrimination Lawsuit

- Refusing to hire or promote a pregnant employee because of her pregnancy.

- Threatening to fire or terminating an employee because of her pregnancy or potential pregnancy.

- Failing to provide the same benefits to all employees regardless of pregnancy.

- Refusing to provide light duty for a pregnant employee while providing light duty for a non-pregnant employee.

- Discriminating against an employee based on a potential or intended pregnancy.

- Discriminating against an employee because she has had or is considering an abortion.

- Refusing to allow a pregnant employee to continue work if she is physically capable of continuing to work and wishes to do so.

- Evaluating a pregnant employee differently from a non-pregnant one when the employer has unilaterally lessened her work load in response to the pregnancy.

- Excluding or permitting exclusion of a pregnant employee from the normal office culture and social circles.

- Reassigning an employee to a lower-paying job because she is pregnant, or changing her job description and then eliminating the new job in restructuring.

- Discriminating against a male employee for his wife's pregnancy or pregnancy-related condition.

- Requiring a note from a pregnant woman's doctor concerning her ability to continue to work if the employer does not require a similar note from doctors of other employees with short-term disabilities.

take leave when possible. An example of this would be giving notice of intent to take leave 30 days before the due date of a birth.

Recent Court Rulings Provide Some Guidance

There are at least a dozen ways employers can illegally discriminate based on pregnancy. **Figure 1** summarizes these instances. Examples range from intentionally eliminating pregnant applicants from the labor pool to unintentionally discriminating against a pregnant woman because of an apparently sex-neutral insurance policy. Each of the following guidelines, based on the latest court rulings, reveals just how far application of the pregnancy discrimination laws can go:

1. An employer may not refuse to hire, refuse to promote, or fire a pregnant employee because of her pregnancy. On top of that, an employee does not have to prove that pregnancy was the only reason for her employer's decision not to hire, to fire, or not to promote her. Instead, she need only show it was considered in the decision.

2. An employer must provide the same benefits to all employees regardless of whether they are pregnant. However, an employer is not required to provide more benefits or special treatment for pregnant employees. Full benefits must be given to spouses of male employees if full coverage is given to spouses of female employees. This was not the situation recently at Newport News Shipbuilding and Dry Dock Company. The firm provided full benefits to the spouses of female employees but provided only limited benefits for pregnancy to spouses of male employees. In the ensuing court case, the U.S. Supreme Court ruled the company's plan discriminatory because protection given to married male employees was not as good as protection given to married female employees.

3. An employer may not refuse to provide light duty for a pregnant employee while doing so for a non-pregnant one. When Charlotte Adams, a patrol officer for the city of North Little Rock, Arkansas, was six months pregnant, she told her supervisor she needed to be placed on light work duty because of her doctor's recommendation. The North Little Rock Police Department denied Adams' request because of a recently implemented leave policy that had been passed in response to a "rash of pregnancies" in the department. According to the policy, employees who suffered non-work-related injuries or illness that included pregnancy, miscarriage, abortion, childbirth, and recovery thereof could not take light duty but must instead use accumulated sick leave, then vacation leave, and finally unpaid leave of absence. Adams continued to work as long as she could and then took an unpaid leave of absence for 26 weeks. Upon returning to the police department, she discovered she had been removed from the patrol officers'

roster. At the same time Adams had requested and was denied light duty, the North Little Rock Police Department had given light duty to a male officer who had a non-work-related disability. This constituted unlawful discrimination.

By contrast, in *Elie v. K mart,* a U.S. district court in Louisiana dismissed a claim against K mart in which the plaintiff did not prove she had been treated differently from non-pregnant employees. The woman, who was 19 weeks pregnant, requested reassignment to a job not requiring heavy lifting. She refused the evening and weekend hours her new assignment required because they were incompatible with her child care needs, and she was subsequently fired. The court ruled that the plaintiff had failed to prove that other employees who objected to new assignments based on medical reasons had not been terminated. The statutes, it said, "protect against employment decisions which are unlawfully motivated by an intent to discriminate. The law does not guarantee that pregnant employees will not suffer any adverse employment decisions."

4. An employer may not discriminate against an employee based on potential or intended pregnancy. This occurred in the case of Charlene Pacourek, who went to work for Inland Steel in 1974. In 1986, Pacourek, who was infertile because of a disability called esophageal reflux, began an experimental in-vitro fertilization treatment to become pregnant. Until that time, she had worked in good standing for the company and had been promoted several times. When she informed her employer she intended to continue the treatments and become pregnant, problems began at work, resulting in Pacourek's termination in 1993. Among other things, evidence indicated that company managers attempted to apply a sick leave policy to Pacourek that they did not apply to other employees; supervisors verbally abused her by expressing doubts about her ability to conceive and be a working mother; and managers told her that her condition was a problem and eventually placed her on probation. A U.S. district court found that the PDA had been violated because the employer's actions discriminated against an employee with a "pregnancy-related condition" (infertility). The court stated that the PDA

... does not affirmatively instruct employers to treat pregnancy, childbirth, or related medical condition(s) in any particular way; rather, it instructs employers to treat those things in a neutral way....

The basic theory of the PDA may be simply stated: only women can become pregnant; stereotypes based on pregnancy and related medical conditions have been a barrier to women's economic advancement; and classification based on pregnancy and related medical conditions are never gender neutral. Discrimination against an employee because she intends to, is trying to, or simply has the potential to become pregnant is therefore illegal discrimination.

5. An employer may not discriminate against an employee because the latter has had or is considering an abortion. Kim Turic, a 17-year-old mother of one, was employed at a Holiday Inn to bus tables in the restaurant and as a member of the room service staff. Upon learning she was pregnant, Turic informed her supervisor that she was considering an abortion. When the other employees heard the news, the ensuing discussions resulted in an "uproar" and conflicts between Turic and the staff. Several days later, Turic was terminated under the pretext of poor work performance. In Turic v. Holland Hospitality Inc., a Michigan court found that Turic was fired because she was considering an abortion, and her dismissal violated the PDA. In its finding, the court deferred to EEOC guidelines:

> The basic principle of the PDA is that women affected by pregnancy and related medical conditions must be treated the same as other applicants and employees on the basis of their ability or inability to work. A woman is therefore protected against such practices as being fired . . . merely because she is pregnant or has had an abortion.

6. An employer will also violate Title VII, and possibly the PDA and the ADA, by refusing to allow a pregnant employee to continue work if she is physically capable and wishes to do so.

7. An employer may not evaluate a pregnant employee differently from a non-pregnant one, especially when the employer has unilaterally lessened the employee's work load in response to the pregnancy.

8. An employer may not exclude or permit the exclusion of a pregnant employee from the normal office culture and social circles because this may cause her to become, as Bennett-Alexander & Pincus (1995) have stated, "less aware of matters of importance to the office or current projects."

9. An employer may not threaten to fire or terminate an employee because of her pregnancy or potential pregnancy. In 1993, a jury awarded $2.7 million to Lana Ambruster because she had been fired from her job upon revealing that she was pregnant. Ambruster was a claims adjuster for California Casualty Insurance Company when she became pregnant. On several occasions her boss had threatened to fire anyone who became pregnant because the firm had no budget for maternity leave. Although the boss claimed during the trial that such statements were made in jest and that the firing was for poor job performance, the jury found that the firm's actions violated pregnancy discrimination laws.

10. An employer may not reassign an employee to a lower-paying job because of her pregnancy. Nor may an employer change a worker's job description and then eliminate the new job in restructuring. Both of these actions violate the PDA. For example, Sundstrand Corporation recently settled a federal lawsuit brought by the EEOC on behalf of present and former Sundstrand workers that alleged such conduct. In June 1995, the company agreed to open jobs to pregnant workers that had originally been off limits to them.

11. Just as an employer cannot discriminate against a woman for pregnancy or a pregnancy-related condition, it cannot discriminate against a man for the same reasons. In the late 1980s, after Judy Nicols announced she was pregnant, she and her husband Scott were subsequently fired from the company where they worked. Managers explained that the dismissals were caused by declining sales and company cash flow problems. But the Nicolses filed complaints with the EEOC alleging pregnancy discrimination. A federal judge in Virginia agreed that the couple was protected by the PDA and could claim discrimination, so the company settled the lawsuit out of court for an undisclosed sum. The judge's ruling indicates that a man can sue for discrimination based on his wife's pregnancy. In states where marital status—or lack thereof—is protected under discrimination laws, this ruling may apply to pregnancies involving unmarried couples.

12. An employer may not require a note from a pregnant woman's doctor concerning her ability to continue work if the employer does not require similar notes from doctors of other employees with short-term disabilities. Such an action violates the PDA because the employer would be treating a pregnant person differently than a non-pregnant person. The PDA does not require an employer to offer maternity leave or take other steps to make it easier for pregnant women to work. However, it does require that the employer ignore the pregnancy and treat both pregnant and other employees in the same manner.

Pregnant Employees And The ADA

The Americans with Disabilities Act is another important law that may affect the rights of pregnant employees. This Act, which applies to companies that employ 15 or more people, requires reasonable accommodations for disabled employees or job applicants if they are qualified for a position. It also requires that an employer disregard a person's disability.

The EEOC recently published its "Compliance Manual Section 902: Definition of the Term Disability" specifically excluding pregnancy as a disability. However, this does not mean the decision is necessarily binding on the courts. Although courts generally give great weight to EEOC regulations, they have been known to disregard these guidelines if they are believed inconsistent with Congress's intent or are unreasonable.

One case illustrates the right of the court to rule in opposition to the EEOC Compliance Manual. In Chapsky v. Baxter Healthcare, decided in 1995, the plaintiff was fired for a single violation of the company's no-smoking policy the day before she was scheduled to undergo surgery for pregnancy complications. A male employee had received progressive disciplinary action, including 23 warnings and probation, before being discharged for violating the policy. Chapsky had consistently received outstanding ratings by her supervisors until her dismissal. So the court found that sex discrimination had occurred. Notably with regard to ADA applications, the court also ruled that she had established a case for disability discrimination, recognizing pregnancy as a disability under the ADA.

The final status of this case is unclear. The court based the disability finding on *Pacourek v. Inland Steel*, which relied on the PDA, not the ADA, and did not address pregnancy from the standpoint of a disability. However, the most recent U.S. district court rulings have refused to extend the ADA to pregnancy and related temporary medical conditions. These courts based their findings on the EEOC regulations stating that conditions such as pregnancy that are not the result of a physiological disorder should not be considered impairments, and that temporary, non-chronic conditions with little or no long-term impact are usually not disabilities. In these rulings—*Johnson v. A. P. Products, Ltd.*, for example, decided in August 1996—the courts noted that plaintiffs' complaints of employment discrimination based on pregnancy are already specifically covered by Title VII in the PDA.

Even in light of these rulings and the EEOC determination that pregnancy is not a disability, EEOC guidelines recognize that pregnancy complications may be a disability under the ADA. As a result, gestational diabetes, toxemia, chronic morning sickness, and other potential long-term complications of pregnancy may require that an employer reasonably accommodate a pregnant employee. For example, she may have to take light or desk duty if she has high blood pressure. If the accommodation is reasonable and does not impose an undue hardship on the employer, the ADA may require such an action on the part of the employer.

IMPLICATIONS FOR MANAGERS

The laws and court cases reviewed here indicate that some managers have engaged in and been held liable for actions that discriminate against pregnant women, women who have announced an intention to become pregnant, women who might become pregnant, women who have had an abortion or plan to have an abortion, and even men whose wives have become pregnant. Companies can avoid the difficulties and costs associated with improper and illegal treatment of female employees by following the suggestions listed in **Figure 2**. Most large corporations have taken the following steps to avoid being held liable for discrimination; smaller companies may want to consider similar actions.

Employment Policies. One important step for companies is establishing, amending, and enforcing policies to meet the legal requirements outlined earlier. Policies should reflect the firm's position on other temporary physical conditions involving its employees, not just pregnancy. Evenhanded treatment of pregnant and non-pregnant employees is crucial to the legality of such policies. It is important not to restrict employees from working as long as they are able to perform job duties effectively and safely. Workers and their doctors should be encouraged to notify the employer in writing when the job cannot be performed without risking health and safety; again, this applies to *all* employees, not just those who are pregnant.

Some organizations, such as police departments, trucking companies, and airlines, have different requirements regarding public health and safety. In these cases, the employer should provide alternative light duty job assignments for pregnant workers if similar assignments are provided for other employees who are unable to perform their jobs because of a tem-

Figure 2

Guidelines For Organizations

Employment Policies

Establish company policies that reflect the firm's position on all temporary physical conditions involving employees, not just pregnancies.

Employee Selection

Focus interview questions and employment applications around the duties and responsibilities of the job. Treat all applicants similarly.

Benefits

In designing benefit programs, treat women affected by pregnancy, childbirth, and related medical conditions the same as other employees.

Alternative Work Arrangements

If alternative arrangements are offered, they should be provided to all employees.

Performance Appraisal

Carefully document *all* employee performance; disciplinary actions for excessive absences and low productivity should begin when performance problems occur.

porary physical condition. The key is a policy that does not demote, harm, or malign an employee because of pregnancy.

Employee Selection. It is important to ensure that interviewers do not ask questions of applicants regarding their families or their intentions to have a family. Focusing the questions around the duties and requirements of the job on the employment application and during the interview protects the manager and the employer from future allegations of illegal discrimination. If a firm's managers attempt to avoid pregnancy discrimination by hiring only men, the managers will be violating Title VII for discriminating against women.

Bona fide occupational qualification (BFOQ) is often used as a defense in discrimination cases. However, managers who treat married and unmarried pregnant employees differently—arguing that unmarried pregnant women are negative role models under the BFOQ discrimination exception—would be violating current law unless they fall within very narrow exceptions, such as religious organizations that counsel young women.

Benefits. Whereas federal law does not require health benefits to be offered to employees, several states mandate that they be provided by many employers. The key for employers who offer health care, disability, sick leave and other benefits—mandated or voluntary—is to treat women affected by pregnancy, childbirth, and related medical conditions the same as other employees. For example, if an employer offers 12 weeks paid disability leave as a benefit for all illnesses, this benefit should apply to pregnancies as well. However, the U.S. Supreme Court has ruled that even if an employer does not offer disability leave to employees, it can (but does not have to) provide pregnancy leave even though male employees do not receive similar benefits.

Alternative Work Arrangements. Various options have been instituted to enable women to succeed and thrive in companies. These include alternative career paths, extended leave, flexible scheduling, job sharing, and telecommuting. Some firms adopted such policies to attract and retain talented women. However, these policies must be applied to all employees to avoid problems with discrimination. Obviously, fathers could also take advantage of such programs, so excluding men would constitute sex discrimination and perhaps pregnancy-related discrimination as well.

Performance Appraisal. Several organizations have fired pregnant workers who were said to be unproductive or incompetent and then lost court cases after discrimination was charged by the fired worker. These decisions raise the question of whether poor performers who are pregnant can ever be fired. Obviously, it is easier to terminate incompetent employees who happen to be pregnant in states that have retained a strong employment-at-will doctrine, particularly dur-

ing an employee's probationary period. However, in many states the employment-at-will doctrine has deteriorated, and often organizations want to demote or fire employees who have been with the company past their probationary period.

Managers are advised to document employee performance carefully and write accurate employee evaluations. If an employee has been having work-related problems, these should be documented and disciplinary action begun immediately, not after the employee has become pregnant. It may appear to a jury that a pregnant worker was unfairly dismissed if her performance appraisals indicate that she did not become "a problem" until after announcing her pregnancy.

Ignoring the issue of pregnancy discrimination carries a high price tag for employers. Costs borne to defend and settle lawsuits are the most obvious result of engaging in discriminatory actions. Another cost is the potential loss of skills if those affected by pregnancy are not accommodated when they are in need. As the labor pool contracts and certain skills become difficult to obtain, companies that have gone an extra mile to oblige employees by instituting family-friendly policies regarding leave and work arrangements will retain those highly skilled employees. They will avoid costs associated with high turnover: training and development of new workers and the performance lapse that occurs while employees of less experience learn how to perform their jobs.

Despite the federal laws, job bias against pregnant women remains an underlying problem. There is a concern that although discrimination laws have aided employees who have faced blatant bias, these protections will negatively affect the hiring and advancement of women in some organizations. Requiring companies to obey laws related to the treatment of pregnant workers may result in subtle discrimination against hiring women of childbearing age. This type of discrimination usually offers no "smoking gun." However, the realities of work force demographics will increase a firm's long-term costs of discrimination against women, pregnant or not.

References

Adams v. Nolan, 962 F.2d 791 (8th Cir. 1992).
D. Bencivenga, "ADA Coverage For Pregnancy Bias Rejected; But Federal Judge Says Other Laws May Be Used," *New York Law Journal,* August 15, 1996, p. 1.
D. D. Bennett-Alexander and L. B. Pincus, *Employment Law for Business* (Chicago: Irwin, 1995).
Chapsky v. Baxter Healthcare, Mueller Div, 66 EPD ¶ 43,573 (1995).
Civil Rights Act of 1964, 42 U.S.C., 2000e2(a)(1964).
Cleveland Board of Education v. LaFleur, 414 U.S. 632 (1974).
Doe v. First National Bank of Chicago, 668 F. Supp. 10 (N. D. II 1. 1987), affd. 865 F.2d.
Elie v. K mart Corp., No. 93-1077 (E.D.La., filed February 11, 1996).

General Electric v. Gilbert, 429 U.S. 125 (1976).

H.R. Conference Report, No. 95-1786, 95th Congress, 2d Sess. 4, reprinted in 1978 U.S. Code Cong. & Admin. News, pp. 4765–4766.

International Union, UAW v. Johnson Controls, Inc., 499 U.S. 187 (1991).

W. Johnston, "Global Work Force 2000: The New World Labor Market," *Harvard Business Review,* March–April 1991, pp. 115–127.

C. Kleiman, "Man Allowed To Sue For Pregnancy Discrimination," *Chicago Tribune,* June 15, 1992, Busn. Sec., p. 5.

M. Lord, "Pregnant—And Now Without A Job," *U.S. News & World Report,* January 23, 1995, p. 66.

Newport News Shipbuilding and Dry Dock Company v. EEOC, 462 U.S. 669 (1983).

Pacourek v. Inland Steel Company, 858 F. Supp. 1393 (D.C. 111, 1994).

Pregnancy Discrimination Act, 42 U.S.C., 2000e(k)(I 978).

F. N. Schwartz, *Breaking With Tradition: Women And Work, The New Facts Of Life* (New York: Warner, 1992).

Shafer v. Board of Public Education of the Pittsburgh School District, 903 F.2d, 243 (3d Cir. 1990).

"Sundstrand Settles Pregnancy Suit," *Chicago Tribune,* June 27, 1995, Busn. Sec., p. 1.

Troupe v. May Department Stores Company, d.b.a. Lord & Taylor, F.3d (7th Cir. 1994).

Turic v. Holland Hospitality, Inc., 858 F. Supp. 759 (W.D. Mich. 1994).

"Woman Wins Suit Over Her Pregnancy," *Chicago Tribune,* November 21, 1993, p. 27.

D. C. Wyld, "Is There A Dan Quayle (Or Role Model) Exception To The Pregnancy Discrimination Act? An Analysis," in C. Boyd, ed., *Southwest Academy of Management Proceedings* (Springfield, MO: Southwest Missouri State University 1995), pp. 81–85.

Zaken v. Boerer, 964 F.2d 1319 (2d Cir. 1992).

Amy Oakes Wren is an assistant professor of business law at Louisiana State University in Shreveport. **Roland E. Kidwell, Jr.** is an assistant professor of management and **Linda Achey Kidwell** is an assistant professor of accounting, both at Niagara University, New York. An earlier version of this article was presented at the Human Resource Management/Labor Issues Track of the Annual Meeting of the Academy of Management, Southwest Division, San Antonio, Texas, in March 1996.

Female Entrepreneurs: How Far Have They Come?

E. Holly Buttner

Women have been starting their own businesses in unprecedented numbers in recent years. They are leaving large corporations to "go it alone" for a number of career reasons: frustration at hitting the "glass ceiling," dissatisfaction with slow career advancement and unmet career expectations, and corporate downsizing. They are also fulfilling personal dreams of entrepreneurship, being their own boss, and achieving success in business.

The rapid increase in women-owned enterprises is important because small business provided the major source of new job growth in the 1980s. Women have been initiating businesses at twice the rate of men. Between 1972 and 1987, businesses owned by women grew from less than 5 percent to 28 percent of all U.S. businesses. According to the *1988 State of Small Business Report*, the number of non-farm sole proprietorships owned by women increased 62 percent between 1980 and 1986. If current startup rates continue, women will own half of U.S. businesses by the year 2000.

Until recently, most of what we have known about entrepreneurs has been based on the study of men who initiated ventures. Because the number of women starting their own businesses has grown so large, it is important now to understand whether their experiences are different from those of their male counterparts. Consequently, we are learning much more about the women who are piloting their ventures in the turbulent seas of the current economic climate. The purpose of this article is to summarize what we

> *Women entrepreneurs share many traits with their male counterparts. With perseverance, success will become one more.*

know about the experiences of today's entrepreneurial women in North America.

The Woman Entrepreneur: Past and Present

When we think of the women initiating businesses ten or 20 years ago, a particular image comes to mind. Historically, women entrepreneurs were divorced, widowed, or at home with small children, starting their businesses out of financial necessity. They often fit the stereotype of working to support the family. Their education was in liberal arts with little or no business experience. The enterprises were usually small service or retailing establishments, started with personal savings or loans from friends or family. The businesses typically remained small, slow-growing, labor-intensive operations. Although some female owners still fit this description, today's modern female entrepreneurs are generally quite different in background and experience.

The female entrepreneur of the 1990s is typically middle- to upper-middle class, married with children, and 30 to 45 years of age at startup. She is often the first-born, college-educated daughter of a self-employed father. She usually has worked in a larger organization, gaining skills and knowledge her forebears lacked. Typically she capitalizes on her training, initiating her business in the same industry. Today, greater numbers of women are venturing out into manufacturing, engineering, transportation, construction, and other traditionally male-dominated fields.

Is the Female Entrepreneur Unique?

There is a commonly held perception that entrepreneurs (typically male) differ from the general population in such personality characteristics as independence and leadership. Male entrepreneurs are indeed higher on these dimensions than many employees of large organizations. Are female entrepreneurs

> "Whereas men generally see entrepreneurship as a business decision, many women view it as a life choice—a way of integrating family and career needs."

more similar to their male colleagues or to their female counterparts in large organizations?

Numerous studies have shown that there are no differences between entrepreneurial men and women in personality dimensions, including achievement motivation, autonomy, persistence, aggressiveness, independence, (non-)conformity, goal orientation, leadership, and risk-taking propensity. A few differences in how men and women manage their businesses have emerged, however. Compared to men, female entrepreneurs are more adaptive, more socially aware, have wider experience in different business areas, delegate more, and engage in longer-term planning.

Overall, men's and women's motivations for business initiation are quite similar. As with male entrepreneurs, females seek independence, autonomy, higher income, and the opportunity to be their own boss. One difference between men and women in their motivation to initiate a business is that men often cite economic reasons, whereas women often cite family needs. Whereas men generally see entrepreneurship as a business decision, many women view it as a life choice—a way of integrating family and career needs. Barbara Noble, in her report on female entrepreneurs (1986), summarized the difference in orientation when she wrote, "For men, being an entrepreneur is a business strategy. For women, it's a life strategy."

Female entrepreneurs are also quite similar to female executives in large corporations. For both groups, the predominant motivations for working are a need to achieve and the desire for job satisfaction and professional recognition. However, female executives tend to be more stable than their entrepreneurial colleagues. In one study of women's work experience, 42 percent of the entrepreneurs had held at least four previous jobs, compared to only 16 percent of the corporate managers. Female executives and entrepreneurs also gave different reasons for their professional success. The executives saw their ability to work with people as the key to their success, while entrepreneurs saw endurance and hard work as their key success ingredients.

What conclusions can we draw about the uniqueness of the female entrepreneur? Male and female entrepreneurs are much more similar in personality characteristics, motivations for initiating a venture, management styles, approaches to strategic management, values, and predictors of success than they are different. Women's migration into entrepreneurship appears to result more from their frustration at hitting the "glass ceiling" or experiencing downsizing than to some unique personality attribute.

Success of Female-owned Businesses

Despite the myth that women lack business savvy, female-owned businesses have a survival rate comparable to men's. Entrepreneurial success, as measured by gross sales and market share, is the same for both male and female entrepreneurs.

Successful female business initiators have previous experience in the field in which they operate their businesses. They also possess financial and communication skills, are adept at establishing long-term objectives and generating new ideas, effectively set up formal organization structures when needed, and are highly motivated by new market opportunities. Again, the men and women initiating new enterprises are remarkably similar. But although men and women may be equally successful, differences in perceptions about their likelihood of success persist among resource providers.

Sex-Role Stereotypes and Female Entrepreneurship

In spite of their success, many female entrepreneurs report that they have to work harder than their male counterparts to prove their competence as business owners to customers, suppliers, and other resource providers. Women maintain that this extra effort is especially critical if they are in traditionally non-female-owned businesses, such as manufacturing, transportation, or construction. There is well documented evidence that women are perceived as lacking attributes associated with successful management. These perceptions of women's lack of fitness for management, which spill over into the entrepreneurial arena, have been a topic of heated debate.

Contrary to the empirical evidence demonstrating similarities in personality attributes, motivation, and success between male and female entrepreneurs, stereotypical perceptions that women are less qualified persist. In a study I conducted several years ago with my colleague Ben Rosen (1988), we asked bank loan officers to rate men, women, and successful entrepreneurs on attributes of successful entrepreneurship. Women were rated significantly lower than men on seven of nine dimensions: leadership, autonomy, readiness for change, risk taking, endurance, lack of emotionalism, and low need for support.

The results of another study provided additional evidence of the predominance of sex stereotypes in entrepreneurship. When asked to describe the personality profile of a successful entrepreneur, employees in female-owned small businesses used masculine characteristics more often than feminine ones. Do these stereotypical perceptions influence resource providers' decisions, including those of bank loan officers? This is a critical issue, because the inability to obtain financing can be an insurmountable roadblock for an aspiring entrepreneur—bank loans are second only to personal savings as a source of capital for women.

A controversial issue has been whether bias exists in the capital funding process. The House of Representatives Committee on Small Business (1988) reported that women still suffer the negative effects of misperceptions and discrimination in capital acquisition. They cited the need for female entrepreneurs to have access to additional management training to overcome these barriers. Female entrepreneurs in numerous surveys conducted in the early 1980s also asserted that they have more difficulty than men in raising startup capital. However, these allegations have been largely unsupported when the funding process is closely examined.

Ben Rosen and I (1989) investigated female entrepreneurs' allegations that loan officers favored men in their funding decisions. We developed a business plan and two videotapes: one interview of a male entrepreneur and one of a female entrepreneur applying for a bank loan to start a biotechnology venture, a field historically dominated by men. We found that in funding recommendations for identical business proposals, the loan officers in our sample treated male and female applicants identically. There were no differences in the

> **"High-performing females are rated more positively than comparably performing males when the women's performance runs counter to stereotyped expectations."**

loan officers' likelihood of recommending funding or the amount of the loan as a function of entrepreneurial gender when they read the business plan. A different sample of loan officers made slightly larger counteroffers to the female entrepreneur after reading the business plan and watching the videotape of the loan application interview. This finding is consistent with other research, which shows that high-performing females are rated more positively than comparably performing males when the women's performance runs counter to stereotyped expectations.

In another study of the financial histories of Canadian entrepreneurs, conducted by Allan Riding and Catherine Swift (1990), the results indicated that, in the aggregate, financial conditions for women appear less favorable. The women surveyed paid a higher interest rate on loans, were required to put up more collateral, were less likely to have a line of credit, and were more likely to have to provide the co-signature of a spouse to obtain a loan. However, closer examination of the data provided a somewhat different picture. Compared to male-owned businesses, the women's companies were younger and smaller (in annual sales), had lower rates of growth, were more likely to be a sole proprietorship than a corporation, and were more often in the retail and service industries. All these attributes made the women's businesses less attractive as potential loan recipients. When the researchers compared the funding histories of women's businesses to comparable male-owned businesses, only one gender-related difference remained: the collateral requirement for a line of credit was still higher for women. This is a notable difference in treatment, since a line of credit is often essential for firm growth. Overall, however, research to date indicates that men and women in comparable businesses are, in most cases, treated similarly by loan officers.

How can we account for the contradiction between the allegations of female entrepreneurs and the research findings to date? Ben Rosen and I conducted a third study (1992) to find an answer to this question.

We asked our entrepreneur participants to imagine that they had applied for a startup loan for a new venture. When we queried them about their views after rejection of the loan, we found few differences in male and female entrepreneurs' attributions about loan officers' funding criteria. They attributed the rejection to bad timing, insufficient collateral, the inability to develop good chemistry with the loan officer, or the excessive size of the loan request, in that order. Gender bias was rated as the least likely reason for re-

> "Women entrepreneurs report that they come home from work too tired to engage in other desired activities and that they have difficulty relaxing at home."

jection by both males and females. Entrepreneurs of both sexes were also strikingly similar in their subsequent actions. Both the men and the women indicated that their most likely next steps would be to revise the business plan and seek funding at another bank, seek advice from other entrepreneurs, and take various measures to strengthen their cases for attracting venture capital.

Female entrepreneurs were significantly more likely to seek funding from a venture capitalist or to attend a venture capital forum than were men. As a result,

these women were generally more active in seeking venture capital funding. It appears that today's female entrepreneurs, who have more business experience than their forebears of a decade ago, may be more aware of the financial requirements for obtaining a loan and less likely to attribute a rejection to gender bias.

Resource Availability in Women's Entrepreneurial Networks

To be successful, entrepreneurs must be well-integrated in their communities. Networking can be a way for an entrepreneur to gain access to resources (information, advice, or capital) needed for initiating and operating a new venture. Entrepreneurs connected to many diverse information sources are more likely to survive and make their business grow.

Women have historically been excluded from the "old boy networks" in large organizations. Perhaps because of these obstacles, they have developed different networking strategies than those used by men. Women represent a source of information significantly more often for other women than for men. Male entrepreneurs have few women in their close business networks of suppliers, customers, bankers, and creditors. If connections bring access to resources, women starting their businesses may be at a disadvantage compared to (better connected) male entrepreneurs.

Women . . . may also have different priorities than men in establishing networking relationships. Men's motives are often more "instrumental" (seeking personal gain), while women have more "affective" considerations in social relationships. As a result of socialization, women may have more difficulty than men in putting personal feelings aside in business relationships. Men rely on such outside advisors as bankers, lawyers, or accountants for information, advice, and support; their spouses typically play a secondary role. Female entrepreneurs, on the other hand, indicate that their husbands are their most important source of support.

The reliance of entrepreneurs on members of the same gender works against women in a different way. Women are underrepresented in fields crucial to entrepreneurial success. For example, loan officers and venture capitalists are predominantly male. Only 7 percent of partners and associates listed in the 1986 Venture Capital Association Directly were female. This underrepresentation of women in the financial industry is important, because networking by gender predominates over networking activities across gender lines. Thus, women entrepreneurs are less likely to have women bankers or venture capitalists in their network.

Managing Family and Work

Although we know relatively little about how entrepreneurs manage work and family life, women appear to experience greater family/work conflict than their male counterparts. Women entrepreneurs have reported that they come home from work too tired to engage in other desired activities and that they have difficulty relaxing at home. Not surprisingly, women who report business success also report greater satisfaction with their home life. This higher level of satisfaction may be attributable to a high crossover between the business and personal dimensions of their lives.

What have we learned over the past 15 years about women who strike out on their own in business? Research suggests that the critical determinants of success for female entrepreneurs involve good business management, drive and ambition, and an ability to exploit opportunities in areas of industry where entrepreneurs have significant business experience. Of course, these critical success factors apply to men as well.

Male and female entrepreneurs are strikingly similar in personality. Women initiate their businesses as a strategy for integrating life and career values, while men are more likely to initiate their businesses for economic reasons. Both groups seek to achieve success through the business and to operate with greater freedom than they have experienced in larger organizations.

Women will continue to struggle with the combined needs of family and business. We still do not have a clear understanding of the experiences these entrepreneurial women have as they try to juggle the simultaneous demands of both aspects of their lives.

To dissipate the enduring perception that entrepreneurship is a predominantly male domain, successful female entrepreneurs need to serve as role models for aspiring female business students and provide mentoring and internships in female-owned ventures. Women will continue to benefit from opportunities to enhance business skills in marketing and finance through training programs offered by the Small Business Administration, Small Business Development Centers, and colleges and universities. Enhanced skills and experience may help women develop greater entrepreneurial self-confidence.

Women need to be aware that the nature of the business they initiate will influence the ease with which they are able to attract venture capital. Service and retailing businesses with slower-growth histories, labor-intensive technologies, and lower profitability will be harder to finance with outside capital than growth-oriented, high-technology ventures. As women-owned businesses mature and develop track records of performance, banks should be more willing to negotiate loans. Bankers need to be careful to review collateral requirements for lines of credit to assure equal access for both male and female entrepreneurs.

Men, on average, have greater longevity in their ventures and therefore have greater entrepreneurial experience. Women entrepreneurs could benefit from concerted efforts to include supportive male colleagues in their networks and draw upon this potential additional source of information, advice, and resources.

In spite of these obstacles, the movement of women into the mainstream of business and entrepreneurship can be viewed in an optimistic light. As women gain business experience, build their own networks, and establish credibility with such network members as bankers, customers, and suppliers, their success and longevity will rival that of their male colleagues.

References

Howard Aldrich, "I Heard It Through the Grapevine: Networking Among Women Entrepreneurs," paper presented at the National Symposium on Women Entrepreneurs, Baldwin-Wallace College, April 7–9, 1988.

Howard Aldrich, Pat Reese, and Paul Dubini, "Women on the Verge of a Breakthrough: Networking Among Entrepreneurs in the United States and Italy," *Entrepreneurship and Regional Development*, 1 (1989): 339–356.

Robert L. Anderson and Kathleen P. Anderson, "A Comparison of Women in Small and Large Companies," *American Journal of Small Business*, 12, 3 (1988): 23–34.

Sue Birley, "Female Entrepreneurs: Different or Not?" *Journal of Small Business Management*, 27, 1 (1988): 32–37.

Candida Brush and Robert Hisrich, "Women Entrepreneurs: Strategic Origins Impact on Growth," in Barry Kirchoff et al., eds., *Frontiers of Entrepreneurship Research* (Wellesley, Mass.: Center for Entrepreneurial Studies, Babson College, 1988), pp. 612–625.

E. Holly Buttner and Benson Rosen, "Bank Loan Officers' Perceptions of the Characteristics of Men, Women, and Successful Entrepreneurs," *Journal of Business Venturing*, 3, 3 (1988): 249–258.

E. Holly Buttner and Benson Rosen, "Funding New Business Ventures: Are Decision Makers Biased Against Women Entrepreneurs?" *Journal of Business Venturing*, 4, 4 (1989): 249–261.

E. Holly Buttner and Benson Rosen, "Entrepreneurs' Reactions to Loan Rejections," *Journal of Small Business Management*, 30, 1 (1992): 59–66.

Alan Carsrud and Kenneth Olm, "The Success of Male and Female Entrepreneurs: A Comparative Analysis of the Effects of Multidimensional Achievement Motivation and Personality Traits," in Robert Smilor and R. Kuhn, eds., *Managing Takeoff in Fast Growth Companies* (New York: Praeger, 1986), pp. 147–162.

Radha Chaganti, "Management in Women-owned Enterprises," *Journal of Small Business Management*, 24, 4 (1986): 18–29.

Jill Charbonneau, "The Woman Entrepreneur," *American Demographics*, 3, 6 (1981): 21–23.

Joe A. Cox, Kris K. Moore, and Philip Van Auken, "Working Couples in Small Business," *Journal of Small Business Management*, 22, 4 (1984): 24–30.

G. Dessler, "Importance of Women in the Market," *The Miami Herald*, January 14, 1985, p. 43.

Ellen Fagenson and Eric Marcus, "Perceptions of the Characteristics of Entrepreneurs: Women's Evaluation," *Entrepreneurship Theory and Practice*, 15, 4 (1991): 33–47.

William Hamner, J. Kim, L. Baird and William Bigoness, "Race and Sex as Determinants of Ratings by Potential Employers in a Simulated Work-sampling Task," *Journal of Applied Psychology*, 59 (1974): 705–711.

Robert Hisrich and Candida Brush, *The Woman Entrepreneur* (Lexington, Mass.: Lexington Books, 1986).

R. Hisrich and C. Brush, "The Woman Entrepreneur: Management Skills and Business Problems," *Journal of Small Business Management*, 22, 1 (1984): 30–37.

Robert Hisrich and Candida Brush, "Women Entrepreneurs: A Longitudinal Study," in N. Churchill et al., eds., *Frontiers of Entrepreneurship Research* (Wellesley, Mass.: Center for Entrepreneurial Studies, Babson College, 1987), pp. 21–39.

House of Representatives, Committee on Small Business, "New Economic Realities: The Rise of Women Entrepreneurs," Report No. 100-736 (Washington, DC: U.S. Government Printing Office, 1988).

M. Humphreys and J. McClung, "Women Entrepreneurs in Oklahoma," *Review of Regional Economics and Business*, 6, 2 (1981): 13–20.

Eileen Kaplan, "Women Entrepreneurs: Constructing a Framework to Examine Venture Success and Failure," in Barry Kirchoff et al., eds., *Frontiers of Entrepreneurship Research* (Wellesley, Mass.: Center for Entrepreneurial Studies, Babson College, 1988), pp. 643–653.

Mollie Longstreth, Kathryn Stafford, and Theresa Maudlin, "Self-employed Women and Their Families: Time Use and Socioeconomic Characteristics," *Journal of Small Business Management*, 25, 3 (1987): 30–37.

Robert Masters and Robert Meier, "Sex Differences and Risk-taking Propensity of Entrepreneurs," *Journal of Small Business Management*, 26, 1 (1988): 31–35.

E. Mellor, "Investigating the Differences in Weekly Earnings of Men and Women," *Monthly Labor Review*, 107 (1984): 17–24.

T. Mescon, G. Stevens, and G. Vozikis, "Women as Entrepreneurs: An Empirical Evaluation," *Wisconsin Small Business Forum*, 2 (Winter 1983): 7–17.

Dorothy P. Moore, "First and Second Generation Female Entrepreneurs: Identifying Needs and Differences," *Southern Management Association Proceedings* (1987): 175–177.

Dorothy P. Moore, E. Holly Buttner, and Benson Rosen, "Stepping Off the Corporate Track: The Entrepreneurial Alternative," in Uma Sekaran and Fred Leong, eds., *Womanpower: Managing in Times of Demographic Turbulence* (Newbury Park, California: Sage, 1991), pp. 85–110.

Linda Neider, "A Preliminary Investigation of Female Entrepreneurs in Florida," *Journal of Small Business Management*, 25, 3 (1987): 22–29.

Barbara Noble, "A Sense of Self," *Venture*, July 1986, pp. 34–36.

Kenneth Olm, Alan Carsrud, and Lee Alvey, "The Role of Networks in New Venture Funding for the Female Entrepreneur: A Continuing Analysis," in Barry Kirchoff et al., eds., *Frontiers of Entrepreneurship Research* (Wellesley, Mass.: Center for Entrepreneurial Studies, Babson College, 1988), pp. 658–659.

Shirley Olson and Helen M. Currie, "Female Entrepreneurs: Personal Value Systems and Business Strategies in a Male-Dominated Industry," *Journal of Small Business Management*, 30, 1 (1992): 49–57.

Eric T. Pellegrino and Barry L. Reese, "Perceived Formative and Operational Problems Encountered by Female Entrepreneurs in Retail and Service Firms," *Journal of Small Business Management*, 20, 2 (1982): 15–24.

Paul D. Reynolds and Brenda Miller, "Race, Gender, and Entrepreneurship: Participation in New Firm Startups," paper presented at the Academy of Management Annual Meeting, San Francisco, August 1990.

Allan Riding and Catherine Swift, "Women Business Owners and Terms of Credit: Some Empirical Findings of the Canadian Experience," *Journal of Business Venturing*, 5, 5 (1990): 327–340.

Eleanor Schwartz, "Entrepreneurship: A New Female Frontier," *Journal of Contemporary Business*, 5, 1 (1976): 47–76.

Robert F. Scherer, James D. Brodzinski, and Frank A. Wiebe, "Entrepreneurship Career Selection and Gender: A Socialization Approach," *Journal of Small Business Management*, 28, 2 (1990): 37–44.

C. Scott, "Why More Women are Becoming Entrepreneurs," *Journal of Small Business Management*, 24, 4 (1986): 37–44.

Donald L. Sexton and Nancy Bowman-Upton, "Female and Male Entrepreneurs: Psychological Characteristics and Their Role in Gender-Related Discrimination," *Journal of Business Venturing*, 5 (1990): 29–36.

Donald L. Sexton and Nancy Bowman-Upton, "Sexual Stereotyping of Female Entrepreneurs: A Comparative Psychological Trait Analysis of Female and Male Entrepreneurs," in Barry Kirchoff et al., eds., *Frontiers of Entrepreneurship Research* (Wellesley, Mass.: Center for Entrepreneurial Studies, Babson College, 1988), pp. 654–655.

Donald L. Sexton and Calvin A. Kent, "Female Executives and Entrepreneurs: A Preliminary Comparison," in Karl Vesper, ed., *Frontiers of Entrepreneurship Research* (Wellesley, Mass.: Center for Entrepreneurial Studies, Babson College, 1981), pp. 40–55.

Larry Smeltzer and Gail Fann, "Gender Differences in External Networks of Small Business Owner/Managers," *Journal of Small Business Management*, 27, 2 (1989): 25–33.

Norman Smith, Gary McCain, and Audrey Warren, "Women Entrepreneurs Really Are Different: A Comparison of Ideally Constructed Types of Male and Female Entrepreneurs," in Karl Vesper, ed., *Frontiers of Entrepreneurship Research* (Wellesley, Mass.: Center for Entrepreneurial Studies, Babson College, 1982), pp. 68–77.

Lois Stevenson, "Against All Odds: The Entrepreneurship of Women," *Journal of Small Business Management*, 24, 3 (1986): 30–36.

The State of Small Business. A Report of the President (Washington, D.C.: U.S. Government Printing Office, May 1985).

Charles Stoner, Richard Hartman, and Raj Arora, "Work-Home Role Conflict in Female Owners of Small Businesses: An Exploratory Study," *Journal of Small Business Management*, 28, 1 (1990): 30–38.

Venture Capital Association, *Directory 1986*.

Frank Waddell, "Factors Affecting Choice, Satisfaction, and Success in the Female Self-employed," *Journal of Vocational Behavior*, 23 (1983): 294–304.

Ellie Winninghoff, "Crashing the Glass Ceiling," *Entrepreneurial Woman*, 1 (1990): 66–70.

E. Holly Buttner is an associate professor of management at the Bryan School of Business and Economics, University of North Carolina at Greensboro.

Unit 7

Key Points to Consider

❖ How can society best cope with the increase of working mothers in the workforce?

❖ Would society be better off if we didn't think of ourselves in terms of gender?

❖ Why is the Million Man March an indicator that there is a growing social, political, and economical problem between the sexes?

❖ Would full military equality for women diminish the effectiveness of the military? Why or why not?

 **Links** www.dushkin.com/online/

These sites are annotated on pages 4 and 5.

The dispute over a woman's nature and her role in society is very much alive as a social and anthropological issue and very much in need of an unemotional examination against its historical background. After nearly 200 years of intermittent struggle between feminists and antifeminists, neither side has been willing or able to make a dis-passionate evaluation of its view of woman's nature without resorting to exaggeration, outright misrepresentation, or special pleading. For instance, more than 14 years ago, feminists spearheaded the move to write absolute equality into the United States Constitution with the Equal Rights Amendment, but antifeminists vehemently opposed the amendment, ultimately leading to its defeat.

The problem inherent in the two sets of competing ideas lead to struggles that play out on a wide scale and for high stakes. These struggles, which may be short-lived but generally last for several centuries, color the pages of history with abrasive confrontations.

This unit is a collection of essays that examines these struggles. Included in the grouping are topics concerned with problems that women experience with their life choices, unrealistic societal expectations, and physical limitations that often put them at a disadvantage. The first article, by Catherine Daily, describes the evolution of American women's roles in society and ways that society can cope with the increasing presence of women in various walks of life.

In the second article, Barbara Kantrowitz examines the psychological adjustment of children with gay parents and finds them as well-adjusted as other children and no more likely to be gay themselves. Then, Françoise Coré and Vasiliki Koutsogeorgopoulou analyze parenting in terms of a changing society and find that through the use of child care and parental leave initiatives employers can keep skilled workers of both sexes. Another serious problem for women, domestic violence, is discussed in Kristen Golden's article, "Behind [Closed] Doors." In the next articles issues of women in the military, the problems that the male labor force faces in a world that has so enhanced women's position in the workforce, and the idea of black sisterhood, as expressed by the Million Women March, are explored. Finally, in "Beyond 'It's a Baby,'" Frederica Mathewes-Green shares her pro-life misgivings about abortion, and suggests that if pro-lifers gave more thought to women's needs, they would better serve children.

Sociology and Anthropology

The (R)Evolution of the American Woman

Catherine M. Daily, Guest Editor

Catherine M. Daily is an assistant professor of management at the College of Business, Ohio State University, Columbus.

To give a woman the vote, according to a U.S. senator in 1866, would be to put her "in an adversary position to man and convert all the now harmonious elements of society into a state of war, and make every home *a hell on earth*" (Rosenberg 1992; emphasis added). Here is an attitude that provides some insight into the difficulty of women's struggle for equality. And nowhere has this struggle been more visible than in the workplace, as generations of women have historically fought to create harmony between their jobs both inside and outside the home. Although the level of participation by women in the work force has fluctuated during the 1900s, their contributions and progress cannot be discounted.

The economic contributions of women have increased substantially over the past century as the influx of women into the workplace has swelled. The recently released Department of Labor report, *Workforce 2000*, noted that by the end of the century women will constitute nearly half of the work force. This is more than twice the rate of participation recorded in the early 1900s, when just over 21 percent of the work force was women (Edwards et al. 1991).

Several factors have contributed to this more than double the number of working women over the past century. Such technological innovations as washing machines and dishwashers have freed them from the time-consuming tasks necessary to managing the home environment. The fertility rate has steadily declined and has recently leveled off. Medical advances

have shortened the amount of time spent caring for sick children. The rise in single-parent families and the increasing need for dual-income households to maintain reasonable living standards have made income-generating work less a choice than a necessity for most women.

Although for many of us our most vivid memories of progress begin with the social and sexual revolution of the 1960s, working women are clearly not a novelty of the past 30 years. Little progress was realized, however, until this struggle affected middle- and upper-class women seeking advancement into the professional ranks—a trend that has risen since the 1920s. Until the 1960s, however, the contributions of these work force participants were typically transitory. Women worked while they were young and unmarried. Two world wars provided employment opportunities for them. With marriage and peace, however, women exchanged their jobs in the marketplace for those in the home.

To begin to understand the evolution of the role of American women, we must appreciate the difficulty of cultural change, as found in the barriers to progress. At the same time, we must recognize and capitalize on those factors that have enabled progress.

A Chronology of Progress

Rosenberg (1992) recently chronicled the history of working women in America during the twentieth century. Until very recently, women were largely considered a reserve work force used to fill positions that were either undesirable, because of low pay or status, or needed in times of crisis, such as that experienced during times of war. Dr. Alice Hamilton, a physician in the early 1900s and one of a handful of pioneers in the women's movement, commented on this mentality, noting that "[t]he American man gives over to the woman all the things he is profoundly disinterested in, and keeps business and politics to himself."

Whereas approximately 40 percent of unmarried women over the age of 14 worked for wages in 1900, the overall participation of women as a percentage of the work force was 21.2 percent. The typical woman's experience involved working while she was a young woman living under her parents' roof—but only until she got married, whereupon she assumed responsibility for the care and maintenance of the home.

Women who sought a life independent of men had few options. Typically they were relegated to communities of women. Jane Addams, an activist in the early 1900s, was one of the initiators of this independent lifestyle. At the turn of the century, she created a Chicago settlement community designed to meet the needs of unmarried, educated women. The women who joined these communities provided each other with the emotional support to lead the women's movement and challenge other women to become active in transforming the role expectations that society placed upon them.

Not surprisingly, these choices were radical in their time. As has been the case throughout this century, women did not speak in a unified voice. Various factions gained followers. The women striving for change at this time in our history typically fell into one of two categories: suffragists and anti-suffragists. A common denominator shared by both groups was the reliance upon argumentation, which emphasized the differences between men and women. The suffragists argued that the differences between the sexes made political support essential. Anti-suffragists, however, believed sex differences meant that women were destined to remain in the home while men participated in business and politics.

The women's movement continued to be plagued by these factions, preventing any widespread, unified effort for bringing equality between women and men into the workplace. Even today, women support the platforms of various groups professing to speak for the majority opinion. Conservative factions left over from the early 1970s, spearheaded by Phyllis Schlafly's campaign to prevent the ratification of the Equal Rights Amendment, are still at loggerheads with such feminist groups as the National Organization for Women. The perpetual infighting of women can easily obscure the progress that began with such women as Alice Hamilton and Jane Addams.

Progress, however, has not been consistent. The stock market crash in 1929 all but obliterated any gains realized during the previous several decades. With unemployment levels reaching 25 percent, few were interested in the economic or social gains of women. In fact, the opinion that working women were the cause of the crash by virtue of taking away men's jobs gained considerable momentum.

The growth of the service sector and the onset of World War II brought some measure of relief from the backlash of the stock market crash. During the war, women's participation in the work force rose to 35 percent, with a doubling of the numbers of married women who worked outside the home. With the recognition that women were essential to the functioning of the economy, employers responded to the needs of women in the workplace as well as in the home. To accommodate married women with children, day care centers were established and employers provided hot meal programs. But as the war ended and the men returned home, not only were these services discontinued, but men rapidly began displacing the women from the higher-paying jobs they had filled during the war. Once again, the backlash was felt.

The most recent gains occurred as a result of the social unrest of the country during the 1960s. Women's resolve to fight for equality was revitalized. The progress made during the modern women's movement has led to a work force composed of 41 percent women, with projections of an even split by the year 2000.

A Women's Place

Every push forward has been answered with resistance. Faludi (1991), in the bestseller *Backlash: The Undeclared War Against American Women*, documents evidence of a societal backlash occurring whenever women appear to be achieving the still elusive goal of workplace equality. With each incremental gain, the push for equality has met cultural resistance strong enough to halt the advance.

As evidence of the difficulty of widespread progress, even when economic necessity forced a married woman to work outside the home, she was castigated by men and women of all social classes. A 1936 Gallup Poll found that 82 percent of respondents, including 75 percent of the women, believed a woman should not work if her husband held a job. These numbers barely changed after World War II, when 80 percent of women and 84 percent of men felt similarly. Remnants of these attitudes persist even today.

A common denominator underlying these attitudes is an unsettling ambiguity of what defines appropriate gender roles. Eleanor Roosevelt, widely believed to be an ardent supporter of women's rights, struggled with the definition of appropriate primary and secondary roles for women:

It seems to me perfectly obvious that if a woman falls in love and marries, of course her first interest and her first duty is to her home, but her duty to her home does not of necessity preclude her from having another occupation.

More recently, Degler (1980) noted that this conflict still exists:

> Women are still the primary child rearers, even when they work, and the purpose of their work in the main is to support and advance the family, not to realize themselves as individuals.

The biological fact of childbearing has provided the basis for an occupational segregation that has persisted into the 1990s. Even today, parenting is still perceived as primarily a female role; conversely, a full-time, uninterrupted career is still perceived as a male role. It is, however, the persistence of this segregation that remains an inexplicable element of today's culture. Childbearing may be a biological function unique to women, but child care is an issue that transcends gender.

Building Glass Walls

The coining of the term "mommy track" recently ignited debate based on the premise that women are responsible for the two full-time roles of mother/wife and wage earner. Career interruptions as a result of family commitments have led to the stereotype of women who leave organizations to bear and care for children.

Once again, perception is greatly divorced from reality. One recent examination (Garland 1991) found that most of the turnover among women in large firms was a result of some factor other than the desire to "rock the cradle." In fact, 73 percent of these women moved to another company, presumably to seek greater career opportunities or a better working environment.

Role segregation is just one of the barriers that prevents women from advancing to the top levels of organizations. Without access to top management positions, women are relegated to a permanent second-class status in organizations. Any disruption in the organizational status quo threatens the economic lock men hold on these senior-level positions. In 1968, women represented 15 percent of managers, yet today a mere 3 percent of senior executives are women, compared to 1 percent in 1981—a net gain of only 2 percent at the senior level in the past decade. If women were advancing at a rate comparable to that of their male peers, we would expect significantly more women (closer to 15 percent) to occupy senior-level positions 25 years later. Complicating this slow pace is men's resistance to change and women's historical reluctance to create change.

Change brings with it costs, some of which are deliberately built into organizational systems to discourage women from persisting when faced with artificial barriers. Such barriers are constructed based on stereotypes and biases that do little to enable the performance of women in the workplace and much to detract from the consistently high levels of performance that women are capable of achieving.

A recent and notable example of one of the most pervasive barriers women face was the resignation of Dr. Frances Conley, professor of neurosurgery at Stanford University. In an act providing evidence that success in the professions remains difficult for women, Conley resigned her tenured faculty position following 16 years of "gender insensitivity," manifested in such indignities as being called "honey" by her male colleagues.

This incident exemplifies a barrier that has received scant serious attention—language differences between men and women. Gilligan (1982) suggests that women and men speak different languages, which each group assumes to be the same. Men, for example, use language to structure hierarchies, whereas women use language to build relationships. The resulting confusion when these two language styles collide often results in unintentional barriers.

Stylistic differences contribute to an array of tradition-bound stereotypes that women continue to face in organizations. The totality of these attitudes and prejudices transcend the proverbial "glass ceiling" and include "glass walls" as well (Lopez 1992). These barriers refer to the subtle biases that have prevented women from advancing in organizations. The lack of upward mobility demonstrates "the abiding . . . sexism of the corporation" (Bradsher 1988). Not only is women's upward mobility stifled, but lateral mobility is limited as well.

The costs to organizations supporting these role distinctions are significant. Mary Rowe, adjunct professor at the Massachusetts Institute of Technology's Sloan School of Management, has termed this treatment "microinequities" (Edwards et al. 1991). Microinequities occur when stereotypes, not actual performance, constitute the basis for workplace treatment. The outcome is often exclusion from critical information (via exclusion from the "old boy network") and skewed performance appraisals based exclusively on subjective measures of performance.

As evidence of stereotypes operating more powerfully than fact, a recent Department of Education report, entitled *Women at Thirty-something*, found that women consistently outperformed their male counterparts at both the secondary and undergraduate educational levels. Nevertheless, these same women faced a tougher labor market than men, experienced higher levels of unemployment, and suffered gross pay inequities (Koretz 1992). Clearly, the skills and abilities of a significant portion of the work force are being grossly underutilized, if not ignored.

The bias continues to exist, in part, because of differences in preparing individuals for advancement in organizations. Those in positions of power typically encourage and advance individuals most like themselves. Exclusion from these formal and informal networks provides some explanation for the abysmal percentage of women in top management positions.

Exploiting the Cracks

Women who have broken into the corporate elite have relied to a large extent on familial ties. Marion O. Sandler, CEO of Golden West Financial, for example, shares her position with her husband. Katherine Graham, chairperson of The Washington Post Co., inherited her position after the death of her husband. While these women have excelled in these positions, the avenue by which they gained access to the corporate elite is a narrow street that very few have the opportunity to travel. Reliance upon familial ties will not benefit the vast majority of qualified women desiring top corporate positions. Being born into privilege is much like being born into royalty—a privilege of nature, not a barometer of one's ability to lead.

Faced with this reality, significant numbers of women elect alternatives to the traditional organization. The growth of women-owned businesses has ballooned. During the years between 1974 and 1984, the rate of women-owned startups was six times that of men. Some of these businesses are born out of the desire to integrate work and family life successfully, an accommodation that few large firms are willing to make.

The trend toward self-employment, though an attractive alternative at an individual level, does little to address the inequities that continue to plague corporate America. Large-scale organizations must work to manage the diversity that women bring to the workplace. Continued pressure to conform to tradition-bound ideals may only drive more women from large organizations, at a cost to both parties.

Some 15 years ago Kanter (1977) suggested that to manage inequities effectively, organizations must alter systems, structures, and management practices to eliminate any subtle barriers that may prevent employees from reaching their full potential. By focusing on these issues, the burden of blame is removed from any given individual. This orientation enables behavior to be explained more as a function of the position one holds in the organization than as a general attitudinal predisposition. Systemic change, however, is unlikely without cultural revolution.

Removing existing barriers in the workplace is an issue that confronts women and men alike. Challenging opportunities, which provide visibility and the potential for success, are crucial to women's advancement. Incentives must be created so that all organizational members approach issues of equality with a progressive mindset. Rather than perpetuate blame, we must embrace change as a vehicle to equality. As Faludi (1991) suggests, those fearful of progress may, in the short term, have the strength to push back advances. It is unlikely, however, that they possess the endurance to outlast those seeking a cultural (r)evolution.

This special issue of *Business Horizons* is designed as a mechanism for opening the doors to such progress. As you read the following articles, be mindful of Gilligan's observation (1982) and make the effort to hear the message:

As we have listened for centuries to the voices of men and the theories of development that their experience informs, so we have come more recently to notice not only the silence of women but the difficulty in hearing what they say when they speak.

References

K. Bradsher, "Women Gain Numbers, Respect in Board Rooms," *The Los Angeles Times*, March 17, 1988, p. 1.
C. Degler, *At Odds: Women and the Family in America from the Revolution to the Present* (New York: Oxford University Press, 1980).
A. Edwards, S.B. Laporte, and A. Livingston, "Cultural Diversity in Today's Corporation," *Working Woman*, January 1991, pp. 45–61.
S. Faludi, *Backlash: The Undeclared War Against American Women* (New York: Crown Publishers, Inc., 1991).
S.B. Garland, "How to Keep Women Managers on the Corporate Ladder," *Business Week*, September 2, 1991, p. 64.
C. Gilligan, *In a Different Voice* (Cambridge, Mass.: Harvard University Press, 1982).
R.M. Kanter, *Men and Women of the Corporation* (New York: Basic Books, 1977).
G. Koretz, "America's Neglected Weapon: Its Educated Women," *Business Week*, January 27, 1992, p. 22.
J.A. Leavitt, *Women in Administration and Management: An Information Sourcebook* (New York: Oryx Press, 1988).
J.A. Lopez, "Study Says Women Face Glass Walls as Well as Ceilings," *Wall Street Journal*, March 3, 1992, pp. B1, B8.
A.M. Morrison and M.A. Von Glinow, "Women and Minorities in Management," *American Psychologist*, February 1990, pp. 200–208.
E. Roosevelt, *It's Up to Women* (New York: Franklin A. Stokes, 1933).
R. Rosenberg, *Divided Lives: American Women in the Twentieth Century* (New York: Hill and Wang, 1992).
F.N. Schwartz, *Breaking with Tradition* (New York: Warner Books, 1992).
A.T. Segal and W. Zellner, "Corporate Women," *Business Week*, June 8, 1992, pp. 74–78.
D. Tannen, *You Just Don't Understand: Women and Men in Conversation* (New York: William Morrow and Co., Inc., 1990).

Gay Families Come Out

SAME-SEX PARENTS are trying to move out of the shadows and into the mainstream. Will they—and their kids—be accepted?

BY BARBARA KANTROWITZ

THERE WERE MOMENTS IN CLAIRE'S childhood that seemed to call for a little... ingenuity. Like when friends came over. How could she explain the presence of Dorothy, the woman who moved into her Chicago home after Claire's dad left? Sometimes Claire said Dorothy was the housekeeper; other times she was an "aunt." In the living room, Claire would cover up the titles of books like "Lesbian Love Stories." More than a decade later, Claire's mother, Lee, recalls silently watching her daughter at the bookcase. It was, she says, "extremely painful to me." Even today, Lee and Claire—now 24 and recently married—want to be identified only by their middle names because they're worried about what their co-workers might think.

same benefits as husbands and wives, and celebrity couples like Melissa Etheridge and Julie Cypher proudly announce their expectant motherhood (interview).

Lily was conceived in a very '90s way; her father, Jim Hough, is a gay lawyer in New York who once worked as Rubenfeld's assistant and had always wanted to have kids. He flew to Nashville and the trio discussed his general health, his HIV status (negative) and logistics. They decided Rubenfeld would bear the child because Alberts is diabetic and pregnancy could be dangerous. They all signed a contract specifying that Hough has no financial or legal obligation. Then Rubenfeld figured out when she would be ovulating, and Hough flew down to donate his sperm so Alberts could artificially

though no one knows exactly how many there are. Estimates range from 6 million to 14 million children with at least one gay parent. Adoption agencies report more and more inquiries from prospective parents—especially men—who identify themselves as gay, and sperm banks say they're in the midst of what some call a "gayby boom" propelled by lesbians.

But being open does not always mean being accepted. Many Americans are still very uncomfortable with the idea of gay parents—either because of religious objections, genuine concern for the welfare of the children or bias against homosexuals in general. In a recent NEWSWEEK survey, almost half of those polled felt gays should not be allowed to adopt, although 57 percent thought

In the most recent Newsweek Poll, 57% of the adults surveyed said they think gay people can be as good at parenting as straight people; only 31% said they didn't think so

Hundreds of miles away, a 5-year-old girl named Lily lives in a toy-filled house with her mommies—Abby Rubenfeld, 43, a Nashville lawyer, and Debra Alberts, 38, a drug- and alcohol-abuse counselor who quit working to stay home. Rubenfeld and Alberts don't feel they should have to hide their relationship. It is, after all, the '90s, when companies like IBM offer gay partners the

inseminate her at home. Nine months later, Lily was born.

Two daughters, two very different families. One haunted by secrecy, the other determined to be open. In the last few years, families headed by gay parents have stepped out of the shadows and moved toward the mainstream. Researchers believe the number of gay families is steadily increasing, al-

gays could be just as good at parenting as straight people. Despite the tolerance of big companies like IBM, most gay partners do not receive spousal health benefits. Congress recently passed—and President Clinton signed—a bill allowing states to ban same-sex marriages. Only 13 states specifically permit single lesbians or gay men to adopt, according to the Lambda Legal Defense and

Education Fund, a gay-rights advocacy group. Even then, usually only one partner is the parent of record—leaving the other in legal limbo. Courts have allowed adoptions by a second parent (either gay or straight) in some of those states, although the law is still in flux. In California, for example, Gov. Pete Wilson has been lobbying hard against his state's fairly open procedure for second-parent adoptions.

Dealing with other people's prejudices continues to be a rite of passage for children in gay families. Merle, 14, lives north of Boston with her mother, Molly, and her mother's partner, Laura. Over the years she has learned to ignore the name-calling—gay, queer, faggot—from kids who know her mother is a lesbian and assume she must be one, too (as far as she knows, she isn't). And there are other painful memories, like the time in fifth grade when a friend suddenly "changed her mind" about sleeping over. Merle later learned that the girl's parents had found out about Molly and Laura and wouldn't let their daughter associate with Merle. One day in sixth-grade health class, the teacher asked for examples of different kinds of families. When Merle raised her hand and said, "lesbian," the teacher responded: "This is such a nice town. There wouldn't be any lesbians living here."

Gays say they hope that being honest with the outside world will ultimately increase tolerance, just as parenthood makes them feel more connected to their communities. "It sort of gets you into the Mom and Dad clubs of America," says Jennifer Firestone, a lesbian mother and gay-family educator in Boston. Having a child can also repair strained family relations; mothers and fathers who may have once turned their backs on gay sons and daughters often find it emotionally impossible to ignore their grandchildren.

Still, the outlook for children in this new generation of gay families is unclear. Only a few have even reached school age, so there are no long-term studies available on what the effects of growing up in such a family might be. Researchers do have some data on kids who grew up about the same time that Claire was living with Lee and Dorothy in Chicago. Most were born to a married mother and father who later split up. If the children were young, they generally wound up living with their mother, as did the majority of children of divorce. Pressures were often intense. The children worried about losing friends, while the mothers worried about losing custody if anyone found out about their sexual orientation. Yet despite these problems, the families were usually emotionally cohesive. In a comprehensive 1992 summary of studies of gay parenting, psychologist Charlotte Patterson of the University of Virginia concluded that the children are just as well adjusted (i.e., they do not have any more psychological problems

and do just as well in school) as the offspring of heterosexual parents. The studies also show that as adults, they are no more likely to be gay than are children of straight parents.

The new generation of gay parents is far more diverse and will be harder to analyze. Often they are already in stable partnerships when they decide to start a family. They include lesbian couples who give birth through artificial insemination (the donors can be friends or anonymous contributors to a sperm bank); gay dads who adopt, hire surrogate mothers or pair up with lesbian friends to co-parent, and the more traditional—in this context, at least—parents who started out in heterosexual unions.

Usually they try to settle in a relatively liberal community within a large urban area like Boston, Chicago, or Los Angeles, where their children will be able to mix with all kinds of families. They often join one of the many support groups that have been springing up around the country, like Gay and Lesbian Parents Coalition International or COLAGE, an acronym for Children of Lesbians and Gays Everywhere. The support groups form a kind of extended family, a shelter against the often hostile outside world.

A decade ago, when gay parents routinely hid their sexual orientation, the issues of differences rarely came up in school. But now gay parents say they try to be straightforward from the first day of class. Marilyn Morales, 34, and her partner, Angela Diaz,

37, live on Chicago's Northwest Side with their son, Christopher, 6, and their 4-month-old daughter, Alejandra, both conceived through artificial insemination. Registering Christopher for school proved to be an education for everyone. Because Morales appeared to be a single mother, a school official asked whether the family was receiving welfare. When Morales explained the situation, the woman was clearly embarrassed. "People don't know how to react," says Diaz. At Christopher's first soccer game, Diaz had to fill out a form that asked for "father's name." She scratched out "father's name" and wrote "Marilyn Morales." Both Morales and Diaz feel Christopher is more accepted now. "At birthday parties people say, 'Here comes Christopher's moms'," says Morales. Dazelle Steele's son Kyle is a friend of Christopher's, and the two boys often sleep over at each other's home. "They're such great parents," Steele says of Diaz and Morales. "Their actions speak louder to me than rhetoric about their political decisions."

To the parents, each new encounter can feel like coming out all over again. Brian and Bernie are a Boston-area couple who don't want their last names used because they are in the process of finalizing the adoptions of two boys, ages 12 and 6. A few years ago, Brian dreaded meeting the older boy's Cub Scout leader because the man had actively tried to block a sex-education curriculum in the schools. But his son Ryan wanted badly to join the Scouts, and Brian

Looking for Comfort Zones

The acceptance of gay men and lesbians as parents varies from state to state. This overview is based on information provided by the Lambda Legal Defense and Education Fund, a gay civil-rights group that looked at adoption law and custody decisions.

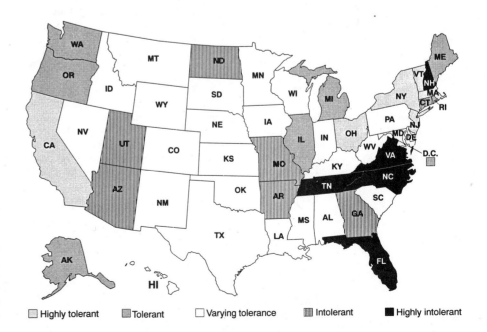

Highly tolerant Tolerant Varying tolerance Intolerant Highly intolerant

felt he needed to tell the man that the boy's parents were gay. As it turned out, the session went better than Brian had expected. "People challenge themselves, and people grow," Brian says. But, he adds, "as out as I am, I still feel the blood pressure go up, I sweat profusely, I'm red in the face as I tell him I'm gay, that I have a partner and that Ryan has two dads. I always think how it looks to Ryan. I'm always hoping he doesn't see me sweat."

Even in the relatively more tolerant '90s, gay parents "always feel threatened," says April Martin, a New York family therapist who is also a lesbian mother and the author of "The Lesbian and Gay Parenting Hand-

him because—according to the questionnaire he filled out at the sperm bank—he was well educated, spiritual and optimistic. "I don't really want a dad," says Sora. "I like having two moms."

But problems can arise even in the most innocent situations. Wayne Steinman and Sal Iacullo didn't truly understand their fragile footing until Labor Day weekend a few years ago, when they drove to Disney World from their home in New York City. As they passed through Virginia, Steinman was at the steering wheel; Iacullo was in the back seat with their adopted daughter, Hope, now 9. They noticed a pickup truck sticking close to them, and when they pulled off the high-

shared joint custody of their daughter, Annie, who was 13 when their marriage fell apart in the early 1980s. But although Annie talked to her father nearly every day of her life, he never told her he was gay. "Several of my friends and even family members had been of the opinion that there might be some real psychological damage and some anger if I didn't make the disclosure," says Kuhlman, now 49 and the ethics counsel for the American Bar Association in Chicago. "That was the bear breathing down my neck." But the timing never seemed right.

Then, one day when Annie was a college freshman, he called to say goodbye as he was about to head off for a Caribbean vaca-

36% of those surveyed think gay couples should have the right to adopt, as compared with 29% in 1994; 47% oppose gay adoption rights, down from 65% in 1994

book." "How can you feel secure when it's still legal for someone to tear apart your family?" The parents are haunted by such well-publicized legal cases as the 1995 Virginia Supreme Court ruling that Sharon Bottoms was an unfit parent because she is a lesbian; she had to surrender custody of her 5-year-old son, Tyler, to her mother. In Florida this summer, the state appeals court ruled that John Ward, who was convicted of murdering his first wife in 1974, was a more fit parent than his ex-wife Mary, a lesbian.

Catherine Harris, 41, a university administrator in Boston, knows only too well the pain of these legal battles. Ten years ago, she was married and the mother of a toddler daughter, Tayler. Then she fell in love with Paula Vincent, now 38, a nurse-midwife. During the divorce Harris's husband fought for custody of Tayler, and Harris's parents, who disapproved of her new identity as a lesbian, testified against her. Her ex-husband won.

Harris is still on rocky terms with her parents and her ex-husband, but she and Vincent have started a new family of their own that now includes Sora, 7, and her twin siblings, Kaelyn and Marilla, 22 months. In contrast to Tayler, Sora knows her biological father only as "the donor." She has seen the vial his sperm came in and knows that her biological mother, Vincent, and Harris chose

way to get lunch the truck followed. Just as they were getting ready to pay the bill, two highway patrolmen walked in and started questioning them. The driver of the pickup had called the cops because he suspected the fathers of kidnapping. Fortunately, Steinman and Iacullo were able to convince the patrolmen that they were, in fact, Hope's parents. "From that point on, we carried the adoption papers in our pockets," says Iacullo.

Legalities aside, gay parents—and those who disapprove of gay families—are also concerned about issues of the children's emotional development. Most same-sex parents say they make a special effort to ensure that their kids learn to relate to adults of the opposite sex. Their situation is not that different from that of heterosexual single parents, and the solution is often the same: persuading aunts, uncles or grandparents to be part of their children's lives. Hope Steinman-Iacullo, for example, often visits with her grandmother, her aunts and her teenage cousins. "There are a lot of female role models," says Iacullo.

Psychologists say the best time to tell kids how their families are different is either in childhood or in late adolescence. Young adolescents—from about ages 11 to 15—are particularly vulnerable because they are struggling with their own issues of sexual identity. George Kuhlman and his ex-wife

tion with a male friend. "She just said, 'Dad, I know. I've known for a long time . . . I just thought you and Tom would have a much nicer time and a happier vacation if you know that I knew and I love you.' I pretty much fell to pieces." Annie, now 24, says she is happy she learned about her father when she was an adult. His sexuality isn't an issue now, she says. "When you have a dedicated parent, it matters less."

And, ultimately, it is the quality of the parenting—not the parents' lifestyle—that matters most to kids. Sexual orientation alone doesn't make a person a good or bad parent. In Maplewood, N.J., Charlie and Marc are raising 17-month-old Olivia, whom they adopted. Last Christmas she had a lead role in their church's holiday pageant. "So you had a little Chinese girl of two gay parents who was the baby Jesus," says Charlie. Adds Marc: "It gives a whole new meaning to the word 'Mary'." As she gets older, Charlie and Marc say, they'll explain to Olivia why her family is unusual. "I think Olivia is so lucky to have the opportunity to be different," says Marc. "And that's what I intend to teach her."

With KAREN SPRINGEN *in Chicago,* CLAUDIA KALB *in Boston,* MARC PEYSER *in New York,* MARK MILLER *in Los Angeles and* DANIEL GLICK *in Denver*

Parental Leave: What and Where?

Françoise Coré and Vassiliki Koutsogeorgopoulou

The past two decades have witnessed some majorchanges in the structure of the labour force because of the growing number of women who work and the increase in dual-income households and single-parent families. It is no easy task for workers to reconcile their responsibilities as parents with the requirements of a job, and they are increasingly demanding a more flexible organisation of their working time. As a result, issues such as child care and parental leave have come to the forefront of domestic— and international—policy debates. Enterprises are likewise having to cope with growing requirements in two central areas of human-resource management, as they increasingly require higher standards of skills and more flexibility. They must be able to attract and keep skilled workers of both sexes. More and more, too, they are rotating workers on some jobs. Granting leave can be a way of meeting these concerns.[1]

Parental leave is granted to parents—both mothers and fathers—to allow them to take care of a young child for a relatively long period. The right to this type of leave, which is distinct from the entitlement to benefits during the leave, is relatively recent in the legislation of OECD countries. Sweden was unquestionably the forerunner, introducing parental leave as early as 1974. Most of the other OECD countries have followed this lead, some quite recently (Table 1). As yet parental leave is rarely included in collective or company agreements, with the noteworthy exception of the public sector, and in particular the civil service. A directive on long-term leave for parents has been under discussion in the European Commission since 1983.

In most countries, long-term leave to take care of a young child initially developed simply as extended maternity leave (as is still the case in Turkey and the United Kingdom). The specific feature of parental leave is that fathers are also given this right, which means that the parents can share the leave as they wish. In most cases the father's right is still derived from the mother's, since he is entitled to the leave only if she also is and waives some or all of her rights.

Several countries have recently taken a radically different approach. The parental-leave legislation of 1991 in the Netherlands and the 1993 family-leave legislation in the United States make leave a strictly individual right to which each parent is entitled. In Denmark, Norway and Sweden, following recent legislative changes, a portion of parental leave is now reserved for each of the parents as an individual, non-transferable right.

The maximum duration of the period of leave has grown considerably longer over time. In one in four OECD countries, the combined duration of maternity and parental leave now amounts to approximately one year. It can be as much as three years, as in Finland, France and Germany. Belgium is a special case, for the five years of 'career breaks' provided for by law can be taken over the parent's entire working life without necessarily being linked to individual children. In the United States, the three-month 'leave for family reasons' is too short to qualify as parental leave.

Initially, parental leave was supposed to follow immediately after maternity leave

1. *1995 OECD Employment Outlook*. OECD Publications, Paris, 1995.

Françoise Coré is an expert in the role of women in the economy in the OECD Directorate for Education, Employment, Labour and Social Affairs, where Vassiliki Koutsogeorgopoulou works as a 'young administrator'.

BACKGROUND

Main Types of Leave for Working Parents

Maternity leave: *leave granted to mothers for a limited period around the time of childbirth.*

Paternity leave: *leave granted to fathers for a limited period around the time of childbirth.*

Leave for family reasons: *leave granted to workers to take care of a sick child or for other family reasons.*

Parental leave: *long-term leave granted to either parent to allow them to take care of an infant or young child.*

and to be taken without interruption, although it now reflects today's job flexibility. In a number of countries parental leave can be taken on a part-time basis (in the Netherlands, this is the only possibility), be broken into segments of varying length, and in some cases be used until the child reaches the age of compulsory schooling. Sweden is remarkably flexible in the way in which parental leave can be used (see box, "The Flexibility of the Swedish Model").

Variations in Benefits

The differing philosophies underlying parental leave—and the differences observed across countries—are most clearly revealed by the varying levels of

From *OECD Observer*, August/September 1995, pp. 15-21. © 1995 by the Organisation for Economic Co-operation and Development. Reprinted by permission.

Table 1

Parental Leave and Benefit[1]

year of introduction

	Leave Year	Benefit Year
Australia	1993	no benefit
Austria	1990	1990
Belgium	1985	1985
Canada	1984	1990
Denmark	1983	1983
Finland	1985	1985
France	1984	1985
Germany	1986	1986
Greece	1984	no benefit
Iceland	1980	1980
Italy	1977	1977
Japan	1992	1994
Netherlands	1991	no benefit
New Zealand	1987	no benefit
Norway	1978	1978
Portugal	1984	no benefit
Spain	1989	no benefit
Sweden	1974	1974
United States	1993	no benefit

1. Ireland, Luxembourg, Switzerland, Turkey and the United Kingdom have no legislation on parental leave; Mexico is not covered by the study.

Sources: national data

benefits provided to parents taking leave. Seven countries have introduced parental leave without any specific allowances or benefits (Table 1). Elsewhere, the right to parental leave and the entitlement to benefits are governed by distinct sets of legislation. These benefits are most often paid as part of sickness/disability schemes, unemployment insurance or family allowances, which determine how they are funded. The eligibility rules are not necessarily the same for benefits and for the leave itself, and benefits do not always cover the whole period of leave.

In some countries, child-care benefits are granted to all parents, irrespective of their employment status. In Germany, where this is the case, parents receive a means-tested, flat-rate allowance. In Finland and Sweden, too, all parents are entitled to parental benefits. Parents who are not working when their child is born (which is relatively uncommon given the female participation rates of 85 and 89% respectively) receive a minimum flat-rate allowance, while working parents receive a high proportion of their earnings, at least during part of the leave (66% of earnings for seven months in Finland, 80–90% for 12 months in Sweden).

In the remaining countries, the allowance is paid only to parents who have worked for a minimum amount of time during an earlier period (the require-

ments vary considerably). Only three countries (Canada, Denmark and Norway) pay benefits which replace earnings at the same level as for sickness or unemployment. The most common practice is a flat-rate allowance, generally low, which is often thought of as a 'parental wage'.

Although the aim is generally to pay the highest possible benefits throughout the entire period of parental leave, it is often ruled out by budgetary constraints on the systems which finance benefits, especially because of the length of parental leave. In some countries, the leave benefits do not always cover the full period of leave, and since the early 1990s benefit rates have been cut back, especially where they are proportional to earnings (as in Canada, Denmark, Finland and Sweden).

Take-up Rates

Once entitlement to leave applies, a very high take-up rate can be observed in most countries. In Finland, Norway and Sweden, practically all parents use the leave when they meet the required conditions. The take-up rate is also very high in Denmark (82%) and in Germany (96% in 1991 in the Western Länder). But these high initial take-up rates are not always the case. In the Netherlands, for example, only 27% of eligible women and 11% of men have used the new leave entitlements introduced in 1991. In France, fewer than 100,000 workers were on parental leave in 1992; in view of the number of children under three years of age with two working parents (the target group for parental leave), this figure again seems to indicate a very low rate of use. After the child's first birthday, the leave is less frequently used because of career considerations and economic constraints which become more pressing as leave is prolonged. The possibility of taking leave on a part-time basis is also rarely used. In Germany, where parents on leave can work up to 19 hours per week, fewer than 1% of mothers avail themselves of the possibility.

In principle, there is a close correlation between take-up rates and the level of benefits. If benefits are very low or nil, many workers, particularly in low-income households, will be unable to use their

rights to parental leave. The high take-up rates in Nordic countries reflect a policy of relatively high earnings-related benefits, at least early on. Similarly, the low take-up rate in the Netherlands and France can be ascribed to the facts that there are no benefits at all in the Netherlands and that in France benefits were payable only as from the third child (now, since July 1994, as from the second child).

In Austria and Germany, on the other hand, take-up rates are high in spite of rather limited benefits. That can probably be explained by the relative lack of child-care facilities for young children. As a rule, the more children in a family, the more frequently the parents use their right to parental leave.

With the exception of Sweden, parental leave is used almost exclusively by mothers. In Denmark, Finland, Germany and Norway, fewer than 5% of eligible fathers take leave. That contrasts sharply with Sweden, where a relatively large number of fathers use at least some of their leave; approximately 25% of eligible fathers claimed parental-leave benefits in 1987, a figure which is rising steadily.

Women in managerial and supervisory positions tend to use parental leave less and for a shorter time than other women; they also opt more often for part-time leave. In addition to the fact that a break from work may affect their career adversely, they can more readily afford private child-care services.

The Return to Work

The assumption underlying parental leave based on the fact that workers are guaranteed reinstatement in their jobs is that in the event they will return to work at the end of the leave. Studies in Finland, Sweden and the Netherlands indicate that most do return to their jobs once their leave is finished. By contrast, in Germany, only half of those on leave return to work, while in Austria only one woman in three resumes employment immediately after leave for a first child.

In some cases, it is impossible to make the job guarantee work because the job has disappeared or because the employment contract has come to an end during the leave. These situations have become more frequent in recent years. In other cases, the decision to return to work or not will be determined partly by financial pressure and partly by parents' individual preferences.

The length of leave is a crucial factor in the decision to return to work at the end of the period of leave. One would expect that the rate of return would be lower the shorter the maximum period of leave. The younger the child, the more reluctant parents may be to return to work and the more difficult and costly it may be to arrange for suitable child-care. Rates of return have gone up over time in most countries, which can be attributed at least in part to the longer periods of leave being granted.

But long periods of leave may make returning to work more difficult, particularly if there has been a substantial number of technological and organisational changes within a firm. Some countries are beginning to recognise and address this problem. In France, where leave can be as long as three years, recent legislation ensures a right to retraining at the end of parental leave. In Austria, small enterprises may receive wage subsidies for up to a year for workers returning to their job after two years' leave.

Paradoxically, since part-time parental leave seems to be rarely used, part-time jobs play an important role when people taking leave return to work. In the Netherlands, over half the mothers and 13% of the fathers who returned to work cut back their working hours so as to have more time for their children. Statistics in Austria and Germany also show that nearly a third of re-entrants returned to work on a part-time basis. In Sweden, by contrast, the proportion of parents who changed from full-time to part-time work after parental leave has dropped: only 7% of parents returned to work on a part-time basis in 1988, as compared with 24% during 1979–81. The drop can no doubt be explained by the fact that longer parental leaves have made it easier to return to a full-time job as far as child-care is concerned, but it must also be borne in mind that part-time work has a number of disadvantages.

any given time (Table 2). The incidence may be higher in jobs which mainly employ a young female labour force. But as parental leave can by definition be foreseen and employers are given advance notice, they are able to adopt appropriate strategies of adjustment.

The extent to which substitutes are used to replace workers while they are on parental leave can have a dynamic

placement strategy adopted, since large firms are better able to replace workers on leave from their own ranks or to make systematic arrangements for replacing leave takers (for example, by having a permanent supply of trainees).

The economic climate naturally has a decisive impact on the extent to which workers on leave are replaced. In Finland, a study in 1986 showed that a sub-

Table 2

Absence from Work through Maternity Leave(A) and for Other Reasons including Personal/Family (B)[1]

		A thousands	B thousands	A+B % of female employment	A+B % of employed women with child(ren) under 5 years
Belgium	1983	10.8	7.8	2.3	7.1
	1992	13.9	14.9	2.6	9.7
Denmark	1983	13.9	12.2	13.1	13.2
	1992	24.5	11.0	4.1	18.4
France	1983	122.7	34.1	2.6	9.6
	1992	157.1	22.5	2.5	9.7
Germany	1983	35.7	27.3	1.0	*
	1992	206.8	163.1	3.7	19.9
Italy	1983	*	*	*	*
	1992	82.9	41.3	3.1	11.5
Netherlands	1983	..	..	..	..
	1992	17.1	5.7	1.2	6.6
Portugal	1983	..	..	..	..
	1992	14.4	*	1.7	6.1
Spain	1983	..	..	..	..
	1992	16.1	15.6	1.7	6.2
United Kingdom	1983	36.0	52.9	1.7	11.0
	1992	123.9	83.7	2.9	13.7
EC (12)	1983	228.5	144.9	1.5	8.5
	1992	667.1	365.0	2.9	12.6

.. not available.
* data unreliable.
1. Women 15–49 years old.

Source: Eurostat (labour-force surveys)

How Businesses Cope

Parental leave usually affects only a small portion of the overall workforce at

impact on both the internal and external labour markets. The use of replacements from the external labour market is subject to the existing legislation on hiring workers on fixed-term contracts. On the whole, firms are more likely to replace less skilled workers than more highly skilled ones. The size of the firm is also a key factor which influences the re-

stitute was used in 77% of cases. At present, because of the sharp decline in business activity and hiring since 1990, the workload of people on leave is now more often divided among other employees inside the firm.

Statistics from the few surveys available show that parental leave generally does not create major problems for

Table 3

Expenditure on Maternity and Parental Leave Benefits

% of GDP

	1985	1990	1991	1992	1993
Austria	..	0.42	0.48	0.67	0.76
of which:					
Maternity	..	0.15	0.17	0.18	0.19
Parental	..	0.26	0.31	0.49	0.58
Canada	0.09	0.11	0.17	0.19	0.18
of which:					
Maternity	0.09	0.11	0.12	0.12	0.11
Parental	−	−	0.05	0.07	0.07
Denmark	0.39	0.49	0.49	0.51	0.51
Finland	0.63	1.04	1.27	1.47	1.39
of which:					
Maternity	..	0.25	0.29	0.30	0.26
Parental	..	0.78	0.96	1.14	1.10
France	..	0.23	0.23	..	..
of which:					
Maternity	0.15	0.14	0.14	..	..
Parental	..	0.09	0.09	0.08	0.08
Germany	0.13[1]	0.23	0.25	0.27	..
of which					
Maternity	0.04[1]	0.04. 0.04	0.04	0.04	
Parental	0.09[1]	0.19	0.21	0.23	..
Italy	0.12	0.09	0.11	0.10	..
Norway	0.17	0.34	0.42	0.47	0.57
Sweden	0.60	0.92	1.01	1.09	1.09
of which:					
Maternity	0.01	0.03	0.02	0.02	0.02
Parental	0.59	0.89	0.99	1.07	1.07

.. not available.
 − not applicable.

1. 1986.

Source: OECD

which benefits are paid. The low take-up rate in some countries has, of course, helped keep down the cost of parental leave.

Yet the rising costs of parental benefits seem to have been curbed in recent years. Because of the recession workers are less willing to take long-term leave, for fear that they will not be able to return to their job. At the same time, increased insecurity about jobs has meant that fewer people are entitled to benefits. Reductions in the level of benefits have cut costs and have also made parental leave less attractive.

The net cost of parental-leave benefits in general public and welfare budgets is in most cases far less than the sums actually paid out to parents, because of the savings made elsewhere in public spending. When parental-leave benefits are financed by unemployment insurance funds and the unemployed are also entitled to parental leave, these benefits directly replace unemployment benefits (and the number of jobless drops accordingly). In Austria, approximately 25% of women who received parental-leave benefits in 1993 were previously receiving unemployment benefits or social assistance. In Denmark, the figures for the recent new program of leave were similar. Leave benefits can also replace other kinds of payments indirectly, as in Belgium, where the 'career break' system requires that a worker taking leave be replaced by a jobless person receiving unemployment benefits.

There are also savings in public child-care services. In Denmark, estimates show that for each month that parental leave is extended, assuming 75% of all mothers or fathers extend their leave, waiting lists are reduced by 2,600 places. In Finland, all children under three years of age are entitled to a place in a public day-care facility; alternatively, parents can take extended leave and receive a flat-rate home-care allowance until the child reaches the age of three.

FOCUS

The Flexibility of the Swedish Model

Sweden has developed a system of parental leave and benefits which takes into account the interests of children, mothers and fathers. It is both very comprehensive and very flexible, to meet the broadest possible range of situations and give parents considerable freedom of choice.

Parental Leave

Parents are entitled to three types of leave:
• full-time leave until the child reaches the age of 18 months; condition: the parent must have worked in the enterprise for six months when the child is born or for twelve months during the two preceding years
• reduction of working time by a quarter until the child is eight years old; condition: the parent must have worked full time in the enterprise for six months.
• leave each time a parental benefit is paid (below)

Three periods of leave are allowed each year.

Types of Parental-leave Benefits

Parental-leave benefits are paid under the national system of social security. The two main types of benefit are:
• an allowance to care for a young child brings an entitlement to 450 days, which can be shared between the parents, and can be taken at any time until the child reaches the age of eight; 30 days are attributed exclusively to each parent, during which 90% of gross salary is paid, with the remaining 390 days sharable between the parents as they wish; in this case the allowance is 80% of salary for 300 days, and a flat rate for the balance
• temporary parental-leave allowance; 120 days per year for each child under the age of twelve, which may be shared between the parents, and used when the child is ill or when the person who normally takes care of the child is ill; the allowance is 80% of salary. The condition is that the parent must have been registered with the social-security system for at least six months to be entitled to a flat-rate allowance, and must have had a declared salary for at least eight months to receive an allowance proportional to earnings.

Paid leave days can be used on a full-time, half-time or quarter-time basis, and the allowance is set accordingly.

firms. Difficulties arise only in small companies and in replacing skilled workers in short supply. In Denmark, for example, the new provisions on parental leave introduced in 1992 caused such a severe shortage of nurses that replacements had to be recruited from Sweden and leave entitlements cut back.

Costs and Benefits

If all allowances and benefits paid to parents on leave are considered together—maternity, paternity and parental benefits—the sums allocated represent a relatively small percentage of GDP (Table 3). They exceed 1% only in Finland and Sweden. But these percentages are rising steadily in most countries, chiefly because of the growing number of beneficiaries and the longer periods over

Municipalities, which are responsible for public day-care services, are allowed to pay a supplementary home care allowance, and most large cities have provided generous additional payments to discourage parents from using public child-care services. But because of the economic crisis this assistance has been cut back substantially.

In the long run, parental leave may have other beneficial effects on public finances. By enabling more women to work and at the same time to have children (this seems to be borne out by women's high participation rates and the increasing fertility rates in several Nordic countries), parental leave should help to improve the dependency ratio, that is, to establish a better balance between the number of people who work and those who do not. This would make it easier to finance the costs created by the aging of the population.

A very different aspect of the benefits and costs of parental leave is its impact on skills and productivity, although it is difficult to evaluate precisely. On the one hand, parental leave is expected to encourage workers to remain with their employers, which increases the incentives for both firms and individuals to invest in skill formation and may benefit productivity and wages. On the other hand, long periods of parental leave may lead to an erosion of workers' skills in industries which are undergoing rapid changes in technology and business practice, which would mean that retraining programmes would be necessary for workers returning after leave.

xxx

Parental leave is a factor of flexibility which is important both to individuals, who are better able to reconcile the demands of work and family life, and to enterprises, which are able to manage their human resources more effectively. But it cannot, on its own, solve the problems involved in reconciling work and family responsibilities. It is merely one of a series of necessary measures, such as flexibility of working time and a broad range of services to families, the most important being child-care. Only in this way will it be possible to meet the requirements of all categories of workers, from the least skilled to those in positions of responsibility, men or women. One of the signal failures of parental leave so far is that so few men have used it.

Because of the economic crisis, the provisions governing parental leave have changed and it has been used to meet new goals, such as reducing unemployment and providing child-care at lower cost. Parental leave has become longer while benefits have declined. It is considerably less attractive to workers, although in most cases they have no alternative. For employers, long-term leave entails replacement and training costs that they are less willing to bear in a period of economic difficulties.

In the future, the impact of parental leave on workers, enterprises and the labour market should be followed much more closely so as to ensure that it is effectively achieving its original goals.

OECD BIBLIOGRAPHY

• 1995 OECD Employment Outlook, 1995
• Women and Employment Restructuring: New Perspectives, 1994
• Françoise Coré, 'Women and the Restructuring of Employment', The OECD Observer, No. 186, February/March 1994.

behind [closed] doors

Domestic violence has an impact on everyone in the family. Here, a mother and daughter tell how it started, how it affected them, and how they stopped it. A few months ago a friend of a Ms. editor's came to her and said: "My mother was beaten by my stepfather when I was a teenager. We'd like to talk about it for the magazine." Theirs is truly a tale from inside the belly of the beast: the mother, Maggie,* who lived through the beatings, believing for too long that her husband would get better or seek treatment; and the daughter, Jennifer, who watched it happen, terrified that one day her mother would be killed. Eventually they fled their home. Leaving is never an easy choice for a battered woman—especially when she is running away from the home she created for herself and her children. Perhaps it was the vision of terror she saw in her children's eyes that persuaded this mother to get out.

Interviews by Kristen Golden

Maggie: When I was growing up, we moved every few years because my dad was an executive who was transferred often. I got to like moving. I'd think: "A whole new life—I'll start fresh and have all these new possibilities." I was married to Jennifer's father from when I was 21 until I was 35. He got cancer in his early thirties. He was treated and was fine for a few years and we forgot all about it, thinking, "This will never come back." Suddenly he had a recurrence. He was in the hospital a while, and then he came home. There was nothing left for the doctors to do. He had a hospital bed in the middle of our living room, so I could take care of him and be with Jennifer, who was about 11 then. His illness took over my life, but I was so busy I hardly noticed.

With all that my husband and I went through together, I discovered that marriage was more important than I had ever thought it was. We got to be so close. I found out that I could hang in there longer than I would've believed possible, and it would probably all be worth it.

After he died, I started going out with somebody we'd been friends with. For years my husband had taken all my attention. I didn't feel restless when he was sick, but when he was gone, I thought, "Wow, here I am, 35, and I'm ready for life." Maybe the timing was wrong, but I think your children are never actually going to like your going out with someone else. Jennifer didn't dislike Peter, but we all had a hard time.

Peter was recently divorced when we started seeing each other. Quite soon we said we'd like to get married, but somehow that didn't happen for a long time. Our situation turned out to be so difficult that our marriage didn't last too long, although I was actually very fond of him. He is the father of my younger daughter, Theresa.

Frank was the next one. I met him through some friends. I thought, "Well, I'll go out with a new person and forget about my troubles." I was still quite depressed about the breakup of my marriage even though a couple of years had gone by. I felt like I needed something. At the same time, I thought I should be doing something completely different with my life. So my kids and I packed up and went on a big trip through South America.

The trip was great. I wanted to do something with my daughters that they'd remember their whole lives. You get pretty close when you're sharing hotel rooms—a rare opportunity, especially for a teenager and her mom! Unfortunately, our money ran out sooner than I expected. I barely had enough to get us home.

I had started going out with Frank right before we went on the trip, and we wrote to each other while I was away. We decided we wanted to get married even though we had only known each other a few weeks before I left. When I got married to Peter, I had been engaged for almost two years, and I thought, "That didn't do any good. Let's try this way." We were together for a couple of months when we got back, but obviously, looking back, it was too fast.

---

*Names and identifying details in this article have been changed.

 From *Ms.*, March/April 1997, pp. 60-67. © 1997 by Ms. Magazine. Reprinted by permission.

In the beginning, Frank and Jennifer didn't have a lot to do with each other. Before he came along, it was just the three of us, and my daughters and I had become closer than ever. Jennifer was trying to be supportive and helpful and make me feel O.K. She wanted me to be happy, so she tried to like Frank as best she could, but she didn't very much. I guess later she felt like she was the one who was right.

Frank was different from most people I'd known. I'm fascinated by things that are different or new. I was feeling somewhat rejected from my last episode, and along comes this truly romantic man. Frank was a very quiet person—articulate but with a quiet voice. He was a real storyteller and pretty interesting for me to talk to. He was fond of my younger daughter. When we were dating, we'd often go out in the evenings, but when we saw each other in the day, my little one was always with us. He seemed to want more children. He had one that he had lost touch with through divorce. I wanted a father for my daughter and I liked the way he was with her.

He had a seasonal job, traveling around selling water sports equipment. We'd been married just a few months when Frank started traveling a lot. Every few weeks, I'd drive to where he was, and stay for several days. Jennifer was 16. She took care of her four-year-old sister and my mom would look in on them.

At the end of the vacation season, when business slowed down, I met him in a resort town for a week. We spent a lot of time together, fishing and water-skiing. We rented a house right next to the water. I loved waking up in the morning and hearing the sound of the waves. These early romantic experiences made the relationship almost worth it.

I don't know exactly when the violence started. I know we hadn't been together that long, maybe a few months. He was really sweet to me before we married, but one eye-opening thing happened on our honeymoon. There wasn't any physical violence, but he had been drinking and he was goading me. He told me what he really thought of my kids. That sure made my alarm bells go off. I don't really have a temper, but everybody has a point. We didn't exactly fight, but I was quite surprised at what he said. Then he was all sweet in the morning. It wasn't really verbal abuse—but in a way, it was.

Gradually Frank started to drink more and push me more. I never figured out what he wanted me to do or say. I felt like he thought he had to make me angry—and inevitably he would. He was intelligent, more so than Jennifer thought. He'd select the things about me that I prided myself on and say that they weren't true. Sometimes I would raise my voice when we fought, which my children were quite shocked at because I had never raised my voice to them.

After about a month and a half of that kind of treatment, I got really angry one night. I'm pretty sure this was the first time he was violent. The kids had gone to sleep. You know how traditionally a woman might slap a man's face once in a while, if he's extremely goading? I felt like he wanted to bring me to that point. I was never one to even spank children, but Frank made me so angry that I slapped him. That seemed to be the signal for him to go wild. I was shocked to suddenly be thrown around the room. Afterward he was all contrite—he had given me a black eye—but he said, "Well, you started it." I guess that's true. I thought, "Well, look what I did."

The next day you could see my black eye. I think anybody whose husband beats them up feels ashamed. I don't know why they should. Husbands should be ashamed, but they don't feel that way somehow. I guess you just feel like such an idiot to be staying with this person that you don't want to talk about it. And you don't suddenly stop loving someone just one night; it takes longer than that.

I still cared about Frank and didn't want to run him down with my children, so I didn't talk about it with the kids. Jennifer was busy with her own life, and her friends were really her life. Frank was very nice after that. I found out later that a lot of these things are just the usual pattern, but I hadn't had any experience with this sort of thing before.

There were a lot of good things in our relationship. The violence didn't really have anything to do with it. Of course, we would argue, but he would be really nice for a while and then gradually he would get back to criticizing me. The violence would always escalate when he'd been drinking, so I'd think, "If only he could give up drinking."

One time when he was drunk, he hit me so hard, I flew across the room and broke my arm. That was scary. I didn't feel like he was going to stop beating me, no matter what happened. I was in so much pain, I could barely talk, so it was hard for me to say anything, but that didn't calm him down. He kept going, even when he started to sober up. I was terrified. Finally, he felt bad and took me to the hospital.

When we got there, I didn't want to tell people what happened. I guess I felt protective toward him. But also, this man is right there glaring at me. Having him go to jail seemed silly, because if I sent him there I would be pretty frightened when he came out. It was a mixture of protecting him and being afraid.

And Frank was genuinely frightened by the possibility that the police might be notified. One time—before the broken-arm episode—he was being violent, and Jennifer called the police. When they arrived, I didn't want to say, "Take this person away." So I said, "I'm all right. I don't want to charge him." The police said, "Are you sure?" I said yes and they went away.

And I *was* sure because I could feel that Frank was so shocked by the police coming that that would be it for that occasion, at least. Jennifer was quite stunned that I did not turn him in. I think your kids often don't understand why you do certain things. If he had ever touched either of my kids, I would have done something. Strange that you can't think more of yourself. And the kids weren't really afraid of him. I would say Jennifer is a fairly strong woman and, if anything, he was probably a little afraid of her. I don't think he would have done anything to the girls. There's something about wives, though.

After the broken-arm thing, of course, I realized this was getting serious. At the hospital he said he was going to give up drinking. He was very contrite, and he asked for one more try. We talked for a few hours and I thought, "Well, one more try," but I suggested that we sell the house we bought together and separate our finances in case it didn't work out. I wasn't feeling too hopeful. Quite often I'm sure women want to leave but don't know what they would do for money. You can't just leave the house and wonder, "How will I get him out of there? How will I support my family?"

When the men are contrite, I think its a good idea to try to make some kind of financial arrangement or at least say, "Well, I'll come back but I want my own bank account with a couple of hundred dollars in it."

In my case, I asked Frank at a time when he was willing to do anything. He felt pretty shocked about what he had done and he really wanted to be with me. So he agreed that we would sell the house. He was an honest person. Even when someone has something really bad about them, that's not all there is to them. But I was feeling like this was the last try. And after a while I noticed he was starting to drink a bit again. So I called a women's shelter just to find out what you do.

A few months later, he beat me again. I decided to leave then and there. After having gone through the episode with my arm, this time I thought it could be life or death, and I wasn't going to let myself be killed. Jennifer had already said to me that while she couldn't make me leave, she wouldn't let me die. I was really scared, but I started to fight back physically. I was quite angry—all those promises and here we were again. But fighting back didn't make me feel powerful.

He just kept hitting me. Finally, I said I had to go to the bathroom and fled the room. I grabbed Theresa and ran out the door. Fortunately, someone was driving by. Although I didn't even know him and my clothes were torn, I flagged him down. I said, "Please help me, this man is trying to hurt me." He told me he'd drive me wherever I wanted to go. I figured he was a better bet than what I was running from. Frank came out of the house, but he just stood there. The abuse plays a little differently when it's outside. I got in the car and asked the man to take us to where Jennifer was working. My little daughter and I sat there and waited until the end of Jennifer's shift, and then we all went to the women's shelter.

I had a very unsympathetic boss at the time. So here I was: I had to go to work, look normal, and then go to the shelter at night. But the shelter was very helpful for me. I got to tell my story confidentially. Everyone was supportive. I got a lot of counseling and coaching on the law, although it seemed

I think anybody whose husband beats them up feels ashamed. I don't know why they should. Husbands should be ashamed.

really quite boring that the whole thing was so predictable. You know: the men are always so sweet afterward and say they would never do it again; they're usually controlling, manipulative people who run down your self-esteem so you think you deserve being hit. The shelter was hard for Jennifer. She was very uncomfortable. She was good to me, but she wasn't pleased about being there.

Theresa used to cry when Frank and I fought. I'd send her to her room when things got bad, but she could hear us. She was pretty scared that last time because I grabbed her and ran out of the house. So the shelter was wonderful for her. There were kids for her to play with. She wanted to stay there forever. That's the hardest part. The women were supportive, but you couldn't stay there forever. Everyone had to get a job and a place to live pretty quickly.

It's been a few years now—four years ago that we got married—so I've pretty much been able to shake what Frank did to me. Maybe I'm not as sure of myself as I would want to be, but he didn't convince me I was a bad person. I think, "Perhaps I'm not really so great, but I still didn't deserve this." These men make you feel so bad about yourself. They have no right to say that you're not a worthy person. No right at all. Every person in the world is much too important to lose.

I'm sorry for my children—it was so hard on them. But I've found it interesting to be able to understand why I did the things I did. I was like everyone else. I used to think, "Why, why do women stay after the first minute of violence?" So if my telling my story gets even just one of those women out, even though it's not much, I'd feel like something in my life has made a difference.

I think my daughters would go at the first sign of violence. The whole thing felt very dragged-out for them. Maybe I felt more in control because I could decide to go, whereas they couldn't make me leave. Jennifer so much resented that I stayed as long as I did.

I never felt that Frank should be prosecuted. I still feel something for him. Less so as the years go by and less so when I remember how it felt being beaten. I actually hope that he can solve his drinking problem and just hope there's not some other woman that he's beating. I think Jennifer is more, well, bitter. She and my mother probably would be glad to prosecute him. I admire them for that.

Jennifer: There was no turbulence in my life when I was a kid, as far as my parents' relationship goes. I don't remember their ever fighting or anything like that. I read a lot as a child. Actually, I hid in my room. We had a really small house and there was a hospital bed in the living room and that's where my father was. We've always had a really loving, close family, but a lot of things are left unsaid. I knew my father was very sick, and he had been in intensive care for at least a month. I guess now, looking back on it, he came home to die. But I didn't realize that, so I was shocked. A little later, my mom said, "I can't believe that you didn't think he was going to die." But when you're a kid you just don't think people are going to die.

Right after my father died, I began to hate going to school. I didn't want to talk to anyone and I thought everyone hated me anyway. I'd pretend that I was sick, and my mom would let me stay home. I almost wished that I could have a nervous breakdown so I wouldn't have to go to school and deal with people.

But then I really made the effort to bring myself together, and I built up a lot of coping mechanisms. I definitely went through a process of self-examination, which I think I get from my mom. I know she does spend a lot of time examining things in herself, but we haven't really talked about it. I've always admired my mother. She is a very quiet, shy person. Everyone who meets her thinks she's so sweet, and she is. I thought of her almost as a saint. She was very loving with us.

My mom is physically very strong. When my dad was sick, she had to turn him in bed, and he was six feet tall. She has really serious biceps. Since she never had any money for anything, she was always walking places or running for the bus. I've always felt my mom was emotionally stable for us. My

mom has been the center of my world. But all of the externals were unstable—what school I was going to, where I was living, what man she might be living with. All of those things were coming and going all the time.

I feel like I've been raised without a father, even though my dad died when I was 11. I eventually developed a sort of father-daughter relationship with Peter, the man my mom married after my father, but I would never call him Father, Dad, or anything like that. Peter and my mom got involved very shortly after my father died. After only six months, they told me they were having a serious relationship. I took the news really badly, because I felt, "How could anyone replace my father? How could she love someone else so soon?"

Their marriage lasted just a few months. Then my mom went out on all these dates through the personal ads. After a while, some friends introduced her to Frank. I think she had only gone out with him a few times, so I was certainly surprised when she told me that they were going to get married. I guess they had kept up some sort of correspondence while we were traveling, but I was totally in the dark.

The trip to South America had been totally incredible for me. I got to leave school for several months. That was so cool. Eleventh grade. When you're a teenager, you don't want to do things with your family anymore, but you make an exception when it's a trip like that. We had a great time. I felt a lot closer to my mother and my sister than ever before. When we got back my mom told us that she and Frank really loved each other and they planned to get married. She was so excited. I knew this was outside my control and I had other things going on in my life. A part of me also believed that whatever my mom did was right. I guess I had these conflicting ideas about my mom. In some ways, she seemed so perfect and wonderful and everything she did must be right, yet I didn't always like everything she did.

Like Frank. There was definitely something about him that I didn't like. Everything he enjoyed, my mom didn't. She doesn't drink, smoke, or gamble, but he took her to Atlantic City for their honeymoon, where that's all everybody does. Occasionally, she went to bars with him. She'd get drunk on one or two beers because alcohol affects her so easily. But it's not like she changed. My mom just likes to be exposed to different ways of living and to absorb the experiences of others.

I can't remember how much I hated Frank before I knew he was hitting my mom and how much more I hated him after. Frank was a total deadbeat. He seemed to have had a lot of jobs and I think he spent a lot of time on unemployment.

I wasn't home a lot, but I had indications that Frank was a questionable character—like the vodka bottles in the cupboard. Normally, we didn't have any alcohol around the house. I'd stare at the bottles, fascinated, because I knew that he was drinking them. One day, I was looking for something in my mom's closet and I saw shotguns hidden away in the back. That made me very uneasy.

Frank would do all this terrible stuff to my mom while he was drunk. Then, when he sobered up, he'd feel guilty and act so sorry. He did go to AA for a while. I just remember thinking he was such a hypocrite. His Bible would be sitting around the house. Here he is pretending he's a religious Christian while he goes around hitting my mom. AA must have been his penance. Maybe he tried to quit drinking as part of an agreement for her to stay with him. I know there was a lot of negotiating going on. I guess she felt she could change him or help him change.

After he broke her arm, obviously I had a lot of resentment toward him. I didn't trust him and I didn't feel safe. When they would fight, I was terrified because this horrible man was yelling at my mom and hurting her, and she was just a quiet victim of his rage. My mom is someone who takes a lot of stuff. Now I see it as a bit of a martyr complex. I wasn't in the same room when they were fighting, so I don't know what she did. I think her technique was to try to calm him down. She'd try to diffuse his rage, but if she couldn't calm him, she would just take it.

Some of these incidents stand out so clearly to me, like there's been a flare thrown on them, but others are really obscure. I think your mind blocks out things that it doesn't want to remember. I can't even remember Frank's last name.

One night, I got a call at work. I worked at a fast-food restaurant. Terrible place. I worked after school until 11 or so in the evening. My little sister, who'd just learned how to use the phone, called saying, "I'm really scared. Mom and Frank are fighting. They're in the other room but I hear them yelling and I think he's hitting her." So I told her I'd come home, but first I called the police and asked them to go to our house.

Since I hated this guy, I felt what he was doing was a crime, but I had never heard about domestic violence. I know the feminist movement was talking about it, but it hadn't reached me or the schools. I just called the police to protect my mom. I was embarrassed because I had to tell my boss what was happening in order to leave. And I had to ask her to drive me home because we lived pretty far away and I didn't have a car. By the time we got there, the police had arrived. They were ridiculous. They asked what was going on and Frank started freaking out, yelling, "Who called the police?" At least the officers were smart enough not to say, "This girl over here called us," so that things would really be a mess. They said the neighbors heard noise and called the police.

> ## I always thought my mom was strong, even when she was taking his abuse. I thought she was strong just for staying alive.

One officer asked my mother if Frank was hitting her. Standing right beside him, of course, she said no. Then they asked my sister, but since she wasn't in the same room, it wasn't enough that she heard all the noise. You knew the next day bruises would come out all over my mom's face. That was the evidence. Since she wasn't going to admit that anything had happened, and my sister hadn't actually witnessed the violence, the police said they couldn't do anything. They told us they'd be in the area, and they left.

I herded the family into my sister's room and locked the door. Then I called my boyfriend—not that I thought he would save us or anything, but I felt like this horrible spell had been cast over my family. I thought the spell would be broken if anyone from outside came, and that Frank wouldn't dare do anything while someone else was there. So I told my boyfriend what was happening and asked him to come right over. He said yes, but then he called back and said he couldn't come. His parents thought it was a bad idea. I was crushed. I felt like there was no one I could depend on.

"One of these days—POW right in the kisser" *Ms.*, August 1976

This is Ms.'s twenty-fifth year of publication; over the years we've had many firsts. One of the most important was our 1976 cover story on domestic violence: we were one of the first U.S. magazines to depict the terror and mayhem that goes on behind closed doors, and to demand that battery be treated like the crime we all knew it to be. This brief excerpt from one of the 1976 articles illuminates how much has changed—awareness of the problem, willingness to blame the batterer and not the victim, and even the official response to violence in the home. But too much remains the same. We know what to do, but as a society we are still trying to implement the prescriptions feminists came up with back then. That's not surprising, given how tough it is to wrench free from abusive people who say they love us and to wrest power from the patriarchy that sanctions their violence. The truth is, the battering of women will not stop until sexual inequality is brought to an end.

—The Editors

The plight of the abused wife has generally been ignored in our society. Assaulted wives have been convinced their ordeal is freakish and shameful—or their own fault. Increasingly, however, these women are beginning to realize that they are not singularly cursed but victims of a crime more prevalent than rape—and just as misunderstood.

In our culture, the attitudes toward abused wives and rape victims are strikingly similar. Just as the rape victim is supposedly a seductive temptress who asked for what she got, the abused wife has provoked her husband into beating her. Secretly, the woman is supposed to enjoy being beaten, just as the rape victim is accused of relishing violent sex. A woman who attempts to charge a man with either crime is assumed to be vindictive; skeptical police and prosecutors must be convinced that she is indeed a "worthy" victim. Though the penalties for assault are less severe than those prescribed for rape, judges are reluctant to impose them when the assailant is married to his victim. Marital violence sometimes ends in divorce, sometimes in murder, but for many women it is a way of life that goes on and on. Often the beatings are a daily, weekly, or monthly ritual instituted early in the marriage and increasing in frequency and brutality over the years. Michigan lawyers Susan Eisenberg and Patricia Micklow conducted extensive interviews with twenty abused wives who had been punched, slapped, kicked, thrown across rooms and down stairs, struck with brooms, brushes, and belts, threatened with knives and guns—frequently after verbal disputes over trifles.

Why do women endure years of such terror and degradation? In large part it's because they feel they have no other choice. Their economic dependence on the men who abuse them usually keeps them in their place. In a country where the courts are notoriously unable to extract child-support payments from unwilling husbands and where female household heads and their children constitute more than 80 percent of all welfare recipients, many women don't see divorce as a possible solution.

Psychological pressures add to the economic constraints to leaving. "Women have been raised and socialized to believe they must make their husbands happy," argues Marjory Fields, an attorney with the South Brooklyn Legal Services Corporation. "So they not only take the beatings; they tend to feel responsible for them."

Marital violence may be kept secret from the neighbors, but chances are that the children know. One mother grimly admits that her six-year-old tried to overrule attempts to put him to bed by threatening to "call Daddy to hit you."

It is vitally important to combat the widespread indifference toward battered wives, and this requires an effort akin to the feminist assault on rape, which in the last few years has won better treatment for rape victims. More shelters and counseling and better law enforcement are indispensable to improve the lot of the battered wife, but they will not themselves eliminate wife beating, just as rape clinics will not eradicate rape. The battered-wife syndrome is rooted in centuries of sexual inequality and will disappear only when that inequality is rooted out.

—Judith Gingold

I was really panicked. I kept thinking, "Oh, my God, what's going to happen?" By this point, Frank was banging on the door and asking my mom to come out. The more she refused to come out, the more irate he became. Finally Mom said she would talk to him. I didn't want her to go, but she did anyway. So when I heard the yelling start again, I thought, "I can't just sit in here and let it happen."

I felt that I should take charge. I was the one who had called the police and my boyfriend, and had tried to deal with the situation. At the same time, I felt so helpless. I wanted to help my family, but I didn't know what to do. I was 17 years old. Earlier, when we were locked in the room away from him, my mom told me that Frank had been strangling her while they were fighting and she had blacked out. Knowing that, I was really scared. I finally decided that the best solution was to go out there and tell Frank to get out of our lives.

So I went out and started yelling at him. "You're ruining our lives," I screamed, "and you're hurting my mother. We all want you to leave. Leave this house right now." Well, that made him totally flip out. He lunged at me, but my mom grabbed him. She looked really scared that he was going to do something to me. That moved her into action more than danger against herself did. She grabbed him and said, "Don't hurt my daughter."

I felt this total adrenaline rush as I confronted him. I shouted, "Go ahead and hit me like you hit my mother." That really made him mad. But Frank finally left the house, and nothing else happened the rest of the evening. That was the only time I took charge. Then I went back to feeling that I had no control over my life. In the end, it was my mom's life, so she had to make the decision.

Finally, during a fight, she left him. She called me at work to tell me she and Theresa were on the way over. That made me happy, but it was the kind of thing that added to my feelings of instability: I never knew when I was going to get a phone call at work or at school saying something terrible was happening to my mother.

Mom brought Theresa to the restaurant and they sat at a table until I finished cleaning up at the end of my shift. Then we sat around and tried to figure out what to do next. Mom said she could call my grandmother but she didn't really want to, because my grandmother already disapproved of her marriage. It would be humiliating. And she did have this phone number of a women's shelter.

Finally, she said she'd call the shelter. We looked for a public phone with a lot of people around, because she thought Frank might be looking for her. We went to our local supermarket. Mom was on the phone with the woman at the shelter when Frank showed up and made a big scene. We were terrified. It was absolutely surreal—being in this place that I went to all the time, in a neighborhood that I knew, where people knew me, and having this guy who was virtually a stranger screaming at us in front of everyone. The supermarket's security guard finally made him leave. We stood and watched his truck drive off. Then we drove to the shelter.

We were there for about a week, while my mom tried to find a new place for us to live. You had to go to counseling sessions all the time. I can understand that they want to make sure you're not going to fly off the deep end after all you've been through, but I really disliked the whole thing. The place was depressing, and I hated the fact that its location was a secret. I felt horrible walking into this place and knowing every other woman in there was an abused woman. I hated seeing so many of these women who, even though they had taken the steps to get away, just looked so subdued by life.

I would always hope that a woman would leave a battering situation, but that's not a lesson that you can give to people. And being a feminist doesn't necessarily teach you how to have good, healthy relationships with men. My mom is educated and intelligent, but she still didn't know how to leave.

I always thought my mom was strong, even when she was staying with Frank and taking his abuse. Making the decision to leave takes a certain kind of mental leap, but taking abuse isn't easy either. I thought she was strong just for staying alive.

I wish she hadn't stayed with Frank as long as she did, but in the context of most abusive relationships, she got out fast—after about a year and a half. I would have left after the first time he hit me. Ever since this happened, I've said to myself, "If a guy so much as touches me, lays a finger on me, I'm outta there." No second chances. My mom, you know, believes in second and third chances.

Kristen Golden is a contributing editor to "Ms."

Tomorrow's second sex

The signs are everywhere in America and Europe: more women at work; girls doing better in school; debate about "feminisation" in America's politics; it's "million-man march" last year. This article summarises the evidence of a growing social problem: uneducated, unmarried, unemployed men

THESE four pages nail the following arguments to the door of debate:
• that boys are doing worse than girls at every age in school, except university where girls are narrowing the gap;
• that women dominate the jobs that are growing, while men (especially those with the least education) are trapped in jobs that are declining;
• that, for some reason, men are not even trying to do "women's work";
• that there is a loose connection between work and marriage: joblessness reduces the attractiveness of men as marriage partners;
• that men do not necessarily adopt "social behaviour" (obeying the law; looking after women and children) if left to themselves; rather, they seem to learn it through some combination of work and marriage (this is a matter of anthropological observation rather than statistical proof);
• and hence, putting these claims together, that men pose a growing problem. They are failing at school, at work and in families. Their failure shows up in crime and unemployment figures. The problem seems to be related in some way to male behaviour and instincts. It is more than merely a matter of economic adjustment. And (considering the growth in "knowledge-based" employment) it is likely to get worse.

The problem is already far worse in some areas than others. Over the past 30 years, professional men have been less badly affected by economic change than their unskilled brethren. And (to the limited extent they want to) some have added so-called "New Man" attitudes to their traditional breadwinning role. They have adjusted reasonably well to social and economic change. But unskilled men have lost on both counts. Traditional family values—husband winning the bread, wife watching the bairns—tend to be strongest (at least in theory) at the poorer end of the labour market. But American working-class men are increasingly unable (or unwilling) to support families; in Europe, high unemployment has fallen on such men disproportionately. And because providing for a family has been central to men's social role, finding a substitute for steady work will be an immensely hard—conceivably an impossible—task.

Trouble in class

The trouble with men appears early: at school. Though men take up half or more university places in most countries (America is an exception), at primary and secondary school girls are increasingly out-performing boys. In England and Wales, for example, girls score higher than boys in tests conducted at seven, nine, eleven and—which is less often realised—at five. In America, boys are much more likely than girls to be held back a grade and twice as likely to drop out of high school.

Both the reasons for this discrepancy and its true extent are hotly debated. In some subjects at some ages boys still do better than girls (for example, mathematics at 16). Traditionally, boys have done less well than girls before puberty but used to catch up afterwards. What is new now is that boys are no longer catching up. English and Welsh 16 year-olds take a series of tests known as GCSES. A standard measurement is the percentage of children who achieve grades A, B, or C in five or more subjects; 48.1% of girls achieve this, compared with 39% of boys. In some of Britain's poorer areas, the disparity is greater. In Hackney, a poor part of east London, for example, a mere 14.9% of boys reached this standard, compared with 30.2% of girls.

The pattern is repeated all over Europe. In 1995, in the European Union, 124 girls got general leaving certificates to every 100 boys. The boys' narrow lead in vocational certificates—they took 5% more—does not close the gap. Girls also tend to stay in school longer: Austria and Switzerland apart, in every West-European country, more girls than boys stay on in education beyond school-leaving age (though the boys who do stay are slightly more likely to go to university, taking 51% of places).

Trouble at work

Because jobs are increasingly "knowledge-based", this disparity in educational attainment is bound to be reflected in employment once today's school children become adults. This does not necessarily mean that girls have better job prospects than boys; other factors, including sex discrimination at work, may intervene. But it does mean that girls are improving their job prospects relative to boys. Moreover, the job market is already moving the girls' way.

Between 1980 and 1992, women accounted for three fifths of the increase in the American workforce and two-thirds of the increase in the European one. Between 1990 and 1993, in ten of the then 12 EU members, women's share of unemployment fell.

But the problem for men is not just that women are taking more jobs; it is that a significant proportion of men are dropping out of the job market altogether as women enter it. In the 1960s, almost all men worked and less than half of women. Not so now. The percentage of working-age men in the EU outside the labour force rose from just 8% in 1968 to 22% in 1993. For women, the trend was reversed, falling from 58% to 44% over the same period.

In America, the pattern is slightly different: while women's labour-force participation has risen from 43% in 1970 to about 60% now, men's has dropped relatively little from 80% to 75% (though there is an important exception: male high-school dropouts—those completing fewer than 12 years of school; in 1970, 86% were either working or looking for work; by 1993, only 72% were). If its employment trends continue, America will be employing nearly as many women as men by 2005.

Overall, then, the picture in the West is as follows: the labour market is increasingly friendly to women (though men still make more money and are more likely to be in work); but there are growing numbers of men outside the labour market in a way that women have been accustomed to but men are not.

The future for men looks bleaker, even if you disregard what is going on in schools. Western occupational surveys show that for the foreseeable future new job-growth will be in work typically done by women. America's Bureau of Labour, for example, forecasts that the five fastest-growing kinds of work between now and 2002 will be residential care, computer and data processing, health services, child care, and business services. Women dominate all these activities: their share of employment in them is respectively: 79%, 68%, 70%, 70% and 51%. In contrast, the five sectors declining fastest will be footwear, ammu-

nition-making, shipbuilding, leather-working and photographic supplies. They are man's work. Men account for at least two-thirds of the workforce in all the categories.

There are numerous explanations for female success in growing businesses: women tend to be better educated; they stay in jobs longer (especially women with children); low-paid jobs are growing quickly and women are readier to accept them than men, who still see themselves as a family's breadwinner; women tend to have the social skills needed for jobs in services (though whether because of nature or nurture is disputed).

For men, the obvious response to such economic shifts would be to move into the bits of the economy which are expanding. But they are not doing this. Social theorists may like to claim that concepts like "men's work" or "women's work" are outmoded. The choices people make in the labour force tell a different story. Even in Nordic countries, which have made sexual neutrality a principle of national policy, sex segregation is the norm. Local government, state-run day-care centres, schools and social services are run by women. Men weld cars and take out the rubbish. The pattern is unchanging. In America's "administrative services" (ie, office work) men accounted for only 19.8% of the workforce in 1985 and 20.5% in 1995.

Why should this be? Part of the explanation no doubt lies in the advantages that women have in the workforce—especially their willingness to accept lower-paid jobs. But there seems to be more to it than that.

Boys and girls at school

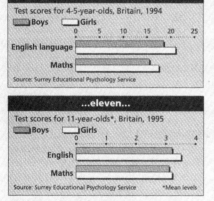

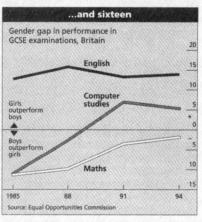

Men and women at work

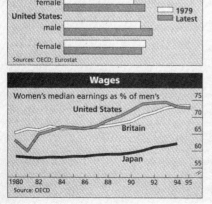

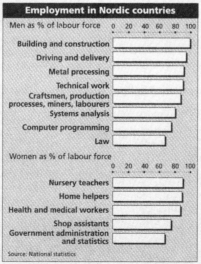

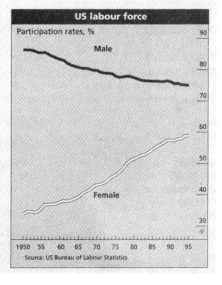

Men continue to spurn even well-paid work that is dominated by women. Less than 5% of America's registered nurses, for example, are men, though the average starting salary of a registered nurse is a comfortable $30,000–35,000. Women account for 96% of America's licensed practical nurses, a responsible but not especially highly-skilled job that pays a full-time worker about $23,000.

The picture is similar in Europe. In Britain, the proportion of men in nursing, 11.6%, has budged little since 1984, when it was 10.2%. As the EU noted in a report on "Occupational Segregation of Women and Men in the European Community", male manual workers are "willing to undertake low-paid and low-skilled jobs provided they are not feminised." In Spain, the share of male office clerks has dropped by a third since 1980—even though this has been a fast-growing field at a time of high unemployment; women, meanwhile, have withdrawn from the textile and footwear industries. In these areas, job separation seems to have increased.

Blue-collar blues

So women are catching up with men for economic reasons ("women's jobs" are growing faster than men's) and social ones (men won't do "women's work"). Both reasons hit unskilled and ill-educated men disproportionately hard.

Jobs that require some tertiary education or training are growing faster than those that require no qualifications. In America's ten largest cities, the number of jobs requiring less than a high-school education has fallen by half since 1970; two-thirds of new jobs created in America since 1989 have been professional and managerial Germany's Ministry of Labour estimates that by 2010, only 10% of German jobs will be appropriate for unskilled workers. In 1976, the proportion was 35%. In 1970, there were more blue-collar workers than white-collar ones in more than half the OECD countries; by 1990, that was true only in Spain.

In principle, unskilled men could accept these changes and kiss their wives goodbye on the doorstep as the little woman goes off to work at the nursing home. In reality, that is not happening. Despite huge social change during the past 30 years, traditional sexual attitudes retain a stubborn hold. A survey for the EU found that more than two-thirds of Europeans (ranging from 85% in Germany to 60% in Denmark) thought it better for the mother of a young child to stay at home than the father. Mothers, said this survey, should take care of nappies, clothes and food; fathers are for money, sport and punishment.

Trouble at home

Among the poor, this combination of traditional sexual attitudes and male unemployment has been deadly to two groups: men in general in high unemployment areas and, especially, young unemployed men there. The reason is that the combination has set off a spiral of harmful and sometimes uncontrollable consequences which is tearing the web that ties together work, family and law-abiding behaviour.

Consider for a moment a neighbourhood in which most working-age women are not in paid jobs. This may conjure up a picture of tidy homes, children at play and gossip. Now think of a neighbourhood in which most men are jobless. The picture is more sinister. Areas of male idleness are considered, and often are, places of deterioration, disorder and danger. Non-working women are mothers; non-working men, a blight.

Men tend to commit most crimes. In America, they commit 81% of all crime and 87% of violent crime. Adolescent boys are the most volatile and violent of all. Those under 24 are responsible for half of America's violent crime; those under 18 commit a quarter. The figures for most western countries are comparable.

Now ask yourself what restrains such behaviour? The short answer is: a two-parent home. Without belabouring the complexity of family policies, two-parent families are demonstrably better at raising trouble-free children than one-parent ones. Fatherless boys commit more crimes than those with father at home; a study of repeat juvenile offenders by the Los Angeles Probation Department found that they were much more likely to come from one-parent backgrounds than either the average child or than juvenile criminals who offended once only.

Having a man in the house (preferably the biological father) is, it seems, more important than any other single factor. William Galston and Elaine Kamarck, two social scientists who worked in the Clinton administration, argue that the connection between crime and having a father at home "is so strong that [it] erases the relationship between race and crime and between low income and crime." That is why it is a worry that, in America in 1991, just 50.8% of children lived in traditional nuclear families (families where both parents were present and the children were the biological offspring of both parents). Among Hispanics, the figure was 38%; among blacks, 27%.

But family is not the end of the matter. Work also plays a part, both in its own right and as a means of keeping men tied to families. In 1949, Margaret Mead, an eminent anthropologist, argued that

> In every known human society, everywhere in the world, the young male learns that when he grows up, one of the things which he must do in order to be a full member of society is to provide food for some female and her young . . . Every known human society rests firmly on the learned nurturing behaviour of men.

When men find it impossible to provide, they also seem to find it difficult to learn the nurturing bits. They may retreat into fundamentalist masculinity—the world of gangs which provide for their members a kind of rule-based behaviour that boys do not get elsewhere. For everyone else (and, in the long run, for boys too), the effects of failing to learn nurturing are universally bad.

For an extreme example of this dynamic, take the studies by William Julius Wilson of mass male joblessness in American inner cities*. Here, for the first time in the West, most men are not working and women are the breadwinners (partly because they are working more than ever and partly because welfare cheques go to them). Mr Wilson argues that joblessness, especially among young men, not poverty is a prime cause of the disintegration of inner cities: "high rates of neighbourhood poverty are less likely to trigger problems of social organisation if the residents are working." Mass unemployment, he claims, destroys the institutions that enforce social behaviour—small firms, clubs, informal networks and, above all, the family.

Mr Wilson demonstrates that, for men, employment is strongly linked to marriage and fatherhood; for a woman, children and work are separate (often competing) worlds. Men who cannot support a family are much less likely to form one; their attractiveness as a marriage partner sags. Among the inner-city blacks in Chicago whom he

---

*"When Work Disappears,", by William Julius Wilson, Alfred A. Knopf. 352 pages. $26.

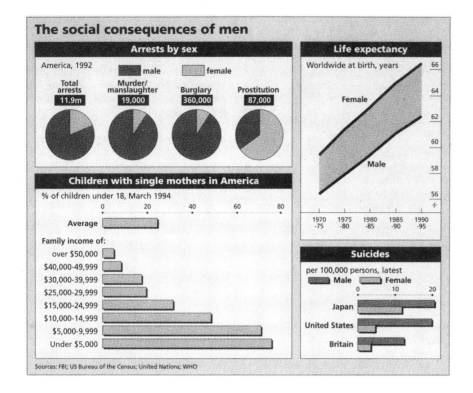

The social consequences of men

Arrests by sex

America, 1992   ■ male   ▨ female

Total arrests	Murder/ manslaughter	Burglary	Prostitution
11.9m	19,000	360,000	87,000

Children with single mothers in America

% of children under 18, March 1994

Average

Family income of:
over $50,000
$40,000-49,999
$30,000-39,999
$25,000-29,999
$15,000-24,999
$10,000-14,999
$5,000-9,999
Under $5,000

Life expectancy

Worldwide at birth, years

Female

Male

1970 -75 · 1975 -80 · 1980 -85 · 1985 -90 · 1990 -95

Suicides

per 100,000 persons, latest

■ Male   ▨ Female

Japan

United States

Britain

Sources: FBI; US Bureau of the Census; United Nations; WHO

about 10% of Americans. And young people make up a disproportionate share of Europe's unemployed (except in Germany) and take even longer to get a job. In France, unemployment among under 25-year-olds is 27%, compared with a national average of 12.5%. More than 60% of European youths who are long-term unemployed have never had work; 40% will take two years or more to find their first job. You do not need a sociology degree to worry about the effects of so many young men with nothing to do.

The Japanese solution? No, thanks

There is one rich country that does not have these problems; where just 1% of children are born to single mothers; where crime is low; where marriage rates are relatively high—and where the labour market is rigged in favour of men. This is Japan. In any recession, the "office flowers" are made redundant first. Women are expected to give up jobs on marriage. In the professions, there is not so much a glass ceiling as a concrete one: hard to miss, painful to hit.

The trouble is that the West is unlikely to copy such a system, which is showing cracks in Japan, too. Just because men—or some of them—are struggling in work and at home, women are not about to stride back to the past, accepting the kitchen and nursery as their allotted spheres.

That is all to the good. But there has been a loser in women's march to something closer to equality and that is the man in the blue-collar uniform. Many of the gains that the West has made through enhancing the economic position of women will be tarnished if the male labourer is pushed to the margins. Once known as the salt of the earth, at the moment his troubles are making countries lose their savour.

studied, almost 60% of those aged 18–44 have never been married and marriage rates are even lower among jobless black fathers than among employed black fathers. And this is true in America as a whole. Black men born in the early 1940s, who came of age during an era of full employment, were more than twice as likely to marry as those born since the late 1950s, who joined the workforce at a time when blue-collar jobs were falling.

So, in the language of social science, "The uncertainties in the labour market are carrying over into uncertainties in the marriage market," as John Ermisch of Britain's Economic and Social Research Centre puts it. Work, it seems, helps determine other aspects of men's lives.

Obviously, the impact upon a neighbourhood of large numbers of jobless single men is influenced by other factors, especially the prevalence of sophisticated deadly weapons. Europe has nothing like Chicago's South Side, the so-called "black belt" that is Mr Wilson's particular area of study. Compared with the South Side, drug use is lower in European cities; gun ownership is much lower; crime is lower; fear of crime is lower. The living standards of the poorest are generally higher. Schools do not have metal detectors.

All the same, if male joblessness is the crucial factor in neighbourhood decline (as Mr Wilson claims), then Europe faces similar problems, though they may be bottled up. Not only is average unemployment more than twice as high as in America, but a jobless European stays that way longer. Of Europe's 19m unemployed, more than half have been out of work for a year or more, compared with

Sex, Lies, and Infantry

Walter A. McDougall

IN A tender love song from the late 1970's, Bob Dylan asked, "Can you cook and sew and make flowers grow, do you understand my pain?" The line outraged feminists. To the ensuing barrage of criticism, the somewhat shaken but unrepentant songwriter replied: yes, women should be free to do whatever they liked, but "when a man says he's looking for a good woman, he isn't looking for an airline pilot."

Two decades later, all manner of media are laboring to purge Americans of such benighted attitudes, and all manner of American institutions are breathlessly acquiescing. The title of one of my five-year-old daughter's favorite bedtime books is *Maybe You Should Fly a Jet*, and the cover shows a woman—a blonde, glamorous woman—at the controls. Children's television programs invariably depict female doctors, police, and mechanics; presidents of women's colleges deplore the fact that one in eight teenage girls still hopes for a career in modeling; and the United States Army encourages women to "be all you can be" by trading cosmetics and cars for camouflage paint and helicopters.

Indeed, one of the central goals of the feminist movement is to establish a fully sexually-integrated military, trained, fit, and ready to engage in combat. To the advocates of this cause, it is an outrage that the United States is not moving at a rapid *enough* pace in their direction; but the truth is that it has moved very swiftly indeed. Thanks to feminism, and thanks as well to the all-too-explicable silence

---

WALTER A. MCDOUGALL *is a Vietnam veteran and a Pulitzer-prize winning historian. His latest book is* Promised Land/Crusader State: The American Encounter with the World Since 1776, *published by Houghton Mifflin.*

of the officer corps, a new, strange—and deeply troubled—future has arrived for the American military.

WOMEN HAVE participated in all of America's wars. In World War II, some 350,000 Wacs, Waves, and nurses saw active service; but they never carried rifles or other arms, and of course their numbers paled beside the millions of male veterans of that war. Only since 1975 has the Pentagon recruited large numbers of women in peacetime. Today, they comprise 14 percent of military personnel, and they perform duties that place them near, at, and, beginning in the 1980's, across the front line.

Creating a sizable female contingent in the military was hardly President Richard Nixon's intention when in 1970 he announced a plan to abolish the draft and create an All-Volunteer Force (AVF). The commission which drew up the blueprint for the AVF calculated that higher pay and other material inducements would suffice to attract a high number of (male) soldiers; it did not even discuss the recruitment of women, which at the time was a non-issue. But in the wake of the Vietnam war, with the morale of the military shot, and the youth of the Make-Love-Not-War and Me generations resisting appeals based on patriotism and self-interest alike, male enlistment plummeted. Worse, a good many of those who did sign up were of inferior physical and intellectual quality. To make the AVF succeed, the Defense Department began to accept women, and not merely as auxiliaries but as regular troops serving beside men in all military-occupational specialties save those involving heavy labor or combat.

Having said A, however, the military very quickly came under fierce pressure to say B. On what basis could female soldiers and sailors be barred from "getting their tickets punched" and proving their mettle in those branches of the service that have always represented the fast track to high honors and rank, where aspiring admirals and generals earn their spurs? The Defense Advisory Committee on Women in the Service (DACOWITS), set up in 1951 to help recruit female auxiliaries during the Korean war, became by the 1970's an assertive lobby on behalf of the full integration of the military by sex. Year after year, its exclusively civilian membership pressured the armed forces and Congress to open a greater range of military-occupational specialties to women, to counter sexual harassment, to reeducate males who objected to the expansion of women's roles, and—fatefully—to design separate (and unequal) standards of training to ensure that women recruits, no matter how faltering their performance, would not fail.

A key if not the decisive turning point came in 1975, when Congress obliged the service academies—the Army's at West Point, the Navy's at Annapolis, and the Air Force's at Colorado Springs—to admit women and treat them as equals to men. Needless to say, most of the females in the entering classes were physically not as strong as their male counterparts, and were certainly not at home in the boot-camp/college-fraternity environment of the academies. In the early years, these female students either suffered in silence or washed out. But among the male cadets there was simmering resentment, both at the lowering of standards and at the abolition of treasured traditions, all to make a handful of young women feel at home.

The rancor boiled over in 1979, when seniors at West Point openly advertised themselves as "the last class with balls." The military brass, which lived in fear of DACOWITS, rushed to the barricades bearing a document entitled "Institutional Plans to Overcome Sexism." Soon all the services were running sensitivity-training programs; rapidly relegated to the past were the hazing and physical challenges that had formerly been employed to instill camaraderie, confidence, and courage in officers-to-be.

The 1980's, under Presidents Reagan and Bush, saw another turning point. This one resulted not from the steady rise in the percentage of women in the AVF but rather from war.

In 1983, American forces invaded Grenada in Operation Urgent Fury; in 1989, they were dispatched to Panama in Operation Just Cause; and finally, in 1991, came the Persian Gulf war. In Grenada and Panama women played a supporting role, but in the war to liberate Kuwait—Operations Desert Shield and Desert Storm—servicewomen were engaged in military action as never before. Fifteen were killed, and one, a truck driver, was captured by the enemy and sexually molested.

Grenada, Panama, and the Persian Gulf gave new energy and new arguments to those pressing to eliminate the barriers against women serving in combat units. For one thing, they claimed, the distinction the Pentagon had attempted to draw between support and combat roles was revealed to be untenable. Support soldiers themselves, after all, came under fire and took casualties. For another thing, women soldiers under fire had displayed both skill and courage. For yet another, the public appeared to take in stride the novelty of female casualties and POW's. Finally, the spectacular display of American technological prowess in the Persian Gulf undercut the old assertion that success in combat depended largely on the kind of brute physical strength possessed by men.

By 1993, when the Clinton administration arrived in Washington, these arguments had prevailed. Tossing out a cautious report that had been commissioned by President Bush, Clinton's civilian appointees in the Defense Department ordered the Navy to deploy female sailors on combat ships and the Army to open 35,000 jobs in military-occupation specialties hitherto reserved for men. Although infantry, armor, artillery, combat aviation, and submarines were still off-limits, those pressing for a sexual revolution in the military had won on the key principle. All that remained was a mopping-up operation to conquer the last preserves of male thinking and male privilege.

GIVEN HOW fast and how far women have come in the armed forces, one might think that feminists would be in a celebratory mood. But to judge by a new book by Linda Bird Francke,* a former "Hers" columnist for the *New York Times*, they remain just as agitated and angry as ever. The reason for their

---

Ground Zero: The Gender Wars in the Military. Simon & Schuster, 304 pp., $25.00.

anger, according to Francke, is clear: from top to bottom, a male-dominated military establishment persists in its repression and persecution of women, and conspires to protect the few remaining male-only units in the name of a "conservative male culture" that cannot come to terms with the presence of women in the ranks.

For those involved in this campaign, Francke writes, the "weapon of choice" is the fact that some female soldiers get pregnant while on active duty and must leave their units at critical times. To Francke, this is a red herring; the Army, she contends, loses fewer days of service to pregnancy than it does to the drug, alcohol, and disciplinary problems that are so rampant among men. Moreover, although it takes two to make a baby, the services act as if pregnancy were a female problem alone, and fail to hold fathers accountable in any way.

But the underlying problem in Francke's eyes is not pregnancy. It is the retrograde nature of the American military ethos itself, and the "masculine mystique" that guides it. Trainees are taught from the start to despise feminine qualities, and are tagged as "pussies" if they fail to live up to the macho ideal. Sexist "Jody songs" (marching chants) and a "torrent of misogynist and anti-individualist abuse" foster a culture of violence that inevitably leads to harassment and rape. In fact, within such a culture, equal opportunity for women can *never* be achieved: women, Francke concludes, are engaged in an "unwinnable war." No matter how they try to fit in, no matter how often they prove their courage in battle, "the dynamic of white male culture" will not permit military men to accept them as equals.

Francke's show of terminal pessimism is instructive, for in her alternately petulant and haranguing way she has actually begun to put her finger on a central issue. That she does not wish to confront this issue, however, is clear from her one-sided presentation of the facts. Her accounts of female heroism in battle, for example, are only so much embroidery over a severely compromised reality.

Take her extended paean to the combat exploits of Captain Linda Bray, whose military-police unit came under sniper fire while storming a dog kennel in Panama. To Francke, this episode proves that women have what it takes to lead infantry assaults. But a close look at Captain Bray's accomplishment tells us something else. The butcher's bill for the fire-fight against the undefended kennel was six enemy dead, all of them canine. One need not minimize Captain Bray's bravery under fire to doubt that this episode proves women can or ought to lead infantry assaults as a matter of course. Nor, for that matter, does Francke's tale of how another female officer, also in Panama, disarmed an assailant by giving him a bonk on the head with her canteen. Would that all our country's enemies were so easily cowed.

On the other side of the coin, Francke simply shrugs off the extent of the Navy's unhappy experience with women at sea: during the Persian Gulf war, 10 percent of the female sailors on board the destroyer-tender USS Acadia (a.k.a. the "Love Boat") had to be removed on account of pregnancy. She dismisses out of hand the wisdom of sending young mothers to fight and die in war. And she never asks whether mixing the sexes in close quarters might in any way be responsible for the kind of trouble we are witnessing in sex scandal after sex scandal and court martial after court martial. Instead of honestly thinking about what these woes mean and whence they arise, Francke insists that the problem rests entirely with the military's incurably sexist men and the refusal of the Pentagon to accommodate its female soldiers.

IN FACT, the problem lies elsewhere. Although Francke, along with other feminists, regards the military as just another workplace, the elementary truth is that the United States maintains a military for one purpose and one purpose only: to protect national security. In order to carry out that job, the military prepares for and, if necessary, fights wars. And to ensure that the armed forces can carry out their mission—a mission which demands that soldiers be prepared to risk and to sacrifice their lives—military life is organized according to a rigid hierarchy and a rigid code of discipline.

Is it really necessary to point out the obvious—namely, that when the sexes are put together in close quarters, especially for prolonged intervals or during periods of great tension, courtships, jealousies, and favoritism will arise; hierarchy will disintegrate; codes of conduct will become unenforceable; and fairness and discipline will break down? Although the case of Israel is frequently adduced by proponents of a mixed-sex combat force, in fact the Israeli example proves the opposite. Israel did experiment with such a mixed force in its 1948 war of independence (as did the Soviets, in desperation, in World War II), but combat effectiveness suffered because of the sub-par performance of some of the women and of almost all the men—who were incorrigibly overprotective of the females fighting next to them. The Israelis quickly reverted to segregated training and all-male combat complements. As Edward Luttwak has put it, "The Army can't do something that eluded the Franciscans. It can't run a mixed monastery."

But that is exactly what the Army is attempting to do, with predictable and widely apparent results. Everyone in the military knows that sexual liaisons are detrimental to order and morale. Everyone knows that pregnancies cause extraordinarily high attrition rates in units attempting to key up for battle—*and* that some servicewoman have courted pregnancy to escape hazardous or inconvenient duty. Everyone knows that to put grizzled sergeants in charge of training nineteen-year-old girls is to invite the former to abuse their authority and the latter to curry favor. And everyone knows that combat units which include women will not perform up to par, whether (as in the Israeli case) because of male overprotectiveness or because of male resentment, or both.

E VERYONE KNOWS—and yet nobody talks, at least in public. "He who is full of courage and *sang-froid* before an enemy battery sometimes trembles before a skirt," Napoleon famously said. And in the Pentagon these days, there is a good deal of trembling. Barbara Pope, Clinton's Assistant Secretary of the Navy, has asserted authoritatively that "We are in the process of weeding out the white male as norm. We're about changing the culture." In such circumstances, to express reservations about sexual integration is, simply, a "career buster." Even those civilian officials critical of the new policy appear unable to speak their minds. When pressed, here is all Caspar Weinberger, Reagan's otherwise sharp-tongued Secretary of Defense, could think to say about placing women in harm's way:

> [E]ither I'm too old-fashioned or something else is wrong with me, but I simply feel that that is not the proper utilization [of women]. And I think, again to be perfectly frank about it and spread all of my old-fashioned views

before you, I think women are too valuable to be in combat.

Such flaccid resistance makes a curiously fitting match with the reckless and often flagrantly contradictory arguments of feminists like Linda Bird Francke. On the one hand, they say women can be just as strong and aggressive as men and deserve the chance to prove it; on the other hand, they damn a "masculine" culture that cultivates martial characteristics. On the one hand, they argue that gender roles, being nothing more than a social construct, are infinitely malleable; on the other hand, they lament the fact that the "masculine mystique" is "innate" and, in Francke's words, "can't go away." As the social critic Jean Bethke Elshtain has observed, feminists have

> not quite known whether to fight men or join them; whether to lament sex differences and deny their importance or to acknowledge and even valorize such differences; whether to condemn all wars outright or to extol women's contributions to war efforts.

In fact, feminists do all these things at once, which may help account not only for their own confusion but for the confusion they have sown in the ranks of their putative adversaries.

In the meantime, the unasked question in this so-called debate is why most women want to join the armed forces at all. From what we know about the overwhelming majority, the answer has nothing whatsoever to do with the military's unique mission of fighting wars. Rather, they are attracted to military service because of the decidedly nonmilitary perquisites it offers, including better pay than they could make on the outside, cradle-to-grave government benefits, and education. Most would not volunteer for combat even if they could, and many who are now posted overseas ache for a stable stateside billet.

In other words, the current concentration of women in clerical work, supply, and other rear-echelon jobs is not, as the feminists would have it, the product of a continuing pattern of discrimination in the military but a reflection—with a few prominent exceptions—of the desires of women themselves. Those exceptions—those few women who, for reasons which it is considered bad form to question, want to storm beaches with an M-60 machine gun or bomb Baghdad from a B-2—are what the fever is about. It is for them that the entire defense establishment of the United States is being invited to turn itself upside down and inside out, at a cost in reputation, morale, and, yes, warfighting capacity that no one has begun to estimate.

Writing in the 1940's in opposition to the ordination of women as priests, C.S. Lewis argued that the issue was not whether females could perform the caring and instructional missions of the clergy as well as or better than men. Rather, the issue was the priesthood itself, which was a burden the Lord had chosen to place upon men. If men had become inadequate to their appointed duty, Lewis wrote, the solution was hardly to call upon those who were not men at all.

Mutatis mutandis, something of the same could be said of our situation today. We arrived at our current military travails for the simple reason that not enough American men could be found to perform a duty that nature has placed on the shoulders of men. If our only solution is to reserve some of the toughest jobs in the military for the fairer sex, then we may soon reach the point where men, as Amelia Earhart predicted in the 1930's, would rather "vacate the arena [of combat] altogether than share it with women." C. S. Lewis, speaking not about priests now but about the modern temperament in general, put the case with lyric precision:

> We make men without chests and expect of them virtue and enterprise. We laugh at honor and are shocked to find traitors in our midst. We castrate and bid the geldings to be fruitful.

This line of argument, of course, is not likely to appeal to Secretary of Defense William Cohen. He has his flanks to cover; all he can say is, "We are not going to turn back the clock." But Bob Dylan had a line for him, too. "How many times can a man turn his head, pretending he just doesn't see?" The answer is blowin' in the wind.

Catherine Horwood looks at how the launch of *Good Housekeeping* in the UK 75 years ago heralded a new image of domestic activity.

HOUSEWIVES' CHOICE—

WOMEN AS CONSUMERS BETWEEN THE WARS

(Below) New broom: the cover of the first UK issue of *Good Housekeeping*, March 1922.

GOOD HOUSEKEEPING
MARCH, 1922   ONE SHILLING

Marie Corelli   William J. Locke   Clemence Dane
Lady Astor   Robert Hichens   Kathleen Norris

In March 1922, America's leading domestic magazine was launched in Britain. Prophetically, publicity promoted *Good Housekeeping* as 'infinitely more than a magazine—a New Institution, destined to play an important part in the lives of thousands of women'. It was claimed that 'no magazine to compare with *Good Housekeeping* has ever been attempted in this country before'. Was this a fair claim? Did *Good Housekeeping* indeed become a trend-setting 'institution'—or was it part of an inevitable growth industry as a sea of consumerism linked to household goods washed over women's lives?

Women's magazines have often been seen as central to the promulgation of a cult of domesticity, and perhaps none more so than *Good Housekeeping*. Its very title seems to confirm this clichéd image. Undoubtedly, many women's magazines have tried to elevate the image of women as home-makers by aiming to dignify what elsewhere could be seen as drudgery. They attempted to do this by raising the status of housework to that of a true 'science' and by encouraging women to buy their way to a new domestic freedom. But whose side were they really on? Were they trying to tip their readers' lives towards an even more domestic bias? Did publishing entrepreneurs see in advertising, a golden opportunity to harness the wealth of the rapidly developing manufacturing industries? Or were they merely answering a need as shifts occurred in the pattern of women's daily lives during these two interwar decades?

Today everyone accepts that we live in a consumer society and that women are prime targets for advertisers of domestic goods. Seventy-five years ago, this was uncharted territory as magazines and manufacturers appeared to join forces to change the status of domestic housework. For middle-class women suddenly life in the early 1920s seemed exciting and full of new opportunities in the form of careers, clothes, cinema, cars, quite apart from the vote. New Woman had arrived. Or had she? Less than twenty years later, by the start of the Second World War, it appeared that in fact she had been propelled back towards the shelter of the home. The enormous strides in terms of women's progress had petered out to be replaced by a domesticity cult reminiscent of the Victorian 'angel in the house'.

This was undoubtedly aggravated by the shortage of domestic help in the home as working-class women looked elsewhere for job opportunities. As the 1930s approached, there were jobs to be had in the 'new' industries and especially in manufacturing consumer goods where the shorter hours appealed, though wages never matched the men's. For many middle-class women, this loss of domestic help was a double blow. The pressure to keep up standards was enormous and the 'servant problem' was a constant topic of conversation among middle-class householders, making the time ripe for a boom in 'service magazines'.

In spite of *Good Housekeeping's* claims, the idea of domestically-orientated or service magazines, as they are known, aimed at British middle-class women was not new. In 1852, publishing entrepreneur Samuel Beeton launched *The English Woman's Domestic Magazine* at the startlingly low price of 2d a copy. An instant success, it had achieved a circulation of 50,000 by 1860 and became the 'blueprint for the modern magazine industry'. It appealed to the rapidly-expanding middle-class sector who relished the mix of fiction, fashion and food, the latter provided by Beeton's wife, the soon-to-be lionised Isabella.

The last quarter of the nineteenth century had also been a boom time for women's magazines. There were forty-eight new launches in the period up to 1900. The most resilient and noteworthy of these was *The Lady* in 1885, an upmarket society weekly but read by the aspiring upper-middle classes as well. However it was 'society' journals such as this that were to suffer the biggest drops in circulation in the aftermath of the First World War as Britain began to attempt to adapt to the social upheaval it had caused. Established magazines such as *The Lady* tried to make allowances for the changing status and interests of their readership, who were

rapidly becoming the 'New Poor', in an attempt to halt the decline. However, *The Lady* failed to follow through with much practical advice and did little to reassure advertisers, the life-blood of the magazine industry, who turned instead to magazines aimed at the 'New Rich', the rising band of aspirant middle-class families who were constantly seeking to improve their standard of living—more often than not by purchasing the latest status symbol: cars and domestic appliances.

The inspiration for these new machines and gadgets undoubtedly came from America where they were well ahead of Britain in the development of domestic equipment. In the US, ice-chests, the forerunners to refrigerators, were common in most homes by the turn of the century. Electric irons had first been patented in 1904, and it was shortly after this that W.H. Hoover put his portable electric sweeper on the market which by 1917 was available nationwide for the very low price of $19.45.

The first to capitalise on the changing lifestyles of middle-class British women was George Newne's *Homes & Gardens* in 1919, to be followed a year later by *Ideal Home* from Odhams Press. These were among the earliest magazines to introduce housewives to the wonders of the electrical appliances that were beginning to appear on the market. But some magazine editorials were cautious and reluctant to recommend them. *Homes & Gardens,* for example, took the rather restrained view that 'unfortunately the new electric vacuum cleaner was not, as yet "practical politics" in the home'.

The US magazine industry was also well ahead in capitalising on middle-class women's need for advice in coping with their new-found servantless state. Considering the popularity of the original American edition of *Good Housekeeping,* the decision to launch a British version was hardly surprising. It had been founded in 1885 by Clark W. Bryan whose aim was 'to produce or perpetuate perfection, or as near unto perfection, as may be obtained in the household'. An instant success, it was sold to the Phelps Publishing Co. in 1900, who instigated a small 'experiment station', known editorially as 'The Bride's First Attempts' and which became the forerunner of the now famous Good Housekeeping Institute.

However, it was the purchase of the magazine in 1911 by Randolph Hearst

in one of his ventures into publishing and its subsequent move to New York as America's leading domestic magazine. Hearst's employment of Dr. Harvey W. Wiley, government promoter of the 1904 Pure Food and Drug Act (known as 'the Wiley Laws') as a nutritional adviser, and his marketing promotion of the magazine's 'Ironclad Contract' which Phelps had initiated in 1902, and which was to lead to the Good Housekeeping Seal of Approval, were to prove an inspired combination. What gave the British *Good Housekeeping* the edge over its competitors was the comparatively high standard of feature writing throughout. In a break from previous magazine practice, the editor, J.Y. McPeake, went to the trade papers for experts, rather than to the 'hack writers of Fleet Street'.

Magazines were the main source of information on new domestic ideas and innovations, but they were also backed up by books such as *The Servantless House* in 1920 which told women that the answer to the vanishing maids lay with 'the equipment of the house rather than with details of any daily arrangement of work'. While the housework debate would rage within the editorial pages of women's magazines, appliance manufacturers were delighted to find these ideal vehicles for their goods. The relative financial security of the readership is confirmed by the heavy advertising investment from the newly-developing consumer industries such as the British Commercial Gas Association, the British Electrical Development Association and their associated suppliers.

Between 1920, a year after the BEDA was established, and 1930, domestic electricity users had risen from one in seventeen households to one in three. An advertisement in an early issue of *Ideal Home* in 1925 encouraged women to increase their use of electricity in the kitchen by investing in a variety of small appliances. In December 1927, *Good Housekeeping* carried advertisements from thirty-four different light, cooking and heating companies, in addition to numerous washing machine and vacuum cleaner companies and other 'labour-saving' devices.

So, while the bread and butter of these magazines' advertising content were the everyday household necessities of life such as soap, shoes and stockings, the icing on the cake came from the mass-produced commodities of the 'new' industries. Advertisers were quick to realise that while their readers were not wage-earners, their influence over the family budget often meant that 'women rather than men held the purse strings' and aimed their marketing strategies accordingly.

A strong relationship between advertising and editorial content was yet to develop but nevertheless the juxtaposition of commercial goods with editorial advice on practical domestic issues was a sound marriage for manufacturers to feel encouraged. Early issues of *Ideal Home* gave a guarantee on advertised goods though this had been dropped by the thirties. *Good Housekeeping* was one of the first to clinch the relationship with the added incentive of the 'Good Housekeeping Seal of Approval'—a refund guarantee—giving every advertiser an enviable endorsement (though there is no record of how successful the guarantee was, or what level of complaints ever materialised).

In the early twenties, in spite of the decrease in servant numbers, the assumption of advertisers was still that they were aiming at women with help in the household. It is evident that labour-saving devices such as the vacuum cleaner were being sold as an aid to the disappearing domestic servant, rather than the lady of the house herself. 'The Hoover', it was claimed, 'is no longer a luxury. It is to-day a necessity. It frees you and your servants forever from the tyranny of the broom', stated an advertisement in July 1923. Another for a washing-up machine claimed: 'there is nothing more disagreeable than to be confronted with the miserable task of washing-up after a good meal' but clearly did not want to assume that the purchaser would be the one to get her hands wet as it ends, 'considerate housewives will install one for lightening the maid's duties'. Such 'consideration' to servants was never so obvious before the servant shortage.

As the 1920s progressed, a gradual shift in emphasis can be seen. The housewife herself became shown using the vacuum cleaner or polishing the furniture in advertisements—although always looking as though she thoroughly enjoyed the experience. By the end of the decade, there is little doubt that the advertisers realized that the majority of women were having to do at least some of their own cleaning. Ironically, the domestic appliances they would use were now being made by the very women who would previously have done these jobs as servants.

Somewhat surprisingly, *Good Housekeeping* in the twenties was suggesting that the housewife 'no longer expends all her energy and hopefulness in domestic labour. She is gaining a little freedom, a little time for culture, and even for pleasure'. As they promised in their launch issue, 'the time spent on housework can be enormously reduced in every home by good household management, and 'there should be no drudgery in the house . . . There must be time to think, to read, to enjoy life . . .'

This was not a sentiment universally echoed in other magazines, however. *Ideal Home,* in an editorial extolling the virtues of the 'Easiwork Kitchen Cabinet' in 1925, believed that 'it is necessary [for a woman] to avail herself of all the short cuts in the domestic routine in order that she may have further time to devote in the interests of her husband and her children'. The majority of magazines of this time were full of similar unintentionally patronising homilies.

The message now being sent to the middle-class woman was that 'the problem of domestic service can be solved mainly by the housewife herself by means of thoughtful organisation and the most up-to-date equipment'. This was reflected by a noticeable shift in the editorial direction to an increasing focus on housecraft. For example, in *Good Housekeeping* in the early 1930s, over half the features now emphasised home and family matters. The development of their 'how to' section reinforced the prevailing notion that a woman's true vocation was to run a home successfully.

For, while the numbers of women in domestic service marginally increased again, only a little over half the number now lived 'in'. One 'char' was having to do the work previously done by two or three maids. By 1938, more than half Britain's households relied on domestic appliances rather than domestic help. The replacement label 'housewife', rather than 'mistress of the household' completed the transformation of middle-class British women into 'a species of home technician, wrapped in a new and powerful aura of homebound femininity'.

The change was further reflected in advertisements which were also now directly aimed at women doing all their own cleaning. Many machines did not live up to their promises, such as one that claimed to wash, rinse, wring, dry, iron and then turn into a vacuum cleaner, but in general, advertisers had little trouble in persuading their new target group to buy the latest equipment, especially with the introduction of hire purchase schemes which tempted many to obtain items otherwise beyond their means. This is illustrated by the fact that at the end of the 1920s there were some 30,000 vacuum cleaners in Britain, but in less than ten years the figure had reached nearly a million. The stigma of buying household goods on credit, still seen by many as a blighting feature of the working classes, was gradually being eroded by editorials which confirmed its acceptability.

Whether these new items actually did improve women's lives is very much open to question. The new technology for washing clothes that was sweeping the US was slow to reach British women and in 1938, 96 per cent of households were still coping with boiling up the copper, a washboard and mangle. The appeal of a gas or electric cooker that could be turned on immediately is obvious against the old coal range that not only involved constant re-fuelling, but also laborious cleaning and clearing. That said, this breed of service magazine definitely contributed to the mania for 'keeping up appearances' by encouraging immaculate cleanliness in the home and which probably involved women in more hours actual work with their new appliances to achieve higher standards than was absolutely necessary for a healthy home.

Women's importance as consumers throughout this period is in little doubt. Advertisers were quick to capitalise on their influence over the major family purchases outside the domestic sphere as well. In both the 1920s and 1930s, large advertisements regularly appear in these magazines from the major car manufacturers such as Ford, Austin and Vauxhall. For many middle-class women living in the new suburbs, a car would have been a lifeline to an otherwise restricted social life. As Virginia Woolf wrote in her diary of 1927: 'we talk of nothing but cars . . . This is a great opening up in our lives . . . Soon we shall look back at our pre-motor days as we do now at our days in the caves'.

In terms of advertising fashion and beauty items, however, it was still early days. There is little mention of make-up in either the editorials or advertisements in women's magazines of the 1920s, although this was the time when Coco Chanel legitimised the suntan, and lipstick and powder were no longer signs of moral decadence—at least among the well-to-do. As Robert Graves observed in 1940, 'the use of facial pigment in Britain [in the Twenties] had not gone very far along the usual course . . . from brothel to stage, then on to Bohemia, to Society, to Society's maids, to the mill-girl, and lastly to suburban women'.

Once into the 1930s, the return to fashion of the curved silhouette confirmed that female emancipation was well and truly over and that the romantic and escapist world of the cinema was beginning to have a major impact on women's dress. But while editorials were encouraging married women to keep making an effort to look good for their husbands, the use of obvious make-up was still very much frowned upon, as a survey in *Good Housekeeping* in 1930 revealed. In one of the first surveys of its kind, this showed that only 20 per cent of their readers used lipstick, 7 per cent, rouge and 5 per cent, scent. The majority used some sort of face cream, however, showing that advertisements for Pond's Cold Cream with the snob-appeal of Mildred, Lady Oranmore and Brown, and Viscountess Moore, was still stronger in influence than the sex appeal of Hollywood film stars to the morally staid women of the British middle classes.

By 1935, however, the pervasive influence of the cinema had gained a hold, a fact acknowledged by *Good Housekeeping* in a 1935 feature, 'What Price Beauty?'. 'Most women spend more conscious effort nowadays on their appearance . . . the films have had much to do with it' the article reported, going on to list the imaginary beauty budgets of six women. Their out-goings should range, the magazine believed, from £3.2s2d. a year for a provincial typist, to a phenomenal £743.14s for an actress in London. In between, the average

budget of £8-£9 a year covered rouge, lipstick and face powder as basics, plus visits to the hairdresser and beauty salons.

In spite of the size of their circulations, it is important not to magnify the influence of these magazines beyond their scope. Compared to the multi-million pound and multimedia industry that exists today, with its international commercial links, *Ideal Home, Good Housekeeping* and their interwar competitors were small-fry. Just as the daily lives of these women were constantly responding to the pressures of society around them, so the magazines can be seen to have similarly adapted in the messages they sent to their readers. Some of these pressures were touched on in their general features, but on the whole, it comes across that their intentions were to help a woman at home in the way they thought best—a practical way—even to the extent of suggesting she breed rabbits at home to 'grow your own fur coat'!

In the predominantly female and often isolated suburban society that these women inhabited, it is not surprising that they looked towards a magazine as a reliable source of reassurance. The magazines in turn steadfastly maintained their adulation of the 'science' of domesticity in a manner which very conveniently mirrored the general view of the role of women at the time, and gave manufacturers a ready market for their products.

Whilst the editorials tried to convince women it was efficiency of their housework that would bring them happiness, the advertisers tried to convince them that it was the equipment they purchased that would change their lives and enhance their social status. The message was clear. The achievement of a perfect home, a happy husband and a healthy family could all be achieved if the right food, dress, vacuum cleaner or gas fire were bought. *Plus ça change . . .*

It is undoubtedly true that for many women between the wars, the lifestyle of the comfortably-off middle-class wife, such as epitomised by Jan Struther's Mrs Miniver, was an idyll they longed to

achieve. 'The carpet and the three-piece suite, the Hoover and the new gas-oven' it has been said, were 'icons of hope and dignity as well as of pride and envy'. *Good Housekeeping* stepped in to answer a need at a time when the somewhat Victorian notion of 'respectability' had reached a much more visible zenith and a woman would be judged by her peers as much by the whiteness of her net curtains as by the cut of her clothes.

It is perhaps ironic that while *Good Housekeeping* started out to be 'revolutionary' in its editorial content, it has ended up so much a part of the establishment that its influence can be seen merely as a reflection of the interests of its readers. Post-war social trends with yet more 'back-to-the-kitchen' regression have done little to dent its position as a domestic 'bible' to its readers. As women have increasingly deserted the kitchen for the workplace, however, only by recognising their changing needs has *Good Housekeeping*, along with the other service magazines, managed to retain its readership and its relevance. The links with consumerism, though, are immutable.

FOR FURTHER READING:
J. Benson, *The Rise of Consumer Society in Britain 1880–1980* (Longman, 1994); B. Braithwaite, *Women's Magazines: The First 300 Years* (Peter Own, 1995); C. Davidson, *A Woman's Work is Never Done* (Chatto & Windus, 1982); J. Giles, *Women, Identity and Private Life in Britain 1900–1950* (MacMillan, 1995); F. Gloversmith (ed.), *Class, Culture and Social Change: A New View of the 1930s* (Harvester, 1980); R. Graves and A. Hodge, *The Long Weekend: A Social History of Great Britain 1918–1939* (Abacus, 1995); C. Hardyment, *From Mangle to Microwave* (Polity Press, 1988); C. White, *Women's Magazines 1693–1968* (Michael Joseph, 1970).

Catherine Horwood lectures in early twentieth-century British History at the University of North London and is completing an MA in Women's History at Royal Holloway, University of London.

DESPERATELY SEEKING SISTERHOOD

It drew more than 500,000 Black women in all their glory, but the Million Woman March was merely a first step.

By Donna Britt

I didn't want them to be right about the Million Woman March.

The sisters who said, "Sorry, I love Black women but I'm not going because *my* girlfriend network is at work, next door and at church"—I didn't want them to be right. I didn't want the established Black women's groups who were rebuffed by march planners to be right, either—the sisters who privately felt snubbed, who had predicted that a national march put together by inexperienced organizers would be chaotic.

I even shushed the voice in my head that asked: *Why didn't the march platform mention more everyday Black woman concerns—day care, domestic violence, spiritual emptiness and strained relationships with our men—instead of things like "mechanisms that will assist Black women who are in 'transitional' experiences which will facilitate them more effectively"?*

I especially didn't want the media to be right, those that had projected a teensy turnout for any march whose planners missed key meetings with Philadelphia city officials, whose publicity was so meager that a week before the event, many sisters didn't realize there *was* a march.

The "no-wayers," naysayers, "home-stayers" had to be wrong. Because I wanted this march to work. I yearned for it to be as soul-stirring as the 1995 march that had hardened brothers hugging, crying and confessing in these streets of D.C. I wanted the same awed, inspired look on my face that my husband, Kevin, had had when he returned from the Million Man March.

The last thing I wanted was what I too often got: hours spent aimlessly wandering with thousands of other searching women. All shifting from location to location. All desperately seeking sisterhood.

More than half a million of us came to Philadelphia that drizzly October Saturday, our numbers alone making a mighty statement. We came with overstuffed backpacks and a heartfelt prayer: That the sisterlove generated by the march would give Black women—whose contributions, needs and beauty are routinely overlooked—some overdue affirmation.

Moment by moment, it did. I got my first taste of sisterhood on a Philly-bound bus from a woman who said with immense poignancy, "I keep searching for how things got to be the way they are now."

Bernestine Singley, 48, had flown from Dallas to ride the bus with a friend who lived in Washington, D.C. She hoped the gathering would prove that Black women, who keep hearing that they need *more*—more skills, more motivation, more education—in truth have it all:

"I want to come away with this belief that we have *everything* that we need, to do what we need to do now," she said.

There was a tense moment at a Philly subway station, miles from the march, where I waited in a line thick with hopelessly delayed sisters. A woman in a kufi gasped when a clerk inside the booth—a Black woman—was asked for 402 tokens. "She's multiplying it by hand?" the hat lady groaned. A second sharper voice asked, "Didn't she learn multiplication in the third grade?"

Suddenly the hat lady checked herself. "We are *sisters* today," she announced. "We can't be bashing no other sisters!"

We were, she reminded us, one: Women in ratty sweats and fur-lined anoraks, in pricey Nautica gear and Kmart parkas. Women with short velvet 'fros and visible weave tracks and expert perms and more braids and locks than there are vines along the Nile. Connected less by our incomes and lifestyles than by our grinding, gimme-some-love need, we came, some of us not fully understanding why.

"I came to find out why I came," said Stacey Jordan, 25, of Hyattsville, Maryland. "I came to find out what the march *will* represent for me."

So did I. And when I focus on how many women showed up, the Million Woman march seems a huge success. When I consider that a group of virtual unknowns put it together, I see an undeniable achievement.

When I focus on feelings, I sense an unrealized opportunity.

Why weren't more of us filled with the kind of joy that animated the woman who raced through the crowd, laying hands on strangers' shoulders, shouting, "I just want to *touch* a million women!"? Her elation inspired Christine Williams, 43, of Philadelphia, to sigh: "I don't feel that warmth from other sisters."

Perhaps that was due to some marchers' puzzling hostility toward one another, the faulty sound system, or the gauntlet of vendors hawking food and memorabilia. Speakers' putdowns of other Black women, such as sexpot rappers Lil' Kim and Foxy Brown, had some women asking, "Where's the sisterhood in *that*?"

Many felt that the absence of warmth stemmed from the organizational problems inherent in a national event for which the march's novice planners could not have been prepared. The Million Man March was organized by Minister Louis Farrakhan, whose guidance guaranteed it the Nation of Islam's resources and his instant credibility among many Blacks. The Million Woman March—which was not sponsored by the Nation, despite its conspicuous presence—was the brainchild of Philé Chionesu, a small-business owner barely known outside Philadelphia.

Embarking on such a mission—let alone pulling it off—took guts and imagination. Chionesu began working on the march almost two years ago after awakening from a dream of a million Black women coming together. With public-housing activist Asia Coney, Chionesu enlisted a circle of local women. Soon they were holding yard sales and car washes across the country to raise the $2 million needed to pay for the event.

Rumors flew early that organizers didn't want mainstream civil-rights and black women's organizations to play a central role. "We wanted to start with the grassroots women," explained Paula S. Peebles, the march's national program chairperson. "We worked our way up to the more affluent women." Among the march's 12-point platform goals: development of Black independent schools, further investigation of the Central Intelligence Agency's involvement in the penetration of crack cocaine into Black communities, and help for female ex-convicts. Actress Jada Pinkett, Representative Maxine Waters (D-CA), Sister Souljiah, Dorothy I. Height and keynoter Winnie Madikizela-Mandela were among the relatively few speakers with more recognition, as a result of organizers' desire to give lesser-known activists a national forum. Planners relied largely on

met—briefly, even intimately, bonding with them, as any decent pickup basketball game proves.

Women's sharing occurs on a smaller scale: whispered over office-cubicle dividers, laughed over steaming plates in church basements, wistfully sighed in warm, comforting hugs. Sparking that soul-lifting vibe between thousands of women just may not be so easy.

But perhaps sisterhood simply wasn't among the essential gear many participants brought to the march. Exhausted from making baby-sitting, meal and travel arrangements, we arrived in Philly the way women arrive everywhere: hefting hastily crammed purses, shopping bags and backpacks. Our baggage, stuffed with makeup, extra clothes, fried chicken and thermoses, caused Monique Smith, 25, of Washington, D.C., to marvel, "The *men* didn't have all these bags."

We'd dragged along other baggage, too: old insecurities and suspicions about Black women with more money, or less, than we have; whose skins are lighter or darker; whose coifs—whether straight, kinky, braided or locked—challenge our own Black-hair

to add their expertise to help create "the lives of all Black women desire."

Just what we needed—another challenge. It's almost enough to make a woman wish she'd stayed home, warm and dry with the naysayers. They were right about some things: Our most satisfying sister networks are close to home. Links that the grassroots organizers hoped to forge were sabotaged early on when they rebuffed offers of help from Black women with more traditional, everday concerns.

But the sisters who marched were right, too. Women who knew each potential problem and saw many of them realized still found moments of connectedness—sweet, warm slices of sisterhood—to savor.

Such as my most unforgettable march moment, after the standing-room-only subway ride to City Hall. Women who were ecstatic at just *being* there flowed like rapids from the train, and a clarion voice rang out:

"Oh, when the saints
Go marching in . . ."

Twenty voices, then a hundred, joined hers. Roaring through the concrete tunnel, the spiritual shimmied down our bones:

'I wanted this march to be as soul-stirring as the one that had brothers confessing in the streets.'

Black·radio, newspapers and churches, and good old word of mouth to spread the news.

When hundreds of thousands of women journeyed to Philly, their numbers testified to the vastness of our hopes and our potential to change our lives. *But where,* many wondered, *was the sisterhood?*

Some felt it got misplaced with the basic creature comforts, like bathrooms and welcoming restaurants, that marchers rarely found. Others thought it got washed away in the rain. "The Million Man March took place on a warm, beautiful day on the mall," a friend pointed out. "Which would *anyone* prefer?" For many, the clear spiritual purpose that fueled the brothers' march for atonement was oddly missing. None of the Million Woman March's written goals mentioned a higher power, a vital concept to most African-Americans.

And then there was the phenomenal success of the Million *Man* March. Hoping for a similar miracle, organizers and participants used that event as a model, forgetting the historic, perhaps visceral differences between men and women. Born into a sporting tradition, brothers learn early to hook up with guys they've never

choices. Related suspicions probably contributed to the planners' initial rejection of veteran organizers' help, and to certain women's assumption that untried activists had no business planning a march. For all our talk of *sisterhood,* we can mistrust one another as reflexively as some Whites mistrust all Blacks.

Ironically, many of the Million Woman March's flaws might have been corrected by an early coalition of the myraid kinds of Black women who showed up—of the women who came together without truly coming together. But looking at those disparate women, I thought: *If the march inspires us to forge more such alliances, we would be a powerful force—and the greatest legacy of the Million Woman March.*

Singley, the Dallas sister I met on the bus, is a Harvard-educated lawyer who creates empowering programs for public-housing residents. She sees the fact that the Million Woman March was put together by grassroots women as "its greatest strength." Its success "completely annihilated the myth that poor Black women just want to sit on their asses and do nothing," she continued. It also challenges established sisters

"Oh I want to be in that number!
When the saints go marching in . . ."

For a fleeting moment, I felt that we *were* saints, joined in a quest so enormous that it linked us to every woman on the streets above, to the sisters who couldn't or wouldn't come. I *felt* the spirit: of my mother who taught me how much black women can survive; of my grandmother who never made a plan without saying "God willing"; of millions of Black women who have never stopped singing of their determination to be counted.

I want more slices of sisterhood like that one, moments that suggest that Black women of every variety can love one another unconditionally. Not morsels or snacks, but enough to make a feast that satisfies us all.

The Million Woman March couldn't fill me. But sister by sister, we can build on what we started by just showing up. Moment by moment, with God's willingness and enough of our own, we can prove Singley's words to be true:

We have *everything* we need, to do what we need to do now.

Donna Britt is a syndicated columnist for The Washington Post.

Beyond 'It's a Baby'

If pro-lifers give more thought to women's needs, they will serve children better as well.

FREDERICA MATHEWES-GREEN

"THIS week is anti-choice week at UB," wrote Michelle Goldberg, a staffer with the student paper *The Spectrum* at the University of Buffalo in New York. "If you see one of them showing their disgusting videos or playing with toy fetuses, do your part and spit at them. Kick them in the head."

In my travels to college campuses—Yale, Princeton, Bryn Mawr, Brown, Wellesley, et al.—no pro-choicer has actually kicked me in the head, but a few have looked as if they'd like to. A few more have delivered dark imprecations in the question-and-answer period, occasionally disguised as questions. And a few more have just glowered at me threateningly, like the wicked witch before the bucket of water hit her.

But most pro-choicers I've met have been distressed, saddened, and deeply ambivalent about abortion. I recall the black woman at an Oregon college who during our question period confessed that she wasn't really in favor of abortion, even thought that it was generally a bad thing, but necessary because "If I got pregnant, nobody would adopt my

Mrs. Mathewes-Green is a columnist for Christianity Today.

baby." This is not only false—babies of every color are adopted quickly—it is sad, and reveals the loneliness and fear of abandonment that lie behind many abortions. "Nobody wants my baby" has echoes of "Nobody wants me."

Similarly, a woman whom I'd seen gleefully leading pro-choice chants at a

---

> *Most pro-choicers I've met have been distressed, saddened, and deeply ambivalent about abortion.*

---

rally was holding forth on her other cause, the evil of child abuse. I asked her why her concern didn't extend to unborn children. She hesitated, then replied with disarming honesty, "It's even

worse than that. You see, I think I believe life begins at conception. I can't help thinking, if it's a baby after it's born, what is it a week before it's born? A month before? Where's the dividing line?"

I've found pro-choicers to be ambivalent not only about the unborn, but about the pain abortion causes women. That is why I've concluded that the usual pro-life message is ultimately ineffective. The usual message is brief and insistent: "It's a baby." Most pro-life communication pushes that message with unwavering persistence: precious-feet lapel pins, "Abortion Stops a Beating Heart" bumperstickers, billboards showing a row of babies, each third one ghosted over, with the legend, "Every third baby dies from choice."

It is the truth, of course, and it is a horrible truth; that's why most pro-choicers who are thoughtful people are troubled about abortion. It was that truth that flipped me over many years ago, back when I was a standard-issue, not-amused, hairy-legged women's libber, and eagerly pro-abortion (none of that sissy "pro-choice" stuff for me).

But then I read an article in *Esquire* magazine titled "What I Saw at the Abortion," in which surgeon Richard

Selzer described the twitching of a poison syringe that had been plunged into a pregnant woman's abdomen. That was enough to convince me. It was indeed a baby, and abortion made it die. No way could I reconcile that with my overriding conviction that it was wrong to use violence to solve social problems. Could that be me in the mirror: vegetarian, anti-death-penalty, sprinkled with anti-war buttons, yet in favor of the killing of our own children?

The mystery is not that "It's a baby" troubles and disturbs; the mystery is that, for so many, it doesn't disturb enough. Not enough, that is, to convince them that abortion should be illegal. Polls regularly show three-quarters agreement with statements like "The fetus is a human baby and killing it is always wrong," and also show two-thirds agreement with "Society should have no say in whether a woman has an abortion." An LA. *Times* poll a few years ago showed 57 per cent of respondents willing to call abortion "murder"—a charged term that thoughtful pro-lifers avoid. (Intriguingly, a more recent CBS News poll found that those most likely to call abortion murder are between 18 and 29 years old.) But among those willing to use the term were a fourth of those who generally favored abortion and a full third of the women who admitted to having had an abortion themselves.

The problem is that "It's a baby" winds up in deadlock with "It's a woman's right." The two statements do not refute each other, and so no resolution is possible. What's more, they continue a pernicious fallacy, that deadly conflict between women and children is a normal state of affairs.

In no sane country are women and their own children assumed to be mortal enemies; any culture that so assumes is slowly committing suicide. This is true both literally and symbolically as well. When we accept as normal the ripping of a child from the mother's womb, we violate something disturbingly close to the heart of the human story. In the land where women kill their unborn children, every lesser love grows frail.

The problem with "It's a baby" is that it's answering a question no one is asking. Since the widespread arrival of ultrasonography, no one doubts that the life in the womb is a baby. The real question to ask about abortion is, "But how could we live without it?"

Proving that it's possible to "live without it" will require a step that's somewhat unusual; we don't need so much to change what we do as what we say. There are three thousand pro-life pregnancy-care centers across the country, where volunteers do the best they can to provide women with the basics—clothing, shelter, and medical care—and with more specific aid like job training, adoption counseling, and assistance resolving post-abortion grief. The pregnancy-care movement is more than thirty years old, and such help centers far outnumber politically oriented pro-life groups.

But It's-a-Baby thinking has tenacious roots. I once asked a stalwart pro-life congressman why he agreed to serve on the board of a pregnancy-care center. Why did he think that work was important? He answered that we have to "convince more Americans that the destruction of unborn children is unjust . . . and we can do that through crisis-pregnancy ministries."

A mental train had just jumped the track. Crisis-pregnancy services don't demonstrate anything about injustice or the sanctity of fetal life. They just demonstrate a commitment to helping women love their own children to life. Yet the impulse to switch back to the default "It's a baby" position is so strong that even someone well-informed and supportive of services to pregnant women couldn't resist the pull.

THIS is not to pretend that a national transition to "living without it" is going to be easy. Abortion is so entrenched in the cultural milieu, is so handy for resolving problems (resolving them the easy way, inside women's bodies), that the average person reels when imagining the disruption that would follow if it were unavailable. Abortion is the handmaiden of the sexual revolution, that great male victory in the war between the sexes. As feminist poet Adrienne Rich says, "The so-called sexual revolution of the Sixties [was] briefly believed to be congruent with the liberation of women . . . it did not mean that we were free to discover our own sexuality, but rather that we were expected to behave according to male notions of female sexuality."

Scientists have finally discovered the cause of unplanned pregnancy: sex. When sexual relations take place in a relationship lacking emotional commitment, any unsought pregnancy is much more likely to be difficult. Abortion allows the *Playboy*-friendly status quo to continue, disposing of the ties that might bind.

The problem is that women's sexuality is deeply tied to commitment and emotional stability, and in this bad bargain women lose. Abortion severs two relationships at once, the woman from her lover and from her child. No wonder pro-choice slogans ring with first-person-singulars: my right, my decision, my body, my choice. The flip side of autonomy is loneliness. Abortion promises to make a woman unfettered, empowered, and free; instead she finds herself isolated, endangered, and sad. And condoms don't solve this problem: you can't put a condom on your heart.

Living without abortion means restoring the sexual balance of power, with respect for women's need for commitment and security—in short, abstinence before and fidelity within marriage. It also means supporting women who get pregnant nevertheless, with pregnancy-care services and adoption counseling.

While the financial and practical needs of these women are great, the surprising thing I learned while researching *Real Choices: Listening to Women, Looking for Alternatives to Abortion* was that women said what they needed most was a friend. As I traveled the country holding "listening groups" with women who had had abortions, I always asked, "What situation caused you to make this decision?" I expected to hear tales of financial woe, yet nearly 90 per cent of the women told me they had had their abortion because of a relationship—because someone they loved, a boyfriend or a parent, told them to. When asked what anyone could have done to help them complete the pregnancy, over and over the answer was: Just stand by me. "I would have had that baby," I heard repeatedly, "if only I'd had one person to stand by me." Pregnancy-care centers may run short of diapers, maternity dresses, and doctor fees, but as long as they can keep the doors open and the lights on they can do that one necessary thing: be that friend.

When I've spoken at colleges and elsewhere, I've found that talking about the women's needs and problems has a disarming and opening effect. Even many who are hostile will say, "I agree with you about all that, but I just don't think abortion should be illegal." If we can agree about all the foregoing, we've come a long way indeed. I do think abortion should be illegal—in any civilization, laws protecting the weak from the strong belong to the irreducible core of justice. But I don't know if I'll see such laws in my lifetime. I'm convinced we can do much to prevent abortions even while the regime of legal availability remains. Tomorrow morning, 4,100 women will wake up and think, "My abortion is today." An amendment to the Constitution is not going to suddenly appear and halt them; in fact, if we miraculously padlocked all the abortion clinics tomorrow, without making any changes in our support system, all we'd have is women banging on the locked doors and crying. We wouldn't have done anything to alleviate the problems

that drove them to the clinic in the first place. What can we do to help them?

ONE thing I don't do any more is debates. Too often these amount to verbal mud-wrestling, a spectacle put on for entertainment, not elucidation. They entrench positions around cheering sections, rather than lead to consensus and change. Besides, an access of cleverness doesn't lead to success; you can't beat someone up until she agrees with you.

Instead, I've become involved with dialogues. Through the Common Ground Network for Life and Choice, based in Washington, D.C., I can meet, for respectful dialogue, with a group of pro-lifers and pro-choicers. We don't expect to change minds immediately or to agree, but we

do seek to comprehend each other's beliefs; we try to clear away the misunderstandings so that we can arrive at genuine, honest disagreement. I've learned a lot there. When I look across the table at a pro-choicer, I don't see a fiend who deserves a "kick in the head"; I see someone troubled by the grim reality of abortion, and seeking a solution she can live with.

I think I've found that solution. I can never doubt my conviction that abortion is a bloody horror, death to children and living death to their mothers. But I know from experience that, at these charged moments, careful listening is the most necessary thing. Because in the pro-choicer I see not only my enemy, and my friend; I see, across the span of twenty years, myself.

Guinier, Lani, 145
Gur, Ruben C., 48, 49, 50

Haire, Doris, 67
harems, 32
Hargreaves, Jennifer, 76, 77
Harrison, Beverly, 120
health, working women and, 54–57
Hebrew language, 94
Hebrews, 94
herbs, for "bringing on the menses", 73
heterosexuality, 52
hidden transcripts, 112
higher education, postwar expansion of, 25
holistic environmental thinking, 131
home: staying at, in Islam, 98, 100; wartime women in the, 23, 24, 26
homefront, women and, 136
homeopaths, 73
homophobia, in sports, 77
homosexuality, 52, 192–194
homosexuals, as parents, 192–194
Hoover, Herbert, 9
Hoover, J. Edgar, 24
hostile work environment, 150–152
House of Representatives, women in, 8
household machines, 218
human sacrifice, 94
husbands, as source of support to female entrepreneurs, 183
Hussein, Saddam, 135, 140
hyper-patriarchy, 32
Hysterectomy Educational Resources and Services (HERS) Foundation, 67

income burden, of women, 27
India, 145
Indonesia, 142
Industrial Age, 32
Industrial Revolution, 18
instant gratification, 140
intuition, women's 130
Islam, 31, 96–102
Islamic nations, women in politics in, 142
Italy, 141

J

James, Jane Elizabeth Manning, 12–13
Japan, 37, 141, 142, 143, 145; men and labor market in, 210
Japanese-American women, 25
jobs, as major issue to women, 28
Judaism, 31
jury service for women, 25

K

Kennedy, Anthony, 116, 117
knowledge-based societies, 53
Korean Americans, and churches, 107–113
Krasnegor, Norman, 50

L

labor, low-wage, women's 142
labor reform, 17–22

law, access of women to profession of, in 1920, 8
learning differences, of girls and boys, 46
lesbian separatism, 31, 33
lesbian studies movement, 51–52
lesbians, female soldiers accused as, 137; as parents, 192–194
life expectancy, female, 102
light duty, and disability, 175, 177
limbic system, 48, 49
loans, females as less-attractive potential recipients of, 182–183
longevity, increase in, 33
Lucilla, 87
Luker, Kristin, 120

Mailer, Norman, 39
make-up, 218–219
male backlash, 31, 32, 33, 189
male myths, 132
management, 142; man's versus woman's way of advancing in, 170–171
marriage: Muslim, 99; working women and, 54–57
martyrs, women, 87–88
Marxism, 51
Mason, Biddy, 13
maternal health and abortion, 116
maternity leave, 101
math anxiety, 47
matriarchs, 33
medical model, in women's health-care, 67
medical research subjects, women as, 62
medical schools, and teaching of abortion techniques, 118
medical trials, 61
men: changes of, 30; coalition with, 29; declining compensation of work of, 27, 29; disadvantage of, 53; downsized, 27, 29; and the priesthood, 215; and public sphere of government, 137; unmarried, uneducated, unemployed, 207–210
men's movement, 33
mentors, 165, 166, 167, 169, 170, 171, 184
methotrexate, 118
Mexico, 141, 145
microloans, 131
micromanipulation, liberation through, 111, 112
midwives, 73
mifepristone, 118
military academies, 212
military service, women's exclusion from, 137
military, women's entry into, 23, 211–215
Millett, Kate, 34, 38
Million Woman March, 220–221
ministerial-level positions, worldwide, 143, 145
misogyny, 31, 213; in the Koran, 97
Mongolia, 141
Moral Majority, 119
morality, of Persian Gulf War, 135
Mormons, 12, 13
Moskowitz, Belle Lindner, 9–10, 11
Mother Teresa, 89–92
Munson, Ronald, 48, 49

Muslims, 96, 97
mythology: Babylonian, 94; Egyptian, 94

National Black Women's Health Project, 67, 68
national health-care reform: and abortion, 71; and health of women, 70
National Latina Health Organization, 67, 68
National Organization for Women, 189
National Women's Health Network, 67
nationalism, in sports, 77
nationality, and women's rights under the UN, 101
Native American Women's Health and Education Resource Center, 67, 68
NCAA, 80
Nelson, Mariah Burton, 76, 77
networking, of entrepreneurs, 183
networks: informal, in the workplace, 168, 169, 183, 184; sister, 221
Nevins, Tish, 15
New Chastity, The (Decter), 41
New Deal, 11
New Independent States of the former Soviet Union, and women's representation, 143
New Zealand, and women's suffrage, 141
Nineteenth Amendment to the Constitution, women's vote and, 8
Nordic countries, 143
North American Free Trade Agreement, 130
nuns, 103–106; clothing of, 103

O

O'Connor, Sandra Day, 116, 117
office, public, right of women to run for, 142
O'Reilly, Lenora, 17–22; oratory of, 19
Our Bodies, Ourselves (Seaman), 67, 69
Our Right to Choose (Harrison), 120
overcompetitiveness, of sports, 77
ownership, by women, of land and housing, 147

P

paganism, 31, 32, 93–95
paid work, 17, 24, 25, 180–185
paradigm shift, in women's roles, 27–28
parental leave, 195–199
partnership model, of male-female relations, 31, 33
patriarchy, continued, 32
penile implants, 61
Perkins, Frances, 10, 11
Perpetua, 88
Petchesky, Rosalind, 120
pill, birth-control, 35, 118, 119
Pleasant, Mary Ellen, 13–14
political attitudes, of women versus men, 146–147
polygamy, 32, 33
poor, aid to, 89–92
pornography, 29
power, political, women and, 141–147
power-over politics, 140
prayer, 90

pregnancy: and guidelines for organizations, 177; in the military, 213; in the workplace, 173–179
pregnancy discrimination, 173–179
priestesses, 95
priests, women, 84, 86, 87
Prisoner of Sex, The (Mailer), 39
privacy, right to, 116
pro-choice politics, 119–120, 222–224; background of, 68; need for leaders in, 119
pro-life politics, 222–224
Progressive Era, 17, 18
public office, difficulty of women getting elected to, during periods of heroism in wartime, 137

Quayle, Marilyn, 11
quota system, in elections, 145–146

racism, in sports, 77
radical feminist ideology, 60
radical feminist movement, 30–33
railroad, women working on the, 158–164
rape, 78, 100, 140, 213
Reagan, Leslie J., 73
reasonable woman (person) doctrine, and sexual harassment, 151–152
reductive biological model, of gay and lesbian studies, 52
religious women, 103–106
remarriage, 87
reproductive policy, and Catholic hospital systems, 63, 65
research inequities, medical (men and women), 69
rhetorical obstacles, of female legislators, 136–138
rights, 101; lack of women's, in Islamic culture, 98
Roe v. Wade, 67, 74, 75; legal future of, 116–117; medical future of, 117–118; political future of, 118–120
role models, 167, 168
Roman Catholic Church, and hospital policies about birth control, 63, 65
Roosevelt, Anna Eleanor, 10, 11
Roosevelt, Franklin, 10

"Saint" Jerome, 85, 87
satisfaction, of successful women entrepreneurs, 184
Scandinavia, 40
scholarship money available to women nationwide, 80
screening, of female patients by female physicians, 70
Seaman, Barbara, 67
separate spheres ideology, 11
sex, casual, 36
sex differences, in brain, 48–50
sex discrimination, 26; in employment, 148–149
sexism, in the Jewish community, 94; in schools, 45; of sports, 77

sex-role stereotypes, and female entrepreneurship, 182–183
sexual harassment, and hostile environment, 150–152; legal evolution of, 148–155
sexual liberation, 37
sexual politics, 28, 29
Sexual Politics (Millett), 34, 38
Shaywitz, Bennett, 48, 50
Shaywitz, Sally, 48, 50
silence: learned, 111; of women on war, 137; on women and war issue, in Persian Gulf War, 134, 136
sisterhood, 36, 220–221
slaves, female, 32
social constructionist nature, of gay and lesbian studies, 52
social work, 90
Socialiam, 20
Society for the Advancement of Women's Health Research, 67
sounding boards, 167
Souter, David, 116, 117
South Africa, 144
South Korea, 141
Southerners, 133
Soviet state, and equality of women, 141
specificity, versus abstraction, in speaking of war, 138
Sporting Females: Critical Issues in the History and Sociology of Women's Sports (Hargreaves), 76, 77
sports feminists, 77
spouses, and career support, 169–170, 183
Stanton, Elizabeth Cady, 8
Steinem, Gloria, 34
stereotypes, 190–191
structural adjustment policies, 146
submissiveness, 25
subordination of women, collapse of, 30
suffering, 92
suffrage, winning of women's, 8, 9, 17, 19, 141
superwoman, image of the, 30
Sweden, 195, 196
Switzerland, 141
Syria, 142

The Stronger Women Get, the More Men Love Football: Sexism and the American Culture of Sports (Nelson), 76, 77
thinking women, 21, 22
Title VII of the Civil Rights Act, 149, 152, 153, 154, 174, 176
Title IX, 25th anniversary of, 79–81
top management, women's underrepresentation in, 142
traffic, in women, UN prohibition of, 101
Training the Body for China: Sports in the Moral Order of the People's Republic (Brownell), 76, 77, 78
trivialization, of female athletes, 78
True Womanhood, 18

ultrasound, 118, 223

unemployment, of men, 207–208, 209, 210
United Nations Declaration on the Rights of Women, 101; and first international women's conference, 143
"Uprising of the 20,000," 20
U.S. senators, female, 8

venture capitalists, and female entrepreneurs, 183
veterans, 123
victimology, 62
virginity, 87
voting blocs, 145

wages, standardization of, 19, 24, 25
wartime, policies about women in, 23–26
Webster v. Reproductive Health Services, 67
When Abortion Was a Crime (Reagan), 73, 75
widowhood, 87
wifebeating, 100
witchburning, 32
witchcraft, 32, 61
Witelson, Sandra, 49, 50
woman, creation of, 94
woman's sphere, 18
woman-to-woman talk, 108
women: African American, 12–17, 24; on the American western frontier, 12–17; battered, 200–206; as breadwinners, 209; changes of, 30; in combat, 212, 213, 214; as consumers between the wars, 216–217; effect of war on, 134–140; employment of, 24, 25; as entrepreneurs, 180–185; in the military, 211–215; as owners of businesses, 180; in politics, 8–11; as pilots in World War II, 121–123; as railroad workers, 158–164; at sea, 213; as sexual war booty, 140; in wartime, 23–26, 134–140
women physicians, in U.S., 69
women's colleges, 46–47
women's emancipation efforts, 141–142, 219
women's groups in the 1920s, 9
Women's Health Initiative, 67
women's healthcare research, lack of, 68–69
women's liberation, 34
women's magazines, 216, 217, 218, 219
women's movement for equality, 28, 34; worldwide, 143
women's rights, 101; and abortion, 120
women's studies programs, 60
Women's Trade Union League (WTUL), 17, 19, 20, 21
work, 32, 208; mothers and, 54–57; protection of women in, 101
Working Girl, 19, 20
working women, 21, 208
World War II, and women, 23–26, 121–123

AE Article Review Form

We encourage you to photocopy and use this page as a tool to assess how the articles in **Annual Editions** expand on the information in your textbook. By reflecting on the articles you will gain enhanced text information. You can also access this useful form on our Web site at **http://www.dushkin.annualeditions.com/**.

NAME: _____ DATE: _____

TITLE AND NUMBER OF ARTICLE: _____

BRIEFLY STATE THE MAIN IDEA OF THIS ARTICLE: _____

LIST THREE IMPORTANT FACTS THAT THE AUTHOR USES TO SUPPORT THE MAIN IDEA:

WHAT INFORMATION OR IDEAS DISCUSSED IN THIS ARTICLE ARE ALSO DISCUSSED IN YOUR TEXTBOOK OR OTHER READINGS THAT YOU HAVE DONE? LIST THE TEXTBOOK CHAPTERS AND PAGE NUMBERS:

LIST ANY EXAMPLES OF BIAS OR FAULTY REASONING THAT YOU FOUND IN THE ARTICLE:

LIST ANY NEW TERMS/CONCEPTS THAT WERE DISCUSSED IN THE ARTICLE, AND WRITE A SHORT DEFINITION:

ANNUAL EDITIONS revisions depend on two major opinion sources: one is our Advisory Board, listed in the front of this volume, which works with us in scanning the thousands of articles published in the public press each year; the other is you—the person actually using the book. Please help us and the users of the next edition by completing the prepaid article rating form on this page and returning it to us. Thank you for your help!

ANNUAL EDITIONS: Women's Studies 99/00

ARTICLE RATING FORM

Here is an opportunity for you to have direct input into the next revision of this volume. We would like you to rate each of the 44 articles listed below, using the following scale:

1. Excellent: should definitely be retained
2. Above average: should probably be retained
3. Below average: should probably be deleted
4. Poor: should definitely be deleted

Your ratings will play a vital part in the next revision.
So please mail this prepaid form to us just as soon as you complete it.
Thanks for your help!

RATING

ARTICLE

1. Why Suffrage for American Women Was Not Enough
2. African-American Women on the Western Frontier
3. "Rights as Well as Duties": The Rhetoric of Leonora O'Reilly
4. Women, War, and the Limits of Change
5. Beyond Gender
6. Women of the Future: Alternative Scenarios
7. A Farewell to Feminism
8. The Education of Alice and Dorothy: Helping Girls to Thrive in School
9. Man's World, Woman's World? Brain Studies Point to Differences
10. Gay- and Lesbian-Studies Movement Gains Acceptance in Many Areas of Scholarship and Teaching
11. The Trouble with Men
12. The Myth of the Miserable Working Woman
13. Warning: Feminism Is Hazardous to Your Health
14. Blocking Women's Health Care
15. Women's Health Movements
16. Abortion in American History
17. Females in Sports: A Book Review
18. Fair Game: Title IX Twenty-Fifth Anniversary
19. Women and the Early Church
20. No Humanitarian: A Portrait of Mother Teresa
21. The Goddess Myth
22. Islam's Shame: Lifting the Veil of Tears

RATING

ARTICLE

23. Whatever Happened to Sister Jane?
24. The Labor of Compassion: Voices of "Churched" Korean American Women
25. The Future of Roe v. Wade
26. The Long Flight Home: Women Served—and Died—in WWII. Now They Are Remembered
27. Sex and Lies
28. Women's Work
29. Women and War: How "Power-Over" Politics Silenced U.S. Congresswomen in the Persian Gulf War
30. Women in Power: From Tokenism to Critical Mass
31. The Legal Evolution of Sexual Harassment
32. The Lady Brakemen
33. Separate and Unequal: The Nature of Women's and Men's Career-Building Relationships
34. Managing Pregnancy in the Workplace
35. Female Entrepreneurs: How Far Have They Come?
36. The (R)Evolution of the American Woman
37. Gay Families Come Out
38. Parental Leave: What and Where?
39. Behind [Closed] Doors
40. Tomorrow's Second Sex
41. Sex, Lies, and Infantry
42. Housewives' Choice—Women as Consumers between the Wars
43. Desperately Seeking Sisterhood
44. Beyond 'It's a Baby'

(Continued on next page)

We Want Your Advice

ANNUAL EDITIONS: WOMEN'S STUDIES 99/00

BUSINESS REPLY MAIL
FIRST-CLASS MAIL PERMIT NO. 84 GUILFORD CT

POSTAGE WILL BE PAID BY ADDRESSEE

Dushkin/McGraw-Hill
Sluice Dock
Guilford, CT 06437-9989

NO POSTAGE
NECESSARY
IF MAILED
IN THE
UNITED STATES

ABOUT YOU

Name _____ Date _____

Are you a teacher? ☐ A student? ☐
Your school's name _____

Department _____

Address _____ City _____ State _____ Zip _____

School telephone # _____

YOUR COMMENTS ARE IMPORTANT TO US !

Please fill in the following information:
For which course did you use this book?
_____

Did you use a text with this *ANNUAL EDITION*? ☐ yes ☐ no
What was the title of the text?
_____

What are your general reactions to the *Annual Editions* concept?
_____

Have you read any particular articles recently that you think should be included in the next edition?
_____

Are there any articles you feel should be replaced in the next edition? Why?
_____

Are there any World Wide Web sites you feel should be included in the next edition? Please annotate.
_____

May we contact you for editorial input? ☐ yes ☐ no
May we quote your comments? ☐ yes ☐ no